A+ Certification Study Guide

Syngress Media, Inc.

Osborne McGraw-Hill

Berkeley New York St. Louis San Francisco Auckland Bogotá Hamburg London Madrid Mexico City
Milan Montreal New Delhi Panama City Paris São Paulo Singapore Sydney Tokyo Toronto

Osborne McGraw-Hill
2600 Tenth Street
Berkeley, California 94710
U.S.A.

For information on translations or book distributors outside the U.S.A.,
or to arrange bulk purchase discounts for sales promotions, premiums, or
fund-raisers, please contact Osborne/**McGraw-Hill** at the above address.

A+ Certification Study Guide

   234567890 DOC DOC 901987654321098

ISBN 0-07-882538-5

Publisher Brandon A. Nordin	**Copy Editor** Ralph Moore	**Illustrators** Lance Ravella Brian Wells
Editor-in-Chief Scott Rogers	**Indexer** Jack Lewis	**Series Design** Roberta Steele
Acquisitions Editor Gareth Hancock	**Proofreader** Pat Mannion	Arlette Crosland
Project Editor Cynthia Douglas	**Computer Designers** Ann Sellers	**Cover Design** Regan Honda
Technical Editor Tony Hinkle	Mickey Galicia Roberta Steele Jean Butterfield	**Editorial Management** Syngress Media, Inc.

From Global Knowledge Network

At Global Knowledge Network we strive to support the multiplicity of learning styles required by our students to achieve success as technical professionals. In this book, it is our intention to offer the reader a valuable tool for successful completion of the A+ exams.

As the world's largest IT training company, Global Knowledge Network is uniquely positioned to offer this book. The expertise gained each year from providing instructor-led training to hundreds of thousands of students worldwide has been captured in book form to enhance your learning experience. We hope that the quality of this book demonstrates our commitment to your lifelong learning success. Whether you choose to learn through the written word, computer-based training, Web delivery, or instructor-led training, Global Knowledge Network is committed to providing you the very best in each of those categories. For those of you who know Global Knowledge Network, or those of you who have just found us for the first time, our goal is to be your lifelong competency partner.

Thank you for the opportunity to serve you. We look forward to serving your needs again in the future.

Warmest regards,

Duncan Anderson
Chief Operating Officer, Global Knowledge Network

The Global Knowledge Network Advantage

Global Knowledge Network has a global delivery system for its products and services. The company has 28 subsidiaries, and offers its programs through a total of 60+ locations. No other vendor can provide consistent services across a geographic area this large. Global Knowledge Network is the largest independent information technology education provider, offering programs on a variety of platforms. This enables our multi-platform and multi-national customers to obtain all of their programs from a single vendor. The company has developed the unique CompetusTM Framework software tool and methodology which can quickly reconfigure courseware to the proficiency level of a student on an interactive basis. Combined with self-paced and on-line programs, this technology can reduce the time required for training by prescribing content in only the deficient skills areas. The company has fully automated every aspect of the education process, from registration and follow-up, to "just-in-time" production of courseware. Global Knowledge Network through its Enterprise Services Consultancy, can customize programs and products to suit the needs of an individual customer.

Global Knowledge Network Classroom Education Programs

The backbone of our delivery options is classroom-based education. Our modern, well-equipped facilities staffed with the finest instructors offer programs in a wide variety of information technology topics, many of which lead to professional certifications.

Custom Learning Solutions

This delivery option has been created for companies and governments that value customized learning solutions. For them, our consultancy-based approach of developing targeted education solutions is most effective at helping them meet specific objectives.

Self-Paced and Multimedia Products

This delivery option offers self-paced program titles in interactive CD-ROM, videotape and audio tape programs. In addition, we offer custom development of interactive multimedia courseware to customers and partners. Call us at 1-888-427-4228.

Electronic Delivery of Training

Our network-based training service delivers efficient competency-based, interactive training via the World Wide Web and organizational intranets. This leading-edge delivery option provides a custom learning path and "just-in-time" training for maximum convenience to students.

ARG

American Research Group (ARG), a wholly-owned subsidiary of Global Knowledge Network, one of the largest worldwide training partners of Cisco Systems, offers a wide range of internetworking, LAN/WAN, Bay Networks, FORE Systems, IBM, and UNIX courses. ARG offers hands on network training in both instructor-led classes and self-paced PC-based training.

ABOUT SYNGRESS MEDIA

Syngress Media creates books and software for Information Technology professionals seeking skill enhancement and career advancement. Its products are designed to comply with vendor and industry standard course curricula, and are optimized for certification exam preparation. You can contact Syngress via the web at www.syngress.com.

ABOUT THE CONTRIBUTORS

Dorothy L. McGee has worked in the computer industry for more than 12 years, and currently holds A+, CNA, CNE, 2 MCNEs, MCP, MCP+Internet, and MCSE certifications.

Tim First began his computer experiences at the age of 10 with a Zenith Z-100. Since then he has gained the credentials of MCSE and MCP+Internet. Tim is presently preparing for the MCSE+Internet and Oracle DBA certifications. Tim can be reached by e-mail at first@bus.msu.edu.

John Barnes has been working with PC hardware for more than 14 years. John currently works as a Systems Engineer for Cylink Corp., and lives in the Washington, DC area. John is currently the lead field engineer for two Cylink product lines. Besides supporting Cylink customers nationwide, he currently supports a nationwide Windows NT network. John holds MCSE and CNE certifications.

David Yorke is a Systems Support Engineer in Phoenix, Arizona. An A+ certified technician with a specialty in DOS/Windows, he is also certified as an MCP in Windows 95 and Networking Essentials, and is pursuing MCSE status. His experience with different computer hardware and software platforms has spanned more than ten years.

Ted Hamilton is on the desktop support team for EDS. He has been involved with computers since 1979. He has graduated from the College of

Wooster with a Bachelor's in Business Economics. He has also completed some work in graduate-level accounting. Seeing the huge demand for computer networking engineers, Ted has changed his career focus to the pursuit of completing the MCSE. You can reach Ted by e-mail at Tjhtjhtjh@aol.com, or reach him on the Web at http://homepage.usr.com/h/hamilton/

Cary Stotland is currently engaged as a Networking Consultant for a Midwest-based systems integration firm. He has worked with microcomputers since their inception, and continues to study their underpinnings. He may be reached at carys@usa.net.

Melissa Craft is a Consulting Engineer for MicroAge in Phoenix, Arizona. She has a Bachelor's degree from the University of Michigan. After relocating to the Southwest, Melissa became involved increasingly with technology and obtained several certifications: MCSE, CNE-3, CNE-4, CNE-GW, MCNE, and Citrix. Melissa Craft is a member of the IEEE, the Society of Women Engineers, and American MENSA, Ltd.

Mark Larma is a Senior Systems Engineer for MicroAge in Phoenix, Arizona. He has an MCSE in both the 3.51 and 4.0 track, with an emphasis on messaging. He currently has certifications on Exchange, versions 4.0, 5.0, and 5.5. Mark taught himself to program in BASIC at the age of 11 and hasn't stopped using the technology since. Mark dedicates his writing to his patient family: his wife Mary Ann, daughters Alexis and Veronica, and newborn son Hunter.

Technical Review by:

Tony Hinkle (A+, MCSE, CNE) is from southern Indiana. He was raised on a farm and holds a Bachelor's degree in business accounting from Oakland City University. His accounting career was quickly terminated by destiny, and he moved into the field of computer services. Although he started as a hardware technician, he knew that operating systems and networking would be his fields of excellence. With the assistance of his employer, Advanced Microelectronics, Inc., Tony completed the requirements to become a CNE, an A+ Certified Technician, and an MCSE.

Tony thanks all of those who have helped to instill in him the knowledge, experience, and self-confidence necessary to excel in his field.

Global Knowledge Network Courses Available

Network Fundamentals

- Understanding Computer Networks
- Telecommunications Fundamentals I
- Telecommunications Fundamentals II
- Understanding Networking Fundamentals
- Implementing Computer Telephony Integration
- Introduction to Voice Over IP
- Introduction to Wide Area Networking
- Cabling Voice and Data Networks
- Introduction to LAN/WAN protocols
- Virtual Private Networks
- ATM Essentials

Network Security & Management

- Troubleshooting TCP/IP Networks
- Network Management
- Network Troubleshooting
- IP Address Management
- Network Security Administration
- Web Security
- Implementing UNIX Security
- Managing Cisco Network Security
- Windows NT 4.0 Security

IT Professional Skills

- Project Management for IT Professionals
- Advanced Project Management for IT Professionals
- Survival Skills for the New IT Manager
- Making IT Teams Work

LAN/WAN Internetworking

- Frame Relay Internetworking
- Implementing T1/T3 Services
- Understanding Digital Subscriber Line (xDSL)
- Internetworking with Routers and Switches
- Advanced Routing and Switching
- Multi-Layer Switching and Wire-Speed Routing
- Internetworking with TCP/IP
- ATM Internetworking
- OSPF Design and Configuration
- Border Gateway Protocol (BGP) Configuration

Authorized Vendor Training

Cisco Systems

- Introduction to Cisco Router Configuration
- Advanced Cisco Router Configuration
- Installation and Maintenance of Cisco Routers
- Cisco Internetwork Troubleshooting
- Cisco Internetwork Design
- Cisco Routers and LAN Switches
- Catalyst 5000 Series Configuration
- Cisco LAN Switch Configuration
- Managing Cisco Switched Internetworks
- Configuring, Monitoring, and Troubleshooting Dial-Up Services
- Cisco AS5200 Installation and Configuration
- Cisco Campus ATM Solutions

Bay Networks

- Bay Networks Accelerated Router Configuration
- Bay Networks Advanced IP Routing
- Bay Networks Hub Connectivity
- Bay Networks Accelar 1xxx Installation and Basic Configuration
- Bay Networks Centillion Switching

FORE Systems

- FORE ATM Enterprise Core Products
- FORE ATM Enterprise Edge Products
- FORE ATM Theory
- FORE LAN Certification

Operating Systems & Programming

Microsoft

- Introduction to Windows NT
- Microsoft Networking Essentials
- Windows NT 4.0 Workstation
- Windows NT 4.0 Server
- Advanced Windows NT 4.0 Server
- Windows NT Networking with TCP/IP
- Introduction to Microsoft Web Tools
- Windows NT Troubleshooting
- Windows Registry Configuration

UNIX

- UNIX Level I
- UNIX Level II
- Essentials of UNIX and NT Integration

Programming

- Introduction to JavaScript
- Java Programming
- PERL Programming
- Advanced PERL with CGI for the Web

Web Site Management & Development

- Building a Web Site
- Web Site Management and Performance
- Web Development Fundamentals

High Speed Networking

- Essentials of Wide Area Networking
- Integrating ISDN
- Fiber Optic Network Design
- Fiber Optic Network Installation
- Migrating to High Performance Ethernet

DIGITAL UNIX

- UNIX Utilities and Commands
- DIGITAL UNIX v4.0 System Administration
- DIGITAL UNIX v4.0 (TCP/IP) Network Management
- AdvFS, LSM, and RAID Configuration and Management
- DIGITAL UNIX TruCluster Software Configuration and Management
- UNIX Shell Programming Featuring Kornshell
- DIGITAL UNIX v4.0 Security Management
- DIGITAL UNIX v4.0 Performance Management
- DIGITAL UNIX v4.0 Intervals Overview

DIGITAL OpenVMS

- OpenVMS Skills for Users
- OpenVMS System and Network Node Management I
- OpenVMS System and Network Node Management II
- OpenVMS System and Network Node Management III
- OpenVMS System and Network Node Operations
- OpenVMS for Programmers
- OpenVMS System Troubleshooting for Systems Managers
- Configuring and Managing Complex VMScluster Systems
- Utilizing OpenVMS Features from C
- OpenVMS Performance Management
- Managing DEC TCP/IP Services for OpenVMS
- Programming in C

Hardware Courses

- AlphaServer 1000/1000A Installation, Configuration and Maintenance
- AlphaServer 2100 Server Maintenance

ACKNOWLEDGMENTS

We would like to thank the following people:

- Richard Kristof of Global Knowledge Network for championing the series and providing us access to some great people and information. And to Patrick Von Schlag, Rhonda Harmon, Robin Yunker, David Mantica, Stacey Cannon, and Kevin Murray for all their cooperation.

- To all the incredibly hard-working folks at Osborne/McGraw-Hill: Brandon Nordin, Scott Rogers, and Gareth Hancock for their help in launching a great series and being solid team players. In addition, Cynthia Douglas, Steve Emry, Anne Ellingsen, and Bernadette Jurich for their help in fine-tuning the book.

- To Michelle Vahlkamp and Esther Kraft at CompTIA, for quickly answering our many questions.

- Thanks to Phil Baruch at MaxIT, Randall Thomas at IBID Publishing, Jim Gardner at MindWorks, Jeff Thorssell at Dali Design, and Mary Anne Dane at Self Test Software for the support in proividing demo versions of their copmanies practice test software.

CONTENTS AT A GLANCE

CONTENTS

Part I
A+ Core Examination

Part II
DOS/Windows Examination

The Global Knowledge Network Advantage

Linking the Classroom to the Real World

Global Knowledge Network is the largest independent IT training company in the world, training more than 150,000 people every year in state-of-the-art network training centers or on location with major corporate customers. In addition, it is a Cisco Systems Training Partner, a Bay Networks Authorized Education Center, a FORE Systems Training Partner, and an Authorized IBM NETEAM Education provider. Now, for the first time, all of Global Knowledge Network's classroom expertise and real-world networking experience is available in the form of this study guide.

This book's primary objective is to help you prepare for and pass the required A+ exams so you can begin to reap the career benefits of certification. We believe that the only way to do this is to help you increase your knowledge and build your skills. After completing this book, you should feel confident that you have thoroughly reviewed all of the objectives that CompTIA has established for the exam.

In This Book

This book is organized around the actual structure of the A+ exams administered at Sylvan Testing Centers. This exam has two parts to it: a core module, and a DOS/Windows module. CompTIA has let us know all the topics we need to cover for the exams. We've followed their list carefully, so you can be assured you're not missing anything.

In Every Chapter

We've created a set of chapter components that call your attention to important items, reinforce important points, and provide helpful exam-taking hints. Take a look at what you'll find in every chapter:

- Every chapter begins with the **Certification Objectives**—what you need to know in order to pass the section on the exam dealing with the chapter topic. The icon shown at left identifies the objectives within the chapter, so you'll always know an objective when you see it!

- **Exam Watch** notes call attention to information about, and potential pitfalls in, the exam. These helpful hints are written by people who have taken the exams and received their certification—who better to tell you what to worry about? They know what you're about to go through!

- **Certification Exercises** are interspersed throughout the chapters. These are step-by-step exercises that mirror vendor-recommended labs. They help you master skills that are likely to be an area of focus on the exam. Don't just read through the exercises; they are hands-on practice that you should be comfortable completing. Learning by doing is an effective way to increase your competency with a product.

- **From the Field** sidebars describe the issues that come up most often in the training classroom setting. These sidebars give you a valuable perspective into certification- and product-related topics. They point out common mistakes and address questions that have arisen from classroom discussions.

- **Q & A** sections lay out problems and solutions in a quick-read format:

QUESTIONS AND ANSWERS

The computer lost its BIOs settings . . .	This is commonly caused by a low CMOS battery. Replace the battery and reconfigure the CMOS.

- The **Certification Summary** is a succinct review of the chapter and a re-statement of salient points regarding the exam.

- The **Two-Minute Drill** at the end of every chapter is a checklist of the main points of the chapter. It can be used for last-minute review.

- The **Self Test** offers questions similar to those found on the certification exams, including multiple choice, true/false questions, and fill-in-the-blank. The answers to these questions, as well as explanations of the answers, can be found in Appendix A. By taking the Self Test after completing each chapter, you'll reinforce what you've learned from that chapter, while becoming familiar with the structure of the exam questions.

Some Pointers

Once you've finished reading this book, set aside some time to do a thorough review. You might want to return to the book several times and make use of all the methods it offers for reviewing the material:

1. *Re-read all the Two-Minute Drills,* or have someone quiz you. You also can use the drills as a way to do a quick cram before the exam.

2. *Re-read all the Exam Watch notes.* Remember that these are written by people who have taken the exam and passed. They know what you should expect—and what you should be careful about.

3. *Review all the Q & A scenarios* for quick problem solving.

4. *Re-take the Self Tests.* Taking the tests right after you've read the chapter is a good idea, because it helps reinforce what you've just learned. However, it's an even better idea to go back later and do all the questions in the book in one sitting. Pretend you're taking the exam. (For this reason, you should mark your answers on a separate piece of paper when you go through the questions the first time.)

5. *Take the on-line tests.* Boot up the CD-ROM and take a look. We have more third-party tests on our CD than any other book out there, so you'll get quite a bit of practice.

6. *Complete the exercises.* Did you do the exercises when you read through each chapter? If not, do them! These exercises are designed

to cover exam topics, and there's no better way to get to know this material than by practicing.

7. *Check out the web site.* Global Knowledge Network invites you to become an active member of the Access Global web site. This site is an online mall and an information repository that you'll find invaluable. You can access many types of products to assist you in your preparation for the exams, and you'll be able to participate in forums, on-line discussions, and threaded discussions. No other book brings you unlimited access to such a resource. You'll find more information about this site in Appendix C.

The CD-ROM Resource

This book comes with a CD-ROM full of supplementary material you can use while preparing for the A+ exams. We think you'll find our book/CD package one of the most useful on the market. It provides all the sample tests available from testing companies such as Self Test Software, Dali Design, Mindworks, MaxIT, and IBID Publishing. In addition to all these third-party products, you'll find an electronic version of the book, where you can look up items easily and search on specific terms. The special self-study module contains another 300 sample questions, with links to the electronic book for further review.

As of the printing of this book, some vendors had not yet made available the upgrades to the A+ exam demos. For updated exams, please visit the following sites:

- http://www.bcpl.net/~jthorsse/apad.html for an update to Dali Design's PREP! for A+

- http://www.maxit.com/ for an update to MaxIT's A+ Certification Exam Testing Demo

- http://www.ibidpub.com/ for an update to IBID's A+ Certification

- http://www.mindwork.com/ for an update to MindWorks' PRELIM Test Preparation Software

- stsware.com for an update to Self Test Software's A+ Test Demo

There's more about the CD-ROM in Appendix B.

How to Take an A+ Certification Exam

This chapter covers the importance of your A+ certification as well as prepares you for taking the actual examinations. It gives you a few pointers on methods of preparing for the exams, including how to study, register, what to expect, and what to do on exam day.

Importance of A+ Certification

The Computing Technology Industry Association (CompTIA) created the A+ certification to provide technicians with an industry-recognized and valued credential. Due to its acceptance as an industry-wide credential, it offers technicians an edge in a highly competitive computer job market. Additionally, it lets others know your achievement level and that you have the ability to do the job right. Prospective employers may use the A+ certification as a condition of employment or as a means of a bonus or job promotion.

Earning A+ certification means that you have the knowledge, the technical skills, and now, the customer relations skills necessary to be a successful computer service technician. Computer experts in the industry establish the standards of certification. Although the test covers a broad range of computer software and hardware, it is not vendor-specific. In fact, more than 45 organizations contributed and budgeted the resources to develop the A+ examination.

To become A+ certified you must pass two examinations: the Core exam and a DOS/Windows specialty exam. The Core exam measures essential competencies for a break/fix microcomputer hardware service technician with six months of experience. The exam covers basic knowledge of desktop and portable systems, basic networking concepts, and printers. Also included on the exam are safety and common preventive maintenance procedures.

With this new revision of the A+ certification, released in July of 1998, you now have only one choice for the specialty exam: DOS/Windows. The previous version of the A+ exam also offered Macintosh OS as a specialty, but because our world is becoming more and more PC-driven, the new exam also reflects this change. The DOS/Windows module covers basic knowledge of DOS, Windows 3.*x*, and Windows 95 operating systems for installing, upgrading, troubleshooting, and repairing microcomputer systems.

Computerized Testing

As with Microsoft, Novell, Lotus, and various other companies, the most practical way to administer tests on a global level is through Sylvan Prometric testing centers. Sylvan Prometric provides proctored testing services for Microsoft, Oracle, Novell, Lotus, and the A+ computer technician certification. In addition to administering the tests, Sylvan Prometric also scores the exam and provides statistical feedback on each section of the exam to the companies and organizations that use their services.

Typically, several hundred questions are developed for a new exam. The questions are reviewed for technical accuracy by subject matter experts and are then presented in the form of a beta test. The beta test consists of many more questions than the actual test and provides for statistical feedback to CompTIA to check the performance of each question.

Based on the performance of the beta examination, questions are discarded based on how well or poorly the examinees performed on them. If a question is answered correctly by most of the test-takers, it is discarded as too easy. The same goes for questions that are too difficult. After analyzing the data from the beta test, CompTIA has a good idea of which questions to include in the question pool to be used on the actual exam.

Test Structure

Currently the A+ exam consists of a *form* type test. This type of test draws from a question pool of some set value and randomly selects questions to generate the exam you will take. We will discuss the various question types in greater detail later.

Some certifications are using *adaptive* type tests. This interactive test weighs all of the questions based on their level of difficulty. For example, the questions in the form might be divided into levels one through five, with level one questions being the easiest and level five being the hardest. Every time you answer a question correctly, you are asked a question of a higher level of difficulty, and vice versa when you answer incorrectly. After answering about 15-20 questions in this manner, the scoring algorithm is able to determine whether or not you would pass or fail the exam if all the questions were answered. The scoring method is pass or fail. You won't find this type of exam for A+ certification as of yet. Currently Novell is employing the adaptive test format.

The exam questions for the A+ test are all equally weighted. This means that they all count the same when the test is scored. An interesting and useful characteristic of the form test is that questions may be marked and returned to later. This helps you manage your time while taking the test so that you don't spend too much time on any one question. Remember, unanswered questions are counted against you. Assuming you have time left when you finish the questions, you can return to the marked questions for further evaluation.

The form test also marks the questions that are incomplete with a letter "I" once you've finished all the questions. You'll see the whole list of questions after you finish the last question. The screen allows you to go back and finish incomplete items, finish unmarked items, and go to particular question numbers that you may want to look at again.

Question Types

The computerized test questions you will see on the examination can be presented in a number of ways. You may see some of the possible formats on the A+ test, and some you may not.

True/False

We are all familiar with True/False type questions, but due to the inherent 50 percent chance of guessing the right answer, you will probably not see any of these on the A+ exam. Sample questions on CompTIA's web site and on the beta exam did not include any True/False type questions.

Multiple Choice

The majority of the A+ exam questions are of the multiple choice variety. Some questions require a single answer, whereas some require multiple answers. The easiest way to differentiate between the number of answers required is the use of a radio button or a checkbox in front of possible answers. The radio button will only allow you to select one item from the given choices. The checkbox allows you to select any or all of the given answers in response to the question.

One interesting variation of multiple choice questions with multiple answers is whether or not the examinee is told how many answers are correct.

EXAMPLE:

Which files are processed immediately upon the completion of POST? (Choose two.)

OR

Which files are processed immediately upon the completion of POST? (Choose all that apply.)

You may see both variations of the multiple answer questions on the exam, but the trend seems to be toward the first type, where examinees are told explicitly how many answers are correct. Questions of the "choose all that apply" variety are more difficult and can be very confusing to the test taker. The majority of questions on the A+ exam are multiple choice with single answers.

Graphical Questions

Some questions incorporate a graphical element to the question in the form of an exhibit either to aid the examinee in a visual representation of the problem or to present the question itself. These questions are easy to identify because they refer to the exhibit in the question and there is also an "Exhibit" button on the bottom of the question window. An example of a graphical question might be to identify a component on a drawing of a motherboard.

Test questions known as hotspots actually incorporate graphics as part of the answer. These types of questions ask the examinee to click on a location or graphical element to answer the question. As a variation of the above exhibit example, instead of selecting A, B, C or D as your answer, you would simply click on the portion of the motherboard drawing where the component exists.

Free Response Questions

Another type of question that can be presented on the form test requires a *free response,* or type-in answer. This is basically a fill-in-the-blank type question where a list of possible choices is not given. More than likely you will not see this type of question on the exam.

Study Strategies

There are appropriate ways to study for the different types of questions you will see on an A+ certification exam. The amount of study time needed to pass the exam will vary with the candidate's level of experience as a computer technician. Someone with several years experience might only need a quick review of materials and terms when preparing for the exam.

The rest of us may need several hours to identify weaknesses in knowledge and skill level and then to work on those areas to bring them up to par. If you know that you are weak in an area, work on it until you feel comfortable talking about it. You don't want to be surprised with a question knowing it was your weak area.

Knowledge-Based Questions

Knowledge-based questions require that you memorize facts. The questions may not cover material that you use on a daily basis, but they do cover material that CompTIA thinks a computer technician should be able to answer. Here are some keys to memorizing facts:

- ■ **Repetition**   The more times you expose your brain to a fact, the more it "sinks in" and increases your ability to remember it.

- **Association** Connecting facts within a logical framework makes them easier to remember.

- **Motor Association** It is easier to remember something if you write it down or perform another physical act, like clicking on the practice test answer.

Performance-Based Questions

Although the majority of the questions on the A+ exam are knowledge-based, some questions are performance-based scenario questions. In other words, the performance-based questions on the exam actually measure the candidate's ability to apply one's knowledge in a given scenario.

The first step in preparing for these scenario type questions is to absorb as many facts relating to the exam content areas as you can. Of course, any actual hands-on experience will greatly help you in this area. For example, knowing how to discharge a CRT is greatly enhanced by having actually done the procedure at least once. Some of the questions will place you in a scenario and ask for the best solution to the problem at hand. It is in these scenarios that having a good knowledge level and some experience will help you.

The second step is to familiarize yourself with the format of the questions you are likely to see on the exam. The questions in this study guide are a good step in that direction. The more you're familiar with the types of questions that can be asked, the better prepared you will be on the day of the test.

The Exam Makeup

To receive the A+ certification, you must pass both the Core and the DOS/Windows exams. You will see between 75 and 100 questions on each exam and you will have two and a half hours to complete each of them. As we are going to press with this book, CompTIA has not yet established the passing rate of the new exam. As it sits, a 72 percent is the passing rate for the Core portion and a 69 percent is the passing rate for the DOS/Windows portion. You would be well advised to check the CompTIA site at www.comptia.org for the most recent information.

The Core Exam

The Core exam is broken down into eight categories. Note that the final category—customer satisfaction—will be tested, but will not count towards the passing or failing of the exam. The score on those particular questions will be posted on your score card, though, so your employer can see how you did on these types of questions. CompTIA lists the percentages as the following:

Installation, configuration, upgrading	30 percent
Diagnosing and troubleshooting	20 percent
Safety and preventive maintenance	10 percent
Motherboard, processors, memory	10 percent
Printers	10 percent
Portable systems	5 percent
Basic networking	5 percent
Customer satisfaction	10 percent

The DOS/Windows Exam

The majority of the DOS/Windows exam will focus on Windows 95 (a whopping 75 percent), with the rest of the coverage divided between DOS and Windows 3.*x*). CompTIA's breakdown of this portion is as follows:

Function, structure, operation, and file management	30 percent
Memory management	10 percent
Installation, configuration, and upgrading	25 percent
Diagnosing and troubleshooting	25 percent
Networks	10 percent

Signing Up

After all the hard work preparing for the exam, signing up is a very easy process. Sylvan operators in each country can schedule tests at any authorized Sylvan Prometric Test center. To talk to a Sylvan registrar, call 1-800-77-MICRO. There are a few things to keep in mind when you call:

1. If you call Sylvan during a busy period, you might be in for a bit of a wait. Their busiest days tend to be Mondays, so avoid scheduling a test on Monday if at all possible.

2. Make sure that you have your social security number handy. Sylvan needs this number as a unique identifier for their records.

3. Payment can be made by credit card, which is usually the easiest payment method. If your employer is a member of CompTIA, you may be able to get a discount, or even obtain a voucher from your employer that will pay for the exam. Check with your employer before you dish out the money.

4. You may take one or both of the exams on the same day. However, if you only take one exam, you only have 90 days to complete the second exam. If more than 90 days elapse between tests, you must retake the first exam.

Taking the Test

The best method of preparing for the exam is to create a study schedule and stick to it. Although teachers have told you time and time again not to cram for tests, there may be some information that just doesn't quite stick in your memory. It's this type of information that you want to look at right before you take the exam so that it remains fresh in your mind. Most testing centers provide you with a writing utensil and some scratch paper that you can use after the exam starts. You can brush up on good study techniques from any quality study book from the library, but some things to keep in mind when preparing and taking the test are:

1. Get a good night's sleep. Don't stay up all night cramming for this one. If you don't know the material by the time you go to sleep, your head won't be clear enough to remember it in the morning.

2. The test center needs two forms of identification, one of which must have your picture on it (i.e. driver's license.) A social security card or credit card are also acceptable forms of identification.

3. Arrive at the test center a few minutes early. There's no reason to feel rushed right before taking an exam.

4. Don't spend too much time on one question. If you think you're spending too much time on it, just mark it and go back to it later if you have time. Unanswered questions are counted wrong whether you knew the answer to them or not.

5. If you don't know the answer to a question, think about it logically. Look at the answers and eliminate the ones that you know can't possibly be the answer. This may leave with you with only two possible answers. Give it your best guess if you have to, but most of the answers to the questions can be resolved by process of elimination.

6. Books, calculators, laptop computers, or any other reference materials are not allowed inside the testing center. The tests are computer based and do not require pens, pencils, or paper, although as mentioned above, some test centers provide scratch paper to aid you while taking the exam.

After the Test

As soon as you complete the test, your results will show up in the form of a bar graph on the screen. As long as your score is greater than the required score, you pass! Also, a hard copy of the report is printed and embossed by the testing center to indicate that it's an official report. Don't lose this copy; it's the only hard copy of the report that is made. The results are sent electronically to CompTIA.

The printed report will also indicate how well you did in each section. You will be able to see the percentage of questions you got right in each section, but you will not be able to tell which questions you got wrong.

After you pass the Core exam and the DOS/Windows exam, an A+ certificate will be mailed to you within a few weeks. You'll also receive a lapel pin and a credit card-sized credential that shows your new status: A+ Certified Technician. You're also authorized to use the A+ logo on your business cards as long as you stay within the guidelines specified by CompTIA. If you don't pass the exam, don't fret. Take a look at the areas you didn't do so well in and work on those areas for the next time you register. Just remember that the Core and DOS/Windows exams must be taken within 90 days of each other to count toward certification.

Once you pass the exams and earn the title of A+ Certified Technician, your value and status in the IT industry increases. A+ certification carries along an important proof of skills and knowledge level that is valued by customers, employers, and professionals in the computer industry.

Part I

A+ Core Examination

1

Installation, Configuration, and Upgrading

I n order to pass the A+ Certification Core Module, you need to study the function, installation, and configuration procedures for all systems components, from the devices themselves to the connectors and cables they use. In doing so, you also need to familiarize yourself with the common tools of the trade and how they are used. This chapter guides you through the terms and concepts that relate to each of the components as well as informs you of the industry standard procedures used in installation and configuration.

CERTIFICATION OBJECTIVE 1.01

Functions of System Modules

When you think of a computer, you generally picture a monitor and a keyboard hooked up to a box. However, there are many components, called *Field Replaceable Modules (FRMs)* or *Field Replaceable Units (FRUs)*, that make up a computer system. Each FRU has a specific function to perform, whether it accepts data from a user or produces data for a user. As a technician, you need to familiarize yourself with the various modules that are available on the market. The following subsections describe each FRU's function and explain the basic terms and concepts related to each module.

System Board

The most important module of every computer system is the *system board*, also referred to as the *main board*, the *motherboard*, and the *planar board*. The system board is made from a fiberglass sheet interlaid with electronic circuitry. This circuitry provides the pathways for electrical signals, referred to as the *bus*, to travel across the board. Every module that makes up a computer system attaches to the motherboard and is able to communicate with other modules through the bus. Also found on the system board are the central processing unit (CPU), memory slots, cache, various connectors, and expansion slots.

Expansion slots come in several varieties, and are labeled according to the type of bus architecture that is used. Examples of bus architecture are Industry Standard Architecture (ISA), Extended Industry Standard Architecture (EISA), Peripheral Component Interconnect (PCI), and Micro

Channel Architecture (MCA), just to name a few. Each bus architecture is responsible for distributing signals back and forth from the expansion slot to the system board, and typically only one or two types are available on any given motherboard (see Figure 1-1). For a more detailed description of bus architectures and available types, please refer to Chapter 4.

Power Supply

Because computers use electrical signals to communicate between the various system modules, a reliable source of power is required for a

| FIGURE 1-1 | A typical motherboard and its components |

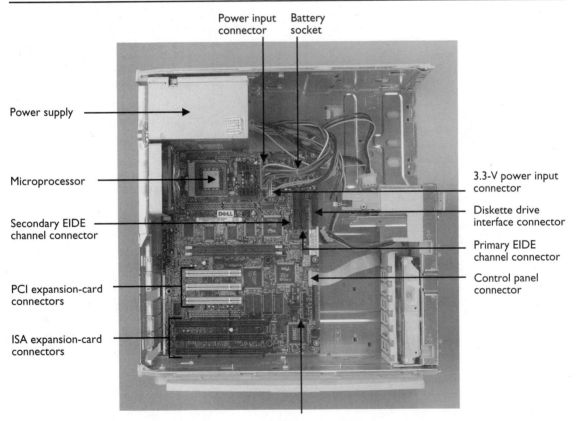

computer to function. Electrical power comes in two forms: *alternating current (AC)*, which is the type that comes out of a wall outlet, and *direct current (DC)*, which is the type that your computer uses. The power supply provides your computer with the electricity it needs by converting AC, or *volts alternating current (Vac)* into DC, also known as *volts direct current (Vdc)*. This current is fed to your computer in each of several forms: +5 Vdc (used to power nearly all chips), +12 Vdc (used to power motors and some communications circuits), -5 and –12 Vdc (required for compatibility, but rarely used in today's PCs). The latest ATX standard also calls for a 3.3 Vdc supply line, used by some of the newest motherboards.

Conventional (linear) power supplies use a diode bridge to convert between current types. All PC power supplies, known as *switching mode* power supplies, add switching transistors to the design, which enables the power supply to be lighter, more compact and more efficient at converting power than a conventional power supply. However, they still generate quite a bit of heat. As a result, power supplies have a built-in fan that is used to prevent them from overheating. An overheated power supply will not only fail, but can damage other components inside the computer.

exam
Watch

Most people have a tendency to glance over these details. However, it is important that you know the voltages generated by the power supply as there will be a question or two on the exam.

Processor/CPU

With all of these electrical signals racing around the system board, a method of directing and controlling these signals becomes necessary. A device, known as the *central processing unit (CPU)*, or merely the *processor*, fulfills this task. CPUs come in different shapes, pin structures, architectures, and speeds.

Generally, the CPU is a square or rectangular chip that attaches to the motherboard through legs, called *pins*, located on the bottom of the chip. Rectangular chips were common in personal computers that predate the early 1980s as well as the original IBM-PC and XT. Since the 80286 CPU was first used in the AT in 1983, all chips through the Pentium have come in a square shape. The newest chips in the PC line-up have returned to a rectangular shape, in two different ways: the PentiumPro is actually two chips with two sets of connections, in one large rectangular chip; and the

Pentium II is actually a rectangular cartridge which fits into a slot and connects to the motherboard through gold fingers, rather than using pins inserted into a socket. The chip itself contains millions of transistors on a silicon base structure like a tiny circuit board. These transistors actually perform the work of directing electrical signals to their destinations and performing calculations.

The pins that attach the chip to the motherboard come in two forms: the *Dual In-Line Package (DIP)* and the *Pin Grid Array (PGA)*. DIP pins are identified as two rows, located on opposing sides of the chip. PCs using either the 8088 or 8086 processor used 40-pin DIPs. The PGA chip has pins arranged in rows on each of the four sides, and was used in PCs using the 80286, 80386, 486 and the first Pentium CPUs (60 and 66MHz). Later Pentiums (75MHz and up) used a slightly different form factor called the Staggered PGA, and the Pentium II dispensed with sockets entirely by going to a cartridge type mounting method called 'slot-1'.

Memory

Just as you need a place at which to work, whether it is a desk in an office or on a countertop in a kitchen, your computer also needs a work area. This area, called *memory*, is used by the computer to store the instructions that comprise your applications and allow for the manipulation of data. Memory is comprised of *integrated circuits (ICs)* that reside on a chip. They work in a manner similar to a light switch in that each circuit can only have one of two states: on or off. Your computer recognizes an "off" switch as a numerical "0," while an "on" switch is translated as a numerical "1." This pattern of 0s and 1s, called *binary*, is how your computer stores, retrieves, and communicates data. Memory is actually broken up into several types: Random-Access Memory (RAM), Read-Only Memory (ROM) and cache memory.

RAM is the most common type of memory chips used for the CPU's main memory, in that the CPU loads your programs into RAM, runs the program's instructions from RAM, loads data into RAM, and manipulates the data while it is in RAM. RAM is sometimes called by its more specific name, DRAM (Dynamic RAM), which is the basis for all main memory chips in all PC systems.

ROM is a type of memory chip that is also part of main memory, except that its contents are written only once, usually at the factory, and when used in a PC system can only be read, hence the name 'Read-Only'. ROM usually only stores the *Basic Input Output System (BIOS)*, which is the set of instructions that your computer uses to boot.

Cache memory is made up of much faster memory called 'SRAM' (Static RAM). Starting with the 80386 CPU, DRAM could not work as fast as the CPU and therefore created a bottleneck that slowed down the CPU. SRAM, which runs up to ten times as fast, could not practically replace DRAM since it also costs ten times as much. However, it was discovered that a small, relatively inexpensive cache of SRAM memory chips could keep copies of the most frequently used main memory locations, and enable the main memory to keep up with the CPU 90% of the time. The faster the CPU, the more cache is needed to maintain that 90% figure. Early 386 systems typically used 64KB or 128KB of cache memory on the motherboard. 486 and Pentium CPUs have added a primary SRAM cache on the CPU chip itself, using a secondary memory cache on the motherboard of 128KB to 1MB in size. The Pentium-II CPU includes a 512KB or 1MB cache built in to the processor cartridge (in addition to an on-chip primary cache of 32KB) and therefore needs no memory cache on the motherboard. All of these design combinations result in an overall memory system performance of 85% to 95% of the theoretical maximum performance, for thousands of dollars less.

Storage Devices

Information has become one of the most important commodities to individuals and businesses today. In the past, data was kept in the form of paper documents held in rows of file cabinets. Storing that information for any length of time became an almost impossible task due to space limitations. When personal computers began populating offices, their storage potential began to be explored. While the first computers used floppy disks and hard drives, today's computers have a wider variety of storage media available, such as CD-ROMs, tape drives, optical drives, Zip drives, and Jazz drives.

Tape Drives

Shortly after the first computers were invented, it was discovered that magnetic tape could store information as a series of 1s and 0s. However, magnetic tape can only store data sequentially, and is most commonly used as a backup medium. As tape drives are not covered on the A+ Certification exam, they only get a brief mention here.

Floppy Drives

Floppy drives write data on disks that are inserted and removed from the drive. The actual disk is encased in an envelope, which has a small opening to allow a read/write head to access the disk. The read/write head passes over the disk, reading data from or writing data to the disk itself. Floppy drives, and the disks used by them, come in two sizes: 5.25" or 3.5".

The 5.25" drives are the older of the two, and are seldom found in actual use today. The original single-sided drives had a capacity of only 180 kilobytes. Double-sided drives and disks were later introduced which increased the storage to 360KB. The 5.25" disks eventually reached a capacity of 1.2MB as technology refined both the accuracy of the drives and the surface of the disk.

As programs began to take up more space, the demand for higher capacity floppy disks increased. 3.5" drives emerged to fill this requirement, and added the extra bonus of using smaller disks encased in a more rigid medium. The first 3.5" disks only held 720KB, but capacity increased as technology progressed. A still newer design allowing 2.88MB was created several years ago, but did not catch on. Today's systems still support the 1.44MB format, while the 720KB and 2.88MB sizes have fallen by the wayside.

Hard Drives

Hard drives work in a manner similar to a floppy drive, but actually contain multiple disks stacked on top of each other inside of the drive itself. The disks reside on a rotating pole, called the *spindle*, and are in constant motion. Several read/write heads pass over the disk, allowing for a more rapid retrieval of data than the floppy drive. While the original hard drives only stored around 10 or 20MB, today's personal computer drive capacities currently reach above 30GB.

CD-ROMs

Compact Disc Read Only Memory or CD-ROM drives, have become increasingly popular and are now a standard component of today's computers. CD-ROMs are used more as a distribution medium than as a true storage medium, but this will change as CD-R (CD-Recordable, a writable standard that is compatible with most CD-ROM readers) writers become more affordable. The drive uses a laser instead of a read/write head to read data off of a compact disc, which is similar to the audio compact discs available at any music store.

As applications increased in size, it became cost-ineffective for vendors to package software on floppy disks. CD-ROMs offer an average capacity of 650MB and allow software manufacturers to store their applications on a single CD-ROM as opposed to multiple disks. This saves the manufacturers quite a bit of money in postage and handling costs. In turn, it saves the customer time by not having to wait around the computer to swap disks. As a result, floppy disks have become the dinosaur of distribution medium.

Monitor

Monitors are an integral part of any computer system, and one with which you must become extremely familiar. However, monitors come in a wide variety of types, ranging from the original monochrome display adapter (MDA), which only permitted text-based characters, to today's high resolution super video graphics adapter (SVGA).

Depending on the type of monitor you are working with, the number of colors and screen resolution varies. However, all monitors function basically the same way. The back of the display screen, called a *cathode ray tube* (CRT), is coated with special chemicals, called phosphors, which glow when electrons strike them. An electron gun, controlled by a monitor's electronics, resides inside the monitor and continuously shoots electrons at the CRT, panning across the monitor from left to right and top to bottom. In a color monitor, each position on the screen, called a pixel (or picture element) has a group of 3 cells—red, green, and blue. The adapter receives a character to be displayed from the computer and converts it into a synchronized series of signals sent to the video monitor, which then uses those signals to light up the correct pixels at the right time, to produce the text and grahics we see on the screen.

Different monitors have the ability to produce a different number of colors and resolution. The original monochrome monitor only supported one color and no graphics. The Hercules monitor was developed to include graphics, but it still only supported one color. Both of these monitors used digital adapters, which only allowed the output to be in a form of 0s and 1s.

Color Graphics Adapters (CGA) provided for four types of digital output. This output was defined with the red, green, and blue colors plus an intensity bit (RGBI). This meant that by combining all three colors, and changing the intensity of those colors, you could get a total of 16 different colors on the display (remember, digital output). However, the display could only show 640 pixels horizontally and 200 pixels vertically, referred to as 640 x 200, on the screen at any time in monochrome, or 160 x 100 in 16 colors.

The next improvement on the monitor was dubbed Enhanced Graphics Adapter (EGA) and added an intensity bit (rgb) to each of the primary colors (RGB) to give a palette of 64 colors. However, while it could only display 16 colors at any given time, it improved resolution by enhancing the maximum pixel resolution to 720 x 350 for text mode and 640 x 350 in graphics mode, even though it still used the old digital output technology.

Monitors were ready for a revolution in technology, and the Virtual Graphics Array (VGA) gave it to us in 1987. It allowed for analog output, meaning that the adapter could control each RGB line incrementally – each wire was no longer restricted to the digital binary value of 'ON' or 'OFF', but could instead use a whole range of analog voltages. By doing so, the monitor was able to display an unlimited range of colors for each individual pixel. The very first VGA adapter cards were limited to only 16 colors, but competitors quickly designed video adapters to display up to 256 different colors at any given time from a virtually unlimited palette. Resolution was improved to 720 x 400 in text mode and 640 x 480 in graphics mode.

Still, there was one more step in monitor technology to be explored, and it was probably the final step. Super Virtual Graphics Array (SVGAs) hit the market and brought us higher resolution standards of 800 x 600, 1024 x 768 (sometimes known as XGA, or eXtended Graphics Array), 1280 x 1024 and even higher. Depending on the amount of RAM included on the video adapter, the number of colors could be 256 or more. 32K or 64K colors are sometimes known as High-Color which is very good, but not quite as good as 16-million color combinations, also known as True-Color. The human eye can only distinguish about 4 million different colors throughout the entire spectrum, so there is no need for any higher color definition.

Monitors are used with *adapters*, or video cards. As stated before, the adapter used must match the type of monitor that is connecting to it. This is because the adapter translates digital information from your computer into the appropriate signal type used by the monitor to generate the picture. If an incorrect adapter is used, the monitor will not work and can result in severe damage to the monitor.

Modem

Today's society has come to rely heavily upon computer systems to facilitate the exchange of information. As a direct result, computers must also have the ability to communicate with other computers in order to send or receive information, regardless of the distance involved. Modems are not only one of the many devices that permit two separate computers to talk to each other, but they're also one of the most common peripherals a technician will work with.

Modems work by translating signals between a computer and a standard telephone line. A computer utilizes binary signals to read, process, store, and communicate data. However, the standard telephone line uses analog signals to carry sound waves, and therefore requires a much wider range of data than a computer. A modem takes data from the sending computer and translates it from digital signals into analog signals before transmitting it across a telephone line, a process called modulation. When a modem receives analog signals from a telephone line, it converts the data back into digital signals, a process called demodulation. As you've probably guessed, the word "modem" is merely an acronym for MOdulator/DEModulator.

Input Devices

Computers live for data, and to give them the data that they crave requires a means for them to accept input. Input devices take data from a user, such as the click of a mouse or the typing on a keyboard, and convert that data into electrical signals used by your computer. Several devices that provide input are: keyboards, mice, trackballs, pointer devices, digitized tablets, and touch screens.

FROM THE FIELD

Use That Screen Saver

There are many misperceptions and rumors regarding screen savers. In recent years, many people have come to the conclusion that they are just something fun to look at. They think that the monitors of today will not get any image burned into them. These people are wrong. In the field, I have seen monitors that have been turned on with the same desktop pattern for 24 hours and they have the image of the desktop burned into them rather deeply. These have been high-quality monitors, which were less than a year old.

Choose your screen saver carefully. I'm sure you have seen the veritable plethora of available screen savers for your PC. Some are simple and some are quite complex. The complex ones usually have 3-D graphics and may contain animation or even have an interactive mode for the user to play a game or whatnot. Remember though that this comes at a price in terms of system resources. As you know, some system resources are very limited. If you are maxing out your system with a screen saver, you may be thrashing on the hard drive as your system is desperately swapping out memory to the disk just to keep this thing running. In the long run, this does run wear on the hard drive.

It has been rumored that the Windows OpenGL screen savers have one option that rarely, but every so often, renders a teapot instead of the tubes, which has been known to bring down systems. This can be tragic on a server. These OpenGL screen savers, and they are not alone, have been the culprit for many systems crashing. When troubleshooting a PC, especially in memory-related freezes and crashes after people come in after lunch, always look at the screen saver they are using as a possible cause. If you think it is their screen saver, change the saver back to the standard ones that don't take up that much memory. It is truly amazing how many times this is overlooked.

—By Ted Hamilton, MCP, A+ Certified

Output Devices

In order for your computer to be useful, it must provide data to you in some form, called *output*. Output devices take electronic signals *from* a computer and convert it into a format that the user can use. Examples of output devices include monitors, which were discussed in a previous section, and printers.

Printers produce paper output, called *hardcopy* or *printouts*. Printouts can include text, graphical images, or both on the same page. Printers come in a variety of types, and many printers now include color. The most common printer types are: dot-matrix, ink jet, bubble jet, and laser printers. For a more detailed description of the various printers available, please refer to Chapter 5.

BIOS

As difficult as it is for you to keep up with all the peripheral devices available in the marketplace, not to mention the different models available from any given vendor, it is even more complex for your computer. And, as if things weren't already rough enough, your computer needs to know how to communicate with every device attached to it, regardless of the operating system software used. The *Basic Input/Output System*, or BIOS, is the mechanism used by your computer to keep track of all this information and still remain independent of the operating system.

The system BIOS is stored in read only memory, or ROM. When an application needs to perform an input-output (I/O) operation on a computer, the operating system makes the request to the system BIOS. The BIOS then translates the request into the appropriate instruction set used by the hardware device. Most system BIOS programs can only run in DOS mode, and are therefore, essentially, DOS mode device drivers for standard devices. Only DOS, early Windows versions, and parts of Windows 95/98 use the system BIOS to communicate with the basic devices. Parts of Windows 95/98, Windows/NT, and many other operating systems (such as UNIX) cannot use the system BIOS and must include their own device drivers for even the basic system devices that are recognized industry-wide.

CMOS

Different FRUs require different settings, such as interrupts, memory address ranges, and input-output ports. To inform the computer of all of the necessary operating parameters every time the computer boots up would, in effect, become tiresome. The CMOS, or *Complementary*

Metal-Oxide Semiconductor, contained in the RTCC (Real-Time Clock/Calendar) chip, allows the computer to store this information even after the computer has been turned off.

CMOS is an integrated circuit manufacturing method using metal-oxide as an insulator between contacts that allows for very low-power operation—the Real-Time Clock/Calendar chip used in your PC can run for 2 to 10 years on the small battery included on every motherboard! Along with keeping track of the date and time even when the system is turned off and unplugged, there are a few extra storage locations (from approximately 50 bytes for older systems, to 2000 for the latest) where data can be written to the chip. While it is commonly identified as CMOS memory, it is really a battery-backed device that is only written to when a new component is installed, such as a hard disk drive or an internal peripheral card that requires component-specific information to be available before the boot process.

Adding and Removing Field Replaceable Modules

As technology increases (often at an exponential rate), new forms of components come into being. These components have to be added to the computer or must replace, or upgrade, an existing one. In addition, some parts will fail as a result of being defective or worn out through use. Therefore, one of the most common tasks every technician has to perform is adding or replacing a system module.

The first, and most important, step that you must take is to power off the computer and disconnect the power cord from the wall outlet. Powering off the computer ensures that no computer activity is occurring while you are working on it, which could cause data loss or worse. And, of course, no circuit boards or devices should be installed or removed while powered up. To do so will likely cause permanent electrical damage. By removing the power cord from the wall outlet, you are ensuring that if you mistakenly hit the power switch while working on the computer, no damage will occur. There may be times when you need to have the power on while inspecting the unit, or testing for voltages; in such cases, be sure the power is turned off while removing the case, as you may cause damage to the system (particularly the hard drive) if it were to receive any sharp jolts while operating. Be careful while performing tests on 'live' circuits, as a misplaced probe or static charges can cause damage to the system. Also, *never open up the power supply* for any reason, as there are dangerous voltages inside the power supply that can be lethal. If you believe the power supply is failing, simply replace it.

Before the cover can be removed from the computer, called the *chassis*, you must ground both the PC and yourself together. This is due to the possibility of an *ElectroStatic Discharge (ESD)* that could damage the computer. ESD occurs when there is a difference in charge between one object and another, resulting in an exchange of electrons that equalize the potential between the two. In order to properly ground yourself to the computer, you must place the chassis on an ESD mat and connect one of the two wires to the computer. The second wire is connected to a ground pin that can be found on any electrical outlet. To ground yourself, wear an ESD wrist strap and attach the wire from the strap to the mat, or to a common ground. ESD and related procedures are more closely explained in Chapter 3.

After you have followed the ESD procedures, the cover can be safely removed. First, remove the screws that hold the cover in place. Some chassis also employ an operating latch to hold the cover in place. Ensure that you disengage any latches if in use. Then, slide or lift the cover from the chassis. Ensure that you place the cover in a location that is out of everyone's way to avoid injury.

At times, it will be necessary to remove expansion cards from the computer as they tend to get in your way. If needed, note their locations and any connectors that attach to them before removal to ensure that you will be able to put everything back in its appropriate spot. To remove cables and power connectors, simply grasp the connector and pull away from the component.

Adapter cards are held in place along the back plane of the computer by screws. Remove all screws holding the card in place and then get a firm grasp on both ends of the board. While using a gentle pulling motion, slightly rock the card from end to end. Some cards may need a bit more effort than others to get out of the expansion slot, but be careful not to exert too much force or you can damage the card and/or the system board. Repeat this procedure for all of the remaining cards that you need to remove.

The following subsections will assume that you have already completed the preceding procedures before continuing.

System Board

Prior to removing the system board, you need to remove all expansion cards, cables, and power connectors attached to the motherboard. Once this has been completed, you need to locate and remove any screws or plastic clips that attach the board to the computer. Once all fasteners have been removed, the system board can then be removed from the chassis.

Once the system board is free of the case, take note of any jumper settings and/or DIP switch settings on the old system board and configure the new board in the same fashion. However, ensure that you have consulted the manufacturer's instruction manual to ensure that none of the settings have changed. At this point, you can move the CPU and memory chips to the new board. Reverse the procedure used to install the replacement system board.

Power Supply

Power supplies are one of the easiest components to replace, as they do not require any jumper or DIP switch settings. The power supply is attached to the system board and the disk drives by power connectors. Follow the procedure in Exercise 1-1 to remove the power supply from your system.

EXERCISE 1-1

Removing a Power Supply

1. Mark the positions of the power connectors so that you can hook up the new power supply properly.

2. Next, firmly grasp the connector and gently pull it from the socket. Never pull on the wires, as they are very easily damaged.

3. Some power supplies have a cable that runs from the power supply to the power switch that must be disconnected as well.

4. After all of the connectors have been detached, the final stage is to remove the mounting hardware used to hold the power supply

in place. Depending on the power supply and mounting hardware, you may need to remove the four screws that hold it in place. With others, you can simply pull or slide the power supply out of the computer.

To install a new power supply, simply reverse the procedures used to remove it, as shown in Figure 1-2. However, you must remember that when you reattach the two power connectors to the motherboard, the black wires that are located on each connector must be facing each other.

Processor/CPU

Some processors are attached to the motherboard by a Zero Insertion Force, or ZIF, socket. If your motherboard has one of these, you operate the lever to remove the chip. In other cases, you use a chip puller to gently grasp the corners or sides of the processor. Use a gentle upward motion to remove the chip from its socket. A slight rocking of the chip is often needed to remove it; make sure you do not rock the chip more than 5 degrees in each direction as you remove it as this can cause damage to the pins that attach the processor to the circuit board.

FIGURE 1-2

Installing a power supply

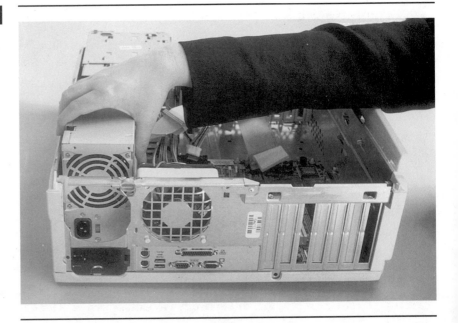

If you are inserting a different speed or type of processor, you must reconfigure the system board. This is done through a series of jumpers or DIP switches that are located on the motherboard. As the board settings differ between the type of board and manufacturer's specifications, refer to the manual provided with the board and configure it appropriately. If the documentation is unavailable, you may be able to consult the manufacturer's Internet site for the correct settings.

Once the system board has been reconfigured, the manner in which you install the new processor differs depending on if you have a ZIF socket or not. If so, simply place the new processor over the socket and operate the lever, or position the processor over the socket and gently push down until the chip is seated. Reinstall any expansion cards or connectors that you removed previously and the installation is complete. A typical processor installation is outlined in Figure 1-3.

Memory

To install memory, follow the procedure outlined in Exercise 1-2 and Figure 1-4.

FIGURE 1-3

Installing a processor

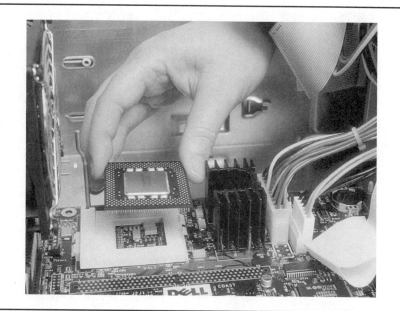

FIGURE 1-4

Installing SIMM memory

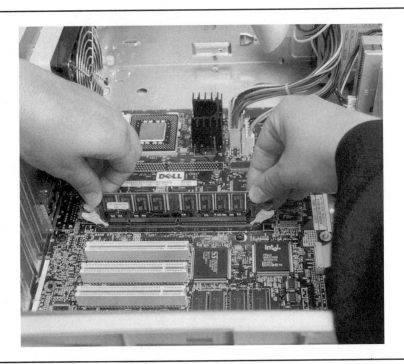

Installing SIMM Memory

1. Place the SIMM memory module over the slot at a 45-degree angle.
2. Gently work the module into the bottom of the socket, and move it to an upright position until it clicks into place.
3. SIMM memory modules are keyed so that they can only fit into the slot one way. If the SIMM module will not go all the way into the socket, then it is probably reversed.

To remove a SIMM memory module, make sure that you disengage the clips from the module first. Then, tilt the chip in the reverse direction from installation and slide it out. If you try to pull directly up on the module you may damage the clips or the electrical contacts in the bottom of the socket.

Nearly all of the latest Pentium and Pentium-II motherboards have a newer kind of memory module called the DIMM (Dual-Inline Memory Module). Where the SIMM had a single row of 72 connecting fingers, each making contact on both sides, the DIMM has two rows of connecting fingers, one row on each side, for a total of 168 connections. The DIMM design and installation method was also changed to help eliminate the common problem of broken clips on SIMM sockets.

Installing DIMM Memory

1. Place the DIMM memory module directly over the slot, so that the notches in the bottom of the module match up with the keys in the socket.

2. Press down carefully on the top of the DIMM module, making sure that the notches are positioned directly over the socket's plastic keys.

3. As the module moves into place, you may notice the side-mounted retention clips moving towards the locked position—you may need to guide them into the locking notches on the side of the DIMM module.

4. When the board is in all the way, the retention clips on the side should be lined up with the notches on the side of the DIMM module—press them into place to lock the module and prevent it from coming out.

To remove a DIMM memory module, simply move the locking retention clips away from the DIMM module. The bottom of the clip will cause the DIMM module to be automatically ejected.

Some older DIMM sockets do not have the locking retention clips—these motherboards should be avoided, as the DIMM memory modules can come loose and cause memory problems.

There are usually no CMOS settings to be concerned about, as memory is auto-sensed by most recent BIOS programs. Even so, you may be required to enter the BIOS Setup program and simply choose the Save Changes option. Some older systems may require you to input the actual amount of memory before saving your changes.

Storage Devices

There are several types of storage devices that are available for computers today, and that number is growing as technology improves. However, the most common peripherals that you will see are floppy drives, hard drives, tape drives, and CD-ROM drives. Hard drives are discussed in later sections under IDE/EIDE and SCSI.

Floppy Drives

To remove a floppy drive, follow the procedure outlined in Exercise 1-4.

EXERCISE I-4

Removing a Floppy Drive

1. Remove the chassis cover from the PC or the front faceplate if you have a proprietary chassis that utilizes rails to mount the drive.

2. Remove the four restraining screws on the sides of the drive or the two screws in the front that fasten the rails to the chassis.

3. Remove the power connector located in the back of the drive that runs from the power supply to the floppy drive. When you remove this connector ensure that you grasp the connector and *not* the wires as you could damage the electrical connections either in the cable connector or in the drive's receptacle.

4. Remove the floppy drive cable which is a flat ribbon cable with a small twist in the wires located in the back of the drive that connects the drive to the floppy controller. In some cases, the floppy controller is on the motherboard.

5. After all of the connectors are free, simply slide the drive out of the computer.

When you install a floppy drive, simply reverse this procedure, as shown in Figure 1-5.

Tape Drives

Tape drives come in two forms, internal or external. With external tape drives, to add or remove them you merely plug or unplug the connector from the adapter located in the back of the computer. With internal drives, you need to remove the power connector and the tape drive cable. After the connectors have been removed, simply slide the drive out of the computer. To install, you reverse this procedure and add one more step. Some tape drives require a device driver installation. This is accomplished through the operating system software. Consult the manufacturer's documentation for more specific details.

Installing a floppy drive

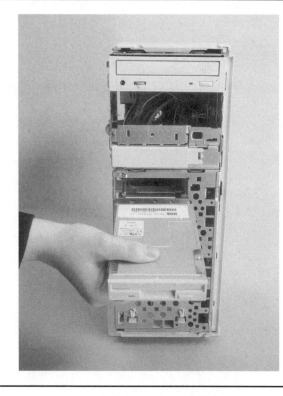

CD-ROM Drives

CD-ROM drive removal and installation is similar to a tape drive with two exceptions. The first is an extra cable that connects the CD-ROM drive to either the controller or the sound board. This cable is used to transmit audio signals from the CD-ROM drive to the controller/sound board. The second difference is that a CD-ROM drive usually requires a device driver installation through the system software, where the tape drive's device driver is usually contained within the application program accompanying the tape drive and usually cannot be used by any other software. Again, consult the product documentation to obtain more details on the particular model you are installing. A typical installation is outlined in Figure 1-6.

Monitor

Although most of the equipment you will deal with isn't too out of date, monitors are the exception. Monitors of all types are still in use today,

FIGURE 1-6

Installing a CD-ROM drive

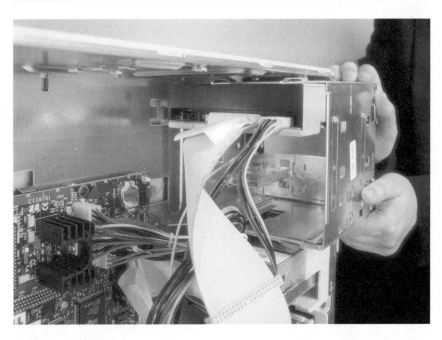

including the old monochrome monitor. When you remove a monitor, you simply unplug it from the back of the computer. If it is a monochrome, Hercules, CGA, or EGA monitor, it is a digital monitor and will have a male DB-9 connector that plugs into a digital adapter. If it is a VGA or SVGA monitor, it will have a male high-density DB-15 connector that plugs into an analog adapter also located in the back of the computer. *Never plug a digital monitor into an analog adapter, or vice versa, as severe damage will result.*

If you need to remove the graphics adapter card, make sure that you note any cable connections to the adapter before removing them. The adapter card itself is held to the chassis by a single screw that must also be removed. Then, gently pull the card out of its socket. To install, simply reverse the procedures.

If you are installing a different model of VGA or SVGA video monitor, be aware that if it is not as capable as the previous monitor, the image on the screen may not be readable. If such is the case, change the video resolution to Standard VGA before installing the new monitor. You may then experiment with choosing the best resolution for the new monitor. However, if you are installing a different type of VGA or SVGA video adapter, ensure that you install the video adapter's device drivers into the operating system. Without changing device drivers, the video adapter will not work correctly, if at all. (Note: If you do not have the drivers for that specific video adapter and operating system available, you can usually specify Generic VGA and most adapters will work—you can then often download the necessary drivers from the video adapter manufacturer's Internet site).

Modem

If you are removing an internal modem, you must be sure to detach the phone cord from the back of the computer before removing the modem card. You can then remove the single screw that holds the modem in place and gently pull upward on the card until it is free from its socket. If it is an external modem, you simply unplug the device from the back of the computer.

To install a modem, you merely reverse the procedures for removing it.

Input Devices

Several forms of input devices are available, such as keyboards and mice. Keyboards are the easiest component to install, as you simply plug them into an available port in the back of the computer. There are two types of keyboard connectors in use, the DIN-5 connector and the Mini DIN-6 connector. DIN-5s are generally found on AT style keyboards and have a round port with 5 pins. The Mini DIN-6 came out with the release of IBM's PS/2 machine, and also has a round port but differs in that it has 6 pins with one square plastic positioning pin.

There are several kinds of mice available, and thus several connectors in use. If you have a serial mouse, it will have a male DB-9 connector and requires a free COM port. A PS/2-type mouse will use a DIN-6 connector and require a free IRQ, almost always IRQ-12. The last type of mouse is the bus-mouse, which is similar to the PS/2-type except that it has to have an expansion card installed to use it. The bus-mouse type is now mostly considered obsolete. Once you have connected the mouse, you have to install the device driver in the operating system software.

While there are a variety of other input devices available, you will not need to know about them for the A+ Certification exam, and thus they are not explained here.

Output Devices

Output devices come in various forms, but the standard devices tested on the A+ exam are monitors and printers. As we have already discussed monitor installation in an earlier section, we will discuss printers in this section.

Printer installation usually requires a cable, a power outlet, and device drivers. The printer cable, which is a flat ribbon type or a round shielded cable, attaches to a parallel port in the back of the computer. Printers have their own power supply inside the unit and must be connected to a power outlet. Once this has been completed, the device driver that shipped with the printer must be installed in the operating system software. To remove a printer, simply reverse the procedures.

CERTIFICATION OBJECTIVE 1.03

IRQs, DMAs, and I/O Addresses

In order to ensure that information is passed between the system modules and the CPU in a timely fashion, devices must be able to directly communicate with the CPU. Because the processor is a busy device, system components must first get the CPU's attention. This is accomplished through a special set of lines, called *interrupt request lines (IRQs)*, in the bus. IRQs are given a number, ranging from 0 through 15, to identify them. In turn, devices are given an IRQ to use. However, with most BIOSs, no two devices in the computer can use the same IRQ or else the processor won't know who is calling it. Some of the newer BIOSs support IRQ sharing, but you need to consult with the vendor's documentation to see if this feature is supported.

Once the CPU receives an IRQ from a device, it can directly communicate with that device through *I/O addresses*, also known as *I/O ports*. I/O ports are assigned a range of numbers which are in turn assigned to specific devices. As with IRQs, no two devices can use the same I/O address.

There are times when some components need to write information directly into main memory. When a device has to do this, it uses a channel called a *Dynamic Memory Access (DMA) Channel,* to do so. This method can be used to improve the module's performance, as you are basically removing the overhead of having the processor move the information from the device to main memory.

Standard IRQ Settings

The computer industry has come up with a set of standard IRQ settings. These settings should be used whenever you are installing a device. Table 1-1 lists the standard IRQ settings.

IRQ 2 is the subject of a good bit of confusion. This results from the fact that the original PC had only 8 interrupt lines, numbered 0 to 7. When the AT was designed, a second interrupt controller was added to provide 8 more interrupt lines (numbered 8 to 15). This second interrupt controller had to deliver its signal through the primary controller on the motherboard, and IRQ 2 was chosen for this task ('cascade' from second controller). Unfortunately, some earlier cards had already made plans to hook into the IRQ 2 signal wire, so on newer machines with the second controller, that signal wire now leads to IRQ 9 on the second controller. The bottom line: For hardware purposes, IRQ 2 and IRQ 9 should be considered the same interrupt signal, and should not be used together in the same system.

exam
ⓦatch

Know your IRQs cold. There are several questions on interrupt assignments on the exam.

Standard I/O Address Settings

In addition to standard IRQ settings, you need to know the standard I/O address settings. Table 1-2 lists the more frequently used port addresses.

exam
ⓦatch

Know your I/O addresses like the back of your hand. You will encounter several questions on the exam pertaining to I/O addresses.

IRQ Number	Standard Device Assignment
NMI (nonmaskable interrupt)	Memory parity error
0	System timer
1	Keyboard
2	On motherboard, cascaded from IRQs 8-15 From device IRQ2, is re-directed to IRQ9
3	Serial port (COM2)
4	Serial port (COM1)
5	Parallel port (LPT2)
6	Floppy controller
7	Parallel port (LPT1)
8	Real-time clock
9	Unassigned (also redirected from IRQ2)
10	Unassigned
11	Unassigned
12	Mouse
13	Math co-processor
14	Hard disk controller
15	Secondary hard disk controller

Differences Between Jumpers and Switches

Interrupts, I/O addresses, DMA channels, and some additional features have to be configured in the hardware. Jumpers and Dual In-Line Package (DIP) switches are used to accomplish configuration.

Jumpers are actually made of two separate components. The first component is a row of metal pins on the hardware itself. The second component is a small plastic cap that has a metal insert inside of it. Each jumper has two positions, either on or off, sometimes described as closed or open, respectively. The particular setting, or combination of settings you choose determines the configuration according to the hardware design,

	Port Address (hex range)	Device
TABLE 1-2	1F0-1F8	Hard drive controller, 16-bit ISA
	200-20F	Game control
Standard I/O Addresses	201	Game I/O
	278-27F	Parallel port (LPT2)
	2F8-2FF	Serial port (COM2)
	320-32F	Hard drive controller, 8-bit ISA
	378-37F	Parallel port (LPT1)
	3B0-3BF	Monochrome graphics adapter
	3D0-3DF	Color graphics adapter
	3F0-3F7	Floppy controller
	3F8-3FF	Serial port (COM1)

which should be described in the device manual. DIP switches are very tiny boxes with switches embedded in them and work exactly the same as jumpers. Each switch is set to on or off, and is sometimes referred to in the manual as 0 or 1, depending on how they are set. You will see two forms of DIP switches in use, but the only difference between the two is the method by which you set the switch. One type of switch is a miniature flip-toggle type switch and the second type is a slide type switch.

Locating and Setting Switches/Jumpers

Regardless of the type of configuration device used, you must locate and set them according to the directions found in the component's documentation. On hard drives, these switches are generally found near the connectors. However, on system boards or expansion cards, you must look around the card. There is no true hard and fast rule used to locate them, but setting these devices can be a bit difficult. To make things a bit easier on yourself when installing a jumper, use a pair of tweezers or the small parts-grabber device found in some toolkits. Never use a pen or pencil point to set DIP switches, as any stray ink or graphite particles can eventually find their way inside the switch and cause intermittent failure. Instead, use a tweezer or the tip of a small screwdriver to press or slide each dipswitch. Always be sure to follow the manufacturer's guidelines for installing. Figure 1-7 shows a typical jumper installation.

Modems

Modems may or may not need to be configured with an IRQ and I/O address depending on what type they are. If they are external devices, they will use an existing serial port on your computer and therefore do not need a separate IRQ or I/O address. However, if they are internal devices, you will definitely have to configure these values. Computers today often have four COM ports, labeled COM1 through COM4. You must choose an unused COM port and I/O address in order to get the modem to function correctly, but most modems are now configured to use either COM3 with an I/O setting of 3E8-3EF or COM4 with an I/O setting of 2E8-2EF. In addition, you need to select a free IRQ. To be sure that these settings will work with your modem, consult the manufacturer's documentation.

FIGURE 1-7

Jumpers

Jumpers

Sound Cards

Sound cards have become popular thanks to the video game industry. Imagine trying to shoot the bad guys with your space ship without having sound to hear those marvelous explosions! Creative Labs has been the industry leader in the sound card business, and as such has set the standard. Typically, sound cards have the following configuration: IRQ 5, DMA 1, and I/O Address 220. These are standard numbers used with SoundBlasters, but as always consult the manufacturer's documentation in case you have one of the esoteric kinds.

Network Cards

Network cards are becoming more common as networks have proven to be a cost-effective method of sharing information. Network cards need to have an IRQ, I/O address, and a memory address configured both on the card and in the device driver. Different forms of network cards, such as Ethernet or Token Ring, have different standards as to their configuration. Figure 1-8 shows the correct procedure for seating an adapter card, but consult the manufacturer's documentation for the appropriate settings.

FIGURE 1-8

Seating an adapter card

CERTIFICATION OBJECTIVE 1.04

Peripheral Ports, Cabling, and Connectors

As a computer technician, your clients expect you to be extremely knowledgeable about *every* facet of a computer's operation. Unless you are one of those lucky few individuals who have been blessed with a photographic memory, this is an almost impossible task. However, you can use a combination of documentation, knowledge, observation, and deductive reasoning to figure out an unfamiliar component's operation, installation, and configuration. In this respect, you become a computer detective, and like any good investigator, you must at least learn the basics of your trade. As you will be working with many different types of FRMs, you need to have a good working knowledge of the various kinds of cables, peripheral ports, and connectors associated with them.

Cable Types

The function of a cable is to transmit electronic signals from one device to another. It does this by sending the signal over some form of medium, such as copper wire or fiber-optics. The medium is enclosed in a tube or a ribbon sheathing in order to protect it from damage. Cables come in two different forms, *shielded* cables and *unshielded* cables, as shown in Figure 1-9. Shielded cables have a wire mesh or Mylar layer added in between the medium and the sheathing that protects the cables from interference. Signals normally follow the medium through the line, but sometimes a signal will stray into the atmosphere producing electrical noise, which is known as EMI (Electro-Magnetic Interference) or, more specifically, RFI (Radio Frequency Interference). Unshielded cables do not have this kind of protection.

Cable and Connector Location—Internal/External

Cables are used to connect peripherals to adapters. Peripherals generally have the connector located in the back of the device while adapters

FIGURE 1-9

Common cable types

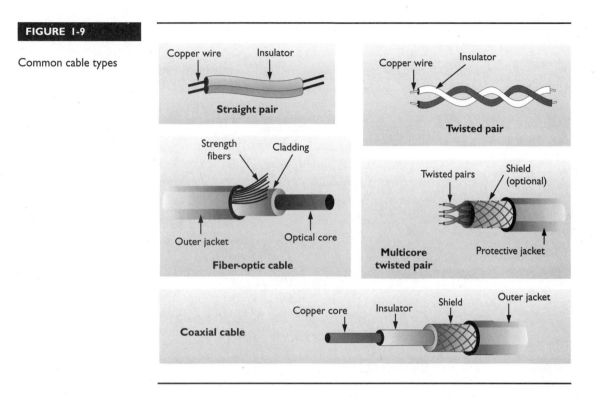

typically have the connector located on the side of the card. Some adapter cards have the connector extending out of the computer in order to enable connection with external devices, while others have it on the side of the card for internal devices.

Serial Versus Parallel

Serial and parallel communications are defined by their transmission characteristics and primary control signals. We explore these forms of communication in the following subsections.

Serial Communication

Serial ports are used for serial communications. PC serial communications ports follow an RS-232C standard. When a device transmits data serially, it is actually transmitting the bits of information sequentially over a single conductor. However, there are two methods used to transmit the data, synchronous and asynchronous.

Synchronous communication uses a single clock circuit in the transmitting device to *synchronize* the data transfer and set the rate of transmission. This synchronization defines the start and end of each and every bit. With asynchronous communications, both the sending and receiving devices have their own clock circuits. Synchronization is established by inserting a start bit in front of the data to be transmitted, then either 7 or 8 data bits, an optional parity bit, and finally one or two stop bits. When the receiver sees the first start bit, it begins its own clocking sequence. As long as the transmitting clock and the receiving clock are approximately the same, the receiver should be able to decode the following bits through the stop bits correctly. Because of the uncertainty of how close the two different clocks correspond, asynchronous serial communications is usually limited to a maximum of 115,200bps (bits per second). Actually, some devices will have problems at anything above approximately 50,000bps.

The primary control signals are summarized in Table 1-3.

Parallel Communication

Parallel communications transmit data over eight parallel conductors. The signals are broken down into two types, data signals and control signals. Control signals are used to control functions or synchronize the devices, called *handshaking*, while data signals contain the actual information. When data is

TABLE 1-3	Control Signal	Description
Primary Control Signals Used in Synchronous Communication	Serial Data Out (TxD)	Used to transmit data. Output from the computer to the device.
	Serial Data Receive (RxD)	Used to transmit data. Input to the computer from the device.
	Data Terminal Ready (DTR)	Used to tell the receiver that the data terminal (computer) is ready.
	Data Set Ready (DSR)	Used to tell the receiver that the data communications equipment (usually a modem) is ready.
	System Ground	Ground reference voltage between the two devices.

sent out using parallel communications, it transmits one byte at a time by transferring 8 bits on 8 separate wires simultaneously (in parallel), versus eight bits transferred one after another on one wire in serial communication.

The primary control signals used in parallel communications are summarized in Table 1-4.

exam
⑪atch

Memorize the primary control signals for the exam. There are several questions that refer to both parallel and serial communications.

Pin Connections

Each pin on a connector is used to carry control signals back and forth from the device. For a listing of the control signals used in serial and parallel communications, please refer back to Table 1-3 and Table 1-4, respectively.

Cable Handling/Routing

When you handle cables, you must be careful with them as they are more easily damaged than you may think. Never place cables near any sharp corners, as any movement or vibration can eventually wear through the

TABLE 1-4	Control Signal	Description
Primary Control Signals Used by Parallel Communications	Acknowledgment	Used to inform the transmitting device that data was received.
	AutoFeed	Used by the processor to inform a printer to generate an automatic line feed.
	Busy	Used to inform the processor that the receiving device cannot receive data.
	Error	Used by the receiving device to indicate an error condition.
	Init	Used by the processor device to initialize the receiving device.
	Slct	Used by the receiving device to acknowledge a Slctin.
	Slctln	Used by the processor to select the device.
	Strobe-Asserted	Used by the receiving device to inform it that valid data is present on the data lines.

insulation. Also, interference with the signals that travel along the cable from high-voltage equipment could cause problems with the proper function of devices that will still try to interpret corrupted signals.

Types of Connectors

Connectors come in two standard flavors, male (pins) or female (sockets). The names in parentheses are due to a new wave of political correctness sweeping through the computer industry that has decided to rename the connectors to something more "acceptable" to society. Male connectors are distinguished by possessing rows of pins, while female connectors are characterized by having sockets. When you attach a connector to a device, you are actually attaching it to another connector. For example, if you are connecting a keyboard to a computer, you are using a male connector to link up with a female connector on your motherboard.

In addition, there are several categories of connectors in use. While there are too many to define, we discuss the connectors most commonly found on the exam.

DB-9

DB-9 connectors are distinguished by their trapezoid appearance. There are 9 pins in the connector, 5 pins in the bottom row and 4 pins in the top row. This type of connector is most commonly used for video display devices and serial ports.

DB-25

DB-25 connectors are similar to DB-9s in that they are trapezoidal in shape. There are 25 pins set into two rows on the connector. This type of connector is used for parallel and serial ports.

RJ-11

RJ-11 connectors are the same connectors that are used to attach a phone line to a phone. It is also used to link a modem to a phone line. These connectors only have two pins, and clip into the modem.

RJ-14

RJ-14 connectors are dual-line phone jacks that can handle up to two phone lines. These types of connectors are not very common in the industry.

RJ-45

RJ-45 connectors are most commonly used to attach an unshielded twisted pair (UTP) cable with a network card. These connectors have 8 pins, and are similar to the RJ-11 connector. This is the most common connector used on an Ethernet network.

PS2/Mini-DIN

PS2/Mini-Din connectors are most commonly used for mice and keyboards. These connectors have 6 pin positions (sometimes with only 5 pins), plus one square positioning key.

CERTIFICATION OBJECTIVE 1.05

Installing and Configuring IDE/EIDE Devices

The earliest hard drives, the ST-506 and the ESDI (Enhanced Small Device Interface) drives, had to utilize a device known as a *controller* in order for the drive to function. The controller's job was to interpret commands from the CPU into the instructions needed by the hard drive. For example, if the CPU was told to write data to the hard disk, it would send the proper software instructions to the controller. The controller would create a set of hardware instructions that would tell the hard drive how to position the read/write heads over the disk, and then actually read the data. Once the drive got to the data, it would send it back to the controller, which would then pass it back to the CPU.

Controllers complicated the installation of hard drives because they were an additional circuit board that had to be configured and installed in the computer. Integrated Drive Electronics (IDE) drives simplified hard drive installation and improved reliability by integrating the controller into the drive itself. It is because of this that IDE drives gained popularity in the computer industry. However, IDE drives are limited by the fact that they are restricted to about 504MB, or about 528 million bytes. The Enhanced IDE (EIDE) drives were created to overcome this limitation, and can be found in a variety of sizes in the gigabyte range.

However, before installing an IDE or EIDE drive, you must have a hard drive adapter connected to the motherboard. Most of the more recent system boards already have an IDE/EIDE adapter built-in, but if it is an older board you merely plug the adapter into the system board, and then plug the drive into the adapter. Once the adapter is in place, you can install the drive into the computer, as outlined in Figure 1-10. The drive is attached to the adapter using a 40-pin cable, which is similar to the floppy drive cable we discussed earlier except that it doesn't have a twist, and it has 40 pins instead of the floppy's 34 pins.

The last phase of your installation is to run the computer's CMOS (Complementary Metal-Oxide Semiconductor) Setup program. Without completing this step, many computers won't even know that the hard drive is there. When you turn on the computer, you should see a message on the screen that states to press a key, or keys, for SETUP. On some of the newer computers, you have to pay strict attention to the monitor or you may miss

FIGURE 1-10

Installing a hard drive

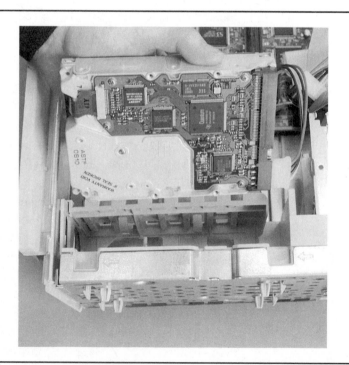

this message. When you press the key combination that brings up the Setup program, enter into the Fixed Disk section and enter the appropriate information needed by the Setup program to identify the drive. This information generally includes items such as the number of sectors, cylinders, and heads that the hard drive has. You can usually find all of the correct configuration information imprinted on the drive itself or in the accompanying manufacturer's documentation.

Master/Slave

The preceding installation information works if you have only one drive to install, but what if there is an existing drive in the computer or you have to install multiple drives at once? Because the IDE interface was designed to emulate the original Western Digital hard drive controller used in the IBM PCs as closely as possible, it has retained the same limit of two drives per controller. To install a second IDE drive, the installation is performed the same way as previously discussed up to the point where you actually install the drive itself. At this point, installation becomes slightly more complex due to the fact that each drive has a controller built into the device itself. When two IDE drives (and two built-in controllers) are attached to the same cable (or channel) at the same time, the adapter that is attached to that cable would get confused as to which controller was "in charge." This problem is resolved through the *master/slave* relationship.

Basically, one drive on each IDE/EIDE channel becomes the *master* drive. All commands that direct the slave drive's operations are passed through the master's controller. Configuring the master/slave drives is accomplished by setting the appropriate jumpers on the individual drives before you install them. First, consult the manufacturer's documentation for the correct jumper setting, set the jumpers accordingly, and install the drives. The rest of the installation is completed as before.

Devices per Channel

With either IDE or EIDE drives, you can have up to four drives installed but you will only be able to put two drives on a single cable (or channel). In order to have three or four drives, you need a separate cable that is connected to the second IDE/EIDE interface. Each connector on the IDE/EIDE controller is given a channel number. The first channel is Channel 0 (primary) and the second is Channel 1 (secondary).

CERTIFICATION OBJECTIVE 1.06

Installing and Configuring SCSI Devices

SCSI (Small Computer Systems Interface), pronounced "scuzzy" in the computer industry, has become more popular in the PC field recently. This interface permits you to connect multiple devices to one cable or SCSI channel in configurations of up to 8, 16 or 32 devices (including the adapter as one device) on a single channel, depending on the SCSI implementation that you are using. In order to properly install or upgrade SCSI devices, there are several things that must be taken into consideration and are discussed in the following sections. We will first discuss the types of SCSI devices that are available.

Types of SCSI Devices

As technology improves, new forms of devices and standards become available. The organization that defines the SCSI standard is the American National Standards Institute (ANSI), and was responsible for releasing the first SCSI standard in 1986. Since then, SCSI has gone through several evolutions. The types of SCSI devices that you may encounter are the topics of the following subsections.

SCSI-1

The original SCSI device had an 8-bit bus that was attached to the devices using either female DB-25 or Centronics-50 connectors for external SCSI devices. Internally, SCSI devices were attached with a 50-pin ribbon cable. Its data transfer rate was a maximum of 5 megabytes-per-second (MBps), and was the fastest drive on the market. However, vendors did not adhere to the standard and made a few small changes in their implementation. As a result, some SCSI devices would interfere with the correct operation of other SCSI devices. This made them a major headache to install and configure when those differences made themselves known.

SCSI-2

In 1994, ANSI released a new standard that was aptly named SCSI-2. This standard allowed for backward-compatibility with the original SCSI-1 devices. However, three different variants of the device have been released because of the different options that the standard permitted. One of the variants, named *Wide SCSI-2*, included a 16-bit bus that enabled large data transfers to be more efficient (a 32-bit version is also available, but is rarely implemented). *Fast SCSI-2* was another option that increased the data transfer rate to 10MBps. However, the final variant combined the features of both options to create *Fast-Wide SCSI-2*. This combination yielded a 16-bit bus with a total transfer rate of 20MBps.

SCSI-3

Because the SCSI-3 standard is so new, relative to the A+ Certification exam, there really isn't anything about it that you need to study for the exam. However, the information is included here as a reference point for real-world situations.

SCSI-3 is the latest SCSI standard issued by ANSI. Like SCSI-2, SCSI-3 also provides for extra options, and at the time of this writing there are only two additional variants on the market. The first one goes by the names Fast-20 SCSI or Ultra SCSI. It was developed for high-performance SCSI devices and comes on an 8-bit bus with a 20MBps transfer rate. The second variation on a 16-bit bus goes by the labels Wide Fast-20 SCSI and more currently Wide Ultra SCSI. Its characteristics are a 16-bit bus with transfer speeds at a maximum of 40MBps.

Address Conflicts

Like IDE drives, there can be more than one SCSI device per channel. Unlike IDE drives, SCSI can have more than two devices on one interface, so it is very important that you be aware of the SCSI ID address used for each device on a particular adapter, and the rules that govern them. Keep in mind the following rules when identifying and setting the SCSI ID for each SCSI device:

- **SCSI ID Address (8-bit)**   For SCSI-1 or SCSI-2 using a standard 25 or 50-pin cable, the ID can only be 0 through 7. The adapter uses one ID which is usually 7. In some rare cases the adapter may use ID 0. Although SCSI ID 7 has the highest priority, this has very little importance since it is only a means of arbitrating which device goes first in the rare situation where two devices try to activate the bus at the very same time (within 2.4 microseconds of each other).

- **SCSI ID Address (Wide SCSI)**   For 16 bit Wide SCSI, there are 16 possible SCSI IDs, 0-15. The additional SCSI ID numbers 8-15 have a lower priority than 0-7, with 8 being the lowest. For 32-bit Wide SCSI, the additional ID numbers 16-23 have the next lower priorities (with ID 16 being the lowest) and ID addresses have priorities that are lower still, with ID 24 having the lowest priority of absolutely all device ID addresses. In a SCSI system with a mixed bus (some 8-bit, some 16-bit for instance), the entire ID addressing for the entire SCSI bus on that adapter will be limited to the smallest limit—in this case, even the Wide-SCSI devices would be limited to ID addresses 0-7. As stated earlier, although the ID addressing limitations are very important, the priority is really unimportant.

- **SCSI ID Address (All)**   No two SCSI devices can use the same SCSI ID address on one particular SCSI Channel. If a PC has two or more SCSI adapters with separate cables (channels), then these rules apply only to each channel independently. Adaptec, for instance, has the capability in most of their SCSI adapters to have up to 4 separate SCSI adapters (and therefore 4 SCSI channels) operating in the same PC at the same time. The SCSI adapter itself is usually ID 7, although a few have been designed as ID 0. For those that can be set to any number, 0-7 must be chosen in order to work with all SCSI devices, and generally 7 should be chosen to help avoid confusion.

- **Bootable SCSI devices**   SCSI devices were not assumed to be boot-type devices such as floppy or hard drives. For this reason, in order to boot to a SCSI device, a supplemental BIOS chip must usually be present on the SCSI adapter. In the most recent motherboard designs, a SCSI adapter may be included on the motherboard and, if so, the SCSI boot code is then likely to be included in the system BIOS. Please check your SCSI adapter (motherboard or not) for actual instructions for activating a SCSI device for boot purposes. In most cases, the SCSI boot device will need to be assigned either ID 0 or 1.

Switch and Jumper Settings

SCSI devices must be manually set to a SCSI ID address prior to their installation according to the addressing rules just discussed. This is accomplished through a series of jumpers or DIP switches located on the back of the device. In order to correctly configure the address, consult the manufacturer's documentation for the appropriate settings. If the documentation is unavailable, configuration information may be found at the manufacturer's Internet site.

Cabling

The kind of cable used to connect SCSI devices is dependent upon whether or not it is an internal or external device, and the speed and width of the SCSI device it is attaching. Internal 8-bit devices use a single, unshielded 50-pin ribbon cable, while external 8-bit devices use either a DB-25 or Centronics-50 cable. For external Fast-SCSI connections, SCSI-2 and SCSI-3 specified a new mini-Sub-D connector, approximately half the dimensions of the Centronics-50 cable but still containing 50 pins. These are all considered the *A-cable* in SCSI-2 definitions, and are for 8-bit operation.

16-bit Wide-SCSI requires new cabling; either a second 68-pin cable called *the B-cable* to be used in conjunction with the A-cable, or a newer single cabling method with 68 pins called the *P-cable*. Internally, the P-cable is a 68-pin ribbon cable with half the pitch (.025-inch conductor spacing, .05-inch contact spacing) of the original internal 8-bit A-cable; externally, a 68-pin mini-Sub-D is defined in SCSI-2 for Wide SCSI operation, which is the same as the 50-pin mini-Sub-D, with the exception of 18 extra pins.

32-bit Wide SCSI is defined in SCSI-3 as using yet another cable, the *Q-cable*, another separate 68-pin cable used in conjunction with the P-cable. Internally or externally, the two cables are used together where the lower 16 bits are transferred on the P-cable while the upper 16 bits are transferred along the Q-cable.

Termination Conflicts

Armed with a unique address and attached to the bus, the circuitry on the SCSI device takes over. When a signal is sent out on the bus, only the device that corresponds to the correct address responds to the initiator. However, that signal doesn't stop at the device but instead continues traveling along the bus. To prevent these signals from hitting the end of the bus and being reflected back down the cable, a *terminator* must be attached on both ends of the bus. Some devices and adapters have the terminator incorporated into the device, in which case you can enable or disable the terminator using a jumper or a DIP switch. Termination on any device in the middle of the bus must be removed or disabled. Keep in mind that if an adapter has both internal devices and external devices attached to their respective cables, the adapter itself must have it's own termination removed or disabled, as it is sitting in the middle of one SCSI bus containing both internal and external devices.

If termination is not set up correctly, any SCSI device on the bus may function intermittently, or not at all. Typically, if no termination is installed anywhere on the SCSI bus, nothing will work. If only one terminator is installed, all SCSI devices may work, but occasionally hang. If two terminators are installed, but not at the end of the cable, any devices located on the unterminated portion of the cable will be subject to failure or hanging. If excessive termination is installed (3 or more terminators), the devices may work intermittently, or fail completely.

Termination Power (TERMPWR)

If *Active Termination* is used on any SCSI device (to find this out, consult your SCSI device documentation), termination power must be enabled on one SCSI device, but only one.

Installation Steps

For the installation of SCSI devices, you will need to configure up to three settings: the SCSI ID addresses, SCSI bus width, and termination. You will find that almost all SCSI problems stem from improperly configuring one or more of these three settings.

1. **SCSI ID addresses**   For each SCSI channel, make sure each SCSI device, both internal and external, has a unique SCSI ID address. Check the ID address for the adapter itself, and make sure no other device is assigned that ID. If you have a choice, you should usually set the adapter to ID 7. If you have a SCSI device that you want to be bootable, you will probably need to set it to ID 0, or possibly ID 1. Check your system documentation to be sure.

2. **SCSI bus width**   If using a mixture of 8, 16 and/or 32-bit SCSI devices on one channel, be sure to place the smaller-width devices closer to the end of each cable (internal or external) than the larger-width devices. For example, if installing one 8-bit and two Wide SCSI (16-bit) devices internally, connect both 16-bit devices to the P-cable coming from the adapter, then use a 16-to-8-bit transition adapter to connect the 8-bit device.

3. **Termination**   Remove or disable termination from all devices, except the device at the end of each cable. If only one cable is used (either internal or external), the terminator on the adapter itself must be enabled or installed. If both cables are in use, the adapter terminator must be removed or disabled.

Configuration

With all of your SCSI devices addressed, installed, terminated, and cabled together, it is time to tell the computer about them. The procedure used depends on whether or not you have a bootable SCSI device installed. If there is a bootable device, you must enable the BIOS on the adapter card. This is performed through a jumper or DIP switch setting that should be listed in the adapter's documentation. Once the BIOS is enabled, you configure the adapter to use a memory area located in reserved memory. Again, you must consult the documentation for the appropriate address and setting information.

If your device is not bootable, such as a SCSI scanner or CD-ROM drive, you must load a device driver in the operating system software. The driver itself should have come on a floppy disk with the SCSI adapter card, but in some cases you may need to visit the manufacturer's Internet site to get it. Be aware that sometimes there might be problems with the drivers themselves, as problems have a tendency to show up after the adapters have hit the market. If you encounter problems, try visiting the manufacturer's Internet site for an updated driver or a small piece of software, called a patch, that will resolve the difficulty.

CERTIFICATION OBJECTIVE 1.07

Installing and Configuring Peripheral Devices

As peripheral devices are the most frequent modules that need to be installed or replaced, it is critical that you understand how to install the many common components available. The following subsections will describe how to install and configure common devices that you should be familiar with.

Remember that when you work with any computer, you must follow ESD procedures. This requires you to ensure that the computer itself is on an electrostatic mat and attached properly, as well as guaranteeing that your electrostatic wrist band is properly secured on your person. The only time that you would not wear the wrist strap is when you are working with monitors. *Never wear a wrist strap when working on monitors as the high voltage section, even with the power turned off or unplugged, may contain a residual charge that can harm you, or possibly even kill you.*

Once you have your ESD procedures completed, you need to remove the screws in the back of the computer to remove the case. These screws are located around the edges of the computer. Some cases must be unlatched before you slide them out, but usually you just have to slide the cover up and away from the computer. Make sure that you place the cover out of everyone's way, including yourself, to avoid unnecessary injury.

With some components, you may be required to remove various expansion cards or connectors that may be in your way. If there are any such cards or connectors, remove them only after marking their placement and connections. This will save you some grief during the installation process.

Monitor/Video Card

Before installing a new monitor, you must take note of whether this is a different type of monitor than was previously installed, for example upgrading from an EGA to an SVGA. If so, you will require a new video adapter as well. If you are only replacing a monitor of the same type, take note of the models, as different model monitors may not work with some features or modes of your video card.

Either way, follow the procedures in Exercise 1-5 when installing the card.

EXERCISE 1-5

Installing a Monitor/Video Card

1. Power off the monitor and unplug it from the back of the computer.

2. If you are replacing the adapter card, make sure that you note the connectors that attach to the card as the new card will probably have the same connector setup, then remove the connectors.

3. Remove the single screw that holds the card to the chassis, then gently pull upwards and away from the computer. If you apply too much force, you may damage the card.

4. Once it is free, replace the card with a new one by reversing the procedures.

5. After replacing any adapter cards, you can now plug the new monitor into the computer.

6. When you boot the computer, you must install the appropriate device drivers if it is a new type of video card or a different brand. Make sure that you follow the manufacturer's documentation when installing new monitors. If you are working with a Windows 95 machine, it will probably detect the new component and step you through the installation.

If there were problems during the installation of a new adapter card, it will have paid off to have the case off of the computer during the testing phase. Once you have ensured that all the components are working correctly, power off the monitor and the computer to replace the case. Simply slide the case back onto the chassis and reinstall the screws. You can reattach the monitor to the computer at this point.

Modem

Most of today's modems use either COM3 or COM4 for the port. When you install a modem, check the back of the computer for any other connections going in.

You may need to move an expansion card to another slot in order to position a modem so it's easy to get at later for troubleshooting purposes, or to change phone lines going into the computer. Modems come in two forms, internal or external. External modems only need a free COM port, and can plug into an existing serial port in the back of the computer with an RS232-compliant cable. However, with an internal modem, you must make sure that you already have a free IRQ, I/O address, and COM port prior to installation. To install an internal modem, you must insert it into one of the expansion slots inside the computer and install the screw that holds it in place. The IRQ, I/O address, and COM port information will also need to be configured in the operating system software or using device drivers.

Storage Devices

Installation and configuration of the various storage devices have already been discussed in previous sections. For floppy drives, tape drives, and CD-ROM drives, please refer back to the section on Adding and Removing Peripheral Devices. If you need to reference information on hard drives, please refer to either the Installing and Configuring IDE/EIDE or Installing and Configuring SCSI Devices sections for the appropriate type of drive.

Associated Drivers

Various peripherals require that a device driver is installed into the operating system. With MS-DOS systems, the information is placed in the AUTOEXEC.BAT or CONFIG.SYS files. With Microsoft Windows 95, the operating system will detect the new component upon boot and step you through the process of installing the driver if there isn't already one available to the system. Depending on the operating system with which you are working, consult the documentation provided by the manufacturer to ensure that you install the driver correctly.

Functions and Use of Common Hand Tools

In order to install or upgrade computer hardware, you must have a good set of tools. Nothing is more frustrating than going to a customer site and not having the proper equipment with you. Worse yet, the customer will get the impression that you may not know what you're doing. There are several items that should be included in any toolkit, and they are discussed in the following sections.

Screwdrivers

The most common tool found in every technician's toolkit is the screwdriver. Screwdrivers come in various sizes and types. The usual assortment of screwdrivers include: flat-blade, Phillips, and Torx, all discussed in the following subsections.

Flat Blade

Flat blade screwdrivers are common and easily recognizable by their flat blade or flat head. The screws have a single slot that runs dead center across its head. While older computers may still use these types of screws, more modern ones seldom do. The reason is that the metal around the slot has a tendency to be easily damaged by the force used to turn the screw, causing the need to replace the screws more often. If you've ever had to remove a case from a computer, you'll know how stubborn some screws are to remove, especially if it hasn't been used in awhile. Phillips, and more recently Torx, screws are more commonly used. Hex drivers are also very common today.

Phillips

The Phillips screwdriver provides more protection against damaging the head of the screw, and is used more frequently in the computer industry. The blade of the screwdriver is in a cross-shape, tapering down to a point. The screw itself has two slots that form an "X" or a cross, depending on how you view it. The extra slot allows for the screwdriver to more evenly distribute the force exerted on the screw itself, reducing the potential for the screwdriver to slip off the screw head. Unfortunately, if a screw has been over-torqued or otherwise damaged, during your attempt to remove it, you can easily cause damage to the screw. With either type of screw, any slippage can cause bits of metal to flake off, possibly causing short circuits in the system later on. When buying bits or screwdrivers, note that Phillips uses a number system, such as #2, to denote the size of the blade. Be sure to get several different sizes into your toolkit, to minimize the chance of slippage and subsequent damage.

Torx

The Torx screwdriver looks somewhat similar to the Phillips screwdriver with its cross shape, except that it has two extra points of contact, and goes vertically into the screw head (instead of angled) to eliminate the chance of slippage and damage. This type of screw and driver is sometimes called a *star* tip or head. This gives even more protection from damage to the screw itself. Currently, you will usually only need this type of screwdriver to work on Apple Macintosh or Compaq systems, but the popularity of this type is increasing. Torx screwdrivers also use a numbering system to denote the size of the blade, but are given a *T* instead of the pound (#) sign.

Hex Driver

IBM, among others, uses hex-head (1/4-inch or 3/16-inch six-sided) type screws, and are nearly as good as Torx for reliable assembly and disassembly of PC components. Although they are very common with the generic computer chassis and components supplied out of Korea and Taiwan, unfortunately the screws are of very low quality and often are not sized accurately for either English (SAE) or metric hex-head tools. A good idea would be to stock your lab with a bulk supply of case, motherboard, and component screws with high-quality hex-head or Torx-head screws in the 3 or 4 common threads used by PC components.

Chip-Puller

In order to remove integrated circuits, a special type of tool called the *chip puller* or *integrated circuit (IC) puller*, is used. The standard IC puller is U-shaped, and has small fingers on the ends that slip between the socket and the chip itself. These fingers ensure that the force used to pull the chip from the socket is spread equally between the two sides to reduce the possibility of damage to the chip. Once you have the puller on the chip, gently pull until the chip comes out of the socket. Some techs find it easier to pull straight up on the tool when removing a chip; others find they cannot modulate the upward force closely enough, and find it easier to hold the tool lower and rock the chip slightly (less than 5 degrees each way) while applying moderate upward pressure.

Never try to remove an integrated circuit with your fingers. For one thing, you could damage the pins that attach the chip to the board. Another reason is that static electricity on yourself (and therefore, your fingers) can discharge to the pins on the chip and damage the internal circuitry. Another "no no" is to attempt to use a pair of pliers or tweezers on chips. These tools magnify the force that you apply to them, risking an overexertion of force and hence damage to the chip.

Multimeter

Computers work by utilizing electricity in their operations. As such, you can use a measuring device, called a *multimeter*, to determine whether certain components are functioning correctly. Most common multimeters enable you to measure current, resistance, or voltage using the same unit. Switching between these functions is accomplished through a button or a dial. The measurements are made through two probes, one colored red for positive (+) and one colored black for negative (-), that are touched on the component that is to be checked. A built-in display shows you the values obtained by the probes.

A multimeter is most commonly used for two situations, either using the resistance (Ohms) position to make a continuity test of switches or cables, or using the DC (volts) position to verify the supply voltages from the power supply are operating correctly.

To test *continuity* of a switch, the leads are placed on both sides of any switch, and then the switch is operated. When the switch is off, the resistance should read *infinite* (open-circuit). However, if the switch is in-circuit at the time, there will be other circuitry that will conduct some amount of electricity, so you should simply see some value of resistance at least 1000 Ohms or more. When you move the switch to the off position you should then read less than 2 Ohms. On some multimeters, any resistance less than 10 ohms or so will cause it to emit a tone signal.

Testing cables is even easier: after removing the cable, placing the test leads across two neighboring contacts should show *open circuit* resistance of at least 20 megohms (million ohms) or more, otherwise the two pins have some kind of defect between them. Placing the two probe leads at the same pin number at opposite ends of the cable should show continuity, less than 5 Ohms. If not, that wire or contact is broken and defective.

Testing for proper positive output voltages of the power supply is easy—switch the multimeter to a range that will allow the correct voltage to be displayed without going over full-scale (for instance, if your choices for full-scale are 2, 20, or 200 volts, for measuring +12 or +5 volts, use the 20-volt range). Then, place the black lead on the ground wire (always black coming from the power supply) and the red lead on the point to be tested. You should then be able to read the voltage from the display. Check the system documentation for allowable value of that supply line.

Testing the negative supply voltages is exactly the same if using a digital multimeter—the display will simply show a minus sign in front of the number. If using an analog (needle-type) multimeter, just reverse the black and red leads, and read the voltage from the meter as a negative number.

Testing the AC supply voltage from the outlet or inside the power supply is strongly discouraged, as the voltage and current together present a lethal combination that can kill. Fortunately, the only dangerous voltages (other than the video monitor mentioned earlier) are inside the power supply itself. All voltages found anywhere else in the PC case are as safe to work around as the voltages found in a flashlight.

Current cannot be measured in any computer circuit without actually breaking the circuit, and so is rarely performed. To actually check the correct operation of most integrated circuits would require a detailed schematic and either an oscilloscope or logic analyzer, and so that level of troubleshooting is left to the manufacturer.

Upgrading BIOS

The Basic Input-Output System (BIOS) contains the program to start the system, and will read various settings from the battery-backed CMOS storage on the Real-Time Clock/Calendar chip located on the motherboard. Most BIOS chips also contain the Setup program (accessed by pressing a special key-combination shortly after powering up) to choose the settings from a menu and save them in the CMOS Clock/Calendar chip for use during the boot-up process. Other systems require the use of a special disk program to change the BIOS boot-up settings.

System BIOS (Flash or Replace)

Occasionally, a system manufacturer may make a BIOS upgrade available to fix a bug or add a feature: For older systems with the BIOS chip installed in a socket on the motherboard, you simply remove the old chip and replace it with the new one. Newer systems use something called EEPROM (Electrically-Erasable, Programmable, Read-Only Memory), also known as Flash-ROM. In those cases, a special program can re-program the Flash-ROM chip without removing it, from a file either supplied on disk or possibly downloaded from the manufacturer's Internet site.

EXERCISE 1-6

Replacing BIOS

1. Follow the ESD procedures prior to removing the case.

2. When the case has been removed, mark and remove any expansion cards or connectors that may be in the way.

3. It is at this point that you can use a chip puller to gently remove the chip from its socket.

4. To install a BIOS, position the chip over the socket, ensuring that the pins are properly in place, and gently push down on the chip until it is seated.

System Hardware

The BIOS boot-up settings contain information on the system hardware and may need to be updated when a new component has been added to the computer. To access the BIOS, you must enter the SETUP program when the computer is booting. Some systems use the DEL key to enter the program, while others may use an ALT-ESC key combination. To ensure that you hit the appropriate key(s), carefully watch the computer as it powers up for a message that tells you how to access the SETUP program.

CERTIFICATION OBJECTIVE 1.10

System Optimization

Sometimes you are required to *optimize* a computer system. This basically involves improving the performance of the equipment. While there is only so much you can do, there are various devices that can be optimized, such as memory, hard drives, and cache memory. The following sections describe each in detail.

Memory

Optimizing memory usually means that you free up conventional memory, which is the memory address range between 0K and 640K, if you are using DOS, basic Windows, or even in some cases, Windows 95 or 98. One of the things you can do to free conventional memory is to load MS-DOS into the High Memory Area (HMA) by adding the following line to the CONFIG.SYS file:

```
DOS = HIGH
```

Another way to free up conventional memory is to load device drivers or *terminate-and-stay resident (TSR)* programs into upper memory. TSRs are just programs that remain in memory and do not do anything until a special condition takes place, such as a screen saver program. The first step is to actually check the system memory configuration by using a special program called MEM.EXE with the /C switch. The /C tells the memory program to *classify*, or individually list the programs that use up memory and what type of memory is being used, as shown in Figure 1-11. In the Conventional column, any number over 0K means that something is using conventional memory.

To move a device driver or TSR to upper memory, you must first load the EMM386.EXE program from the CONFIG.SYS file if it is not already doing so. For device drivers, use a DEVICEHIGH=<*drivername*> line in the CONFIG.SYS file to load the driver into upper memory. With TSRs, you need to use a LOADHIGH <*TSR_name*> line in the AUTOEXEC.BAT

FIGURE 1-11

Output of the
MEM /C Command

Modules using memory below 1 MB:

Name	Total		Conventional		Upper Memory	
MSDOS	17,648	(17K)	17,648	(17K)	0	(0K)
SETVER	848	(1K)	848	(1K)	0	(0K)
HIMEM	1,168	(1K)	1,168	(1K)	0	(0K)
SMS_10X	27,808	(27K)	27,808	(27K)	0	(0K)
IFSHLP	2,864	(3K)	2,864	(3K)	0	(0K)
WIN	3,648	(4K)	3,648	(4K)	0	(0K)
vmm32	3,424	(3K)	3,424	(3K)	0	(0K)
COMMAND	7,504	(7K)	7,504	(7K)	0	(0K)
Free	590,176	(576K)	590,176	(576K)	0	(0K)

Memory Summary:

Type of Memory	Total	Used	Free
Conventional	655,360	65,184	590,176
Upper	0	0	0
Reserved	393,216	393,216	0
Extended (XMS)	66,060,288	188,416	65,871,872
Total memory	67,108,864	646,816	66,462,048
Total under 1 MB	655,360	65,184	590,176

Total Expanded (EMS)	66,584,576	(64M)
Free Expanded (EMS)	16,777,216	(16M)
Largest executable program size	590,160	(576K)
Largest free upper memory block	0	(0K)

MS-DOS is resident in the high memory area.

file instead. The following illustrates the lines needed by the CONFIG.SYS file and the AUTOEXEC.BAT file.

In the CONFIG.SYS file:

```
DEVICE=C:\DOS\EMM386.EXEDEVICEHIGH=<drivername>
```

In the AUTOEXEC.BAT file:

```
LOADHIGH <tsr_name>
```

Hard Drives

Hard drives have a tendency to become *fragmented*. By fragmented, we are talking about the way in which they store files and file locations. When you save a file to a hard disk, it is not necessarily stored in consecutive areas on the disk. Instead, the drive locates the first areas available and dumps whatever will fit there, then moves on to the next location and so on until the file is stored. A *pointer* is used to tell the drive where the next piece of data that constitutes the file is located. Sometimes the pointers become *corrupt*, or the data itself may be damaged. Also, as the drive has to search in different locations just to retrieve a single file, the speed at which the drive can retrieve the information is slowed down. To *defragment* the drive, you must run a utility, such as Microsoft's Defragmenter (DEFRAG.EXE).

There are also some software packages on the market that are used to optimize hard drives, such as Norton's SpeedDisk, which you can purchase at any computer software store.

Cache Memory

The only thing that you can do to improve the performance of cache memory is to add more. By adding more cache memory, you enable the computer to store more of the frequently accessed instructions and information. Generally, any cache beyond 1MB will not show much additional improvement.

CERTIFICATION SUMMARY

This chapter has provided you with the knowledge of what each system module does and how it works. Understanding this material provides you with the insight necessary to proceed with installing, removing, and configuring the various components that are used by a computer system. Also discussed were the various addressing methods and communications aspects of system components. Armed with this knowledge, you should be able to identify unfamiliar devices by the manner in which they connect to the system, as well as by their function. And if that wasn't enough information, you were presented with system optimization techniques to improve the performance of the equipment.

✓ TWO-MINUTE DRILL

- ❑ When installing a new power supply, remember that when you reattach the two power connectors to the motherboard, the black wires that are located on each connector must be facing each other.

- ❑ Always wear an electrostatic wrist band to ground yourself when removing the computer's chassis.

- ❑ Never wear an electrostatic wrist band when working near a monitor, as the high-voltage circuits may contain residual charge, even when unplugged, that can hurt you, or possibly even kill you

- ❑ Every module that makes up a computer system attaches to the motherboard (also called the *system board, main board*, or *planar board*) and is able to communicate with other modules through the bus.

- ❑ Electrical power comes in two forms: *alternating current (AC)*, which is the type that comes out of a wall outlet, and *direct current (DC)*, which is the type that your computer uses.

❏   The DC current is fed to your computer in one of several forms: +5 volts, +12 volts, -5 volts and −12 volts. The newer ATX and NLX standards provide for an optional +3.3 volt supply voltage as well.

❏   All PC-compatible power supplies, known as *switching mode* power supplies, use transistors in addition to diodes to convert current and are much more efficient at converting the AC power from the wall outlet to the DC power needed inside the PC.

❏   An overheated power supply will not only fail, but can damage other components inside the computer.

❏   Memory, of which there are several types (cache memory, random access memory (RAM), and read only memory (ROM)), is comprised of *integrated circuits (ICs)* that reside on a chip.

❏   Monitors come in a wide variety of types, ranging from the original monochrome display adapter (MDA), which only permitted text-based characters, to today's high resolution super video graphics adapter (SVGA). Other types are CGA, EGA, and VGA.

❏   A modem takes data from the sending computer and translates it from digital to analog signals before transmitting it across a telephone line, a process called modulation. When a modem receives analog signals from a telephone line, it converts the data back into digital signals, a process called demodulation.

❏   The *Basic Input/Output System*, or BIOS, is the mechanism used by your computer to essentially provide device drivers for basic system devices for the DOS/Windows operating system, and also contains the program to initially perform a basic test and boot up of the system.

❏   The CMOS, or *Complementary Metal-Oxide Semiconductor* (an integrated circuit containing the Real-Time Clock/Calendar circuitry and related battery-backed storage) allows the computer to store this information even after the computer has been turned off.

❏   The first, and most important, step that you must take before adding or replacing a system module is to power off the computer and disconnect the power cord from the wall outlet.

❏ Always note the locations and any connectors that attach to expansion cards before removal to ensure that you will be able to put everything back into its appropriate spot. Make it a habit to mark such things when removing and installing modules.

❏ To install most SIMM memory modules, place the SIMM over the slot at a 45-degree angle and gently push the chip into place by moving it to an upright position until it clicks into place.

❏ Never plug a digital monitor into an analog adapter, or vice versa, as severe damage will result.

❏ There are two types of keyboard connectors in use, the DIN-5 connector and the Mini DIN-6 connector. DIN-5s are generally found on AT style keyboards and have a round port with 5 pins. The Mini DIN-6 also has a round port but differs in that it has 6 pins plus one square plastic positioning pin.

❏ Devices request attention from the CPU through a special set of lines, called *interrupt request lines (IRQs)*, in the bus.

❏ Once the CPU receives an IRQ from a device, it can directly communicate with that device through *I/O addresses* or *I/O ports*.

❏ Refer back to Table 1-1 and review the standard IRQ settings.

❏ Refer back to Table 1-2 and review the more frequently used I/O addresses.

❏ Interrupts, I/O addresses, DMA channels, and some additional features have to be configured in the hardware. Jumpers and Dual In-Line Package (DIP) switches are used to accomplish configuration.

❏ Cables come in two different forms, *shielded* cables and *unshielded* cables. Shielded cables have a wire mesh or Mylar layer added in between the medium and the sheathing that protects the cables from interference.

❏ Refer back to Tables 1-3 and 1-4 and memorize the primary control signals for serial and parallel communication.

❏ IDE/EIDE drives can have up to four drives installed, but you will only be able to put two drives on a single cable.

❏ Small Computer Systems Interface (SCSI) devices permit you to connect multiple devices to one cable, or "chain" them, in configurations of up to 7 to 15 devices on a single cable depending on the SCSI implementation that you are using. 32-bit Wide SCSI is rarely available at present, but will allow 31 devices plus the adapter to work together on one 32-bit SCSI channel.

❑ Common tools in every computer technician's toolkit include each variety of screwdriver, a chip puller, and a multimeter.

❑ BIOS boot-up settings contain information on the system hardware and may need to be updated when a new component has been added to the computer.

❑ Flash BIOS means that the BIOS chip can be reprogrammed with new settings. This type of BIOS requires special software, called a *flash program*, and a special data file in order to replace the instructions that drive the BIOS.

❑ One of the things you can do to free conventional memory is to load MS-DOS into the High Memory Area (HMA) by adding a simple line to the CONFIG.SYS file.

❑ To defragment a fragmented hard drive, you must run a utility, such as Microsoft's Defragmenter (DEFRAG.EXE).

SELF TEST

The following Self Test questions will help you measure your understanding of the material presented in this chapter. Read all the choices carefully, as there may be more than one correct answer. Choose all correct answers for each question.

1. When installing a new power supply, the connectors are attached to the system board by:

   A. Green wires facing each other

   B. Black wires facing away from each other

   C. Green wires facing away from each other

   D. Black wires facing each other

2. When removing an integrated circuit, such as a processor, from the system board you would use a:

   A. Pair of pliers

   B. Pair of tweezers

   C. Chip puller

   D. Your fingers

3. When working inside a monitor, you must ensure that you remove your:

   A. Clothing

   B. Jewelry

   C. Electrostatic wrist band

   D. Headphones

4. You have just installed a 16-bit SCSI controller to the computer and are now ready to address your brand new SCSI hard disks. Which of the following address ranges are you permitted to use:

   A. Starting Address: 0
      Ending Address: 32

   B. Starting Address: 0
      Ending Address: 8

   C. Starting Address: 0
      Ending Address: 16

   D. Starting Address: 0
      Ending Address: 15

5. A PS/2 mouse uses a:

   A. Mini-DIN connector

   B. DB-25 connector

   C. DIN-9 connector

   D. DB-9 connector

6. The work area used by the computer is called:

   A. Central Processing Unit

   B. Cache memory

   C. Memory

   D. BIOS

7. When optimizing memory, you want to _____ conventional memory.

   A. Load DOS into

   B. Free up

   C. Remove

   D. Load device drivers into

8. When you transmit a byte of data using several conductors, you are using _____ communications.

   A. Parallel

   B. Byte communications

   C. Network

   D. Serial

9. Interference of a signal is called _____.

   A. Noise

   B. Static electricity

   C. ESD

   D. EMI

10. Power supplies operate in the _____ range.

   A. ± 5 Vdc and ± 10 Vdc

   B. ± 7 Vdc and ± 10 Vdc

   C. ± 5 Vdc and ± 12 Vdc

   D. ± 4 Vdc and ± 7 Vdc

11. A(n) _____ signal is used to indicate that valid data is present when using parallel communications.

   A. Acknowledgment

   B. Data Present

   C. Strobe-Asserted

   D. Init

12. Every device that attaches to the computer is connected to the _____. (Choose all that apply.)

   A. System Board

   B. Main Board

   C. Motherboard

   D. Back Board

13. When installing most SIMM memory modules, you place the chip over the slot in an _____ angle

   A. 10 degree

   B. 45 degree

   C. 90 degree

   D. 145 degree

14. Never use a(n) _____ with a digital monitor.

   A. Analog adapter

   B. Digital adapter

   C. Female D-9 connector

   D. EGA monitor

15. When you transmit data using asynchronous serial communications, synchronization is performed by:

   A. A clock circuit located in both the transmitting and receiving devices

   B. Shaking hands

   C. A clock circuit located in the transmitting device

   D. Using start bits before the data begins and stop bits after the data stops

16. Tape drives are commonly used to:

    A. Store applications

    B. Store data

    C. Back up the hard drive

    D. Play music

17. Floppy controllers normally use the _____ I/O address.

    A. 370 - 37F

    B. 3F0 - 3F7

    C. 2F0 - 2F7

    D. 1F0

18. When optimizing memory, you include the line _____ to load DOS into the HMA.

    A. LOAD DOS=UPPER MEMORY

    B. LOAD DOS=1024K

    C. DOS=HIGH

    D. LOAD C:\EMM386.EXE

19. The _____ signal is used to indicate that data has been received.

    A. Acknowledgment

    B. Data Received

    C. Busy

    D. Slct

20. Parallel port LPT1 uses the _____ I/O address.

    A. 2F0 - 2F7

    B. 378 - 37F

    C. 278 - 27F

    D. 1F0 - 1F8

21. ESD stands for:

    A. Electrostatic Dimming

    B. Electrostatic Discharge

    C. Electrical Sending Device

    D. Electronic Signaling Device

22. BIOS boot-up settings are stored in the _____Clock/Calendar chip so that they may be restored after a computer has been turned off.

    A. Complementary Metallic-Oxide Service

    B. Computer Module Off Switch

    C. Complementary Metal-Oxide Semiconductor

    D. Computer Mode Off Saftey

23. EGA monitors can display images in _____ resolution.

    A. 640 x 350

    B. 720 x 350

    C. 1024 x 800

    D. 600 x 800

24. Serial communications use the _____ signal as a reference voltage.

    A. Ground Reference Voltage

    B. Zero

    C. Reference Point

    D. Timer

25. IRQ 2 is _____.

    A. Keyboard

    B. Mouse

C. Floppy Controller

D. Re-directed to IRQ 9

26. When installing two IDE drives on one cable, one is set to be the _____ and one is set to be the _____.

   A. Master, servant

   B. Master, slave

   C. Dominant, submissive

   D. Primary, second best

27. When determining what device drivers and TSRs are in conventional memory, you use the _____ program.

   A. MEMORY.EXE

   B. CONFIG.SYS

   C. MEM.EXE

   D. AUTOEXEC.BAT

28. You can attach up to _____ EIDE drives to a computer.

   A. One

   B. Two

   C. Three

   D. Four

29. When installing SCSI devices, you must use a _____ on the last drive on the cable and on the adapter.

   A. Resistor

   B. Transmitter

   C. Terminator

   D. End connector

30. RAM is an acronym for:

   A. Random Access Memory

   B. Random Access Module

   C. Read Access Memory

   D. Read And Memorize

31. Parallel port LPT2 uses which IRQ:

   A. IRQ 3

   B. IRQ 5

   C. IRQ 7

   D. IRQ 12

32. Your phone uses a(n) _____ connector.

   A. RJ-45

   B. RJ-11

   C. RJ-14

   D. DB-9

2

Diagnosing and Troubleshooting

W hen diagnosing any component connected to a computer system, it helps to know some of the basic troubleshooting procedures. In addition, if you are armed with the knowledge of common symptoms and problems that relate to each device, the time spent locating and repairing the problem is significantly reduced. In this chapter, we explore basic troubleshooting techniques along with the common trouble spots that afflict individual devices.

CERTIFICATION OBJECTIVE 2.01

Symptoms and Problems

When attempting to troubleshoot a problem, it helps if you are knowledgeable about how the various symptoms relate to common problems. Many field replaceable modules have several parts to them, and some of these parts may be the cause of the problem. In the next subsections, we look at each module and the common causes of problems.

Processor/Memory

When the processor has a problem, it may be related to the Complementary Metal-Oxide Semiconductor (CMOS). For example, if you notice that the time is constantly incorrect, then the CMOS battery is running low on power and needs to be replaced. However, other problems usually show themselves during the Power On Self Test (POST) that occurs during boot time. These errors usually are preceded by a 1**, where the ** can be any set of numbers. The descriptive messages inform you of what type of problem is discovered and you can act accordingly. If the computer displays an error code, before replacing the processor see if the chip has become slightly loose in the socket, a phenomenon called chip creep.

Memory problems are also detected when POST runs at boot time. These types of errors are usually preceded by a 2**, again where the ** can be any set of numbers. Check the descriptive message that comes with the error code and proceed accordingly.

Input Devices

Input devices are the easiest types of components to check, as there are fewer things that can go wrong with them. We discuss the various types of input devices in the next subsections.

Keyboards

When troubleshooting a keyboard, there are only a few symptoms that you have to worry about. These items include:

- Non-functional keyboard
- Sporadic keys
- Sticking keys

The first item, the non-functional keyboard, usually leads to an error message from the computer at boot that reads:

```
KEYBOARD ERROR
PRESS <F1> TO CONTINUE
```

You can check that the keyboard connector is snugly secure in the socket, but if it is, then you may need to replace the keyboard itself.

exam
ⓦatch

Keyboard errors usually generate a 3** error code when POST runs at boot time.

With sporadically functioning keys or sticking keys, you need to give the keyboard a good cleaning. This type of problem is fairly obvious, as most customers have a nasty habit of eating and drinking over keyboards. You can purchase a keyboard cleaning kit at any computer or electronics store to use, but if the problem isn't resolved after a cleaning, you will have to replace it. The good news is that keyboards are relatively inexpensive items and that any replacement takes less than one minute.

Mice

Diagnosing mice is similar to keyboards, with just a few exceptions. The items to consider in mouse troubleshooting are:

- Dirty mouse
- Conflicting address

■ Device driver

■ Adapter card, if any

A dirty mouse is the most common problem reported. The problem is that the roller bars inside of the mouse tend to pick up dust and dirt from the track ball when it rolls over a mouse pad. A symptom of a dirty mouse is when you attempt to move it across the mouse pad and get little, sometimes jerky, response. You can remove the screws from the bottom of the mouse and physically check these bars. If needed, clean them with alcohol, reassemble the mouse, and try again.

If another device is using the same IRQ or I/O address as the mouse, then it probably won't work at all. This is because the results are being returned to the conflicting device. Try checking IRQs and I/O addresses with diagnostic software to ensure that there is not another device using either of these.

Device drivers control how the mouse communicates with the processor. If the driver is configured incorrectly, such as a wrong address or an incorrect sensitivity setting, the mouse will have slow to non-functional symptoms. In addition, if the device uses an adapter card, there may be a problem with the card itself. If you suspect that this is the case, you can try to replace the adapter card and see if the problem is resolved.

Trackball

Most of the time that you will encounter a trackball is with a laptop computer. With laptops, the trackball is integrated into the keyboard and the repair process becomes a bit more difficult. However, trackballs work in the same manner as a mouse and, as such, have the same symptoms and causes as mice. If the device is unresponsive, you have to replace it. On many laptop machines, this also requires that you replace the entire keyboard unit. However, if the response is slow or sporadic, you probably can give it a good cleaning to resolve the problem. Check with your local computer or electronics store for the appropriate cleaning kit, as well as the manufacturer's recommendations listed in the documentation.

If you are working on a personal computer, the trackball is a peripheral device and is not integrated into the keyboard. If the device is non-responsive, check the connection into the computer to ensure that it has not come loose. Also, check any adapter cards and device drivers that are associated with the trackball. Usually, there is a device driver configuration error or driver corruption that causes the problem. You can also check these items with a sporadic problem, but most likely you will need to clean the device to resolve the problem.

Pen/Stylus

With the increased graphical capabilities of today's computers, the stylus is becoming very popular with graphics-oriented shops. These tools look similar to a pen that is attached to a drawing tablet via a cable. Most of the time, the stylus is not the problem but the drawing tablet is. If the tablet is dirty, try cleaning it with a damp cloth. Also look for device driver problems, such as in the configuration or driver corruption, as well as any cable connection from the tablet into the computer.

Scanners

There are two types of scanners that you will come into contact with: the flat-bed scanner and the hand-held scanner. Both work in a similar fashion, except that the flat-bed can scan a full sheet at a time while the hand-held works primarily with smaller images. When troubleshooting these devices, take the following into consideration:

- Dirty scanner surface
- Cable and power connections
- Adapter card, if used
- Device drivers

A dirty scanner surface usually results in smudged or poor-quality images. With flat-bed scanners, it is merely a manner of cleaning the glass surface with a good glass cleaner. However, with hand-held scanners, you need to consult the manufacturer's documentation for the recommended method of cleaning.

Always ensure that the cable connection from the scanner to the computer is properly attached. A loose connection usually results in a non-responsive scanner. However, if you are diagnosing a flat-bed scanner, you also need to check the power connection if the device does not power up.

Adapter cards do the work of translating signals between the scanner and the computer. As such, they are good suspects when you encounter communication-related errors. However, most problems with scanners that are not resolved by cleaning the unit are device-driver related. The driver is the software interface between the computer and the adapter card, and may have been inadvertently modified by the customer. If not, ensure that the driver is not corrupted. If you have determined that the device driver is corrupted, you can reinstall it from the original floppy or floppies that came with the scanner.

Microphones

Microphones are being utilized more and more with computers these days. These devices enable the user to control the computer through speech recognition software, and some software packages even interact with word processing applications to accept dictation. And even though the technology is still in its infancy, microphones pick up your voice in the form of audio signals for video conferencing. However, there is not much that you can do to clean or repair a microphone. You can check the device driver configuration for conflicts and the application software for a correct configuration. The manufacturer's documentation should specify these items. However, if one goes bad, you have to replace the device.

Touch Pad

Touch pads are relative newcomers to the computer industry, but have a wide variety of applications. If you have stopped at a fast food restaurant or visited the mini-market inside of a gas station, you will notice that the cash registers have plastic sheets that the cashier presses rather than depressing buttons, to ring up your order. These registers are early forms of touch pads, and work by having a dollar amount associated to each square on the pad. When the cashier presses the square, a small button or a sensor is triggered that rings up the price. Computer touch pads work the same way. They are pads that have either thin wires running through them, or specialized surfaces that can sense the pressure of your finger on them.

If touch pads need repair, usually a good cleaning with a damp cloth (no detergents) will resolve the problem. You can verify that any device driver or application software has a correct configuration, but beyond this you may need to replace the device.

Floppy Drive Failures

When troubleshooting floppy drive failures, there are a myriad of components that you must take into consideration as the true point of failure. These items include the following:

- Media errors
- Drive incompatibilities
- Dirty read/write heads
- Cabling or connection errors
- Floppy controller card
- Device Driver errors
- Drive failure

Commonly, what seems to be a floppy drive error is not actually a drive problem but a media error. Floppy disks are susceptible to physical and magnetic corruption, giving the customer the appearance of a bad drive with "Error reading disk" or "Error writing to disk" messages. At other times, there are drive incompatibilities so that when one drive writes to a disk, another drive can't read it. This is common, for example, when you copy files from one PC and try to read them on another PC that has an incompatible drive. If you encounter this type of a problem, try reading from another disk, preferably one that was written to by the suspect drive, or writing to a second disk. If the drive can perform the operation on a different disk, it probably is a media error.

Media errors can also be caused by dirty read/write heads on the floppy drive. Dirt can get into a computer through the vents used to pull in fresh air, and as such will stick to the read/write heads. Also, while floppies have less chance of getting dirty from the plastic encasement, there is still some dirt deposited on the media when it is in use by the drive. Floppy drive cleaning kits can be purchased rather cheaply at any computer store, and you should follow the manufacturer's instructions for using them.

Another thing to check for is that there is nothing stuck in the drive itself. Sometimes, people put items in the drive that do not belong there, such as the wrong type of media. Small children are also notorious for placing items into a floppy drive just as they are with VCRs. However, even though you want to believe that people wouldn't do these types of things, you cannot take anything for granted and must check that no foreign objects have been placed into the drive.

Cabling can also lead to drive problems. If you have just installed a floppy drive and you are experiencing a problem with the drive, such as the drive light won't go out, you probably have the cable on backwards. The red stripe on the floppy cable must be connected to pin 1 on the adapter *and* on the drive. Also, there will be times when you think that a cable is firmly seated on the drive, or on the adapter, and it might be a hair off. This can cause communication problems between the drive and the adapter. Try pressing on both connections to see if they move at all.

If the drive isn't getting power, it won't work. Sometimes the power connector isn't properly seated in the power connection. You can attempt to push the power connector to see if it moves. If it doesn't move, and the drive still isn't getting any power, then you have to replace the drive.

Communication problems between the drive and the adapter may also be caused by an improperly seated controller card. You must gently, but firmly, press down on the adapter card. If it hasn't moved, then you may want to check the contacts. Contacts can get dirty and may require cleaning with isopropyl alcohol. If you suspect that the contact might be defective, you can attempt to check it using a multimeter. However, if you believe that you have a problem controller card, you can test it by installing a second floppy drive. If you can successfully use the second drive, then the controller probably isn't the problem.

If the problem doesn't fit into any of the previously mentioned categories, you must check for possible software problems. The device driver used by the operating system software may have become corrupt, in which case you can try reinstalling the driver. However, if the computer has been losing its BIOS settings from a dying CMOS battery, you have to enter the SETUP program to re-enter the settings. With newer computers, this shouldn't be a concern as the BIOS can usually auto-detect the drive. Unfortunately, older computers require you to re-enter these settings manually.

At this point, if you are still encountering problems, then the drive itself is at fault and must be replaced. The good news is that floppy drives are relatively inexpensive items, and they only take around 15 minutes at most to replace.

Hard Drives

Hard drives can be tricky to diagnose or relatively simple, depending on the source of the problem. Some areas to consider when troubleshooting a hard drive problem are:

- Power connection
- Cabling
- Addressing conflicts
- Hard drive controller or SCSI interface
- BIOS settings
- Fragmented or corrupt drives

Without power, the hard drive is useless. One of the first things to try is listening to the hard drive itself. If you cannot hear it, it probably has no power. Verify that the power connection is snugly in the socket and that the power supply is working. This is a common problem with newly installed drives.

Communication takes place between the hard drive and the controller via a cable. This cable could be loose or may have gone bad. This is also common with newly installed drives rather than those that have already been functioning properly. Check the cable connection to ensure that it is connected properly, and if it is try swapping cables. If you have more than one hard drive in the computer, verify that the master/slave configuration is correct.

The controller card may also be a problem for the hard drive. Verify the address settings for the controller and ensure that there are no conflicts with another device. If another hard drive is attached to the controller and functioning properly, you probably do not have a controller problem.

If you feel that you have file corruption or bad sectors on the disk, you can use a utility such as Microsoft's Scan Disk or Norton Disk Utilities to repair or remove damaged files, as well as check and mark any bad sectors on the disk. File corruption or bad sectors can be caused by several things: faulty cables, physical damage to the hard drive data surface, incorrectly configured controller, or even a computer shutdown while the file is in use. A scanning utility can be used to check each sector on the disk and allow you several repair options, depending on the software. If the utility finds a bad sector on the disk, it flags the spot as bad so that it is not used by the drive.

Tape Drives

Problems that are encountered with tape drive systems include the following:

- Media problems
- Dirty read/write heads
- Cabling and power connections
- Controller card
- Device drivers

When diagnosing tape drive problems, it is a good idea to rule out the possibility of media problems first. As with floppy drives, tape cartridges wear out with use and can become corrupted. In addition, if the cartridge has been written to by another device, you might have an incompatibility problem arising between the two devices. The last type of media problem could actually be a result of the software. Most available backup software, such as ArcServe or Legato, put an expiration date on the tape's internal label. The standard expiration date is one year, and if the cartridge has been in use longer than that, it is probably time to dispose of it. Try using another cartridge to determine if there is a media problem.

If you are able to rule out the cartridge, the next step is to inspect the power connection. If the device is not getting power, it will not work. Try checking the power cable and ensuring that the power connector is firmly seated. If the connector is not properly seated, it may be slightly shaken as the drive motors are in operation, and thus cause sporadic power problems. Also check to see if a power strip is in use, as surges or lapses in power can "trip" the power strip, causing it to require a reset.

Another possibility is the cabling from the drive to the adapter card. If the cables are not connected properly, then the drive will experience communication problems. Try to push down on all the connections, as well as on the adapter card itself, to see if there is any perceptible movement. If there is, you have probably found the problem, although sometimes the cable itself may be defective. In this case, replace the cable to see if the problem goes away.

Because device driver software resides on the computer's hard disk, there is also the potential for the driver to become corrupted. There are two ways that you can check this angle. The first method is to verify the software configuration; the second method is to reinstall the driver. Always check the software configuration first, as it is also possible that the customer may have inadvertently made a configuration change, referred to as *operator error*. If you see any garbage characters in the configuration, then you definitely have a corrupt driver and must reinstall it. However, if the values have been slightly altered, you probably have an operator error.

CD-ROMS

When troubleshooting CD-ROM drives, there are several things that should be checked. These items include:

- Media problems
- Cable and/or connectors
- Address conflicts
- Controller board
- Device drivers

One good troubleshooting tool that comes in handy is any diagnostic program that may have come with the CD-ROM drive or the controller board. While not all manufacturers package diagnostic software with the hardware, you may be able to check their Internet site for any of these aides. If you have access to a diagnostic utility, try running it against the equipment and view the results. Often, these programs are able to pinpoint the problem and save you some time.

One of the most common problems reported to the technician with regard to CD-ROMs is that the customer cannot read a CD-ROM disk. There are several things that can cause this, but usually having the customer verify that there is, in fact, a compact disk in the tray or that it was not inadvertently inserted upside down commonly solves this problem. In addition, if the customer is using a CD-ROM tower or a disk changer, they may have forgotten to perform a software mount on the CD, which is usually performed with a MOUNT command. When there is still a problem accessing the disk, try having the customer read from another disk to ensure that there is not a media problem. If the drive can successfully read a second CD, there may be a problem with the original disk through an incompatible CD-ROM format or a corrupted disk.

When you cannot successfully access a second disk, verify that you can hear the motor on the drive. This is usually a high-pitched whirring sound that is easily heard. If you cannot detect the noise, there may be a problem with the drive itself or its power connections. However, if you do hear the drive, try checking the cabling to ensure that there is not a loose connection. Also, do an I/O address check to ensure that there isn't an address conflict going on with another device.

If none of these measures solve the problem, verify that the proper device driver for the CD-ROM and/or the controller card has been installed and that it is configured correctly. Ensure that the driver hasn't become corrupted as a result of a bad spot on the hard disk. If necessary, try to reinstall the driver and see if the problem is resolved before replacing the CD-ROM drive.

If the computer doesn't boot after you have installed a CD-ROM, you may have either an address problem, a cable problem, or a connector problem. First, make sure that the address has been configured properly and that there are no address conflicts with another device. Next, check the cable between the controller board and the drive itself, ensuring that it is properly attached with the red stripe facing pin 1. Verify that the power connector is snugly in the socket. Lastly, ensure that the proper device drivers have been installed for the drive and the controller board.

When the computer will boot, but the CD-ROM drive isn't being recognized, you may have a communication error between the computer and the drive. If you have diagnostic software with you, it is easier to pinpoint the problem. If not, the first things to check for are the device drivers and their configurations. Ensure that you do not have any conflicts with another device, such as an incorrectly addressed drive. Also, verify that the controller board does not have a problem, whether it is the cabling, addressing, or the board itself.

Parallel Ports/Serial Ports

Parallel and serial ports rarely fail, as opposed to the peripherals that connect to them. As such, they are usually the last item to be considered. To diagnose parallel or serial port problems, you need special diagnostic software in order to verify that the ports are working. If you find that you are having a port problem, you need to replace the Input/Output (I/O) adapter card that contains the port.

Sound Card/Audio

The most common problem with sound cards is related to configuration problems with the software driver configuration. This is in the form of IRQ, I/O Address, or DMA channel conflicts. The first thing that you can do to check for these types of problems is to run software diagnostics, such as Windows Diagnostics or Norton Utilities, that show where the conflict is occurring. If there is no conflict found, then you should check the speakers used in conjunction with the card. Often, the customer turns the sound down and doesn't realize it, or battery-operated speakers have run out of power.

You can also ensure that the device driver is not corrupted, and whether it has to be reinstalled from the original disk. If you are working with an older card, you may want to check the manufacturer's Internet site to see if the driver has been updated. However, do not rule out the possibility that the card is defective, even if it is a new card.

Printers

Printers are one of the most complex systems that you will diagnose. Some items to consider when you troubleshoot a malfunctioning printer are:

- Paper faults
- Toner cartridges or ink ribbon
- Mechanical parts
- Cabling
- Interface cards
- Device drivers
- Application software configuration

A paper fault can be a symptom of the use of poor quality paper, such as recycled paper, or an impeded pathway. While we are all environmentalists at heart, and we should recycle everything we can, recycled paper and printers do not mix.

An impeded pathway can also cause paper jams, but usually the jam occurs in the same location every time. It only takes a small bit of paper to cause the problem, and usually you have to take the printer apart to find it. If you open the printer and find a lot of paper dust, you need to clean the whole unit to ensure that the dust isn't the cause of the problem as well, as dust and dirt can carry a small charge and cause the paper to stick to metal parts just enough to cause a jam.

When you encounter a printer that produces blank pages, the usual suspect for dot-matrix printers is the ribbon or the print head. The print head is made up of pins that strike the ribbon onto the paper to form text or graphics. These pins can get dirty and stick, and if the characters are missing spots, you should clean or replace the head.

Printers are basically mechanical devices, whether you are working with a dot-matrix or a laser printer. As with any mechanical device, parts become worn out with time and heavy use. It is important that you check for any signs of wear on all internal components and replace any that exhibit symptoms of deterioration, as worn out parts can also cause an excessive amount of page jam. In addition, ensure that all mechanical parts are properly lubricated.

Cabling can be a problem when you are faced with a non-responsive printer. The connectors between the printer and the computer may have been jostled loose enough that the signals are not being transmitted or received properly. This includes the power connectors to the printer.

Interface cards are also responsible for proper communication between the computer and the printer. Check the card to see if it has failed. If a printer has an internal or external network interface, incorrect configuration of the network interface can disable it from communicating on the network. These settings can be changed with the printer's control panel or from a PC with software designed to manage network printers. The card can also experience hardware failure, which can result in either intermittent or consistent problems.

Software applications also have printer settings. Most of the newer software packages use the operating system information to enable a user to choose between various printers to which they may be connected. However, some of the older packages may require that you specify these settings. Verify all software applications that have a problem interfacing with a printer.

Monitor/Video

Monitors are a necessary item on a computer, but they do not last forever. Some items that you should check for when diagnosing monitors include the following:

- Power and power connections
- Brightness and/or contrast controls
- Sync frequencies
- Cables
- Video adapter card
- Device drivers

One of the most common complaints you will encounter is the "dead" monitor, one that has no picture at all. One of the first things to check, and one of the most forgotten, is to see if the monitor is turned on. You hear jokes about it, but it's true: Technicians receive countless calls from frantic customers who can't make a transmission by the deadline because of a "dead" monitor, and it turns out that they have forgotten to turn the monitor on. With the newer power-saver monitors, it may take a couple of key strokes or movements of a mouse to turn the monitor back on when the power saver has kicked in.

Another possibility is that the customer has the brightness and/or contrast controls turned all the way down. This is another common problem with video displays. Readjusting these controls may revive the display and save quite a bit of time and money in the repair. If the monitor still does not work, try replacing it with one of the same type. If another monitor works, then the original monitor needs repair. Note that you must check with the customer as to whether or not it is under warranty. To get a replacement, most manufacturers require the client to ship the original monitor back. Never try to repair the monitor itself unless you have experience in monitor repair, as monitors are high-voltage equipment and you could accidentally injure or kill yourself.

Monitors use a *sync frequency* to control the refresh rate, which is the rate at which the display device is repainted. If this setting is incorrect, you get symptoms such as: a "dead" monitor, lines running through the display, a flickering screen, and a reduced or enlarged image. This setting is configured through the device driver. In order to ensure that you are using the correct frequency for the type of monitor being used, consult the vendor's documentation.

If a monitor swap doesn't do the trick, you may have a problem with the cables or the adapter card. First, check that all of the cables are properly seated before attempting to replace them. This includes the power cable, as the power cord probably connects to a power strip. Make sure that the power strip is on and that it hasn't been "tripped" by a momentary power lapse.

If you suspect that there is a video adapter problem, check that the card has been correctly configured. This requires you to consult with the manufacturer's documentation to ensure that all jumpers and/or DIP switches are properly set. You may also want to check that any memory installed on the card hasn't suffered from chip creep, and gently press on the memory chips to ensure that they are seated correctly. When you have determined that the card's configuration is accurate and that any on-board memory is seated, proceed to swap video cards. This should solve the problem of a "dead" monitor.

Sometimes you will be called on to diagnose a monitor that has poor image quality. As stated earlier, monitors do not last forever. You can still check for such problems as a brightness/contrast change and cable problems, but most likely the problem lies in either a defective adapter card or a configuration error. To ensure that the adapter card is not the problem, follow the procedures discussed in the previous paragraph. However, when there is a configuration error, it is usually found in the device driver. Check the configuration of the device driver. Remember, if you spot any garbage characters in the configuration information, you probably have a corrupted driver and must reinstall it. However, the most common cause of configuration problems after a monitor has been working awhile is operator error.

Modems

Complaints with modems are frequent, and diagnosing them can become difficult. However, some of the things that you should check for include:

- Power connection
- Cabling
- Phone line
- Communication software
- Device driver

When diagnosing a modem, it is important to first determine if the modem is an internal modem or an external one. External modems are easier to diagnose, as you can see the signals from the display panel. If you have an internal modem, there isn't a display panel for you to look at, making troubleshooting a more difficult problem. You also have to determine if the problem stems from a nonfunctioning modem or a sporadic problem.

With a nonfunctional modem, the first thing to check is the power connection. If it is an external modem, you can power on the modem and see if any of the lights on the control panel are lit. If none of the lights come on, the modem isn't getting power and you must check both the power connector leading into the modem and the connection to the power outlet. Sometimes, the power outlet may have a problem and you can move the connector to another outlet. Power strips cause another problem if there has been a momentary lapse or surge in power and may need to be reset. If the modem still has no lights, then you have to replace the modem. However, if you have an internal modem, you have to open the case and gently push down on the power connection. At this stage, try using the modem to make a connection to see if the problem is resolved.

The next phase in modem diagnosis is to check on the cabling. Sometimes, the cable connections between the modem and the computer become loose, especially if the computer is moved around. This also includes the phone line leading into the modem as well as the wall socket. A common problem with phone lines is that the locking tab on the cable itself breaks off, resulting in a loose connection. In both cases, you need to replace the problem cable and test the modem again.

Besides the phone-line cable, there may be another problem stemming from the phone line itself. With a sporadic problem, it could be that the modem and the office fax are hooked up to the same phone line, which is commonplace in the office environment. If a fax machine is in use when the problem occurs, you may be encountering this type of situation. Another possibility is that the modem could be sharing a phone line with a regular phone, as is typical in home/office environments, which may also explain some sporadic problems. If either one is the case, you may want to recommend that the customer lease a separate line for the modem. However, if this isn't the case, should physically check the phone line itself. To do so, simply unplug the phone line from the modem and plug it into a regular telephone, then pick up the handset. If you do not get a dial tone, the line is dead and you need to turn over the problem to the phone company.

Connection problems are the most common problem you will encounter when diagnosing a modem. Some of these problems are caused by static, or *noise*, on the phone line itself, particularly on the Hayes 14.4 Optima modems. When you connect to another modem, both of the modems have to agree on the method of communication used, called *handshaking*. When noise is present on the line, the analog signals that are transmitted back and forth between the modems may be misinterpreted and result in a failed connection. Static can also cause problems in the transmission of data for the same reason, leading to bad data transmissions, dropped connections, and garbage characters appearing at random intervals. You check the phone line for noise by plugging the phone cable into a regular phone and picking up the handset. Listen for a minute and see if you can hear any noise on the line. If there is, you must get the phone company to look into the problem.

If none of these solutions resolve the problem, you need to check the I/O port used. In order to do so, you can either use diagnostic software designed specifically to test I/O ports. Most port testing software can be more thorough if you have a loopback adapter, a small inexpensive device that exists for this sole purpose.

Another consideration with modem problems is the communication software itself. Ensure that the baud rate, stop bits, parity bits, and communication protocol used are correct for the session that the customer is attempting to establish. The most common symptom for an incorrect configuration is receiving garbage characters after making a connection. For example, if the software is configured to use an Even Parity and the connecting modem expects the parity to be set to None, you will see a steady stream of garbage coming across the screen right after connection. Try different configuration settings if the customer is unsure of the communication parameters, but only after you have noted the current configuration somewhere.

An important item that should be checked is the device driver installed in the operating system software. A corrupt, or improperly configured, driver causes many of the symptoms that have been discussed. Also ensure that you check the IRQ and I/O address of the modem as it is possible that there is a conflict with another device configured in the system. Sometimes a reinstall of the driver solves the problem, but be prepared to replace the modem if it doesn't.

POST Audible/Visual Error Codes

The Power On Self Test (POST) happens every time you boot the computer. It is used to diagnose system-related problems, such as are found in memory or BIOS settings, and is a two-fold alert system: the audible series of beeps, which alerts the operator to a problem, and the on-screen error code/message combination, which specifies the exact error encountered. Typically, anything other than a single beep during this time indicates an error. The most common errors are a keyboard error and a CMOS low, or battery failure, error.

The error codes that you see on the screen fall into a particular range that can be associated with a specific component. Table 2-1 lists these ranges and their associated devices.

TABLE 2-1

Common POST Error Code Ranges and Related Components

Error Range	Component
100-199	System board problem
200-299	Memory error
300-399	Keyboard problem
400-499	Video problems, monochrome
500-599	Video problems, color
600-699	Floppy disk errors
1700-1799	Hard disk problems

BIOS

The most common problem with the BIOS is when the Complementary Metallic-Oxide Semiconductor (CMOS) battery begins to run low on power. Usually, a message is displayed at boot time that states "CMOS battery low." If this is the case, you need to replace the battery and reconfigure the BIOS. However, there are times when the BIOS goes bad and must be replaced. Usually, this is indicated by an obvious message during the POST that occurs when you boot the computer.

Power Supply

As the power supply is the computer's source of power, problems of this nature usually exhibit themselves as a computer that does not boot or an overheated system that constantly reboots itself. Power supplies include a fan in the unit to cool it down, thus preventing overheating. If the fan is not moving on the power supply while the computer is running, it is a good bet that it is time to clean it with compressed air or replace it entirely. However, if the system does not boot at all, then the power supply is shot and must be replaced.

Device Drivers

Device drivers are the computer's translators with the various devices installed on them. If they are to perform their job, they must be configured correctly. Always check the configuration against the manufacturer's documentation, as customers have a tendency to attempt to improve upon a device's performance and forget to mention their modifications.

Because device drivers are stored on a hard disk, you want to ensure that the driver has not become corrupted. This occurs when the hard disk has begun to fail or is experiencing problems, and sometimes when a computer has had a power surge. If you see garbage characters appearing in the device driver description or in its configuration, then it is definitely a corruption problem. Try reinstalling the driver according to the vendor's instructions.

Slot Covers

Most people do not think that a missing slot cover can cause a problem, but your computer knows better. Computers are designed to allow for proper air flow going into and out of the case. Should the air flow become impeded or its route modified, you run the risk of overheating a component in the computer case. If you are experiencing sporadic problems or symptoms of overheating on one or more of the computer's components, be sure that you have all of the slots in the back of the computer covered. Without slot covers you could be causing unintentional damage to the computer components.

Troubleshooting Tools

Several types of troubleshooting tools are available, ranging from hardware to software solutions. For software, there are several excellent diagnostic tools such as Microsoft's Windows Diagnostics and PC Medic, Check-It Pro, and Norton Utilities, just to name a few. These software programs can do everything from verifying the status of the hard drive to ensuring that there are no conflicts with interrupts, I/O addresses, or DMA channels.

Hardware tools are used to verify the status of hardware, and can range from a network analyzer, which displays data about the packets of information traveling over your network, to a multimeter that checks for a variety of things. The multimeter is a favorite topic on the A+ Certification exam, and it is prudent to understand its function. Remember from the discussion in Chapter 1 that the multimeter is actually a multi-measuring tool that measures current, resistance, and voltage. If you suspect that a device is not getting current, you can turn the multimeter to the Amperes, or amps, and measure the current that flows through the device. However, if you need to check a component, such as a battery, any voltage you set the multimeter to will measure volts. The most common use of a multimeter is the resistance measurement, which is measured in ohms. This feature is used to locate the breaking point in a wire by determining if there is resistance on the wire, which is indicated by an infinite reading.

Basic Troubleshooting

When troubleshooting computer-related problems, you are putting on your detective's cap and searching for clues that identify the problem. In your search, you need to gather all the information that you can from the customer, scrutinize the environment, use your observational skills on the equipment and software, and attempt to re-create the problem itself. By combining these steps, you should be able to isolate the problem and complete the repair.

Information Gathering

The first step in diagnosing the problem is to gather as much information on the problem as you can. These are your "clues" that help point you in the right direction. As with any good mystery, you need to question the customer about the problem. Items that you want to include in your information-gathering constitute the computer's environment as well as the symptoms exhibited before, during, and after the problem. We discuss both of these in detail in the following subsections, and round it off with some of the more common problem situations in which you might find yourself.

Customer Environment

Observation is also an important skill to have. Your audio, visual, touch, and olfactory senses all play a part in observation. When you walk into the customer's office, take note of the environment around you for possible environmental causes to the problem. Is there excessive heat in the office? Computers absolutely hate heat, and an overly warm office could be the cause of some sporadic problems. Is the computer near high-voltage equipment? Computers are susceptible to interference caused by high-voltage equipment.

FROM THE FIELD

How To Prepare a Good Repair Arsenal; Pack Your Bags

PC technicians should always try to pack into a case as many repair tools as they can carry comfortably. They should always have most of the equipment to deal with any situation. What exactly goes in this case depends on the types of repairs that you plan to do and the operating system and hardware that you expect to encounter.

I prefer to have a sturdy briefcase, which is about 1 ½' by 2' by 6". Do not pick a flimsy material for this case, because it will most likely be used a lot. Do not buy tools haphazardly. Stick with the kits that you can find in a computer store. Try and get the most tools that you can afford. These kits range from simple to quite elaborate. You'll do well in the $30 to $50 range.

You also need your array of disks. Get startup disks for all the operating systems that you are using. Also, get disks with drivers for all the hardware that you think you'll encounter. Get disk holders for these disks. If you are working on systems with CD-ROM's, get a CD-ROM holder and pack it with ten of the best CDs for repairs. Pack your bag with compressed air, anti-static wrist guards, and

books. Why books? Because there are some indispensable books out there that will save you a lot of time when you are in the field. Try to get a small book that lists all the manufacturers settings for computers, hard drives, error codes, company phone numbers, and so forth. These can be found for under $10. Most operating systems have good books that can be used as reference. Find a good one and keep it in your case. Also, include miscellaneous items that you will always need. Converters, networks cables, computer cables, bolts, adapters, extenders, phone lines, and the like will all prove handy and will save you a trip to go back and get what you need.

Also in this case keep plenty of pens and a note pad. I've seen some techs even carry a sandwich in their repair cases. This is nice if you happen to have a really big repair around lunch time. Always keep your eyes on what other people carry around in their cases. Just make sure you can carry all that you put in it, or you may end up having to move equipment as well as carrying your case.

—By Ted Hamilton, MCP, A+ Certified

If the physical environment is not a problem, you need to verify the computer environment. One of the first things you can check is if there were any changes made to the system of which you might not have been informed. This enables you to verify that any modifications that may have been made aren't the source of the problem. This could be in the form of hardware or software upgrades, including any changes that might have been made to a network to which the customer connects.

If the customer is on a network, find out if software applications are loading from the network. Sometimes, a software upgrade may have put the newer application in a different directory and the new drive mappings haven't been properly implemented. If their operating system loads directly from the network, it is also possible that a device driver has been moved or deleted. Ask the customer if it is a constantly recurring problem or if it is a sporadic problem. Sporadic problems are harder to isolate as they are difficult to re-create.

Verify device drivers and their configurations. Does the customer load their operating system, such as Windows 95, from the network? If so, the device driver may not be in the root directory of the operating system or possibly a different version has overwritten the original one. The customer may have inadvertently made changes to the driver configuration. These are all things that you should check on.

Symptoms/Error Codes

When examining the symptoms, it helps to get any information on error messages or codes received by the customer when the error occurred. Oftentimes, the customer may not have noted the exact message and is unable to supply you with this information. If this has happened, you have to try to re-create the error if the symptoms do not lead you directly to the problem itself.

Most error codes occur during the POST diagnostic routing that is performed during boot time. These codes are listed later on in the chapter, but a few of the more common ones are listed in Table 2-2.

	Error Code	Error Message	Description
TABLE 2-2 Common Error Codes, Messages, and Their Descriptions	161	CMOS battery failure	CMOS battery needs to be replaced.
	164	Memory size error	Occurs after a memory upgrade. Run the SETUP program and the error should disappear.
	201	Memory test failed	One or more of the Random Access Memory chips failed the test. May need to try replacing them one at a time to find the defective chip.
	301	Keyboard did not respond	Indication that the keyboard probably needs a cleaning.
	303	Keyboard or system unit error	Indicates a bad keyboard that needs to be replaced.
	423	Parallel port test failed	Reported with monochrome adapters. Will need to replace the adapter.

Problem Situations

When working in the computer industry, it is surprising how the same problems occur over and over again. Patience with users, who usually know little or nothing about how a computer operates, is not just a virtue but a necessity. Some of the more common problems and their resolutions are listed as follows.

Isolation of Problems and Procedures

When you are faced with a problem, you have to use the information that you have gathered and come up with a plausible cause of the problem. Start with the easiest item to test and work your way upward. This type of method is known as the "bottom-up" method, as you are starting from the ground. For example, if you have a floppy drive error, start with the media used and work your way up to the drive.

QUESTIONS AND ANSWERS

My computer is getting a keyboard error.	Either the keyboard needs cleaning, the connection has worked its way loose, or the keyboard must be replaced.
The computer lost its BIOS settings.	This is commonly caused by a low CMOS battery. Replace the battery and reconfigure the CMOS.
My monitor is dead.	Several issues revolve around this one. If it is a power-saver monitor, try hitting a few keys and see if it comes on. Check that the monitor is actually powered on and that the cable connection is secure.
The mouse moves sporadically.	This is a symptom of either a dirty mouse or an incorrectly configured mouse. If it is a configuration problem, you probably have to raise the mouse-sensitivity property higher than it currently is.
My printer won't print.	Run the printer's diagnostic routine, or *self-test*, and see if there is any problem. If it passes, the printer is not at fault and you need to check that the cable is correctly attached. Verify the device driver configuration, and if necessary, the software application's configuration. If the printer has a network adapter card, the printer may have lost its configuration and you have to use the configuration utility and ensure that the settings are still intact.
The output on the page from my printer is fuzzy.	If you are working with a dot-matrix printer, check the print head for stuck pins. However, a laser printer probably needs a good cleaning.

If you have encountered a problem similar to the reported problem, then use that knowledge to isolate the cause. Once you have encountered a similar problem, you can apply that knowledge to the situation at hand, resulting in a faster diagnosis and repair. Some technicians even keep a notebook with them to log problems and their resolutions to reference when a situation is unusual or infrequent. Keeping a log that references specific sites can also be useful, as you may be called on to troubleshoot the same problem you resolved before.

Hardware/Software Problems

Determining if you are faced with a hardware or software problem can be easy, such as with a completely dead component, or complex, as with configuration problems. Most of the time, the customer is absolutely sure that the problem resides in the hardware itself. Use any error codes from the POST diagnostic routine to isolate hardware problems, as well as any diagnostic software that can be applied to the device and its adapter cards.

With software problems, you need to check for device driver problems, such as configuration errors or corrupted software. Also, verify any application settings that relate to the device itself. If you suspect that an application is at fault, you may have to reinstall the software to resolve the situation.

CERTIFICATION SUMMARY

In this chapter, we have gone over the basic procedures used to troubleshoot hardware and software problems. This formed the basis for diagnosing hardware and/or software errors, even when you encounter an uncommon error. We have also discussed some common items to look for when working on specific hardware devices. Armed with this knowledge, you are pointed in the right direction for isolating the offending component and speeding the repair time.

✔ TWO-MINUTE DRILL

- ❏ CMOS (Complementary Metal-Oxide Semiconductor) which is an integrated circuit composed of a metal oxide that is located directly on the system board.

- ❏ Chip creep is a phenomenon whereby a computer chip becomes loose within its socket.

- ❏ Input devices are the easiest types of components to check, as there are fewer things that can go wrong with them.

- ❏ Keyboard errors usually generate a 3** error code when POST runs at boot time.

- ❏ With sporadically functioning keys or sticking keys, you need to give the keyboard a good cleaning.

- ❏ A dirty mouse is the most common mouse-related problem reported.

❏ If another device is using the same IRQ or I/O address as the mouse, it probably won't work at all.

❏ If a trackball on a laptop is unresponsive, you have to replace it, which on many laptop machines also requires that you replace the entire keyboard unit.

❏ A dirty scanner surface usually results in smudged or poor-quality images.

❏ Most problems with scanners that are not resolved by cleaning the unit are device-driver related.

❏ Sometimes the most obvious solution will solve your problem. With most components, the first thing to do is check that the power is turned on or that the power supply is snugly in place.

❏ Floppy disks are susceptible to physical and magnetic corruption, giving the customer the appearance of a bad drive with "Error reading disk" or "Error writing to disk" messages.

❏ File corruption or bad sectors can be caused by several things: corrupted or invalid device driver, faulty controller cable, an incorrectly configured controller, or even a computer shutdown while the file is in use.

❏ Problems that are encountered with tape drive systems include media problems, dirty read/write heads, cable and power connections, controller card, and device drivers.

❏ For CD-ROM problems, one good troubleshooting tool that comes in handy is any diagnostic program that may have come with the CD-ROM drive or the controller board.

❏ One of the most common problems reported to the technician with regard to CD-ROMs is that the customer cannot read a CD-ROM disk.

❏ If the computer doesn't boot after you have installed a CD-ROM, you have either an address problem, a cable problem, or a connector problem.

❏ To diagnose parallel or serial port problems, you need special diagnostic software in order to verify that they are working.

❑ The most common problem with sound cards is related to configuration problems with the software driver configuration, which is in the form of IRQ, I/O Address, or DMA channel conflicts.

❑ A paper fault can be a symptom of the use of poor quality paper, such as recycled paper, or an impeded pathway.

❑ Printers are one of the most complex systems that you will diagnose.

❑ When you get a complaint of a "dead" monitor, one of the first things to check (and one of the most forgotten) is to see if the monitor is turned on.

❑ Monitors use a *sync frequency* to control the refresh rate, which is the rate at which the display device is repainted.

❑ External modems are easier to diagnose than internal modems, as you can see the signals from the display panel.

❑ When one modem connects to another modem, both of the modems have to agree on the method of communication used, called *handshaking*.

❑ A null modem cable is a special cable that has the send and receive lines reversed on the connector.

❑ A Power On Self Test (POST) is self test performed by the computer that occurs during boot time. It is used to diagnose system-related problems.

❑ Refer back to Table 2-1 and review the error code ranges and components they relate to.

❑ The most common problem with the BIOS is when the CMOS battery begins to run low on power.

❑ Power supplies include a fan in the unit to cool it down, thus preventing overheating.

❑ Device drivers are programs that translate necessary information between the operating system and the specific peripheral device for which they are configured, such as a printer.

❑ When troubleshooting computer-related problems, you need to gather all the information that you can from the customer: scrutinize the environment, use your observational skills on the equipment and software, and attempt to re-create the problem itself.

❑ Refer back to Table 2-2 and review error codes and their meanings.

❑ Patience with users, who usually know little or nothing about how a computer operates, is not just a virtue but a necessity.

❑ When you are faced with a computer problem, start with the easiest item to test and work your way upward.

SELF TEST

The following Self Test questions will help you measure your understanding of the material presented in this chapter. Read all the choices carefully, as there may be more than one correct answer. Choose all correct answers for each question.

1. When faced with a laser printer that produces blank pages, the usual suspect is the:

   A. Ribbon

   B. Paper supply

   C. Toner cartridge

   D. Tractor feed

2. Your customer calls you and says, "I can't read my CD." You would:

   A. Tell them that the CD is defective and to throw it away.

   B. Tell them that the drive needs to be replaced.

   C. Go in and check the adapter card.

   D. Ask them to try another CD.

3. You have reported to a customer site to diagnose a keyboard, and notice that it is dirty. You would first:

   A. Replace the keyboard.

   B. Change the keyboard port.

   C. Clean the keyboard using soap and water.

   D. Clean the keyboard using a keyboard cleaning kit.

4. At boot time, how many beeps indicate a problem with one of the system components?

   A. One

   B. Two

   C. Three

   D. Zero

5. Power supply problems are usually indicated by: (Choose all that apply)

   A. The fan is not working.

   B. The computer frequently reboots itself.

   C. You get an error code during POST diagnostics.

   D. The computer does not boot.

6. When you begin to diagnose a problem, you should first:

   A. Isolate the failed component.

   B. Gather information.

   C. Replace components.

   D. Reboot the computer.

7. Once you have determined that a monitor has power and that the brightness/contrast controls are not at fault, the easiest way to determine that the problem isn't with the monitor is to:

   A. Check the adapter cable.

   B. Replace the monitor with a newer type.

C. Verify the device driver.

D. Replace the monitor with a similar type.

8. Error codes relating to memory problems are in the _____ range.

A. 200 - 299

B. 300 - 399

C. 400 - 499

D. 500 - 599

9. You are troubleshooting a modem problem and connect to a remote system. However, you receive garbage characters across the screen that will not stop. This is typically a symptom of:

A. Incorrect stop bit or parity setting

B. Static on the line

C. Modem cable has become loose

D. No power to the modem

10. A printer is beginning to have a problem with page jams. You should check: (Choose all that apply)

A. Paper quality

B. Toner cartridge

C. Adapter card

D. Paper pathway

11. You have just installed a floppy drive and turned on the computer. However, the drive light will not go out. You have probably:

A. Put the cable on backward

B. Forgotten to configure the BIOS settings for the drive

C. Installed a defective drive

D. Incorrectly configured the device drivers

12. Your customer is complaining that their word processor terminates abnormally when they load a particular document. You probably have to:

A. Replace the hard drive

B. Run a disk-scanning utility

C. Tell them that the file is history

D. Replace the cable

13. You are diagnosing a laser printer that has excessive page jams. When you attempt to print several test pages, the paper jams in the same location. This is a symptom of:

A. Poor quality paper

B. A bad toner cartridge

C. Dirt or paper particles impeding the paper from proper movement

D. Static electricity

14. Your customer calls to report that they are unable to perform a tape backup due to an error reported on their only tape cartridge. The mostly likely cause of the problem is:

A. The tape has expired.

B. The tape is not formatted.

C. The drive is about to fail.

D. The cable needs to be replaced.

15. You have installed and configured a new SVGA monitor. However, when you boot the computer, you notice that the screen flickers. To resolve this problem, you need to:

    A. Replace the monitor.

    B. Replace the adapter card.

    C. Change the Sync Frequency.

    D. Configure the monitor as a VGA.

16. When walking into the customer's office, you would:

    A. Ask questions.

    B. Remove the case from the computer.

    C. Note the environment for problems.

    D. Put on your wrist strap.

17. Printers that communicate using TCP/IP use a _____ card.

    A. NIC adapter card

    B. Jet Direct adapter card

    C. Device drivers

    D. Special cabling

18. You have just installed a new CD-ROM drive, and now the computer does not boot. You would verify: (Choose all that apply)

    A. Address

    B. Cabling

    C. Compact Disk

    D. Application software

19. One of your customers is attempting to work with several graphic files that have disappeared from the directory in which they were located. You have run the SCANDISK.EXE and MS Defragment programs, and neither reports an error. You also know that the customer attaches to a Novell 3.11 server. You would:

    A. Retrieve the files from the last good backup.

    B. Tell the customer that the files have been deleted.

    C. Ask the system administrator if any network applications have been upgraded.

    D. Replace the hard drive in case other files disappear.

20. POST stands for:

    A. Power Off Software Test

    B. Peripheral Operating System Test

    C. Power On Self Test

    D. Peripheral On Self Test

21. Keyboard errors usually generate a _____ error code.

    A. 1**

    B. 2**

    C. 3**

    D. 4**

22. While troubleshooting a modem, you make a connection with a remote computer. However, after you have connected, you notice that garbage

characters appears at random. This is typically a symptom of:

A. Incorrect stop bit or parity setting

B. Static on the phone line

C. Modem cable on backwards

D. The remote system software has bugs

23. A customer calls to complain that their monitor is dead. The first thing you would ask them to try is:

A. Adjust the brightness/contrast controls.

B. Power on the monitor.

C. Check the connection into the monitor.

D. Nothing. You have to go in and replace it.

24. Most problems with sound cards stem from: (Choose all that apply)

A. The card itself

B. Cabling

C. DMA channel

D. IRQ

25. The method used in troubleshooting that starts with the easiest component and works up to the actual device is called the _____ method.

A. Top down

B. Bottom top

C. Sequential

D. Bottom up

26. You have just replaced a hard drive and restored its contents from tape. However, you are now experiencing printer problems. You check the printer and printer cable without finding any errors. The most likely problem is:

A. The device driver is corrupted.

B. The system board is bad.

C. There is a problem adapter card.

D. Static electricity.

27. You reboot a computer and it gives you a processor error. After opening the case, you press down on the chip and discover that it is loose in its socket. The processor is said to have suffered from

_____.

A. Old age

B. Chip creep

C. Socket syndrome

D. Post Operational Stress

28. You are having communication problems between a floppy drive and the computer. You have already checked the address configuration and the cable. The next likely suspect is:

A. Controller card

B. Power connector

C. Floppy drive

D. Device driver

29. You have just installed an external modem. However, when you turn it on,

none of the lights are active. The most likely suspect is:

A. Corrupted driver

B. Bad RS232-C cable

C. Power connection

D. Address conflict

E. None of the above.

30. If you are working on a hard drive, you need to ensure that the device driver configuration is correct for _____ types of drives:

A. MTM

B. IDE

C. EIDE

D. SCSI

31. Floppy disk media errors can be caused by: (Choose all that apply)

A. Defective disk

B. Adapter cable problems

C. Dirty read/write heads

D. Incompatible floppy drives

32. A symptom of a dirty mouse is:

A. Little or poor response from mouse

B. No response from mouse

C. Addressing error message

D. POST error message

33. When diagnosing a software error, you would check for: (Choose all that apply)

A. POST error codes

B. Device driver errors

C. Incorrectly addressed adapter

D. Application problems

34. Smudged or poor-quality images from a flat-bed scanner are symptoms of a:

A. Dirty glass

B. Application problem

C. Device driver configuration error

D. Cable problem

35. The most common problem with the system BIOS is:

A. Configuration errors

B. Low CMOS battery

C. Bad chip

D. Software errors

3

Safety and Preventive Maintenance

I n the previous chapter, we discussed troubleshooting and repair procedures. In this chapter, we discuss the products and procedures used for preventive maintenance of computer systems and associated peripherals. Following this, we discuss safety issues that you should become familiar with to ensure that you do not injure or kill yourself during the repair or upgrade process.

CERTIFICATION OBJECTIVE 3.01

Preventive Maintenance Products and Procedures

Preventive maintenance is something that customers often forget or do not believe is necessary. However, nothing could be further from the truth. For example, suppose you have a customer who frequently reschedules their preventive maintenance time. Because you are unable to perform the maintenance, neither of you would be aware that the fan in the power supply had stopped working. As a result, instead of just having to replace the power supply, the processor and some of the memory failed due to the excessive heat. In addition, the unscheduled downtime resulted in a loss of productivity and a larger bill from you.

As you can see from the preceding example, by performing regular maintenance on computer equipment, you can extend the life of the components themselves as well as locating potential problems. In the long run, this will save the customer time and money. In the next subsections, we discuss the various products available on the market along with the proper procedures for using them.

Manufacturer Suggested Guidelines

Before beginning any preventive maintenance procedures, it is critical that you consult the manufacturer's documentation. Vendors include the information on the proper cleaning materials to use when cleaning or maintaining their components. Failure to follow these guidelines could result in either component degradation, complete failure, or a voided warranty. Never assume that you already know what you can use with what device; instead, take the time to review the documentation. Remember that customer service is not only solving problems, but also ensuring that you do not generate them.

Liquid Cleaning Compounds

There are several liquid cleaning compounds that are used when you perform preventive maintenance. However, it is important to keep in mind that you should always refer to the manufacturer's documentation prior to using any cleaning compound on a component. This is because every vendor may use different materials in the component itself. In addition, some vendors require specialized cleaning compounds that can be purchased from them.

Various forms of alcohol are frequently used in cleaning computer components, such as isopropyl alcohol and denatured alcohol. These items are generally used to clean contacts and are applied to special disks used for cleaning floppy drive read/write heads. Mild detergent can be used on the outside of the monitor, the computer case, and on keyboards.

Cleaning Contacts and Connectors

Few people realize, or remember, that contacts and connectors require cleaning. The reason people forget is because connectors are seldom removed from their respective sockets. Nevertheless, these items do get dirty over time and do require cleaning. Most components can be cleaned with a cotton swab that has been coated with isopropyl alcohol. However, many manufacturers recommend that you use a pencil eraser to clean the contacts on expansion cards. As with most computer components, it is important that you consult the vendor's documentation to ensure that their product will not have an adverse effect from the materials that you use.

Cleaning Tools

There are several cleaning tools that you should keep in your maintenance kit. One nice item to have is a rubber knife. When you are called upon to remove hardened residue from metal components, you can use a rubber knife to dislodge particles that the vacuum or dust-free cloth could not remove. Never use a metal knife or other metallic object when cleaning the computer or its components, as you can either damage them or cause injury to yourself through electrostatic discharge (ESD). ESD occurs when two charged objects come into contact with each other, such as your hand against a door knob. The charge is transferred between the two objects until both objects have an equal charge.

Compressed air comes in handy when you are cleaning components, such as a keyboard, or areas that a vacuum can not get to (or shouldn't get to!). Compressed air is distributed in an aerosol-type can and is available at any computer or electronics store. The air is compressed in the can, hence its name, by extreme pressure and dispelled through a nozzle that is similar to the old aerosol cans. You would use compressed air when you need to blow dust, dirt, or other unwanted debris out and away from a component.

Dust-free, lint-free disposable cloths or wipes are also cheaply available and should be used whenever you need to wipe the surface of a component. Normal cloths naturally attract lint and dust, while dust-free or lint-free cloths do not. This helps to ensure that you are not contributing harmful materials to sensitive components.

Floppy Drive and Tape Head Cleaning

When you've determined that the read/write heads on a floppy drive need cleaning, you need to obtain a floppy drive cleaning kit. The kits contain a special cleaning disk that looks like a normal floppy and a small bottle of isopropyl alcohol. The disk has an access hole, similar to a regular disk, on which you place a few drops of the isopropyl alcohol. Then you insert the disk into the drive and the drive will spin up. When the read/write heads attempt to read it, the disk will spin over the heads and clean them. These kits are relatively inexpensive and can be found at most computer and electronics stores.

When you clean a tape drive, you are performing the same function as with a floppy drive. The only difference is that you would use a special tape-cleaning cartridge instead of a cleaning disk with isopropyl alcohol. The cleaning cartridge looks exactly like a normal tape cartridge, although some manufacturers use a different color (usually white or beige) casing around a cleaning cartridge to help differentiate it from a normal cartridge.

Hard Drive Maintenance

Because hard drives are sealed units that can only be opened in a "clean room," there is nothing you can do to clean the read/write heads. However, hard drives have a tendency to become fragmented over a period of time or with excessive use and should be defragmented as a part of normal preventive maintenance. To perform a defragmentation, you can use a special software program that was designed specifically for this purpose, such as Norton Utilities or Microsoft Disk Defragmenter.

Another problem with hard drives is that the disk surface can become corrupted over time. If the drive attempts to read or write to these corrupted sections, the computer could crash or exhibit strange symptoms that are difficult to pin down. Some software utilities, such as the Microsoft Scandisk utility, are designed to locate and mark corrupted sections on the disk. The mark tells the hard drive to ignore this section of the hard drive. This process should be performed on a regular basis in conjunction with a disk defragmentation.

Determining Wear and Tear

Computer peripherals are not only electrical components, they are also mechanical components. These components wear out over time and eventually fail. As a service technician, you should inspect peripherals for signs of deterioration and replace any components that are about to expire. By doing so, you will save the customer time and money from untimely downtime when the component finally fails. Signs of wear can include thin spots on belts, bends or tear in cables, and moving parts that are only sporadically functioning.

Vacuuming

Most people do not realize it, but it is important to vacuum the inside of a computer case whenever you open it. Dust and dirt particles get sucked into the case through the air ducts and deposit themselves anywhere they can. These particles can conduct an electrical charge, resulting in possible damage to the delicate electronic components inside. Most offices do not have a vacuum that you will be able to use, as there are usually cleaning crews that carry their own equipment with them. However, small, portable vacuums are available for as little as $20 and are well worth the investment.

Whenever you have to open a printer for repair, it is important that you vacuum out the interior. Bits of paper and dust have a tendency to accumulate on the inside of a printer at a faster rate than the interior of a computer. The reason that this happens is due to the nature of the printer — that is, producing output on paper medium. Small bits of paper can tear off and become lodged inside the printer from clearing a paper jam. The dust produced during the printing process itself also contributes to the mess. As stated earlier, dirt and dust can carry an electrical charge. This small charge can be enough to damage the electrical components inside of a computer, as well as causing excess wear and tear on mechanical components that will have to work a bit harder against the dirt.

CERTIFICATION OBJECTIVE 3.02

Environmental Hazard Protection

Computers must have a reliable source of power in order to function. However, there are many problems with our power supply that have the potential to damage computer systems and their individual components. The uninterruptible power supply (UPS) is a device that was designed to protect your computer and its components from possible injury from the problems that are inherent with today's existing power supply structure.

Power Issues

With society's increasing demand for power comes a price. The power utility companies have been hard-pressed to keep up with the present demand, leading to problems in dealing with future increases. As a result, brownouts, which are the momentary lapses in power supply, have become more common than they used to. Brownouts can cause problems with computer components that are not designed to withstand these events. Blackouts are similar to brownouts, as they are also lapses in power, but they are long-term power outages.

When there is a power spike, there is a sudden, huge increase in power that lasts for a split second. Power spikes can literally fry computer components. A power surge is similar to a spike, except that a power surge may not have the intensity that a spike can have.

As stated previously, noise creeps into a power line and is transmitted to the computer. This noise is almost impossible to keep out of the power line due to the vast distances involved and the technology used to transmit power. Noise is a one of the most prevalent problems with the power supply today.

UPS (Uninterruptible Power Supply)

Today's UPS units are populating homes and businesses at an increasing rate as the cost has decreased substantially from the early days of computer history. The UPS is designed to protect your computer from sudden lapses in power, power spikes or surges, and "dirty" current. This is accomplished by several components in the UPS, such as suppressors, noise filters, and surge protectors. Each of these items is discussed in the following paragraphs.

Suppressors

At times, your power outlet will experience momentary surges of current, called *spikes*. Spikes can harm computers and their components much in the same way as ESD damage. However, the damage that results is usually on a much greater level, with catastrophic damage becoming more frequent. A suppressor is designed to either absorb or block the excess power and thus save computer components from injury.

Noise Filters

When someone refers to "dirty current," they are talking about the noise present on the power line itself. This noise is caused by *electro-magnetic interferance (EMI)* and can stray, or leak, from the current into nearby components. When EMI leaks from power current, it is called a magnetic field and can easily damage computer components. UPS's contain a special filter, called a *noise filter*, that reduces the amount of noise present in electrical current and eliminates magnetic fields caused by noise, thus providing some protection to the components that utilize the current or are nearby.

Storage of Components

A UPS is essentially a battery that is designed to take over when there is a power loss, in addition to ensuring that only the proper type and form of current are passed on to the computer. When you need to store a UPS, you must ensure that is has not been discharged. A discharged UPS that is stored for a long period of time may lose some of its capacity to store power or may become unable to accept a charge at all. To ensure that your UPS is stored in the proper manner, review the manufacturer's documentation for any other recommended procedures.

With other computer components, you need to protect them from damage resulting from electrostatic discharge (ESD). ESD occurs when two charged objects come into contact with each other and energy is transferred between them. This transference of energy happens to equalize the charge between these two objects. A good example of ESD is when you grab a door knob, or other metal object, and get shocked. Computer components are very sensitive to ESD and can even be rendered useless. Whenever you store computer components, you must place them in an anti-static bag to ensure their safety from ESD. Anti-static bags are designed so that static build-up is contained on the outside of the bag rather than on the inside, thus protecting the delicate components.

Lasers and High-Voltage Equipment

Whenever you work around lasers or high-voltage equipment, you must be extremely careful not to injure yourself. These forms of equipment can cause damage in the form of burns, eye-related problems including blindness, or even death. There are procedures that should be followed whenever working with either high-voltage equipment or lasers. These procedures are discussed in the following subsections.

Lasers

Lasers employ a high-intensity light beam that can cause severe damage to your eyes, including blindness. *Never* look directly into a laser beam. Some lasers can cause severe burns when they come into contact with skin, or even death depending on the intensity of the beam and the location on you. However, the lasers employed in CD-ROM drives are Level 3 laser beams and are of a significantly lower intensity than those employed in construction or scientific applications. As a result, you will not get a severe burn from them but should nevertheless be cautious when working with them.

The laser that is employed in laser printers is also a Level 3 type of beam. However, laser printers do generate an excessive amount of heat, and components that reside inside these printers *can* cause severe burns. It is for this reason that you should be extremely cautious when working inside a laser printer.

High-Voltage Equipment

You should exercise extreme caution when working around any high-voltage equipment, including any equipment near the computer itself. You can spot these items from one of two types of labels on the equipment itself. The first type of label is a Warning label that usually informs you of the potential of equipment damage as well as personal injury. The second

FROM THE FIELD

Common Sense May Not Be So Common

In the years that I have been doing PC repairs, I think I've seen it all. Many techs (who of course are not A+ certified) make big mistakes that can ruin hardware and jeopardize data. One would think that a tech would not plug a monitor in after carrying it in a downpour of rain. The result: lots of smoke, and an expensive monitor that needs to be replaced.

Or how about the tech who tries to "hot dock" hardware accessories on a system that does not support this method. (Hot docking is the ability of a system to accept new accessories while it is plugged in.) I'll tell you from first-hand experience that a hard drive will not be able to be plugged into the system while the power is on. If you try it, the result is a hard drive that is completely erased.

Never force anything. This is how RAM sockets get broken, causing replacement of the motherboard. If the processor does not fit right, do not try to force it in. The result will be spending the next hour with needle-nosed pliers trying to get all the pins straight again,

or worse—a broken pin and a fun time explaining to your supervisor what happened.

If you drop a screw in the machine, never just leave it there. It could end up against two contact points and really mess things up. Take the time to find and remove the screw. Plug a power cord in backwards and you will see smoke. Turn the power switch on the back of the machine from 120volt to 240volt and you might as well grab some marshmallows. Start trying to repair the monitor when you don't fully understand the voltage involved, and I'll say a prayer for you.

Be careful in what you do. Fires, lost data, personal injury, and damaged hardware are very real events. Your best protection is to know exactly what you are doing at all times and to be careful. If you are in doubt about anything that you are doing, do not be afraid to ask someone who knows. No one is supposed to be able to fix everything. If you are in over your head, do not proceed.

—By Ted Hamilton, MCP, A+ Certified

type of label is a Caution that tells you of possible personal injuries that can occur. Most labels refer to a procedure or set of guidelines to be performed whenever you work on the equipment, although some refer you the equipment's documentation for more information. It is always important to follow the manufacturer's guidelines whenever working on or around high-voltage equipment. Failure to follow these instructions to the letter can result in severe burns or electrocution.

There are a few considerations that you should keep in mind whenever you are working on or around high-voltage equipment. First, never wear an ESD strap around this form of equipment, as the electrical charge could kill you. Second, be especially aware of the electrical pathways on your person. This means that you should never use both hands on the equipment itself. If you do, you are forming a "live" circuit between you and the equipment, resulting in an electrical pathway that leads from one hand and passes through your body to the other hand. The first sensation is one of extreme pain as your skin is cooked where you have come into contact with it. The second is the acrid odor of burning flesh. When electric current passes through your heart, the end result is death as your heart cooks and your blood boils from being heated by the electricity. If the current reaches your head, your brain will become well-done and your eyes could burst out of their sockets. *If this is an intensive, sickening graphical description of what can happen when you are not careful, good!* It cannot be stressed enough how important it is for you to be extremely cautious around any high-voltage equipment and to be aware of the environment around you.

Power Supply

A power supply is the perfect example of high-voltage equipment. As discussed in Chapter 1, these devices convert the alternating current (AC) that comes from your regular power outlet into the direct current (DC) that your computer uses. Therefore, you want to ensure that the computer is turned off and that the power cord has been disconnected from the power supply.

When the power supply performs the power conversion process, some of that energy is lost and converted into another form of energy: heat. The heat generated by a power supply can cause severe burns. Therefore, it is important for you to ensure that the power supply has had sufficient time to cool down before coming into contact with it.

If you ever open a power supply, you risk severe shock or even electrocution from the electrical charge stored in the capacitors located within the power supply itself. This is true even if the power supply has been off for a long time, as the static electricity that builds up over time can get into deadly ranges. As a result, *never* remove the case from a power supply. Remember, while a power supply is a replaceable component, you aren't.

CRT

Monitors are high-voltage components that should only be repaired by experienced personnel. When working on monitors, it is important to remember that extreme caution should be taken at all times, as any built-up charge can be lethal. However, the first thing to remember is *never wear an ESD wrist strap when handling monitors.* After you have removed your wrist strap, ensure that the monitor is powered off and disconnected from the power outlet. This is an important step because you have to discharge the monitor.

To discharge a monitor, you need to have a jumper wire and a screwdriver with a non-conductive handle. First, connect one end of the jumper wire to a ground such as the screw on an electrical outlet. Next, wrap the free end of the wire around the metal shaft of the screwdriver. When you do this, make sure that the wire is as far away from the handle of the screwdriver as possible. This helps to prevent any accidental contact between you and the wire.

Assuming that you have already removed the casing from the monitor, locate the anode lead that is attached to the glass inside the monitor. An anode lead looks like a small suction cup with a wire connected to it. *Do not touch the anode lead or the wire!* Using the tip of the screwdriver against the underside of the anode lead, gently pry the lead away from the monitor until you hear a small "pop" or the lead is free of the glass. The small "pop" sound is any built-up charge that has accumulated on the glass. This charge will pass into the screwdriver and follow the jumper wire into the ground. If you should come into contact with either the shaft of the screwdriver or the jumper wire while the monitor is being discharged, part of that charge will enter your body and can cause severe injury. However, at this point, the monitor has been safely discharged.

exam

!

Ⓦatch

Know the procedure for properly discharging the monitor. Not only for your own safety, but because most people who take the exam get two or three questions on this procedure.

CERTIFICATION OBJECTIVE 3.04

Disposal Procedures

Once you have replaced a component, the next question is what to do with it. Landfills used to be the answer, but these areas have proven to be only a short-term solution. Environmental concerns have also become an issue as harmful chemicals have a tendency to leak into the water table and contaminate our drinking water supply. As a result, most states have enacted stringent rules and regulations regarding the disposal of any item deemed harmful to the environment. Recycling of these hazardous substances has become a more viable, long-term solution. As a service technician, you need to dispose of the various computer components and chemicals that you use in an environment-friendly manner.

For more information regarding hazardous waste and proper disposal procedures not discussed in the following subsections, you can visit the EPA's Hazardous Waste Resource Conservation and Recovery Act page at http://www.epa.gov/epaoswer/osw/hazwaste.htm.

Batteries

Batteries contain environmentally harmful substances and should *not* be disposed of through a convenient trash can. The Battery Act passed by Congress on May 13th, 1996 was designed to phase out the use of mercury in batteries and to provide for the recycling or proper disposal of nickel-cadmium batteries. However, each state has different rules and regulations regarding the proper reclamation and disposal of batteries. To ensure that you follow the appropriate procedures for your location, check with your state's environmental regulatory office before disposing of used batteries.

For more information on The Battery Act, obtain the document from the United States Environmental Protection Agency Web site at http://www.epa.gov/epaoswer/hazwaste/state/policy/pl104.txt.

exam
ⓦatch

Every A+ Certification Exam will have at least one question on battery disposal.

Toner Kits/Cartridges

Toner cartridges are recyclable items. Normally, the vendor will take your old toner cartridges when you order new ones, and will even give you a small credit for doing so (who says recycling doesn't pay?). However, if you are unable to exchange the cartridge, ask the vendor if they have any information or suggestions on the proper disposal method. If, for some reason, they cannot assist you, contact your state's environmental regulatory office for the appropriate disposal measures.

Computers

Old computers need not be thrown away if they are still usable. There are many churches and public schools in dire need of computers, and will accept them as a donation. By doing so, you receive a write-off on your taxes for a charitable contribution. However, if the computer is so antiquated as to be useless or the computer is beyond repair, there are many companies that will buy them for spare parts or as scrap metal.

Chemical Solvents

Chemical solvents are materials that are considered hazardous waste. The reason for this is the liquid gets absorbed in the ground and eventually makes its way into the water table. *Never dispose of these items by emptying them into a sink or toilet.* Proper disposal of chemical solvents is regulated by the Environmental Protection Agency and your local state government. As each state's rules and regulations are different concerning the disposal of these materials, you need to check with your state's environmental regulatory office for the proper procedure.

CRTs

If a monitor still functions, it is a good idea to keep at least one around for testing purpose. However, if you have enough monitors on hand, you can donate them to any church or public school for a tax break. If the monitor is useless, check to see if the manufacturer included disposal instructions with the monitor or contact the manufacturer directly. Some manufacturers will accept the monitor and give you a small credit when you purchase a new one. However, if neither of these options is available, you need to check with your state's environmental regulatory agency for proper disposal procedures, as monitors are no longer acceptable to landfills.

MSDS (Material Safety Data Sheet)

Material Safety Data Sheets (MSDS) are white pages that contain information on any substance that is deemed hazardous, most notably cleaning solvents. MSDS is required by the United States Department of Occupational Safety and Health Administration, and must be posted in obvious locations. The purpose of MSDS is to inform employees about the dangers inherent in hazardous materials and the proper use of these items to prevent potential injuries from occurring. For more information on MSDS, please consult their Internet site at http://www.osha.gov.

CERTIFICATION OBJECTIVE 3.05

ESD (Electrostatic Discharge)

A computer is not just a valuable resource, it is a costly one. As we become more dependent on them in our everyday lives, the most expensive feature is the time wasted by a malfunctioning computer, called *downtime*. As an example, suppose you have over 600 people on a network server that goes down for over four days. While they wait for the server to be repaired, they are not only unable to perform any work, but you still must pay them. Once the server is operational again, it could take an entire week's worth of overtime for them to catch up with the workload, costing you even more money and many missed deadlines. It is because of these types of expenses that you must ensure that the computer is repaired as soon as possible.

One of the things that can cause downtime is damage to delicate computer components through a common phenomenon called *electrostatic discharge (ESD)*. Everyone has been shocked at least a dozen times when grabbing a doorknob or other metal object, and you probably even see a spark when it happens. When an object can conduct electricity, such as a computer component or the human body, it has a tendency to retain some of that energy. That energy, known as *static electricity* because it doesn't move, builds up in an object over time, and is said to be *charged*. When two objects come into contact with each other, electrons are transferred between them until they both have an equal charge. This electron transfer is an electrostatic discharge.

ESD—What It Can Do

While ESD may not hurt you, it can still harm a computer component. Most devices operate between the three- to five-volt range, and can be damaged by ESD charges as low as 30 volts. When you actually feel the shock caused by ESD, that energy transfer is over 3,000 volts. Even worse, if you can see a spark when ESD occurs, that discharge is in the vicinity of 20,000 volts. Unless precautions are taken, you can actually destroy a device without even realizing it. This type of damage is called *catastrophic damage* because the device is rendered inoperable.

One other type of ESD damage can be caused: *degradation*. A component that suffers from degradation may continue to operate for days, or even months, before failing entirely and could damage other components while it is functioning. Depending on the severity of the damage, a device may even pass a diagnostic test. However, the components can cause intermittent problems in the computer that are extremely difficult to pinpoint, causing frustration to both the client and the technician and extending the downtime required to repair the computer.

Hidden ESD

The term "hidden" ESD refers to a couple of things. A static discharge that you do not feel can be considered hidden ESD because you will not even realize that it has occurred. Remember that when you feel ESD, you are receiving a charge around 3,000 volts. Charges that are below 3,000 volts can still damage electronic components.

Another form of hidden ESD is in the form of dust and dirt. As discussed in an earlier section, dust and dirt particles are capable of carrying an electrical charge. This charge is capable of destroying computer components over time, as the particles can pick up a charge and transfer it to a component several times. Unless you can keep your computer in a "clean room," which is a special sealed room that contains almost no dust or dirt, you will have to schedule regular cleanings for your computer system to cut down on the chances of catastrophic damage to computer components.

One last item to consider is the humidity level in the room. A humidity level below 50 percent tends to lead to static electricity. You will notice this especially in the winter months, when humidity levels are low naturally. Ensure that you check any air-handling equipment in the room for a properly set humidity level. However, ensure that the humidity is not set too high, as high levels condense the water particles in the air and these particles stick to computer components. Remember, water is a natural conductor of electricity as well!

Common ESD Protection Devices and Procedures

There are several forms of ESD protection devices, such as mats, wrist straps, and bags. These items should be used whenever you are working with computer components to prevent ESD damage.

ESD mats are made of an insulate material that is designed to slowly bleed away any excess charge from whatever comes into contact with it. There are two wires with alligator clips, one clip connected on the end of each wire, that are attached to the mat. When you use an ESD mat, you should first lay out the mat on a flat surface, such as a desk or a workbench, that is near an electrical ground. Next, you attach the first wire to an electrical ground, such as the screw on an electrical outlet, using the alligator clip. *Never attach the clip to the electrical socket itself as you can electrocute yourself in this manner!* Place the computer, or component, on the mat and connect the second wire to the computer. This safely transfers any static electricity that has stored up in the computer or the device and directs the charge into the ground. However, if you are working on a monitor, do not connect the second wire as you need to discharge the monitor according to the procedures discussed earlier in the chapter.

ESD wrist straps are also made of an insulate material and are worn on your wrist to safely bleed off any excessive charge stored in your body. The strap commonly has a Velcro fastener on it and a metal button that has a wire attached to it. To properly use an ESD wrist strap, you need to put it on and connect the wire to an electrical ground. The wire connects to the ground using an alligator clip that is attached to the end of the wire. Make sure that the ground is close to the work area and that you are aware of where the wire is at all times. Some ESD straps have a long wire that can be tripped over as you move around the work area.

ESD bags are the anti-static bags in which computer components are shipped. These bags are designed to collect stray electrical charges on the outside of the bag as opposed to the inside. Thus, the component stored inside the bag is kept safe from ESD damage. Always store computer components in ESD bags to ensure that they are kept as free as possible from dust and dirt as well as from ESD damage. As these bags are handy items to keep around, ensure that you have a good supply of them for storing old, but still functional, computer components. You can do this by keeping the bags that new components have shipped in rather than throwing them away. This saves you money, as you need not purchase them at an electronics store, and it helps protect the environment by keeping them out of landfills.

You can also purchase anti-static sprays to use on carpets and fabrics to reduce the build-up of static electricity. It is a good idea to spray these surfaces that are anywhere near your work area. In addition, ensure that you are wearing shoes that contain a rubber sole so that you do not build up any static electricity between yourself and the carpet as you walk around.

Hazardous Situations

Because there are many hands that touch the electronic components, from the people who manufactured the equipment to the packaging plant, ESD is not something that you can entirely eliminate. However, there are things that you can do to control the potential for harm to electronic devices and injury to yourself. The first thing is to ensure that you are not wearing any jewelry while working on a computer system. Watches, rings, necklaces, bracelets, and earrings all contain metal parts that conduct electricity. In addition, these items themselves can cause damage to components, as well as you, if the jewelry gets caught on anything inside the chassis. If you still don't believe it, imagine an earring getting caught on a cable as you lift your head out of the chassis!

Another thing that you can do to minimize the possibility of injury to yourself and computer components is by always following the ESD procedures discussed earlier in this section. Always place components on an ESD mat and, unless you are working on a monitor or a high-voltage device, always wear your ESD wrist strap. *It cannot be emphasized enough that you must remember to take off the wrist strap when working around monitors or high-voltage devices.* The charge that builds up in monitors, even after they have been powered off for a long period of time, can prove lethal. And never pack computer components in anything other than ESD bags. You can place the bags in boxes or packing peanuts, but only after the bag has been properly sealed with the component inside.

While the newer computer operating systems, especially network servers, enable you to repair them while the computer is still running, it is extremely important that you follow the manufacturer's guidelines to the letter. When live current is running through a computer, you are faced with the possibility of severe burns or even death. All it takes is a moment's contact with the wrong component and you could become history. Always take the extra time to review the vendor's guidelines before performing the repair.

CERTIFICATION SUMMARY

Preventive maintenance is one of the most important aspects in ensuring a healthy computer system. The tools and materials that are used during this process are equally important, as using improper equipment or cleaning products can result in harm to the delicate components. In addition, it is important to remember that the computer can become dangerous if you are not careful when working on it. Hazards can include anything from high-voltage equipment to electrostatic discharge, and preventive measures must be taken to ensure that you and the computer are not damaged. This chapter has discussed all of this in detail in order to arm you with the knowledge to prevent severe injury, or even death, to you.

✓ TWO-MINUTE DRILL

❑ A discharged UPS that is stored for a long period of time may lose some of its capacity to store power or may become unable to accept a charge at all.

❑ As a service technician, you should inspect all computer peripherals for signs of deterioration and replace any components that are about to expire.

❑ The lasers employed in CD-ROM drives are Level 3 laser beams and are of a significantly lower intensity than those employed in construction or scientific applications.

❑ Batteries contain environmentally harmful substances and should *not* be disposed of through a convenient trash can.

❑ ESD occurs when two charged objects come into contact with each other, such as your hand against a door knob. The charge is transferred between the two objects until both objects have an equal charge.

❑ It cannot be emphasized enough that you must remember to take off the ESD wrist strap when working around monitors or high-voltage devices.

❑ A component that suffers from degradation may continue to operate for days, or even months, before failing entirely and could damage other components while it is functioning.

❑ It is important to keep in mind that you should always refer to the manufacturer's documentation prior to using any cleaning compound on a component.

❑ Never use a metal knife or other metallic object when cleaning the computer or its components, as you can either damage them or cause injury to yourself through electrostatic discharge (ESD).

❑ ESD mats are made of an insulate material that is designed to slowly bleed away any excess charge from whatever comes into contact with it.

❑ Always take the extra time to review the vendor's guidelines before performing any repair.

❑ Noise is a one of the most prevalent problems with the power supply today.

❑ One of the things that can cause downtime is damage to delicate computer components through a common phenomenon called electrostatic discharge (ESD).

❑ Power spikes can literally fry computer components.

❑ When you are called upon to remove hardened residue from metal components, you can use a rubber knife to dislodge particles that the vacuum or dust-free cloth could not remove.

❑ Signs of wear on peripherals can include thin spots on belts, bends or tear in cables, and moving parts that are only sporadically functioning.

❑ The laser that is employed in laser printers is also a Level 3 type of beam.

❑ Never remove the case from a power supply, else you risk severe shock or even electrocution from the electrical charge stored in the capacitors located within the power supply itself.

❑ To discharge a monitor, you need to have a jumper wire and a screwdriver with a non-conductive handle.

❑ Various forms of alcohol are frequently used in cleaning computer components, such as isopropyl alcohol and denatured alcohol.

❑ When a power supply performs the power conversion process, some of the energy is lost and converted into another form of energy: heat.

SELF TEST

The following Self Test questions will help you measure your understanding of the material presented in this chapter. Read all the choices carefully, as there may be more than one correct answer. Choose all correct answers for each question.

1. When working on any monitor, you must first:

   A. Wear gloves

   B. Remove your ESD wrist strap

   C. Wear an ESD wrist strap

   D. Disconnect it from the computer

2. When disposing of chemical solvents, you can:

   A. Empty them into the sink.

   B. Flush them down a toilet.

   C. Contact the state's environmental regulatory office.

   D. Tightly seal them in a bottle and throw the bottle away.

3. It is a good idea to _____ the inside of a computer whenever you have removed the case.

   A. Dust

   B. Vacuum

   C. Air out

   D. Repair

4. Catastrophic damage occurs when:

   A. The component is dropped on the floor and rendered inoperable

   B. The component is rendered inoperable due to ESD

   C. The component has ESD damage but continues to function

   D. The component was deluged with water

5. If you look directly into a CD-ROM's laser while it is on, you risk:

   A. Severe burns

   B. Blindness

   C. Electrocution

   D. Nothing

6. A brownout is:

   A. A momentary lapse of power

   B. Noise in the line

   C. Total power loss

   D. A fried computer component

7. When disposing of a dead battery, you can:

   A. Throw it in the nearest trash can.

   B. Recycle it.

   C. Recharge it.

   D. Reuse it.

8. When working around high-voltage equipment, you should never:

    A. Turn the power off

    B. Use both hands on the equipment

    C. Use only one hand on the equipment

    D. Remove your ESD wrist strap

9. When working on a computer, you should:

    A. Follow ESD procedures.

    B. Remove all jewelry.

    C. Turn the computer off.

    D. Remove the power supply.

10. A _____ is a special white paper that contains information on possible personal injury.

    A. Materials Supply Data Sheet

    B. Materials Section Display Sheet

    C. Materials Safety Data Sheet

    D. Momentary Surge Dispelling Substance

11. You are about to replace the power supply on a customer's computer. Even though the computer has been down for several days, you should still be cautious while replacing the power supply as you could get a severe electrical shock from:

    A. Static electricity.

    B. Live current.

    C. Nothing. Heat is the true problem.

    D. Nothing. The power supply is now safe.

12. To dispose of toner cartridges, you can:

    A. Exchange them for new ones.

    B. Throw them away.

    C. Take them to the landfill.

    D. Pour more toner in them.

13. When storing a UPS, you must ensure that:

    A. You discharge the UPS

    B. You store it in a high-humidity environment

    C. You have not discharged the UPS

    D. You have put it out of the way

14. Prior to performing any preventive maintenance to a computer or its components, you should:

    A. Assemble your tools.

    B. Remove the cover from the chassis.

    C. Review the manufacturer's suggested guidelines.

    D. Nothing. Begin the maintenance.

15. When discharging a monitor, you wrap a jumper wire around a screwdriver that has a non-conductive handle. Before you can safely pry the anode lead off of the CRT's glass surface, you must

    A. Attach the free end of the jumper wire to the monitor.

    B. Attach the free end of the jumper wire to a ground.

    C. Attach the free end of the jumper wire to yourself.

D. Nothing. You can proceed with the repair.

16. You need to replace a secondary hard drive in a computer that is still operating from the primary hard drive. You should first:

    A. Open the case.

    B. Power down the computer.

    C. Discharge the hard drive.

    D. Remove the power cord.

17. When you connect an ESD mat to an electrical ground, you can use:

    A. The pin on an electrical outlet

    B. The socket on an electrical outlet

    C. Another ESD mat

    D. Nothing

18. To discharge a monitor, you can remove the anode lead from the glass using:

    A. Your fingers

    B. A gloved hand

    C. Screwdriver with a grounded jumper wire

    D. Rubber knife

19. UPS stands for:

    A. Uninterruptible Power Surge

    B. Unused Power Supply

    C. Uninterruptible Power Supply

    D. Unnecessary Power Supply

20. Never use a(n) _____ when working on high-voltage equipment.

    A. ESD mat

B. ESD wrist strap

C. Metal object

D. Table

21. Power supplies tend to generate a lot of _____ from power lost during the power conversion process.

    A. Static electricity

    B. Current

    C. Voltage

    D. Heat

22. To reduce the potential for static electricity in the room, you can set the humidity level to:

    A. Between 10% and 30%

    B. Between 30% and 50%

    C. Between 50% and 70%

    D. Between 70% and 90%

23. Noise present on a power line is caused by _____ .

    A. Power surges

    B. Brownouts

    C. EMI

    D. ESD

24. You can use _____ to clean some computer components.

    A. Mild liquid detergents

    B. Isoprophyl alcohol

    C. Pencil eraser

    D. Glass cleaner

25. When a component has been damaged by ESD, yet still passes the diagnostic software, the device is said to have suffered _____.

    A. Degradation.
    B. Catastrophic damage.
    C. ESD damage.
    D. Nothing. The device still functions.

26. To clean the read/write heads of a floppy drive, you would use:

    A. Dust-Free cloth
    B. Mild detergent
    C. Special cleaning disk
    D. Rubber blade

27. To dispose of a functioning monitor, you can:

    A. Donate it to a church or school.
    B. Keep it as a spare.
    C. Throw it away.
    D. See if the vendor will give you credit toward a new one.

28. _____ labels are used to alert you to possible equipment damage or personal injury.

    A. Caution
    B. Warning
    C. Important
    D. Notice

29. A _____ is used to reduce noise in power currents and eliminate EMI.

    A. EMI filter
    B. Surge protector
    C. Noise Filter
    D. There is no such thing

30. You are prying the anode lead off of a monitor. As the anode lead becomes detached from the glass, you hear a small "pop." This sound is caused by:

    A. A small electric charge
    B. Rush of air going into the suction cup
    C. The rubber partially melted on the glass
    D. Your imagination

31. ESD is also known as _____ .

    A. Static electricity
    B. Electrostatic Device
    C. Electronic Systems Device
    D. Electronic Safety Device

32. To prevent possible communications problems with a device's connection, you should:

    A. Periodically replace the device
    B. Periodically clean the contacts
    C. Regularly replace the connectors
    D. There is nothing you can do

33. "Hidden" ESD refers to:

    A. Dust and dirt particles.
    B. ESD that you cannot feel.
    C. Hidden Electronic Static Data.
    D. Nothing. There is no such thing.

34. Common cleaning tools include:

    A. Alcohol
    B. Rubber blade
    C. Screwdriver tip
    D. Dust-free cloths

35. A huge increase in power that lasts for a split second is called a _____.

    A. Power surge
    B. Power spike
    C. Noise
    D. Excessive power

4

Motherboard/ Processors/ Memory

Threader computer industry is one in which technology increases at an exponential rate. Yesterday's technology has already become outdated as soon as it hits your desk. While it can be overwhelming at times, if you understand the basics behind each current component, you will form the foundation necessary to understand new technologies as they are developed. This chapter focuses on the most important components of every computer: processors, memory, motherboards, and the CMOS.

CERTIFICATION OBJECTIVE 4.01

CPU Chips

The *central processing unit (CPU)*, or simply the processor, is the operations center of a computer. Its job is to provide the devices attached to the computer with directives that retrieve, display, manipulate, and store information. Therefore, the rate at which the CPU can process electronic signals is a determinant factor in the speed of the computer.

CPU chips are integrated circuits that contain thousands to millions of transistors. These transistors are used to process information in the form of electronic signals. The more transistors a CPU has, the faster it can process data. Several evolutions of CPUs have allowed for the chips to hold more transistors than their predecessors, and therefore process information at increasing speeds. As a technician, you will encounter several different types of processors in operation and must familiarize yourself with their various characteristics and features. The following subsections describe each chip in detail.

Popular CPU Chips

As with everything in the computer industry, chip architectures change rapidly. Chip architectures are defined by the number of transistors in the chip and the size of the bus. One of the earliest IBM PCs contained an Intel

8088 chip, which only contained 29,000 transistors and an 8-bit bus. Today's Intel Pentium II processors contain 7.5 million transistors and support a 64-bit bus. As discussed in the previous paragraph, the number of transistors inside a chip is one of the determining factors in the rate at which a chip can process information. For example, the 8088 chip only processed data at approximately 4.77 MHz, while the Pentium II is reported to run at speeds of 233 MHz to 400 MHz.

386

The leading processor manufacturer of the time, Intel Corporation, released the 80386 chip in 1985. This chip featured a 32-bit register size, a 32-bit data bus, and a 32-bit address bus and could handle up to 16MB of memory. However, the 386 did not have an internal math co-processor and users who required heavy calculations had to purchase one separately.

Prior to the 386 chip, Intel would license its technology to its competitors. But the competition found ways to make cheaper, and in some cases faster, processors. Consumers were buying these less expensive chips at an increasing rate, which cut into Intel's market share and reduced its status as the leading manufacturer. Intel's competitors came out with their own version of the 386 chip.

The 386 processor was also the first instance where there were two versions of the same basic processor, the SX version and the DX version. The 386SX processor came with a 16-bit data bus, a 24-bit address bus, and a 32-bit register size. The 386DX processor's data bus, address bus, and register size were all 32 bits. Both the SX and DX chips operated at 16 MHz, 20 MHz, 25 MHz, and 33 MHz.

486

The 486 processor is also broken down into four types: 486SX, 486DX, 486DX2, and 486DX4. The 486SX chip did not increase the processor speed, which remained at 33 MHz, or enlarge the bus size from 32-bit. It did introduce an on-board cache to the processor, which was an 8-bit cache, along with an on-chip math co-processor. Unfortunately, the math co-processor was disabled at the factory and a secondary chip had to be purchased to obtain the benefits.

When the 486DX was released, it had the same characteristics as the SX version, only the math co-processor was enabled. A later version of the chip, the 486DX2, was still able to run at 33 MHz externally, but doubled the processor speed, or clock speed, internally and brought it up to 66 MHz. Following that, the 486DX4 chip was released, which increased the clock speed even more and brought it up to 133 MHz.

586 or Pentium Class

Intel decided that it wanted to break away from the standard naming convention when it couldn't trademark the 80x86 name. With the 586 chip, Intel named its chip the Pentium chip and introduced several new features and improvements. The first improvement was in the register size and the data bus size, which was doubled to 64-bit. It also doubled the on-board cache size from 8-bit to 16-bit and increased speeds to a range of 60 MHz up to 200 MHz.

Along with the improvements came a significant change in processor architecture and capabilities. The chip combined two 486DX chips into one, called the *Dual Independent Bus Architecture*, which allowed each processor inside the chip to execute instructions simultaneously and independently from each other, called *parallel processing*. The end result was a faster chip, but required a special motherboard that was able to withstand the enormous amount of heat generated by the chip. Heat sinks also had to be employed to help remove the excess heat from the chip or it would burn itself out.

686 or Pentium II Class

Intel's Pentium II chip outpaced the other chips by offering speeds ranging between 233 MHz to 400 MHz. Another improvement was the integration of Intel's MMX technology, which speeds up the processing of video, audio, and graphical data. MMX does this by employing an enhanced instruction set and the Single Instruction Multiple Data (SIMD) technique. According to Intel, SIMD works by allowing a single instruction to operate on multiple pieces of data when an application is performing a repetitive loop.

Chip Characteristics

Table 4-1 provides an overview of the different varieties of chips and their respective characteristics.

Table 4-2 provides an overview of the different varieties of processors along with their bus sizes.

TABLE 4-1 Characteristics of Different Types of Chips

Processor	Physical Size	Voltage	Speed (MHz)	Heat Sink	Cooling Fan	On Board Cache	Sockets	Pins
8088		5	5 10	No	No	No	DIP	40
80286		5	6 10 12	No	No	No	LLC PGA PLCC	68
80386SX		5	16 20 25 33	No	No	No	PGA	100
80386DX		5	16 20 25 33	No	No	No	PGA	100
80486SX		5	16 20 25 33	No	Yes on 33 MHz	Write-Through	PGA	100
80486DX	345 square	5	25 33 50	No	Yes on 33 MHz	Write-Through	PGA SQFP	168 208
Pentium	1.95 x 1.95	2.9 3.3 5	60-200	Yes	Yes	Write-Back	PGA	296
Pentium Pro	2.46 x 2.66	2.9	233-266	Yes	Yes	Write-Back	PGA	387

	Processor	Register	Data Bus	Address Bus
TABLE 4-2 Bus Sizes of Different Processors	8088	16-bit	8-bit	20-bit
	80286	16-bit	16-bit	24-bit
	80386SX	32-bit	16-bit	24-bit
	80386DX	32-bit	32-bit	32-bit
	80486SX	32-bit	32-bit	32-bit
	80486DX	32-bit	32-bit	32-bit
	Pentium	64-bit	64-bit	32-bit

exam
ⓦatch

Know Table 4-2 cold for the exam, as there are several questions that will test your knowledge of the different processors' bus size.

CERTIFICATION OBJECTIVE 4.02

RAM (Random Access Memory)

When the processor needs to perform calculations or store data, it needs a temporary storage area to hold the information. As discussed in Chapter 1, memory is your computer's work area. Memory is composed of integrated circuits that connect to the system board, or to an expansion card, located inside the computer. These circuits can be either on or off, and therefore represent data as a series of 1s and 0s, respectively. This representation is called *binary*, and is the language that your computer understands.

In order to understand memory, you need to get a feel for some of the terms related to memory, such as that which describes memory sizes. Each individual 0 or 1 is called a *bit*, and written as a lowercase "b." To try and keep track of the millions and billions of bits would prove a laborious task, so bits are grouped into sets of eight called a *byte*, which is written as an uppercase "B". Since computers work with large numbers of bytes, it would still get a bit tedious listing file sizes of 500,000 bytes or 5,000,000 bytes.

Instead, we use a form of shorthand that cuts the numbers down to a more manageable size. There are three common denotations that are used to represent computer numbers: a *kilobyte (KB)* is 1,024 bytes, a *megabyte (MB)* denotes 1,048,576 bytes, and a *gigabyte (GB)* means 1,073,741,824 bytes! So, if you had 16MB of memory on your computer, you actually have 16,777,216 bytes of memory available. If you are wondering why a kilobyte, for example, isn't equal to 1,000 bytes it is because the computer works on powers of 2 rather than 10. Thus, when we calculate 2^10, we get 1,024 bytes instead of 1,000 bytes. If we were trying to get a megabyte, we would calculate 2^20.

Memory comes in several forms, but generally the processor accesses *random access memory (RAM)*. RAM gets its name from how the memory is physically accessed. Data can be accessed by one of two methods, either sequentially or randomly. When you store data sequentially, you cannot get immediate access to the data that you need. Instead, you must go through all of the information that has been stored before actually getting to the data that you need, which is the way that magnetic tape stores and retrieves data. However, with random access, you can bypass the data that you don't need and go directly to the location where the information is stored. RAM allows your computer to store and retrieve data in *random* locations in memory.

There are several forms of RAM available, each with its own method of random access and differing physical characteristics. We discuss each in the following subsections.

Terminology

As we mentioned in the preceding paragraphs, memory stores data as a series of 0s and 1s. These 0s and 1s are stored electronically, but signals on memory chips can degrade unless power is constantly fed to it. To ensure that those signals are correct, memory chips are constantly updated, a process called *refresh*. The rate at which the chips are refreshed is called the *refresh rate* and usually occurs around 60 or 70 nanoseconds, or about 60 to 70 billionths of a second. When your computer loses power, all of the circuits are set back to 0s and anything stored in RAM is wiped.

Static RAM (SRAM)

Static Random Access Memory, or *SRAM*, does not need to be constantly refreshed, hence it is *static*. However, while it doesn't need a constant update, it does require a periodic update and tends to use excessive amounts of power when it does so. SRAM chips were used in the original IBM PC and XT computers and employed transistors to store information, leading to a large chip size. Unfortunately, an SRAM chip can only hold approximately 256KB of data per chip and are relatively expensive.

Dynamic Random Access Memory (DRAM)

Dynamic Random Access Memory, or *DRAM*, chips abandoned the idea of using the unwieldy transistors and switches in favor of using the smaller capacitors that could represent 0s and 1s as an electronic charge. This resulted in the ability to store more information on a single chip, but also meant that the chip needed a constant refresh and hence more power.

Windows Accelerator Card RAM (WRAM)

Microsoft Windows has become one of the most popular client operating systems (OS) in use today due to its graphical nature and ease of use. However, in some environments, it can be a slow one. To help speed up the OS without purchasing a new processor, and in some cases a new motherboard to go with it, the Windows Accelerator Card was introduced into the market. This card utilizes memory that resides on the card itself to perform the Windows-specific functions, and therefore speeds up the OS.

Extended Data Output RAM (EDO RAM)

Extended data output RAM (EDO RAM) is a DRAM memory chip designed for processor access speeds of approximately 10 to 15 percent above fast-page mode processors. This requires both a motherboard and processor that is capable of supporting EDO RAM.

RAM Locations and Physical Characteristics

Random access memory (RAM) is the place that your computer temporarily stores the instructions that make up an application, as well as the actual data it manipulates. As mentioned in the previous section, RAM comes in several forms and possesses differing characteristics.

Memory Bank

A memory bank is the actual slot that memory goes into. The original memory chips were installed individually in sockets designed to hold only one chip at a time. Newer memory components are installed in special slots designed to hold one card that contains multiple memory chips. With both types of memory, the socket or slot is located on the motherboard and uses the system board's circuitry to communicate directly with the processor. In cases where a device uses a DMA channel, such as with sound cards, the component itself can communicate directly with RAM.

Parity Versus Non-Parity Chips

Parity is an error-checking mechanism that enables the device to recognize single-bit errors. Parity comes in two forms: even parity and odd parity. With odd parity, the number of ones in a byte are added up and checked to see if it is an odd number. If it is, an extra bit set to zero (0) is added to the byte, thus ensuring that the total number of ones result in an odd number. However, if the number of ones add up to an even number, the extra bit added on is set to one (1), thus ensuring that the total number of ones results in an odd number.

Even parity works in the same manner, except that the total number of ones must add up to an even number. Therefore, if the sum of ones equals an even number, the extra bit is set to zero. However, if the sum of ones equals an odd number, the extra bit is set to one. Should one of the data bits switch, say from a one to a zero, the total number of ones will not result in the correct odd number (for odd parity) or even number (for even parity). The problem with this is that if two of the bits were switched, the data would still pass the parity test.

Parity is not just used with memory, but is utilized in hard drives and communications. While it is not a 100-percent guaranteed method of ensuring that your data is intact, it is still better than having no parity at all. With a non-parity chip, you have no guarantee that the data that is stored on the chip is what was truly sent.

Memory Chips (8-bit, 16-bit, and 32-bit)

Memory chips communicate with the processor or peripherals through the bus. As stated in Chapter 1, the bus is the actual pathway used to transmit electronic signals from one device to another. The number of bits that can be transmitted or received simultaneously is one of the determining factors of bus architecture. Bus configurations come in 8-bit, 16-bit, 32-bit, and 64-bit.

SIMMs (Single In-line Memory Module)

Before the Single In-Line Memory Module, or SIMM, memory chips were purchased individually and placed on the motherboard in separate sockets. With SIMMs, you get a card that has several DIP chips embedded on one side of the card. Each SIMM module is given a pin designation, such as a 30-pin SIMM card, and is called the SIMM type. The "30-pin" refers to the number of fingers, or pins, that are on the connector.

SIMMs come as either 30-pin or 72-pin cards, but each card has a different format. The format is broken down as follows:

```
Capacity of the Chip x Data Bits
```

The capacity is the amount of data the card can hold, usually denoted in megabytes. However, the data bits determine if the SIMM utilizes parity. If the data bits equal 8 or 32, the SIMM does not use a parity bit, but a 9 or 36 will indicate that parity is in use (8 + 1 parity bit or 32 + 4 parity bits).

DIMMs (Dual In-line Memory Module)

Dual In-Line Memory Modules (DIMMs) are very similar to SIMMs except that they have memory chips embedded in both sides of the chip. Thus, the memory card can hold twice as many chips and twice as much memory as a SIMM. DIMMs come in 32-bit or 64-bit configurations, as well as a variety of pin types. However, as 64-bit motherboards are more common, the DIMM is becoming the memory type of choice.

Motherboards

The most important component of any computer is the motherboard. The motherboard is made of a fiberglass sheet that has miniature electronic circuitry embedded in it. This circuitry provides the pathways for electronic signals to flow between devices. However, not every motherboard is created equal. In the next sections, we will discuss different types of motherboards, their components, and give you some basic compatibility guidelines.

Types of Motherboards

Motherboards come in various shapes and sizes, but there are two basic types of motherboards: AT and ATX. Both motherboards provide the same basic services to the computer, but they are not interchangeable. In the next sections, we take a brief look at both forms of system boards.

AT (Full and Baby)

The AT motherboard actually comes in two different types: Full and Baby. The primary difference between the two types is a matter of size, with the Full form at approximately 12" wide and the Baby at about 8.5" wide. The Full form is usually found with 386 or earlier computers and fits in a wider case. However, most AT-type motherboards in today's computer systems are usually Baby ATs.

Regardless of which type of AT motherboard you are working with, the characteristics are basically the same. The processor is normally located in the front of the board, which has been an annoyance to many technicians attempting to install a new expansion card. The serial and parallel ports are actually located on the back of the case, and attach to the motherboard by headers.

ATX

The ATX motherboard specification was introduced by Intel and has become an industry-accepted standard. While the ATX system board is smaller than a Full AT, it is approximately the same size as the Baby AT. However, the processor has been moved to the back of the board and out of the way of expansion cards. In addition, the ATX form integrates the serial and parallel ports on the motherboard.

Components

A motherboard is composed of several components that work together as a unit. As a service technician, you should familiarize yourself with each of these components and know what their function is. By understanding each component's job and how it works, you will be able to troubleshoot problems with these components much quicker. The following paragraphs discuss each component and what it does.

Communication Ports

A computer lives to process information of all kinds, but in order to receive that data, it has to have a method of communicating with peripheral devices. Internal components attach directly to the motherboard through expansion slots. However, for external devices to connect to the motherboard in this fashion would require the computer's case to be left off. Instead, the communication ports on the system board allow external devices to attach directly to the processor without having to remove the case.

There are two types of communication ports found on a motherboard: serial and parallel. Serial ports transmit data sequentially, bit by bit over a single conductor. This type of communication is usually found with modems and mice. However, a parallel port allows transmission of data over eight conductors at one time. An example of a device that utilizes a parallel port is a printer.

CMOS

The Complementary Metallic-Oxide Semiconductor (CMOS) stores the settings used by the Basic Input-Output System (BIOS). When the computer is rebooted or has lost power, the BIOS is incapable of retaining its settings. To avoid having to reenter these settings, a task that can prove tedious to say the least, the CMOS uses a battery to store the settings and then provide them to the computer's BIOS upon reboot.

SIMM AND DIMM

Single In-line Memory Modules (SIMM) and Dual In-line Memory Modules (DIMM) are the memory types that are used on the motherboard. These types of memory were discussed in depth earlier in the chapter.

Processor Sockets

The processor socket is the actual socket used to attach the processor to the motherboard. In earlier computers, the processor was actually soldered onto the motherboard. When it came time for an upgrade, you would usually have to purchase a new motherboard. With today's computers, the processor is not soldered onto the motherboard and can be removed when necessary.

External Cache Memory (Level 2)

Cache memory is used to store frequently used instructions and data so that they can be accessed quickly by the computer. While many processors offer an integrated cache, it is useful to increase the capacity of the cache memory to speed up the computer's performance. The motherboard contains cache memory slots, or external cache memory slots, that allow you to put additional cache memory onboard the system board.

ROM

Read-Only Memory (ROM) is a form of memory that is only read from, rather than written to. This is because the memory chips were permanently written to by the manufacturer. Types of ROM include the Basic Input-Output System (BIOS) chip, and Complementary Metal-Oxide Semiconductor (CMOS).

Bus Architecture

The bus allows a device to communicate with the motherboard and its underlying circuitry. It is defined by how many data bits can be transmitted at any given instant, such as an 8-bit or 16-bit bus. In general, motherboards only have one or two types of bus architecture on any given board. This is due to the fact that the processor's data bus determines what types of architecture can utilize it. There are several architectures available on the market.

- **Industry Standard Architecture (ISA)** was introduced after the IBM AT computers were released. AT computers allowed for a 16-bit data bus, but the peripherals at the time were still stuck on the 8-bit bus. To improve the communication speed of the devices, and to provide for an industry standard, several of the larger companies got together and developed ISA technology. This now allows for peripherals to utilize the 16-bit data bus that is available with 286 and 386 processors.

- **Extended Industry Standard Architecture (EISA)** was introduced to compete against IBM's Micro-Channel Architecture (MCA) devices, which increased their peripheral's bus size from a 16-bit bus to a 32-bit bus. Because MCA was expensive and proprietary, the original companies that developed ISA got together and created a 32-bit card that was not only cheaper, but retained backward compatibility with the 16-bit ISA cards. This type of bus architecture is used in conjunction with 386 and 486 processors.

- **Peripheral Component Interconnect (PCI)** was designed in response to the Pentium class processor's utilization of a 64-bit bus. Until the development of the PCI bus, peripherals were tied to the processor architecture as well as the processor data bus. However, PCI buses are designed to be processor independent. They are able to accomplish this feat by utilizing a special bridge circuit along with a processor-dependent configuration program.

- **Universal Serial Bus (USB)** is a relatively new bus architecture that is still under development. The USB is designed to allow for true

Plug-and-Play peripherals without your ever having to open the computer case. According to Intel, the USB can handle up to 12 Mbps and will accommodate most peripherals utilizing the Plug-and-Play technology.

■ **The VESA Local Bus** (VL-Bus) was originally created to address performance issues. One of the problems with earlier bus designs was that they could only handle a maximum clock speed of only 8 MHz, while processors could run at much higher clock speeds. The idea was to create a bus that would have the same clock speed as the processor, known as a *local bus*. Components that utilized the local bus increased their performance, and thus several types of components were designed to take advantage of the faster speed.

Of the kinds of components that used the new bus architecture— hard drive cards, memory cards, cache cards—video cards became the most prevalent. However, compatibility issues arose as vendors used proprietary local bus slots and cards. This meant that you had to purchase the vendor's card in order for it to work in the vendor's slot. The Video Electronics Standards Association (VESA) was formed to address this compatibility problem.

VESA created the standards for the local bus architecture that were incorporated into the manufacturer's products. This ensured that a card from one vendor would work in another manufacturer's computer. The VL-Bus used a 32-bit slot and was built upon ISA bus architecture. This meant that the bus was backward-compatible with ISA and that configuration would require the old jumper and/or DIP switch configuration methods.

■ **The Personal Computer Memory Card International Association** (PCMCIA), or the less hard to remember PC Card, bus was first created to expand the memory capabilities in small, hand-held computers. The bus itself is about the size of a credit card and is only 16-bit. While some computers utilize the PC Card bus, the 16-bit size is somewhat restricting in computers that are capable of handling 64 bits. Therefore, a new standard is currently under construction to increase the PC Card to a 32-bit standard.

Make sure that you know the differences between each type of bus and what each acronym stands for. While most of the acronyms seem intuitive, the exam will throw in a few that will seem to be just as plausible.

Basic Compatibility Guidelines

Whenever you have to determine if an expansion card is compatible with an expansion slot, you should always first refer to the manufacturer's documentation. A good rule of thumb is to remember that an expansion card must be of the same type as the expansion slot (i.e., a VL-Bus card can only go into a VL-Bus expansion slot). However, ISA cards are an exception to the rule and can go into an ISA slot, an EISA slot, and a VL-Bus slot.

CERTIFICATION OBJECTIVE 4.04

CMOS (Complementary Metal-Oxide Semiconductor)

The Basic Input-Output System (BIOS) can only hold its settings as long as the power is kept on. Once it loses power, it loses the settings and has to get them from somewhere. The Complementary Metal-Oxide Semiconductor (CMOS) was designed to store these settings and therefore drastically cut down on the number of times that the user would have to input them. However, the CMOS utilizes a battery that does not have an infinite life, and it is always prudent for you to note down the CMOS settings in a safe location in the event that the battery begins to fail.

Basic CMOS Settings

There are several basic CMOS settings that you should familiarize yourself with, as at some point you will have to reconfigure these settings as a result of a dead battery or a system upgrade. While we discuss these items in the following sections, it is always recommended to consult the manufacturer's documentation in case these settings are slightly different.

Printer Parallel Port

- **Unidirectional**   A single directional mode for the parallel port. Data travels only from the computer to the printer in this mode.

- **Bi-directional**   A two directional mode for the parallel port. Data travels both from the computer to the printer and vice versa.

- **Disable/enable**   Enables or disables the parallel port.

- **ECP–Extended Capability Port**   ECP mode offers the same features as bi-directional in addition to the use of a DMA channel for data transfer. This speeds up data transfer rates by bypassing the processor and writing the data directly to memory.

- **EPP–Enhanced Parallel Port**   EPP mode offers the same features as bi-directional and offers an extended control code set.

exam
ⓦatch

Know the different types of parallel ports for the exam, as many people get stuck on these types of questions.

Com/Serial Port

- **Memory address**   All serial ports require a memory address. The memory address is used to receive commands from the processor that are destined for the device attached to the COM port. Each device must have a unique memory address in order for it to function.

- **Interrupt request**   Every COM port must have a unique interrupt. It is through this interrupt that the peripheral attached to the COM port notifies the CPU that there is data available to be retrieved from the peripheral. An example is when the modem receives data. The modem will fire an interrupt on the COM port, which in turn triggers the CPU to pick up data from the modem.

  The standard COM1 interrupt address is 4 and the memory address is 03F8. With COM2, the interrupt address is 3 and the memory address is 02F8. This has a tendency to seem counterintuitive, as COM1 would be listed before COM2.

exam
ⓦatch

Remember the interrupt and memory addresses for both COM1 and COM2 for the A+ Certification Exam.

■ **Enable/disable**   The enable/disable either enables or disables the COM port for use.

FROM THE FIELD

BIOS Fears

Improper handling of the BIOS can cause big headaches and much wasted time. The good news is that the BIOS are improving over the years. They now auto-detect most hardware and set themselves without too much user intervention. The bad new is that most of the BIOS that you will work with will be old.

Over time, batteries become depleted and this resets the BIOS. This causes you to have to replace the battery and reset the settings. You need to choose between all the types of hard drives, or worse, fill in the blank for the cylinder numbers, heads, and so forth. Well, if you have a good hard drive, you can usually find this labeled on the drive. If not, you can always look up this information in a book if you have the manufacturer and the serial number. You will in time find some of these that have none of this information on them. I've seen techs reboot 79 times only to find out that the drive is not one of those preset in

the CMOS. Only third-party software and much time can be the answer to this dilemma.

Get a good idea of when these batteries often die. If you find out that a certain model of computers are losing their batteries after a certain amount of time, make sure you replace the other computers that were bought at about the same time. If the clock starts losing time, you can bet that the battery is to blame. Your best defense, however, is to keep track of the BIOS settings. There are some software programs out there that will save this data and let you print it. Do so, and keep this information with the log for the computer. Not only are hard drives tough to set in the BIOS, but some BIOS have settings that are very difficult to decipher. With your list, you will never have to guess if you should have a setting activated or not.

—By Ted Hamilton, MCP, A+ Certified

Hard Drive

■ **Size**   The size of the drive is automatically calculated from the number of cylinders, sectors, and heads on the drive. If you need to calculate the size of a drive, you would use the following formula:

```
(# of cylinders) * (# of sectors) * (# of heads) * 0.5 KB
```

The 0.5KB constant is due to the fact that most hard drives have 512 bytes per sector.

■ **Primary master/secondary slave**   Each hard drive has a controller built into the drive itself that actually controls the drive. When you have more than one hard drive attached to an adapter card, the adapter could get confused as to which controller was in charge. In order to distinguish which controller is actually being used, one of the drives is designated as a master drive and its controller is used to control the other drives, which are called slaves. When you look at the CMOS configuration screen, you will note that you have to fill in the primary master section for the master drive, and the secondary slave section for the slave drive.

■ **Tracks**   A hard drive is made up of several disks mounted on a spindle. Each disk can be broken down into rings of concentric circles, where each ring is called a track.

■ **Sectors**   As you can break down a disk into tracks, you can further subdivide the disk into sectors. This is done by "slicing" the disk up as you would a pie. Each piece of that pie is called a sector. The number of sectors on a hard drive is usually printed on the outside case of the drive itself.

■ **Cylinder**   When you combine the same tracks on each of the disks in a hard drive, you have what is known as a cylinder. The number of cylinders in a hard drive is also printed on the outside case of the drive itself.

■ **Drive type**   Older systems provided a number of cylinder-head-sector configurations associated with a standardized number. Older models of drives could be set up by simply indicating which type of drive it was, e.g., a 13 or a 16. For drives that did not fit on e the defined types, you would select 'user' and enter the number of heads, cylinders, and sectors manually. Newer systems will automatically detect all of the information needed to set up a hard drive, and also include other drive types including CD-ROM and removable.

Floppy Drive

- **Enable/disable drive**   When installing a floppy drive, you do have the option to disable it. To do this, you must set Drive A to None.

- **Density**   Drive types are usually defined by the capacity and size of the media. There are five standard types available. They are:

  - 5.25" 360KB

  - 5.25" 1.2MB

  - 3.5" 720KB

  - 3.5" 1.44MB

  - 3.5" 2.88MB

5.25" drives are a rarity in today's computers as they are the original floppy drive technology, and purchasing a replacement drive is almost an impossibility. Most computers today utilize the 3.5" 1.44MB drive even though the 3.5" 2.88MB can hold twice the amount of data. There are several factors that have kept the 3.5" 2.88MB drive from becoming commonplace, but you should familiarize yourself with them for environments that do utilize them.

Boot Sequence

When your computer boots, it has to look for the location of the files and settings that are needed during the boot process. The boot sequence tells the computer where to start looking for these files and in what order to search the various storage devices. For example, if you have the boot sequence set up for floppy drive, hard drive, and CD-ROM, the computer first goes to the floppy drive. If it can't find what it needs on the floppy drive, it then proceeds to the hard drive, and so on.

While most people have this set up to search for a floppy drive first, you may want to set the machine to look to the hard drive first. Many customers have a tendency to leave their data disk in the drive when they turn their computers off. When they boot, the computer can't find an operating system to load and it produces an error message. You can cut down on the number of calls by setting the boot sequence to check for the hard drive first, and the floppy drive second. However, the drawback to this is that if you do need to boot from a floppy, you will have to reconfigure this setting.

Memory

As mentioned earlier in the "RAM (Random Access Memory)" section of this chapter, memory is the workplace of the computer. When it comes to configuring memory in the CMOS, there is really nothing that you need to be concerned about because memory is automatically detected and configured. However, there are some cases when you may get a memory error after installing new memory that requires you to enter the CMOS. If this does happen to you, all you need to do is select the EXIT AND SAVE option from the menu and the computer will begin to reboot.

Network Interface Card

Unless you are using a motherboard that has an integrated network interface card (NIC), there is no CMOS setting for this component. If you do work with a computer with an integrated NIC, you must consult with the manufacturer's documentation for the correct settings. Integrated NICs are not a common component found in computers.

Date/Time

The system date and time are stored in the CMOS. This ensures that the user does not have to reenter the date/time every time they boot their computer. This feature is not only utilized by the user, but is used by the operating system and by application software for certain routines that require timing components.

Passwords

Most customers do not implement the password feature of CMOS, as they have enough passwords and codes to remember as it is. However, if you work at any high-security sites, they may have the CMOS password feature enabled. To enable it, you will have to type in a password twice, once for the initial setting and a second time for verification. Then, whenever the computer boots, the CMOS will require that password to be entered in order for the computer to complete the boot sequence.

CERTIFICATION SUMMARY

In this chapter, you have learned about the various types of processors that have been used in the computer industry. These chips defined the types of memory and peripherals that could be used by the motherboard itself. We have also discussed the motherboard and its various components, such as memory, communications ports, and CMOS settings. Armed with this knowledge, you should have a good grasp of how these components work together.

✓ TWO-MINUTE DRILL

- ❑ The CPU's job is to provide the devices attached to the computer with directives that retrieve, display, manipulate, and store information.

- ❑ Today's Intel Pentium II processors contain 7.5 million transistors and supports a 64-bit bus.

- ❑ SIMM stands for Single In-Line Memory Module, which is a type of RAM chip.

- ❑ The Intel 586 (Pentium) chip combined two 486DX chips into one, called the *Dual Independent Bus Architecture*. This allowed each processor inside the chip to execute instructions simultaneously and independently from each other, which is called *parallel processing*.

- ❑ The PCI (Peripheral Component Interconnect) was designed in response to the Pentium class processor's utilization of a 64-bit bus. PCI buses are designed to be processor-independent

❑ Review Table 4-2, which provides an overview of the different varieties of processors along with their bus sizes.

❑ As a service technician, you should familiarize yourself with each of the motherboard's components and know what their function is.

❑ There are three common denotations that are used to represent computer numbers: a *kilobyte (KB)* is 1,024 bytes, a *megabyte (MB)* denotes 1,048,576 bytes, and a *gigabyte (GB)* means 1,073,741,824 bytes!

❑ DIMM stands for Dual In-Line Module, which is a type of RAM chip.

❑ To ensure that the signals on memory chips are correct, they are constantly updated, a process called *refresh*.

❑ WRAM, which was design specifically for the Microsoft Windows operating system, utilizes memory that resides on the card itself to perform the Windows-specific functions, and therefore speeds up the OS.

❑ The number of transistors inside a chip is one of the determining factors in the rate at which a chip can process information.

❑ A memory bank is the actual slot that memory goes into.

❑ There are two basic types of motherboards: AT and ATX.

❑ ISA (Industry Standard Architecture) is an industry standard bus architecture that allows for peripherals to utilize the 16-bit data bus that is available with 286 and 386 processors.

❑ On the AT motherboard, the processor is normally located in the front of the board, which has been an annoyance to many technicians attempting to install a new expansion card.

❑ The communication ports on the system board allow external devices to attach directly to the processor without having to remove the case.

❑ While SRAM doesn't need a constant update, it does require a periodic update and tends to use excessive amounts of power when it does so.

❑ A serial port transmits data sequentially, bit by bit, over a single conductor and is most commonly used with modems and mice.

❑ A parallel port transmits data over eight conductors at one time and is most commonly used with printers.

❏ The processor socket is the actual socket used to attach the processor to the motherboard.

❏ Cache memory is used to store frequently used instructions and data so that they can be accessed quickly by the computer.

❏ EISA (Extended Industry Standard Architecture) is an industry standard bus architecture that allows for peripherals to utilize the 32-bit data bus that is available with 386 and 486 processors.

❏ Originally created to address performance issues, the VL-Bus was meant to enable earlier bus designs to handle a maximum clock speed equivalent to that of processors.

❏ The *Personal Computer Memory Card International Association (PCMCIA)*, or the less hard to remember PC Card, bus was first created to expand the memory capabilities in small, hand-held computers.

❏ Make sure that you know the differences between each type of bus and what each acronym stands for. While most of the acronyms seem intuitive, the exam will throw in a few that will seem to be just as plausible.

❏ Know the different types of parallel ports for the exam, as many people get stuck on these types of questions.

❏ The memory address is used to receive commands from the processor that are destined for the device attached to the COM port. Each device must have a unique memory address in order for it to function.

❏ The standard COM1 interrupt address is 4 and the memory address is 03F8.

❏ With COM2, the interrupt address is 3 and the memory address is 02F8.

❏ Each hard drive has a controller built into the drive itself that actually controls the drive.

❏ The number of heads, sectors, and cylinders on a hard drive is usually printed on the outside of the drive.

❏ Integrated NICs are not a common component found in computers.

SELF TEST

The following Self Test questions will help you measure your understanding of the material presented in this chapter. Read all the choices carefully, as there may be more than one correct answer. Choose all correct answers for each question.

1. RAM stands for:

    A. Random Access Mode

    B. Random Array Memory

    C. Random Access Memory

    D. Random Array Mode

2. The 386DX chip could run at speeds of:

    A. 16 MHz - 20 MHz

    B. 16 MHz - 33 MHz

    C. 16 MHz - 133 MHz

    D. 20 MHz - 66 MHz

3. When the computer is rebooted or loses power, the _____ is used to restore those settings.

    A. BIOS

    B. CMOS

    C. Battery

    D. OS

4. The _____ provides a computer's peripherals with directives that retrieve, display, manipulate, and store information.

    A. Memory

    B. Adapter

    C. Controller

    D. Processor

5. A _____ is composed of the same track numbers on each disk of the hard drive.

    A. Cylinder

    B. Sector

    C. Track

    D. Disk

6. The process by which memory chips are constantly updated is called a _____ .

    A. Timing

    B. Rate

    C. Refresh

    D. Update

7. The Pentium, or 586, chip allowed for parallel processing by using a _____.

    A. Dual Inter-Dependent Bus Architecture

    B. Double Inter-Dependent Bus Architecture

    C. Dual Independent Bus Architecture

    D. Double Independent Bus Architecture

8. 3.5 floppy drives come in capacities of:

    A. 360KB

    B. 720KB

    C. 1.44KB

    D. 2.77KB

9. The _____ is used to receive commands from the processor that are

destined for the device attached to the COM port.

A. Interrupt line

B. Parity

C. Serial port

D. Memory address

10. The _____ was built upon ISA architecture, had a 32-bit data bus, and utilized the local bus.

A. ISA

B. VL-Bus

C. EISA

D. PCI

11. The _____ memory card has memory chips embedded on both sides of the card.

A. SIMM

B. ROM

C. RAM

D. DIMM

12. _____ is a form of error checking where the sum of 1s is added up.

A. CRC

B. Parity

C. Even

D. Odd

13. If you want the computer to request a password before completing the boot sequence, you would enable the _____ password.

A. DOS

B. Windows

C. BIOS

D. CMOS

14. The difference between the 486SX and 486DX processors was that the _____ was disabled on the _____ CPU.

A. Cache Memory, 486DX

B. Math Co-Processor, 486DX

C. Cache Memory, 486SX

D. Math Co-Processor, 486SX

15. Dynamic Random Access Memory chips used _____ to store small electrical charges.

A. Transistors

B. Capacitors

C. Cells

D. Electricity

16. A computer stores information in the form of 1s and 0s, called _____ .

A. Electrical charges

B. Binary

C. Switches

D. Capacitors

17. When modifying the CMOS settings on a computer that has more than one hard drive, which controller is used to control the hard drive?

A. Master

B. Second

C. Primary

D. Slave

18. What is used by a device to get the processor's attention?

   A. Memory address

   B. Dynamic Memory Access channel

   C. Interrupt line

   D. Nothing

19. Which type of RAM does not need a constant refresh rate?

   A. DRAM

   B. EDO RAM

   C. WRAM

   D. SRAM

20. The problem with using parity as an error-checking mechanism is that:

   A. It does not work.

   B. If only 1 bit is changed, the data will be accepted.

   C. If only 2 bits are changed, the data will be accepted.

   D. There is no problem with using parity.

21. To calculate the size of a hard drive, you would use which of the following formulas?

   A. cylinders * sectors * tracks * heads * 0.5

   B. cylinders * sectors * heads * 0.5

   C. cylinders * tracks * heads * 0.5

   D. sectors * tracks * heads * 0.5

22. SIMMS come in what pin sizes? (Choose all that apply)

   A. 16-pin

   B. 30-pin

   C. 64-pin

   D. 72-pin

23. The Pentium II chip runs in speeds ranging between _____ MHz.

   A. 33 - 66

   B. 66 - 133

   C. 133 - 166

   D. 233 - 266

24. The 8088 chip used a _____ bit data bus.

   A. 8

   B. 16

   C. 20

   D. 24

25. External devices attach to the motherboard through the:

   A. Cable

   B. Adapter

   C. Communications port

   D. Connector

26. What type of memory is used to store frequently accessed instructions and data?

   A. Cache

   B. Extended

   C. RAM

   D. ROM

27. Which bus uses a special bridging circuit and special configuration software to allow it to be processor independent?

A. ISA

B. EISA

C. VL-BUS

D. PCI

28. Which bus architecture used a 16-bit data bus and was the first to provide an industry standard?

A. ISA

B. EISA

C. VL-Bus

D. PCI

29. Which bus architecture was originally developed for small, handheld computers?

A. EISA

B. MCA

C. PCI

D. PCMCIA

30. The _____ tells the computer where to locate the files and settings, as well as the search order, that it needs to boot.

A. Boot sequence

B. Power On Self Test

C. CMOS

D. BIOS

31. EISA is an acronym for:

A. Extended Independent System Architecture

B. Extended Industry Standard Architecture

C. Enhanced Independent System Architecture

D. Enhanced Industry Standard Architecture

32. The VL-Bus is more commonly used for:

A. Hard drive components

B. Video components

C. Floppy drive components

D. Audio components

33. What types of communication ports are available on the motherboard? (Choose all that apply)

A. Serial

B. Dual

C. Parallel

D. Single

34. What is used to connect the processor to the motherboard?

A. Processor socket

B. Processor connector

C. Cable

D. Processor port

35. Which processor was the first to have the SX and DX designations?

A. 80286

B. 80386

C. 80486

D. Pentium

5

Printers

Tbere's no denying it. The business world revolves around paperwork. As the processing power of computers continues to increase, the need to put the data processed into a tangible, easy-to handle format called a *hard copy* becomes more and more apparent. It may be quite a while before industries that thrive on computer information services go totally paperless (if and when that ever occurs), so until then, the need for providing data in printed form will remain.

A printer is simply an electro-mechanical device designed to translate electronic impulses into a format that it can understand and transfer that format to a page. This chapter reviews the principles of operation, configuration, and maintenance of various printing devices. By the end of this chapter, you should have a working knowledge of all that's involved with operating and servicing printers.

CERTIFICATION OBJECTIVE 5.01

Printer Operations and Components

Printers are actually very simple devices. They exist for the sole purpose of taking the data that you see on your computer monitor and placing it on the printed page. Printers can be used to print documents from your favorite word processor, create envelopes, banners, labels, full-color photographic -quality images, and T-shirt transfers, just to name a few functions. This section upgrades your knowledge on the types of printers and their common field replaceable units (FRUs).

Types of Printers

There are many different types of printers available on the market, each having its advantages and disadvantages. When choosing a printer, it's best to determine what your needs are and select a printer that best meets those needs. It really comes down to what the printer is going to be used for. Printers can be classified into two major groups: Impact and Non-impact.

Impact printers, like the name suggests, require the impact with an ink ribbon to print characters and images. Non-impact printers do not use an ink ribbon, and therefore do not require direct contact with the paper for printing. The easiest way to differentiate between an impact and a non-impact printer is to determine whether or not multi-part form documents could be printed with them. Images and characters formed on impact printers are actually impressed upon the page, creating copies on all pages, whereas non-impact printers do not.

Daisy Wheel Printers

Daisy wheel printers are the first and most archaic type of impact printers we discuss. They have a wheel with raised letters and symbols on it that looks like a daisy, which is how the printer got its name. This type of printer is probably the computer peripheral most similar to the typewriter. When the printer receives the command to print a character, it sends a signal to the print head, which, in turn, spins the wheel on the print head until the appropriate character lines up. An electromechanical hammer (also called a *solenoid* or *resistive coil*) is energized, causing it to strike the back of the "petal" containing the character. The character impacts a printer ribbon, which then strikes the paper, leaving the image of the character in its place.

Daisy wheel printers were one of the first types of printers developed. Though they are not the fastest printers available, the advantage these have is that they are very capable of creating multi-part forms, which are still used by small businesses today. The main disadvantage of this type of printer is the amount of noise it creates from banging the characters against the page. Although measures have been taken in design to muffle the noise from these machines, they still remain the noisiest printers available.

Dot Matrix Printers

All dot matrix printers form characters and images a few dots at a time. They perform this by creating the image or character in a "matrix" of dots, hence the name *dot matrix*. There are two modes by which these types of printers can operate: Font mode, and dot-addressable.

In Font mode, the printer already has all the pins programmed for every character in its font set. When the printer receives the message to print the letter "R," for example, it looks up the letter "R" in its character table in ROM and sends the correct pin sequence to the print head. This allows a single input to produce many dots on the page, representing the character desired.

In dot-addressable mode, each printed dot requires an input. This provides for a lot of flexibility to users because they are not limited by the fonts available in the printer's memory, but only limited by the software they use. The downside to this mode is that this printing method is much slower than font mode, because multiple dots require multiple inputs.

The print head on a dot matrix printer is a series of pins each controlled by its own solenoid (or resistive coil), which is similar in function to the solenoid on a daisy wheel printer. When the solenoid is energized, the pin is forced away from the print head and impacts the printer ribbon and ultimately the paper, thus impressing the dot on the page. Like the daisy wheel, the advantage of this type of printer is that multiple-page paper may be fed through, as in making carbon copies. The earliest print heads had 7 pins, whereas printers today have up to 24.

When a solenoid is energized on the printhead, its associated pin is forced outward coming into contact with the printer ribbon and finally impacting the page, creating a dot. The print head travels horizontally along the page, striking dots all along the way. It may take several passes to create one line of characters. Some printers are bi-directional, printing both from left to right and from right to left, whereas older dot matrix printers only printed in one direction.

Color of the output is dependent upon the color of the printer ribbon that is installed in the printer. Early dot matrix printers were limited to a single color printer ribbon, but today's models offer ribbons with multiple colors, allowing for color output.

Bubble Jet Printers

Unlike daisy wheel and dot matrix printers, where contact with the paper is required, bubble jet printers do not require contact with the paper. By use of small nozzles on the print head, a bubble jet printer "spraypaints" the image on to the page.

Bubble jet printers are actually an advance in technology from the older ink jet printers. Ink jet printers used an ink reservoir, pump, and ink nozzle to put the ink on the page. This method was inefficient as well as noisy and messy. Bubble jet printers improved on this concept by changing the means by which the ink is propelled towards the page.

Every bubble jet printer operates the same way. Bubble jets are comprised of a disposable ink cartridge that contains the print head nozzles and ink reservoir. This ink cartridge must be replaced when the ink runs out. Although possible, it is not recommended to have the cartridges refilled with ink. Replacing the cartridges not only provides the printer with a fresh source of ink, but it replaces the nozzles that get worn out by the bubble jet process.

Inside the ink cartridge are several chambers. At the top of each chamber is a metal plate with a tube leading to the ink supply. The bottom of each chamber contains a single microscopic pinhole used to spray the ink onto the page. The print head passes across the page horizontally, just like a dot matrix, spray-painting each dot along the way.

When a chamber receives the command to spray ink, an electrical signal is sent to energize the heating element. The heating element, in contact with the ink, heats up very quickly causing the ink to vaporize, resulting in a buildup of pressure in the chamber. This pressure forces the ink out the pinhole forming a "bubble" of ink on the page. As the vapor expands, the bubble gets large enough to break off into a droplet. The rest of the ink is drawn back into the chamber due to the surface tension of the ink. This process is repeated for each drop that needs to be sprayed.

Laser Printers

Laser printers are an entirely different breed of printers altogether. Using a combination of light, electricity, chemistry, pressure, and heat, they have the ability to create very high-quality images and text on the printed page. Lasers are classified as non-impact type printers.

Laser printers are also referred to as page printers because they receive their print job instructions one page at a time. Laser printers can perform this feat through use of a Page Description Language (PDL). Rather than the printer receiving instructions for each dot on the page, the PDL encoded in the printer receives commands from the computer on how to print the page. Using simple line drawing commands rather than printing each dot along that line greatly simplifies the instructions that must be passed to the printer.

The main components of a laser printer are listed as follows:

- **Cleaning Blade** This rubber blade extends the length of the photosensitive drum. It removes excess toner after the print process has completed and deposits it into a reservoir for re-use.

- **Photosensitive Drum** This light-sensitive drum is the core of the electrophotographic process inside the printer. This drum is affected by the cleaning, charging, writing, and transferring processes in the six-step printing process we discuss in detail later in this section.

- **Primary Corona Wire** This highly negatively charged wire is responsible for electrically erasing the photosensitive drum, preparing it to be written with a new image in the writing stage of the print process.

- **Transfer Corona** This roller contains a positively charged wire designed to pull the toner off of the photosensitive drum and place it on the page.

- **Toner** Toner is comprised of finely divided particles of plastic resin and organic compounds bonded to iron particles. It is naturally negatively charged, which aids in attracting it to the written areas of the photosensitive drum during the transfer step of the printing process.

- **Fusing Rollers** These rollers comprise the final stage of the Electrophotographic Print (EP) process, bonding the toner particles to the page to prevent smearing. The roller on the toner side of the page has a non-stick surface that is heated to a high temperature to permanently bond the toner to the paper.

exam
ⓦatch

Understanding the theory of the Electrophotographic Print process is a key to passing the Printers section of the exam.

The Electrophotographic Print (EP) process for putting the image on the page is divided up into six distinct steps. Though some sources disagree on which step occurs first, the important thing to remember is that this process occurs as a cycle within the printer, so order of the steps is critical. During this process, the printer cleans and charges the photosensitive drum to prepare it for the image. A laser beam "writes" the data to the drum. Toner is then attracted to the areas of the drum where the laser "wrote" the image. The image is then transferred and bonded to the page for final output. Each step of this process is explained as follows:

1. **Cleaning** Before any image formation can occur, the photosensitive drum must be cleaned and electrically erased. For the photosensitive drum to be cleaned, a rubber blade extending the length of the drum gently scrapes away any residual toner left over from the previous cycle. If this step is omitted, you would see random specks of black on your printed documents. The toner that is removed is deposited in a debris cavity or recycled for use again in the main toner supply area.

   Electrical erasure is accomplished by a series of erasure lamps aligned within close proximity of the photosensitive drum. The photosensitive drum is just that—photosensitive. Any light at all will erase the image on it. This step ensures that the drum has been electrostatically erased so that it can receive a new image. Now the photosensitive drum is ready for the next step, charging.

2. **Charging** Charging involves applying a high-voltage negative charge to the photosensitive drum. The voltage can reach as high as −5000Vdc. Because the primary corona wire and the photosensitive drum share a common ground, applying a large negative charge to the corona wire creates an electrical field between the two. At low voltages, the primary corona would have no effect on the photosensitive drum, but when a high voltage is applied, this ionizes the air gap between the wire and the drum. This ionization causes negative charges within the drum to migrate to the surface.

3. **Writing** Now that the photosensitive drum has been prepared, the writing process can begin. A laser sweeps the entire length of the drum, cycling on and off with respect to the image to be created. When the laser is "ON," this neutralizes the highly negative charge

on the drum, making the point where the laser strikes much less negative, almost neutral (approximately −100Vdc). The laser is precisely turned on and off as it sweeps across the drum, optically "writing" the image to the drum.

4. **Developing**   So far, the only evidence of an image in the printer is a series of highly negative and almost neutral charges across the photosensitive drum. The electrostatic image must be converted into a visual image before it can be transferred to the paper. Because the toner is negatively charged by nature, it is attracted to the areas of the photosensitive drum that are less negatively charged. Because the remaining areas of the drum are highly negatively charged, the toner will not be attracted to these areas. Finally, the image is beginning to take form, but we're not there yet.

5. **Transferring**   Once the image has been set in toner on the photosensitive drum, it must be transferred to the print medium, the paper. Because the toner is attracted to the drum, it must be pried away by an even stronger charge to get it to the paper. A transfer corona is a positively charged wire positioned on the opposite side of the paper that is used to serve this purpose. The transfer corona creates a strong positive charge on the paper sufficient to pull the toner particles from the drum. Once the toner is on the paper, the only force holding it in place is a weak electrostatic charge on the paper and gravity.

6. **Fusing**   Due to the electrostatic properties of toner, it will stick to about anything. Toner has a negative static charge and the paper has a positive charge. In order to permanently bond the toner particles to the paper, a fusing process must take place. If this step were omitted, the toner would smear and smudge on the page, not creating a very professional look. The paper is pressed firmly between two rollers, one being a nonstick roller. The nonstick roller is heated by a high intensity lamp, creating the heat necessary to bond the toner to the page.

Common Field Replaceable Units (FRUs)

There are several components that function together to make a printer work. These components make the printer more modular in design and facilitate the replacement of these components should they fail. Rather than having to replace the whole printer when it fails, you simply replace the component that failed. As you've read in previous chapters of this book, these components are known as Field Replaceable Units (FRUs). All printers' FRUs are removed and installed in different manners, so it's important that you consult the manufacturer's guidelines when replacing these components.

Paper Feeder Mechanisms

The role of the paper feeder mechanisms is to move the paper through the printer as images and text are printed to it. These mechanisms are in place to get the paper from the paper tray, through the printer, and out to the output tray.

Primary Power Supply Boards or Assemblies

Primary power supply boards provide power to the entire unit. This power is distributed to the various circuits within the printer.

High-Voltage Power Supplies

For laser printers, the EP printing process requires high-voltage electricity. It is the high-voltage power supply that provides this power. It steps up standard AC current (120V and 60Hz) to the higher voltage required for the printer. This high voltage provides power to the primary corona and the transfer corona.

System (or Main Logic) Boards

The "brain" of the printer is the system board, shown in Figure 5-1. This board houses the central processing unit (CPU), which controls all the input and output within the printer.

Typical printer system board

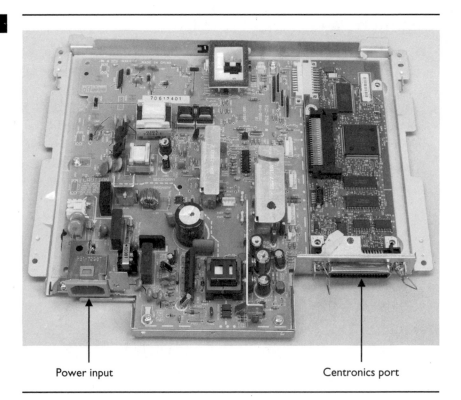

Power input   Centronics port

Sub Logic Boards

Some printers may contain more than one board in their circuitry. Based on the design of the printer, it may have one or more dependent logic boards, as shown in Figure 5-2, for processing the data.

Motors

The voltage is transformed down to approximately 24Vdc to provide power to the various motors used to move the paper through the printer. The main motors that are found within printers are:

- Main drive
- Paper feed
- Transport

FIGURE 5-2

A printer's sub logic board

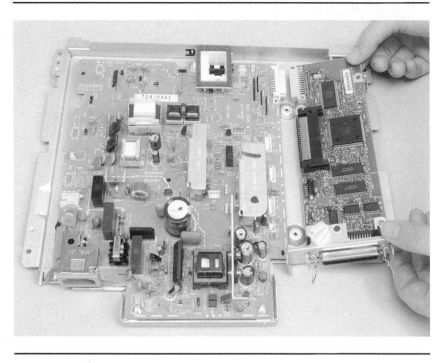

Installation of printer motors varies from type to type and model to model, so you must follow the manufacturer's suggested guidelines for installation procedures. Figure 5-3 shows a typical printer motor.

Fusers

The fuser consists of three main parts: a halogen heating lamp, a rubberized pressure roller, and a Teflon-coated aluminum fusing roller. The fuser heats the fusing roller to anywhere from 165C to 180C. As the paper passes through the two rollers, the pressure roller forces the paper against the hot fusing roller, bonding the toner to the page.

Rollers

Rollers are located inside the printer to aid in the movement of paper through the printer (see Figures 5-4 and 5-5). There are four main types of rollers: feed, registration, fuser, and exit.

FIGURE 5-3

Typical printer motor

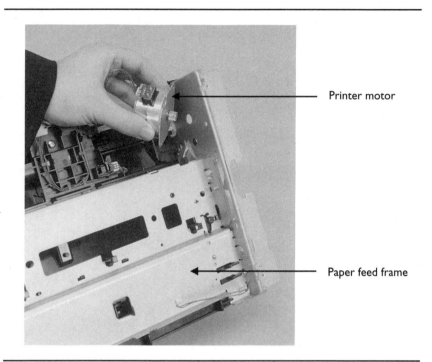

Printer motor

Paper feed frame

The feed rollers (also known as paper pickup rollers), when activated, rotate against the top page in the paper tray and roll it into the printer. The feed rollers work together with a special rubber pad to prevent more than one sheet from being fed into the printer at a time.

The registration rollers synchronize the paper movement with the writing process inside the EP cartridge. The registration rollers do not advance the paper until the EP cartridge is ready to process the next line of the image.

Fuser rollers, as discussed previously, use a combination of heat and pressure to bond the toner to the paper.

Exit rollers aid in the transfer and control of the paper as it leaves the printer. Depending on the printer type, they direct the paper to a tray where it can be collated, sorted, or even stapled.

FIGURE 5-4

Printer rollers, front view

Pickup roller assembly

Delivery assembly   Separation assembly

Sensors

Sensors may be located in various places within the printer to aid in the paper movement during the printing process. For example, one sensor may detect a paper jam and send a signal to the printer control circuitry to generate an error message.

Switches

Switches (also called DIP switches) provide a means for the user to modify a preset hardware configuration to meet his or her particular needs for the printer. For example, a DIP switch might control whether the printer defaults to printing in draft mode or letter quality. The use of these switches

FIGURE 5-5

Printer rollers, side view

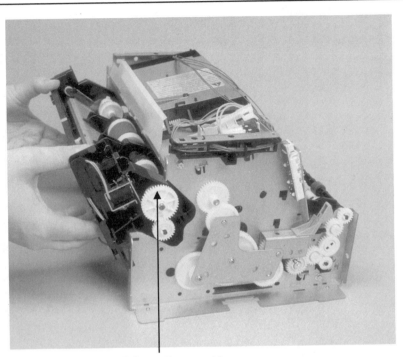

Pickup roller assembly

is diminishing as more and more printers are designed with flashable firmware that allows the printer configuration to be updated with software.

Cables

Cables for the most part are the means of connecting the computer to the printing device. There are normally three separate cable types used to provide the connectivity: parallel, serial, and network.

A parallel cable consists of a male DB-25 connector that plugs into the computer and a male 36-pin Centronics connector that connects to the printer. The recommended length for a parallel cable is ten feet. Lengths any longer than ten feet run the risk of crosstalk, which causes signal degradation and communications to become unreliable.

Serial cables consist of either a DB-9 or DB-25 female connector that plugs into the computer to a DB-25 male connector that plugs into the printer. Because information on a serial cable is only traveling along one wire, serial cables are not as susceptible to crosstalk as are parallel cables, and the cable length can extend up to 25 feet.

Network cables vary from network to network, depending on the media type of the network. Most printers configured with a network interface provide a standard RJ-45 type connector (looks very much like a phone cable). The maximum recommended cable length is specified by the type of network the printer is connected to (for example, a 10BASE2 Ethernet network maximum segment length is 185 meters).

Other types of field replaceable cables may be found inside of the printer assembly. These cables may connect power supplies, motors, print heads, and other components to each other as required. The number and type of cables inside the printer can usually be found in the technical manual.

exam

ⓌatchWatch

Minimize your cable lengths for reliable communications. Parallel cables should be limited to 10 feet; serial cables to less than 25 feet.

Printheads/Toner Cartridges

Print heads and toner cartridges are just about the only FRUs that the printer manufacturer gives the end user responsibility for replacing. Most print quality problems can be remedied by replacement of these components.

RAM SIMMs

Just like a computer, a printer's memory can also be upgraded. Installing additional memory in a printer greatly enhances the amount of information the printer can retain during a print job. This is good news to the computer, because it can resume with other applications and processes once the print job has been completely sent to the printer.

CERTIFICATION OBJECTIVE 5.02

Care and Service Techniques

Proper care and service of the printer greatly extends the life of the printer and maintains the quality of the documents processed. Like the engine in your car, proper care and maintenance will keep the printer operating and performing like new for many years.

Feed and Output

Most of the problems experienced when operating a printer fall into two major categories: feed and output. Either the printer doesn't properly feed the paper, causing a paper jam, or the quality of the printer output is not as desired. We discuss the common problems experienced in these two areas in the following sections.

Paper Jams

Paper jams are one of the most frequent errors that occur in any machine that processes paper. They occur any time something goes wrong with the paper feeder assembly that would prevent proper feeding of the paper through the printer. They can be caused by the feeder mechanism inadvertently feeding two or more sheets of paper at the same time. Sometimes the paper can be torn and small pieces of paper get lodged in the paper path. Paper jams can happen for a variety of reasons, but are usually easily remedied by opening the printer and removing the faulty page(s). Some printers, especially laser printers, have interactive help that walks you through which compartment or paper tray to open to find the jam.

Print Quality

Print quality is usually affected by the failure of a printing mechanism or from the fact that the printer needs cleaning. Most print quality issues can be narrowed down to one of these two causes. Print quality problems vary with each type of printer. Some of the most common ones are covered in the following sections.

FROM THE FIELD

The Printer Top-10 List

Studies have proven that printers are the cause of the most help desk calls. Here are the top ten causes of these printer calls:

1. Bad driver for the printer installed.
2. Dirty rollers.
3. Ink or laser cartridges empty.
4. Paper jam.
5. Bad print job clogging the print queue.
6. Poorly formatted document sent to printer.
7. Actual mechanical breakage.
8. Open paper cabinets, panels, and so forth.
9. Network problems (on network printer).
10. Improper media used.

Printers can be very confusing for new users. If I had a dollar for every "out of paper" ink jet call I've had... Improper media can practically ruin a printer. Have you ever seen mailing labels sent through an ink jet that rolls the paper instead of keeping it flat? Not a pretty sight or a joy to clean up. The all-too-frequent call about a dead printer that is simply turned off will start to get annoying. Assume nothing when troubleshooting a printer—it could be something really obvious or highly complex. Printer problems may stem from software, network, and cabling problems. There are printer problems that have nothing to do with the printer except for how that particular model of the printer reacts to what is being sent as a print job. Some applications mixed with some operating systems mixed with some network privileges mixed with certain computers mixed with certain printers will have problems. I've seen printer problems so mysterious that all the king's horses and all the king's men and Einstein to boot (plus 5 MCSE's and Technet and Microsoft and Hewlett Packard) could not figure out. The only solution was to change computers and print the same print job from another computer. Not a total solution but it worked. The more you know about printers and their idiosyncrasies, the further you'll excel in this field.

—By Ted Hamilton, MCP, A+ Certified

Safety Precautions

In addition to observing basic electronic safety precautions, there are a few things to keep in mind when working with printers. All printers are composed of moving parts that advance the paper through the machine. Be sure that you don't have any loose clothing, or you may find your tie or clothing caught on the plate or other moving parts inside the printer.

Another thing to keep in mind is that components inside a printer can be very dirty. Be careful with your hands around your own clothing and especially around a customer's work area. Everything from ink, toner, and grease is easily spread from one area to another and is difficult to clean.

There are specific tools and measurement equipment provided by the manufacturer for cleaning and to verify proper laser operation. Never take shortcuts with the recommended procedures. Also, some printers have built-in safety interlocks to prevent technicians from injuring themselves. *Never* override an interlocked switch without being advised to do so by the printer service manual.

Preventive Maintenance

One of the easiest ways to ensure trouble-free operation of a printer is by performing periodic preventive maintenance. Although the thought of performing maintenance may not be appealing, taking a few minutes every few months can save you lots of money and unnecessary downtime. Simply put, non-performance of preventive maintenance can lead to expensive, more time-consuming corrective maintenance. As with any piece of equipment you're performing maintenance on, always refer to the procedures outlined in the appropriate user and/or service manuals. Most printer technical manuals will outline the maintenance that should be performed. The most common types of maintenance include vacuuming, cleaning, lubricating interior components, and general cleanliness of the external case. As you've learned, each printer is designed and put together differently, requiring different methods of cleaning and troubleshooting. Keep this in mind as you work on a printer. When in doubt, follow the procedure.

Laser Printers

Print quality problems that can occur with laser printers include the following:

- Blank pages
- Speckled pages
- Ghosted images
- Smudged images

Blank Pages

There's nothing more frustrating than sending a print job to a printer and having it spew out page after page of nothing. Most of the time, this is caused by an application on the computer sending corrupt data, but other reasons a laser printer may send blank pages include:

- **No toner**   If there's no toner in the cartridge, no images will be transferred to the page.
- **Transfer Corona failure**   If this wire fails, no toner will be attracted from the photosensitive drum to the paper.
- **HVPS failure**   If the high voltage power supply isn't providing the voltage necessary to either the primary corona or transfer corona, the printing process will not work correctly.

Speckled Pages

Sometimes a print job may result in little specks of black on the page, random or not. This may be due to a failure of the cleaning step of the EP printing process. Another cause may be a scratch or defect in the EP drum, causing toner to remain in these recesses during the cleaning step.

"Ghosted" Images

"Ghosting" is what occurs when a portion of the image previously printed to the page is printed again, only not as dark. One cause of this is if the erasure lamp fails to operate correctly, not completely erasing the previous image from the EP drum. Another cause of ghosting may be due to a malfunction in the cleaning blade such that it doesn't adequately scrape away the residual toner.

Smudged Images

If an image smudges, then an element of the fusing process has failed. This could be a result of the halogen lamp burning out, failing to melt the toner to the page.

Bubble Jet

The majority of problems experienced with bubble jet printers are print quality issues. Most of these issues can be resolved by replacing the ink cartridge. If the printer sits idle for a prolonged period of time (a week or more), the ink can dry out in the printhead nozzles and clog them.

A corrective measure for a dry ink cartridge should never be refilling the ink cartridge! Replacing the cartridge not only replenishes the ink, but replaces the old worn-out nozzles with new ones.

Dot Matrix

Dot matrix print quality issues normally boil down to two things: ribbon replacement or print head replacement. If the output is beginning to fade, it is time to change the ink ribbon. If there are white horizontal streaks on your page, this would indicate that a pin is not firing, requiring the print head to be replaced.

CERTIFICATION OBJECTIVE 5.03

Printer Connections and Configurations

There are a variety of ways to provide a connection between your computer and the printing device. Current connections make use of the ports available on the back of your machine, and, if you're on a network, a network connection. There are three major types of connection methods: parallel, serial, and network. A connection method that is not yet as common but has its place in this section is infrared, which is discussed briefly. Other connection methods may be available, but are not as commonly used as the methods discussed here.

Parallel

Most printers are configured to communicate via the parallel port. The parallel port consists of a 25-pin connection that allows transmitting of information along eight different wires (hence parallel). When a printer uses parallel communications, it transmits 1 bit per wire, giving it the ability to transmit 8 bits at a time (1 byte). The parallel port allows for fast communication, which is needed especially when transmitting complex images and graphics to the printer.

Serial

Some printers can be configured to communicate via the serial port. When a printer uses serial communications, it transmits one bit at a time along a single wire. Similarly to modems, the serial port must be configured with communication parameters (bps, parity, start and stop bits, and so forth) on both the printer and the computer before communications can occur.

The serial port consists of either a 25-pin or 9-pin connection that allows transmitting of information along a single wire. The bits are sent one after another in a single file line. Because there is only a single wire carrying the transmission, serial cables are not as susceptible to crosstalk as parallel cables are. Cable lengths for serial cables may extend up to 25 feet with no signal attenuation.

Network

Some of the more recent printers coming out on the market have a special interface that allows them to be accessed on a network. These printers come equipped with a network interface card (NIC) that allows them to be plugged directly into the network. ROM-based software allows the printer to communicate with the servers and workstations on the network.

Because virtually everyone in an office environment needs access to a printer, buying a printer for each workstation is not the most economic solution. Networked environments allow for many different users to share printer resources, saving thousands of dollars on printer costs. Printers can be shared when plugged into a workstation through the parallel or serial port, but this requires that the workstation be up and running in order to share that resource.

Infrared

A recent development in printer technology now allows data communications to exist over a beam of light. Some laptops are equipped with an infrared serial port that allows you to transmit to any device that has an infrared port just as if you were physically connected. This is a line-of-sight technology, which requires that the transmitting port be directed to the infrared interface on the printer. We will not go into great detail in this method of printer communication but you should know that the method is available.

CERTIFICATION SUMMARY

There are a variety of ways of presenting information on the written page. Having an understanding of the different printing technologies and a logical method of troubleshooting problems when they arise will not only help you out on the A+ examination, but is invaluable information for a technician in the computer industry. The majority of what you will learn about printers will more than likely be from hands-on experience, where the printer's technical manual should be your guide.

✓ TWO-MINUTE DRILL

❑ A printer is simply an electromechanical device designed to translate electronic impulses into a format that it can understand and transfer that format to a page.

❑ Printers can be classified into two major groups: impact and non-impact.

❑ Daisy wheel printers have a wheel with raised letters and symbols on them that looks like a daisy, which is how the printers got their name.

❑ One advantage of daisy wheel printers is that they are very capable of creating multi-part forms, which are still used by small businesses today.

❑ In the Font mode of a dot matrix printer, the printer already has all the pins programmed for every character in its font set. In dot-addressable mode, each printed dot requires an input.

❑ The print head on a dot matrix printer is a series of pins each controlled by its own solenoid (or resistive coil), which is similar in function to the solenoid on a daisy wheel printer.

❑ The earliest dot matrix print heads had 7 pins, whereas printers today have up to 24.

❑ By use of small nozzles on the print head, a bubble jet printer "spraypaints" the image on to the page.

❑ Replacing the ink cartridges on a bubble jet printer not only provides the printer with a fresh source of ink, but it replaces the nozzles that get worn out by the bubble jet process.

❑ Using a combination of light, electricity, chemistry, pressure, and heat, laser printers have the ability to create very high-quality images and text on the printed page.

❑ Laser printers are also referred to as page printers because they receive their print job instructions one page at a time.

❑ The main components of a laser printer are: cleaning blade, photosensitive drum, primary corona wire, transfer corona, toner, and fusing rollers.

❏ The six-step EP process is as follows: Cleaning, Charging, Writing, Developing, Transferring, and Fusing. Know this process!

❏ During the Cleaning step of the EP process, the toner that is removed is deposited in a debris cavity or recycled for use again in the main toner supply area.

❏ The Charging step of the EP process involves applying a high-voltage negative charge to the photosensitive drum. The voltage can reach as high as −5000Vdc.

❏ In the six-step EP process, an image begins to appear in the Developing step.

❏ In order to permanently bond the toner particles to the paper in the laser printing process, a fusing process must take place.

❏ The main motors that are found within printers are the main drive, paper feed, and transport motors.

❏ The fuser consists of three main parts: a halogen heating lamp, a rubberized pressure roller, and a Teflon-coated aluminum fusing roller.

❏ There are four main types of rollers: feed, registration, fuser, and exit.

❏ Switches (also called DIP switches) provide a means for the user to modify a preset hardware configuration to meet his or her particular needs for the printer.

❏ There are normally three separate cable types used to provide printer connectivity: parallel, serial, and network.

❏ A parallel cable consists of a male DB-25 connector that plugs into the computer and a male 36-pin Centronics connector that connects to the printer.

❏ Minimize your cable lengths for reliable communications. Parallel cables should be limited to 10 feet; serial cables to less than 25 feet.

❏ Most print quality problems can be remedied by replacement of the print head or toner cartridges.

❏ Most of the problems experienced when operating a printer fall into two major categories: feed and output.

SELF TEST

The following Self Test questions will help you measure your understanding of the material presented in this chapter. Read all the choices carefully, as there may be more than one correct answer. Choose all correct answers for each question.

1. Which is the correct sequence for the EP printing process?

    A. Charging, Cleaning, Writing, Transferring, Fusing, Developing

    B. Cleaning, Charging, Writing, Developing, Fusing, Transferring

    C. Cleaning, Charging, Writing, Developing, Transferring, Fusing

    D. Charging, Cleaning, Writing, Developing, Transferring, Fusing

2. Toner cartridges should be _____ when they run out.

    A. Refilled with the correct toner

    B. Replaced with a new toner cartridge

    C. Replaced with an ink cartridge

    D. Serviced

3. What is the maximum recommended cable length for a parallel cable?

    A. 5 feet

    B. 10 feet

    C. 20 feet

    D. 50 feet

4. Which component transfers the toner from the electrostatic drum to the paper?

    A. Fuser

    B. Transfer corona

    C. Transfer assembly

    D. Primary corona

5. Which type(s) of printers can be used to print multi-part forms? (Choose all that apply.)

    A. Dot matrix printers

    B. Daisy wheel printers

    C. Laser printers

    D. Bubble jet printers

6. Which of the following are possible interfaces for printers? (Choose all that apply.)

    A. Parallel

    B. IDE

    C. Serial

    D. Network

    E. Game port

7. The most likely cause for random specs of ink on a laser printed page is:

    A. Improper voltage on corona wire

    B. Parallel cable too long

    C. Photosensitive drum dirty

    D. Improper paper type

8. Which type of printer is most similar to a typewriter?

   A. Page printer
   B. Typeset printer
   C. Laser printer
   D. Daisy wheel printer

9. In the charging step of the EP process, the voltage can reach to as high as:

   A. 120 volts
   B. 1200 volts
   C. 5000 volts
   D. 50,000 volts

10. The most likely cause for a white line across the page while printing with a dot matrix printer is:

    A. Pin not firing
    B. Clogged nozzle
    C. Print head misalignment
    D. Ink ribbon needs replacement

11. In order to permanently bond a laser's toner particles to paper, a _____ process must take place.

    A. Chemical
    B. Magnetic
    C. Charging
    D. Fusing

12. _____ is the dot matrix mode by which characters are stored in ROM.

    A. ROM addressable
    B. Memory mapping
    C. Font addressable
    D. Font matrix

13. Concerning the EP printing process, the primary corona wire has a _____ charge, the transfer corona has a _____ charge, and toner naturally has a _____ charge.

    A. negative, positive, positive
    B. positive, negative, negative
    C. negative, positive, negative
    D. positive, positive, negative

14. What does "PDL" stand for?

    A. Printer-Defined Language
    B. Page Description Language
    C. Paper Driver Latch
    D. Printer Device Logic

15. The print head on a dot matrix printer is a series of pins each controlled by a:

    A. Capacitive coil
    B. Resistive coil
    C. Solenoid
    D. Spring coil

6

Portable Systems

Portable computing represents a rapidly growing and specialized niche in the computer industry. In many offices today, portable computers are replacing the desktop PC as the computer of choice. Portable Systems include any computer that is built with portability in mind. This includes laptops, notebooks, and sub-notebooks.

Servicing these unique computers requires a skill set beyond what is necessary to service desktop computers. Every portable computer, even between different models from the same vendor, is slightly different. In this chapter, we discuss some of the many components that are unique to the world of portable computing.

Because manufacturers are constantly driven to make components smaller and smaller, very few standards exist in the world of the portable. As a result, portable computers are all very proprietary. Steps are being taken to make components more interoperable, but we are still a long way from where the desktop PC industry is in terms of standards. Some components are not even compatible between different portable computers from the same vendor. Also, repairs and upgrades to portable computers remain much more expensive compared to desktop PCs.

As with the rest of the computer industry, portable computer technology is rapidly evolving. Almost as soon as one technology is released, another is released behind it, rendering the old technology obsolete.

CERTIFICATION OBJECTIVE 6.01

Battery Types and Installation

Portable computers need power when connection to a standard AC power source is not available. Portable computers have rechargeable batteries to provide power on the go. These batteries provide DC power when the portable is not connected to an external AC power source and are recharged when they are connected to an AC source. There are many types of battery currently used in portable computers.

FROM THE FIELD

Laptop Versus Desktop

If you are contemplating buying a laptop or recommending one to someone else, these are points to consider. Laptops also bring up unique repair issues. For one thing, they are more challenging to get into. For another, many things just won't work on a laptop. You cannot slave the drive to a desktop, nor swap out any parts to test them, unless you have another similar laptop. Because most repairs you will do are on desktops, you may not be all too familiar with the repairs you may encounter on laptops. With the scarcity of laptops, it can be tough to find an extra one lying around to use for spare parts.

Pros of a laptop

- Portable
- All-in-one components
- Ability to use docking stations
- Does not take up much space
- Better resale value

Cons of a laptop

- Easily stolen
- Less bang for the buck
- Easily dropped
- Harder to repair
- Components are more expensive
- Screen image is not as good
- Not as upgradable
- Limited space physically limits expansion
- Hardware and drivers more difficult to find
- Mouse and keyboard may be hard to use
- Limited battery life
- May not work until it's thawed if left in the cold
- More fragile

—By Ted Hamilton, MCP, A+ Certified

Nickel Cadmium, or NiCad, batteries are rarely used in portable computers today. NiCad batteries must be recharged more often than other batteries, and a full recharge can take as much as 12 hours. Furthermore, when a NiCad battery is recharged before it is fully discharged, the battery loses the ability to fully recharge again. This symptom is known as the memory effect. NiCad batteries also contain Cadmium, which is highly toxic. NiCad batteries are limited to about 1000 recharges.

Nickel/Metal Hydride, or NiMH, batteries offer several advantages over NiCad batteries. Compared to the same size NiCad, a NiMH battery can produce 33-50 percent more power. Advances in NiMH technologies have all but erased the memory effect. NiMH batteries are also more environmentally friendly because they do not contain heavy metals.

Lithium Ion, or LiIon, are the best computer batteries commercially available. LiIon batteries, although slightly more expensive that NiMH batteries, offer many advantages. A smaller, lighter LiIon battery can produce more power than a NiMH battery. LiIon batteries are also becoming available in high-end cellular phones and video camcorders.

exam
Ⓦatch

Portable computer batteries must be disposed of properly. Check the label of the battery and with local agencies for disposal directions. Do not just throw batteries in the trash!

Installation of batteries in portables is easy for the end user, as demonstrated in Figure 6-1. Many people buy a second battery that they keep charged to use as a spare. Most batteries either install from the bottom or the side. Many have an easy-to-remove plastic cover that must be removed first. Generally, there is a row of contacts on the battery itself that meet with spring loaded contacts inside the computer. If a battery is not charging properly, it may help to clean these contacts.

If you replace a battery in a portable computer, do not just throw it away! Consult your local waste management company to find out local requirements for battery disposal.

With many different types of batteries available, which one should you use? LiIon is the best choice if it is available, although it is slightly more expensive. NiMH is more common and less expensive, but is slightly heavier and produces less power. Stay away from NiCad batteries if at all possible.

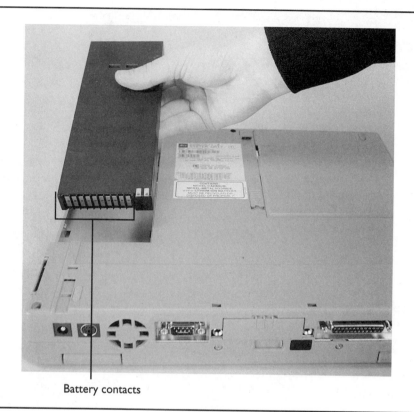

FIGURE 6-1

Installing a portable system battery

Battery contacts

AC Adapter

Each portable computer comes with an AC adapter. This AC adapter serves two roles. The first is to convert either 110v AC or 220v AC to DC to run the portable computer. The second and equally important role is to recharge the battery. AC adapters come in two types, with either an internal or external power transformer. An internal transformer adds weight and bulk to the portable, but is more convenient than carrying an external transformer.

AC adapters for different models and manufacturers of computers have varying output voltage. Before testing, check with the manufacturer to determine the proper voltage. If a computer is not charging properly, it is easy to replace the AC adapter with another and see if that solves the problem.

Portable Displays

Portable displays have come a long way from where they were ten years ago. Older portable computers actually used a Cathode Ray Tube (CRT) for a display. These behemoths were about the size of a small suitcase! Imagine, having a "portable" computer that is too big to fit in the overhead bin on an airplane. Fortunately, we now have flat liquid crystal displays (LCD) that are much thinner, lighter, and require much less power than the small CRTs from ten years ago.

Two major types of LCD displays dominate the market in laptop computers today. The major differences between the two are in the quality of the image displayed, the amount of power used, and the cost of manufacturing.

Passive matrix displays make up the bulk of the laptop displays today. They are cheaper to produce and draw far less power than active matrix displays. Passive matrix displays are easily recognized by poor display quality when viewing the screen from an angle.

Passive matrix displays are made of a grid of horizontal and vertical wires. At the end of each wire is a transistor. In order to light a pixel at (X, Y), a signal is sent to the X and Y transistors. In turn, these transistors then send voltage down the wire, which turns on the LCD at the intersection of the two wires.

Passive matrix screens have problems with images that change quickly. This is very apparent when a cursor is moved quickly across the screen. The cursor will fade from view, and then appear again once the movement has stopped. In fact, Microsoft added the mouse trails option primarily so people wouldn't lose their cursors on passive matrix displays.

Active Matrix displays provide much better image quality at the expense of higher energy consumption and higher cost. Active matrix displays are based on Thin Film Transistor (TFT) technology. Instead of having two rows of transistors, active matrix displays have a transistor at every pixel. This allows much quicker display changes and produces display quality comparable to a CRT.

Just like a traditional CRT display, LCD displays need to be cleaned often. This should be done with a damp cloth or a cleaner specifically designed for cleaning computer displays. Be careful not to drip moisture into the keyboard or other parts of the portable when cleaning the display, as it may have undesirable results.

LCD displays are not a serviceable part. If a LCD display is damaged or broken, it must be replaced. This can be extremely expensive, as the parts will need to come from the original manufacturer. Active matrix screens can easily cost more than $1,000 to replace.

CERTIFICATION OBJECTIVE 6.03

Docking Stations

Docking stations allow users to add "desktop-like" capabilities to their portable computer. Most people would prefer to use a larger monitor and a full-size keyboard when they are available, especially when in the office or at home. A docking station provides an easy and quick way for people to do this, and at the same time, allows expansion of the portable in ways that would otherwise be impossible, such as adding PCI or ISA slots.

Normally, if a user wanted to use an external monitor, keyboard, or mouse, they would have to plug each one into the portable computer every time that they wished to use it. They would also need to have the appropriate connector available on the portable itself. Then, when they wanted to take the portable computer with them when they left, they would have to unplug all of the peripherals they were using. This is both cumbersome and inconvenient.

A docking station allows a user to install their monitor, external keyboard, and mouse to the docking station. Then, whenever they wish to use these peripherals, they can simply connect their portable computer to the docking station. This is a much more convenient and easy way for users to use full-size peripherals when in the office.

Some operating systems (OSs), such as Windows 95, automatically detect when the portable computer is installed with a docking station. The

OS can then use the appropriate hardware settings and user preferences for your docking station. This is extremely convenient, especially for changing screen resolutions for different displays.

Port replicators are the cheapest and simplest version of the three types of docking stations. Most portable computers have external VGA, keyboard, and serial connections. Port replicators simply provide a copy of the interfaces that already exist on the back of the portable computer. Port replicators often ship with a second power cable so the user can leave it plugged into the port replicator. Port replicators are generally the least expensive way to add these types of capabilities to your portable, and for most people this is more than enough.

Enhanced port replicators extend the capabilities of port replicators slightly by adding interfaces not available in the portable computer alone. Extended port replicators often add enhanced sound capabilities and more PC Card slots.

A true docking station gives your portable the greatest amount of expandability and power. Docking stations can give your portable all of the same capabilities usually found in a desktop computer. In addition to everything you get with an enhanced port replicator, docking stations may add ISA slots, PCI slots, and SCSI or EIDE capabilities. They may also provide for full-size drive bays for installing full-size hard drives and CD-ROM drives.

A portable computer that has docking capabilities usually does so via a proprietary interface somewhere on the back. Unfortunately, this means that a docking station for one computer will usually not work with a different type of computer, even from the same manufacturer.

Each manufacturer provides slightly different features with their docking stations, and some features available from one manufacturer may not be available from another. Please consult your manufacturer's guidelines for installing a docking station. Figure 6-2 shows what a docking station typically looks like.

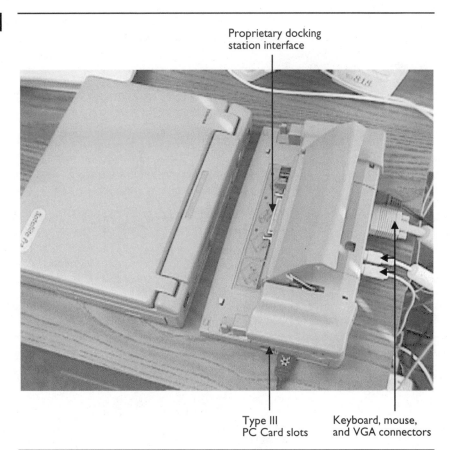

FIGURE 6-2

A portable computer and
a docking station

Proprietary docking
station interface

Type III
PC Card slots

Keyboard, mouse,
and VGA connectors

Hard Drive

Portable computers employ some of the same standards in hard drives as
desktop PCs. Unfortunately, this conforming to standards only applies to
the signal, and not the physical interfaces used. Most portable computers at
the time of this writing are shipping with 2.5-inch EIDE or UDMA hard
drives. Manufacturers use different interfaces and different footprints and
are not necessarily compatible. For this reason, it is necessary that a
replacement hard drive be made for that particular computer.

Replacing a hard drive in a portable computer is generally easy. For most portables, simply follow the steps in Exercise 6-1.

Replacing a Hard Drive

1. Usually there is a small plastic cover underneath the computer that must be removed.

2. Once the cover has been removed, a few screws usually hold in the hard drive.

3. Be careful not to bend the male connectors when removing the hard drive.

4. Insert the new hard drive, again being careful not to bend the connectors.

5. Replace the screws.

6. Replace the cover.

Figure 6-3 shows the removal of a typical portable hard drive.

FIGURE 6-3

Removing a hard drive from a portable system

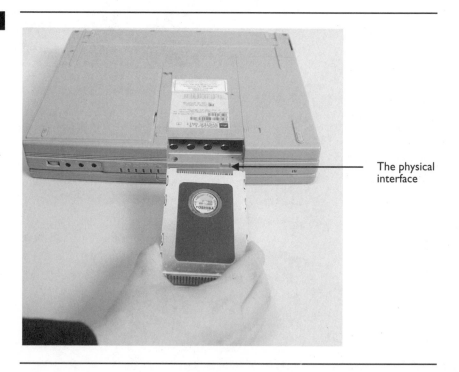

The physical interface

CERTIFICATION OBJECTIVE 6.04

PCMCIA and PC Cards

The PCMCIA, or PC Card interface, defines a standard interface to add credit-card-sized peripherals to PCs. PCMCIA actually refers to the Personal Computer Memory Card International Association, the non-profit organization that defines the specifications for these credit-card-sized peripherals. PCMCIA was founded in 1989 by a consortium of vendors to create and maintain these standards and guarantee interoperability.

The 1.0 version of the PCMCIA specification was released in June 1990 and was originally intended only for memory cards. PCMCIA version 1.0 defined the 68-pin interface that we currently use as well as the physical specifications for the Type I and Type II cards.

The 2.*x* release of the PCMCIA standards expanded the features of the same 68-pin interface and added support for Type III PC Cards. Type III cards are generally reserved for rotating mass storage, such as hard drives. PCMCIA 2.x is backward compatible with PCMCIA 1.0 PC Cards.

In 1995, PCMCIA released the latest standard, officially using the name "PC Card." All PCMCIA cards are now referred to as PC Cards. This latest specification added support for DMA, Bus Mastering, Zoomed Video (ZV), and 32-bit CardBus operation. ZV is a direct data connection between a PC Card and host system that allows a PC Card to write video data directly to the video controller. The 32-bit CardBus specification allows speeds of up to 133 Mbps at 33MHz.

The PC Card specification defines PC Cards as having a length of 85.6 mm and a width of 54.0 mm. Type I cards are the thinnest, measuring only 3.3 mm thick and are generally only used for memory. Type II cards are 5.0 mm thick and are generally used for I/O devices such as modems, network adapters, or SCSI adapters. Type III cards are 10.5 mm thick and are usually used for mass storage devices such as removable hard drives. Most portable computers now come with at least one Type III slot built in.

exam
ⓦatch

All PC Cards are 85.6 mm by 54.0 mm. Type I cards are 3.3 mm thick, Type II are 5.0 mm thick, and Type III are 10.5 mm thick.

Windows 95 supports hot-swapping PC Card devices. This means that you can swap PC Card devices without rebooting your computer. Windows NT currently does not support this feature.

Socket Services is a layer of BIOS level software that isolates PC Card software from the computer hardware and detects the insertion or removal of PC Cards.

Card Services software manages the allocation of system resources such as memory and interrupts automatically once the Socket Services software detects that a card has been inserted in the PC Card slot.

If your operating system does not come with support for PC Card services, check with the manufacturer for support.

The PCMCIA is continuing to develop new technologies for PC Cards. PC Cards are also useful in other electronic devices besides computers. Many digital cameras now use PC Cards for storage.

Uses for PC Cards today include:

- CD-ROM interface
- Cellular phone interface
- Smart Card readers
- Ethernet LAN adapters
- GPS (Global Positioning System) cards
- Hard drives
- ISDN cards
- Memory cards
- Modem/ethernet combination cards
- Modem cards
- Parallel port interface
- SCSI adapters
- Sound cards, input, and output
- Token ring LAN adapter cards

FIGURE 6-4

Installing a PC Card in a portable system

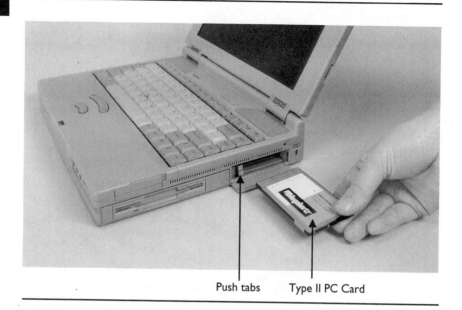

Push tabs   Type II PC Card

Information about the PCMCIA and PC Cards is available on the Web at www.pc-card.com. Figure 6-4 shows the simple installation of a PC Card.

CERTIFICATION OBJECTIVE 6.05

Memory Upgrades

One of the most frequently upgraded components in portable computers is memory. Most portables have some RAM on the motherboard. Manufacturers usually provide a proprietary expansion slot for additional RAM. Memory may also be added in the form of a PC Card.

The manufacturer should provide documentation on installing additional memory. This is generally a simple task. An example is shown in Figure 6-5.

Should the memory on the motherboard itself go bad, it may be necessary to replace the entire motherboard.

FIGURE 6-5

Installing portable
computer memory

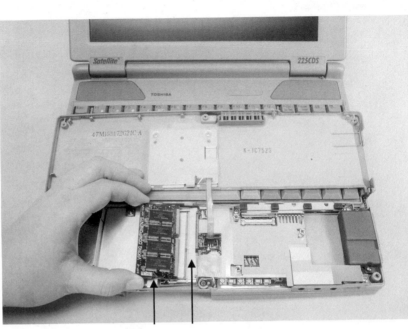

Memory   Contacts
module

CERTIFICATION OBJECTIVE 6.06

Pointing Devices

Pointing devices for portable computers differ slightly from their desktop
counterparts. Manufacturers have come up with some ingenious ways to
provide the same functionality as a desktop mouse, but with a much smaller
footprint. We discuss the three most common types of pointing devices,
their advantages, disadvantages, and maintenance.

Trackballs

Fewer and fewer trackballs are being seen in portable computers. Trackballs are built the same way as an opto-mechanical mouse, except upside-down with the ball up.

Trackballs contain the greatest amount of moving parts and require the most maintenance. As the trackball is rotated inside its case, it constantly picks up dust and oils. This dirt and grime builds up inside the rollers and eventually impairs the trackball movement. This can be cleaned in the same manner as an opto-mechanical mouse. First, the ring holding the trackball must be removed. Rotating the ring counter-clockwise usually does this. Once removed, the trackball can be lifted out.

Pointing Stick

More common than the trackball is the pointing stick-type mouse. This is a smaller pencil-eraser-size piece of rubber in the center of the keyboard. One of the best features of the pointing stick mouse is the fact that your hands never have to leave the keyboard. In fact, they look so much like an eraser, people often call them just that. Maintenance of pointing stick mice is usually limited to replacing the rubber cover.

Touch Pads

Touch pad mice are quickly becoming the pointing device of choice with portable computers. The touch pad is a small plastic square usually located beneath the keyboard. To operate the touch pad, place a finger on the surface, and then move in the desired direction. Touch pads require absolutely no maintenance and have no moving parts. The touch pad may also serve as one of the mouse buttons by just tapping on it.

The type of pointing device that you choose comes down to two things: availability and personal preference. I personally prefer the pointing stick, but many people prefer touch pads and track balls.

CERTIFICATION SUMMARY

Portable computers represent the most proprietary sections of computer hardware. Although the technology between manufacturers is similar, components are not compatible between them. It's important to understand the components that are part of portable systems, as well as their capabilities, because more and more people are taking advantage of these devices and their maintenance requires a skill set that is unlike that for traditional desktops. Especially with the use of docking stations, portable systems are becoming more and more popular with computer users and, in some cases, are even replacing the traditional desktop. This chapter has equipped you with the knowledge that you need to work with portable systems.

✓ TWO-MINUTE DRILL

❑ Some portable system components are not compatible between different portable computers from the same vendor.

❑ Type I PC Cards are generally only used for memory.

❑ Port replicators are the cheapest and simplest version of the three types of docking stations.

❑ Portable computer batteries must be disposed of properly. Check the label of the battery and with local agencies for disposal directions. Do not just throw batteries in the trash.

❑ Passive matrix displays make up the bulk of the laptop displays today.

❑ Most portables have some RAM on the motherboard, but manufacturers usually provide a proprietary expansion slot for additional RAM.

❑ Microsoft added the mouse trails option primarily so people wouldn't lose their cursors on passive matrix displays.

❑ Be careful not to drip moisture into the keyboard or other parts of the portable when cleaning the display, as it may have undesirable results.

❑ A docking station allows a user to install their monitor, external keyboard, and mouse to the docking station rather than to their portable system.

❑ Type III PC Cards are generally reserved for rotating mass storage, such as hard drives.

❑ When a NiCad battery is recharged before it is fully discharged, the battery loses the ability to fully recharge again, which is known as the memory effect.

❑ All PCMCIA cards are now referred to as PC Cards.

❑ All PC Cards are 85.6 mm by 54.0 mm. Type I cards are 3.3 mm thick, Type II are 5.0 mm thick, and Type III are 10.5 mm thick.

❑ Socket Services is a layer of BIOS level software that isolates PC Card software from the computer hardware and detects the insertion or removal of PC Cards.

❑ Touch pad mice are quickly becoming the pointing device of choice with portable computers.

❑ Type II PC Cards are generally used for I/O devices such as modems, network adapters, or SCSI adapters.

SELF TEST

The following Self Test questions will help you measure your understanding of the material presented in this chapter. Read all the choices carefully, as there may be more than one correct answer. Choose all correct answers for each question.

1.   Of the different battery types currently available, which provides the most power with the lease amount of weight?

   A.   Nickel Cadmium

   B.   Lithium Ion

   C.   Nickel Metal Hydride

   D.   Lead Acid

2.   After using her laptop for only a short time, Mary recharged the battery in her computer. She is complaining now that her battery only holds a charge for a short time. You know Mary's computer uses a NiCad battery. What could be the problem?

   A.   Mary's computer is not configured properly for that type of battery.

   B.   Mary's computer is using a high color display that uses a great deal of power.

   C.   Mary's battery is suffering from 'memory effect' and will need to be replaced.

   D.   Mary's battery needs to be fully discharged before it will fully recharge again.

3.   The AC adapter on a portable computer changes one type of power to another. What types?

   A.   110v AC to 220v AC

   B.   220v AC to 110v AC

   C.   110v AC or 220v AC to DC

   D.   12v DC to 110v AC

4.   Portable computers now use which type of display technology?

   A.   Liquid Crystal

   B.   Light Emitting Diode

   C.   Cathode Ray Tube

   D.   8514/A

5.   Which type of display uses a transistor at each pixel?

   A.   Cathode Ray Tube

   B.   8514/A

   C.   Light Emitting Diode

   D.   Active Matrix

6.   Joe is complaining that when he moves his mouse quickly, his cursor disappears. What can you do to help him out?

   A.   Change his display mode from Passive to Active.

B. Set the mouse trails option to On.

C. Adjust the contrast of the display.

D. Tell him not to move the mouse as quickly.

7. A docking station can provide which of the following?

A. PCI slots

B. ISA slots

C. Enhanced sound capabilities

D. All of the above

8. Docking stations use what type of connector?

A. Centronix

B. DB-50

C. DIN

D. Proprietary

9. Patty wants to upgrade the hard drive in her portable computer. You have many new hard drives for other portable computers in your office. What should you do to upgrade her system?

A. Use one of the hard drives that you already have.

B. Compare the old hard drive with a new one. If they look the same, it should work.

C. Buy a hard drive made for her particular computer.

D. Suggest that Mary get a new portable computer. You cannot upgrade a hard drive in a portable.

10. PC Cards were originally intended for what technology?

A. Hard drives

B. Hard drive adapters

C. Memory

D. Network adapters

11. Type III PC Cards are intended for what type of peripherals?

A. Modems

B. LAN cards

C. Rotating mass storage

D. Memory

12. This BIOS level software detects insertion or removal of PC Cards.

A. Card Services

B. Socket Services

C. Windows 95

D. DOS

13. This software manages the allocation of system resources once a PC Card has been inserted.

A. Card Services

B. Socket Services

C. Windows 95

D. DOS

14. Uses for PC Cards today include:

A. Hard drives

B. Network cards

C. Memory cards

D. Global Positioning System cards

E. All of the above

15. What types of pointing devices are found in portable computers today?

    A. Trackballs

    B. Touch pads

    C. Pointing stick

    D. All of the above

16. This type of pointing device has the most moving parts.

    A. Trackballs

    B. Touch pads

    C. Pointing stick

    D. Mouse

7

Basic
Networking

Networking is by far one of the most quickly expanding fields in the computer industry. With the surge in popularity of the Internet in the mid 1990's, a great deal of interest in networking has arisen. Whenever two or more workstations are connected together, a Local Area Network (LAN) is created. Nearly every major company has, at a minimum, a LAN installed.

There are some basic networking concepts that you will run into time and time again as a technician. Whether you have an interest in networking or not, it will be in your best interest to be familiar with these basic concepts.

After you have a firm grasp of some basic networking concepts, it is also important to have a general understanding of how to configure a Network Interface Card (NIC). Configuration of a NIC is extraordinarily simple in most cases, and will be useful to you during your career.

CERTIFICATION OBJECTIVE 7.01

Basic Networking Concepts

As a base for your networking abilities, you need to understand some basic networking concepts. Everything in the world of networking revolves around these concepts, and a firm grasp of them is extraordinarily important. These basic concepts include:

- Cabling
- Network Interface Cards
- Network Access
- Protocols

Cabling

Obviously, in order to create a network, you have to somehow physically connect the devices that will be on the network. This is accomplished using cables. There are many different types of cables, each having its own advantages and disadvantages. In the next few sections, we discuss three types of cabling: Twisted Pair, Coaxial, and Fiber Optic.

Twisted Pair

Twisted pair is by far the most common type of network cable, primarily because of its low cost. Physically, twisted pair consists of pairs of wires, usually four. Each of the wires in a pair is wrapped around the other to help avoid interference. Twisted pair requires that each workstation be attached to a hub (see Figure 7-1). A hub receives data from one of its ports, and then transmits it to all of its ports. Twisted pair cable is considerably less expensive than the other types of cabling. In larger network installations, the lower price of cable offsets the cost of a hub and makes twisted pair the most cost-effective networking solution.

Twisted pair can be referred to by many different names. Some of these names include unshielded twisted pair, UTP, shielded twisted pair, 10BaseT, and 100BaseT; UTP is the most popular. As shown in Figure 7-2, twisted pair is configured in a star topology, in which each device is connected to a central device, usually a hub. In the event of a cable being cut or broken, the device that is connected to that cable will no longer be able to communicate on the network, but will not affect any other devices on the network.

| FIGURE 7-1 | A hub is a device to which each device on a network connects |

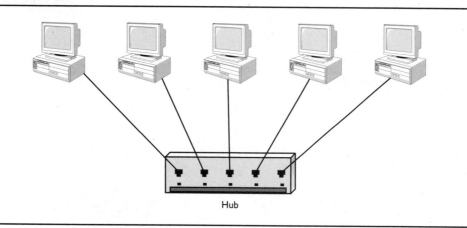

Hub

FIGURE 7-2　　　　A twisted pair network is usually configured in a star topology

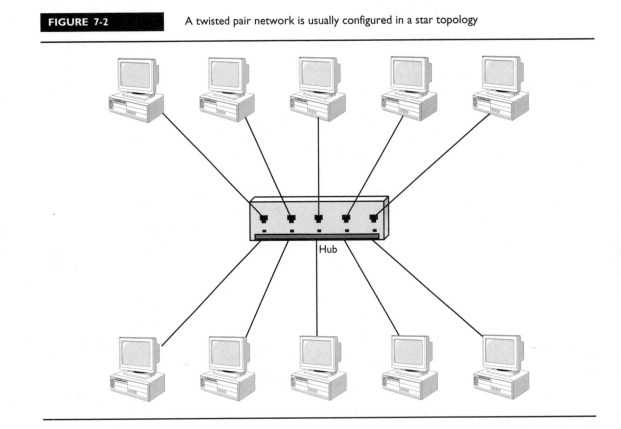

Coaxial

Coaxial, while not as common as twisted pair, is also a popular type of network cable. Physically, coaxial cable consists of a central wire that is surrounded by a screen of fine wires. Coaxial cable is most common in smaller networks, where it is cheaper to purchase the coaxial cable instead of purchasing both the UTP cabling and hubs. Like twisted pair, coaxial can also be referred to by many names. Some of these names include BNC, ThinNet, and 10Base2; ThinNet is the most popular. Each device must be connected to a T-connector, shown in Figure 7-3. Each T-connector is connected to the next with a coaxial cable. After all of the devices are connected, the ends of the cable must then be terminated with a 50Ω terminator. As shown in Figure 7-4, a coaxial network is configured in a bus

FIGURE 7-3

A T-connector is required
between each device on a
network utilizing coaxial
cabling and the coaxial
cable

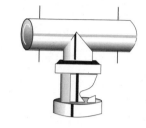

topology. In the event of the cable being cut or broken, the network will
cease to operate.

e x a m
ⓦ a t c h   *Coaxial cable requires that each device be connected to a T-connector,*
which is then connected to the coaxial cable. In addition, each end of
the cable must have a 50Ω terminator installed.

Fiber Optic

Fiber optic is by far the least common of the three types of cabling. Fiber
optic cabling is usually found where long cable lengths are required, where

FIGURE 7-4   A coaxial network is usually configured in a bus topology with each device connected to
a main cable or bus

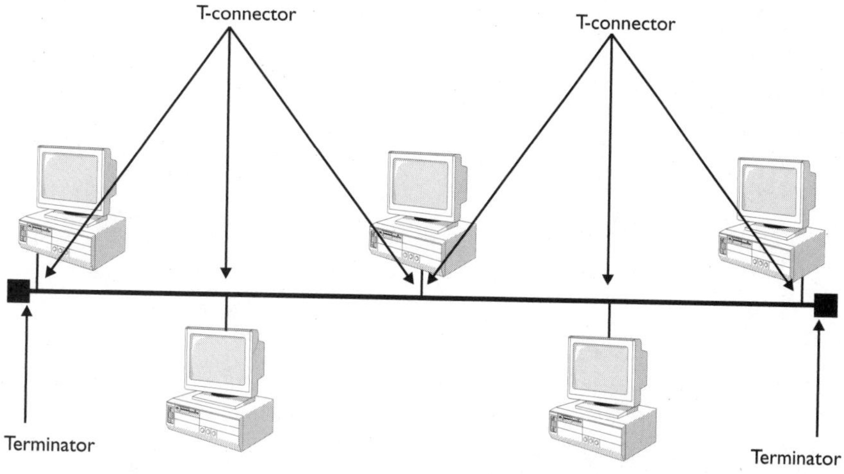

T-connector   T-connector

Terminator   Terminator

extremely high speed is desired (at extremely high cost), or where there is high EMI radiation or other environmental difficulties. Traditional copper-based cables such as twisted pair or coaxial cables are very susceptible to radiation and other environmental difficulties. Fiber optic cable is much less susceptible to these environmental difficulties because it uses light signals rather than electrical signals. Light signals offer much more protection from environmental interferences than electrical signals. Fiber optic is used when long lengths of cable are required because it is able to sustain longer distances without environmental interruption.

Fiber optic is usually referred to simply as *fiber*. Each segment of fiber optic cable must be connected at each end with a special fiber optic connector. As shown in Figure 7-5, a fiber optic network is configured in a ring topology. In the event that the fiber optic cable is cut or broken, the network will cease to operate. (Most fiber optic installations actually include two rings in order to provide redundancy and fault tolerance.) Table 7-1 lists and compares each of the cable types discussed in this section.

| FIGURE 7-5 | A fiber optic network is usually configured in a ring topology where a token is passed around a ring |

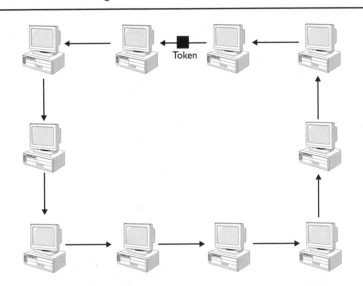

TABLE 7-1			Comparison of Important Characteristics of Cable Types	
Cable Type	**Topology**	**Maximum Distance**	**Transmissi on Speed**	**Other Required Devices**
Twisted Pair	Star	100 Meters	10 or 100 Megabits per second	Each networked device must connect to a port on a hub.
Coaxial	Bus	180 Meters	10 Megabits per second	Each networked device must be connected with a T-connector and terminators must be connected to each end.
Fiber Optic	Ring	Theoretically no limit	Theoretically no limit (100 Megabits per second most common)	Each end of a cable segment must have a special fiber optic transmitter connected.

e x a m
ⓦa t c h *Twisted pair cable is capable of transmitting a maximum of 100 meters, coaxial is capable of a maximum of 180 meters, and fiber optic cable theoretically has no limit.*

Network Interface Cards

Network interface cards (NICs) are the devices that, when installed in a PC, connect the PC to the network cable. NICs must be matched to the type of network and the type of network cable that you are using. It is important to choose a NIC that corresponds to your network. Recently, most NIC manufacturers have introduced models that can connect to either twisted pair or coaxial networks.

Full Duplex

Networking is described as full duplex when it is capable of transmitting in both directions at the same time. In simpler terms, a full duplex network medium has the capability of sending and receiving simultaneously. The most common application of true full duplex networking is in fiber optic cabling.

Network Access

Network access (or *access method* as it is more commonly referred to) is the method by which devices communicate on the network. Without some type of control on the network, any device could transmit at any time, quite possibly at the same time as another device. As we humans have a problem when two people attempt to communicate simultaneously, devices on the network have a similar problem. Network access provides a standard that all devices that wish to communicate on the network must abide by in order to solve this problem. Common types of network access are:

- Carrier Sense Multiple Access/Collision Detection
- Token Passing

Carrier Sense Multiple Access/Collision Detection

Carrier Sense Multiple Access/Collision Detection (CSMA/CD) is somewhat similar to how we humans communicate. With CSMA/CD, a device transmits data onto the network. The device then detects if any other devices have transmitted onto the network at the same time. If it detects that another device has transmitted data onto the network, the device then waits an unspecified random amount of time and retransmits its data. CSMA/CD is most commonly found on Ethernet networks, which most commonly use twisted pair or coaxial cable as the physical cable type. CSMA/CD is one of the faster access methods available, but performance can become an issue on busier networks.

Token Passing

Token passing is a bit more organized than CSMA/CD. Using token passing, a token is passed from device to device around a virtual (and frequently physical) ring. Whenever a device receives the token, it is then allowed to transmit onto the network. Token passing is most commonly found on fiber optic and token ring (which we will not discuss because it is becoming less commonly used) networks. Token passing, although more organized than other methods, is a bit slower because it requires that devices wait until they hold the token prior to transmitting onto the network. In the event that the token were to be lost, the network could be rendered useless until a new token is created, which could take from a few seconds to a few hours. The use of token passing is advantageous where total organization is required, such as in fiber optic backbones.

Protocols

Data cannot simply be transmitted onto the network. Protocols establish standards for such transmission of data. Both the sending and receiving device must be capable of communicating using the same protocols. Some common protocols are:

- TCP/IP
- IPX/SPX
- NetBEUI

TCP/IP

TCP/IP, Transmission Control Protocol/Internet Protocol, is the most common protocol used today; it's the protocol upon which the Internet is built. TCP/IP was originally designed in the 1970's to be used by the Defense Advanced Research Projects Agency (DARPA) and the Department of Defense (DOD) to connect systems across the country. A requirement of this design was the ability to cope with bad network conditions. An advantage of TCP/IP is that it is routable or can be passed beyond a router. A router is a network device that connects two or more networks together. The router allows all traffic destined for the network on the other side of the router to cross. TCP/IP's largest disadvantage is that it requires quite a bit of configuration prior to use.

IPX/SPX

IPX/SPX, Internetwork Packet Exchange/Sequenced Packet Exchange, is the protocol most commonly used with Novell NetWare. IPX/SPX is a very fast and highly established protocol, but is not used on the Internet. Novell developed IPX/SPX for use in NetWare. Like TCP/IP, IPX/SPX is routable and requires some configuration, though nowhere near as much as TCP/IP.

NetBEUI

NetBEUI, NetBIOS Extended User Interface, is a transport protocol that is commonly found in smaller networks. NetBEUI is an extremely quick protocol with very little overhead that was first implemented with LAN Manager products. NetBEUI is not routable and requires little configuration, if any at all.

Ways to Network a PC

So far, all of our discussion has involved using a NIC to connect two or more computers together. There are a few other ways to network workstations.

Dial-Up Networking is when a modem is used to connect two or more workstations together. The majority of people who connect to the Internet from home use Dial-Up Networking on a daily basis. It is considerably slower than using NICs, but can accomplish the same tasks.

A direct cable connection is when two computers are networked using either a serial or parallel cable. Direct cable connections are considerably faster than modem connections, but are still slower than networking using a NIC. Direct cable connections are limited to networking a maximum of two computers and are limited by physical cable restrictions.

CERTIFICATION OBJECTIVE 7.02

Configuring Network Interface Cards

Network Interface Cards (NICs) are fairly simple to configure. Most NICs require an IRQ and an IO memory address. Once the resources that the NIC uses have been configured on the NIC (most newer NICs use a software utility rather than the more traditional jumpers or dip switches; consult your NIC's documentation for exact specifications), the Network Operating System must be configured with the same settings (consult your Network Operating Systems documentation for details, and see Chapter 11 of this book). Configuration will be a less difficult process if the same type of NIC is used in each workstation on your network.

Problems on the Network

As the saying goes, all good things must come to an end. Someday your beautiful network will not continue to operate exactly as it used to. This could be the result of many different things. Some common causes of network problems include:

- Physically damaged cable
- Damaged Network Interface Card
- Excessive traffic on the network
- Incorrectly operating hub
- Missing or incorrectly operating terminator
- Magnetic fields
- Incorrectly configured network devices

Reduced Bandwidth

Reduced bandwidth occurs when users' data transmissions across the network begin to take longer, and begin to be timed-out by the applications requesting the transmission. Reduced bandwidth can be caused by any of the common network problems mentioned in the preceding section. The most likely cause of reduced bandwidth is excessive traffic on the network. Excessive traffic usually is not a result of an equipment failure, but instead a result of equipment success. The only solution to excessive traffic is to modify the network configuration in order to allow more traffic, or to separate high-traffic users from others. The most common method of modifying the network configuration to allow more traffic is to upgrade a 10 Megabits/Second LAN to 100 Megabits/Second by replacing hubs, NICs, and possibly the cabling.

FROM THE FIELD

A Real-World Networking Lesson

It is very important to understand the limitations of the networks on which you work. Bandwidth costs money, and some corporations try to run their networks on the minimum amount of bandwidth. Once, I was swapping a computer with another computer for a user and I needed to transfer the user's data to the new computer. Being naïve, I copied all the user data onto a network drive to copy back to the new computer. Because I assumed the network could handle this procedure, I did not ask anyone about bandwidth or server drive size. Well, guess what? My copying took over 25 percent of the network bandwidth and sent all sorts of server alerts to the administrators. Not only was the bandwidth a problem, the network drive I was copying to became totally full. Luckily, everything worked out okay. I deleted the copied data and the network only slowed down a bit rather than coming to a screeching halt. Always find out the capabilities and limitations of a network before doing any kind of work on it. By the way, I copied the data over by slaving the drives after that and it worked well.

From this example, even if you are on a network that can handle this, you must ask yourself a few questions before doing anything that might strain the network. Are there other people on the network doing something similar to what you want to do? If so, will the combined effect of your collective actions cause network problems? Are there people working on the network who might be slowing things down to a level that would be aggravated worse by your actions? Is there another way to do what you are trying to do without using the network? I've seen many techs carry around a portable hard drive with them all day to do data transfers and software installs. Not only are they saving valuable network bandwidth, but they are probably getting their data sent faster. In addition, they can carry all the drivers and repair software on this drive.

—By Ted Hamilton, MCP, A+ Certified

Loss of Data

Loss of data can be a result of nearly any of the common network problems mentioned previously. Most methods of data transmission provide some type of assurance that the data has been transmitted successfully. Data loss is therefore usually caused by some type of failure, and not by excessive traffic. Excessive traffic results in slower delivery of data rather than loss of data in most cases.

Network Slowdown

Network slowdown occurs whenever users notice that the network is not operating as quickly as they are used to. In most cases, this is a sudden change, rather than a gradual change (a more gradual change would be a loss of bandwidth). Because the change appears to be sudden, it is more than likely a result of a hardware problem, rather than a result of excessive traffic.

CERTIFICATION SUMMARY

This chapter has offered you a general understanding of basic networking concepts, including the various methods by which networks operate and an overview of some of the more common networking problems. A firm grasp of networking fundamentals is becoming an increasing necessity in today's growing network-oriented computer industry.

As you have learned, Local Area Networks (LANs) are most commonly created by connecting workstations that have Network Interface Cards (NICs). These workstations are usually connected using either twisted pair, coaxial, or fiber optic cabling. Communication on the network cable is governed by network access methods such as Carrier Sense Multiple Access/Collision Detection (CSMA/CD) or Token Passing.

Common network problems can be caused by a number of factors, including physically damaged cable, damaged NICs, excessive traffic on the network, an incorrectly operating hub, missing or incorrectly operating terminator, or magnetic fields. Results of some of these causes can include reduced bandwidth, loss of data, and network slowdown.

✓ # TWO-MINUTE DRILL

❏ A Network Interface Card is more commonly known by its acronym, NIC.

❏ Basic networking concepts include cabling, NICs, network access, and protocols.

❏ Common cabling types include twisted pair, coaxial, and fiber optic.

❏ Twisted pair cable is organized in a star topology, and requires that each network device be connected to a port on a hub.

❏ Coaxial cable is organized in a bus topology, whereby each device is connected to a T-connector that is then connected to the cable that has a 50Ω terminator connected to each end.

❏ Fiber optic cable is organized in a ring topology, and requires that each end of the cable be connected to a special fiber optic connector.

❏ Twisted pair cable is capable of transmitting a maximum of 100 meters, coaxial is capable of a maximum of 180 meters, and fiber optic cable theoretically has no limit.

❏ NICs are the devices that connect a PC to the network cable. NICs must be matched to the type of network cable that you are using.

❏ *Network access* defines the method by which devices can communicate across the network.

❏ Some common network access methods include Carrier Sense Multiple Access/Collision Detection (CSMA/CD), which is commonly used with twisted pair and coaxial cable, and token passing, which is commonly used with fiber optic.

❏ CSMA/CD is an access method by which a device transmits data onto the network and then detects if any other devices have transmitted onto the network at the same time.

❏ Token passing is an access method by which a token is passed from device to device around a virtual ring, and the device can only transmit data when it receives a token.

❑ Protocols, which ensure that both the receiver and the sender can understand the data that is sent, are used to define how devices communicate with each other.

❑ Some common protocols include Transmission Control Protocol/Internet Protocol (TCP/IP), Internetwork Packet Exchange/Sequenced Packet Exchange (IPX/SPX), and NetBIOS Extended User Interface (NetBEUI).

❑ Most Network Interface Cards require an IRQ address and an IO Memory address in order to operate correctly.

❑ Common network problems can be caused by a physically damaged cable, a damaged NIC, excessive traffic on the network, an incorrectly operating hub, a missing or incorrectly operating terminator, or magnetic fields.

❑ Common results of network problems can include reduced bandwidth, loss of data, or network slowdown.

SELF TEST

The following Self Test questions will help you measure your understanding of the material presented in this chapter. Read all the choices carefully, as there may be more than one correct answer. Choose all correct answers for each question.

1. What does the acronym NIC stand for?

   A. Network Interface Card

   B. Network Interference Carrier

   C. Network Interface Carrier

   D. Network Interference Card

   E. None of the above

2. What does the acronym CSMA/CD stand for?

   A. Carrier Sense Multiple Address/Carrier Detection

   B. Carrier Sense Multiple Access/Carrier Detection

   C. Collision Sense Multiple Access/Carrier Detection

   D. Carrier Sense Multiple Access/Collision Detection

   E. None of the above

3. What does the acronym TCP/IP stand for?

   A. Timely Cautious Protocol/Internet Protocol

   B. Transmission Control Protocol/Internet Protocol

   C. Totally Controlling Packets/Internet Protocol

   D. Time Controlled Packets/Internet Protocol

   E. None of the above

4. The basic networking concepts introduced in this chapter include all of the following except:

   A. Cabling

   B. Network Interface Cards

   C. Network Access

   D. Network Repairs

   E. Protocols

5. A common cable type used for networks is:

   A. Twisted Pair

   B. Fiber Optic

   C. Coaxial

   D. All of the above

   E. None of the above

6. What is the maximum distance that coaxial cable can successfully be used?

   A. 100 ft.

   B. 100 meters

   C. 180 ft.

   D. 185 meters

   E. None of the above

7. What is the maximum distance that twisted pair cable can successfully be used?

A. 100 ft.

B. 100 meters

C. 180 ft.

D. 180 meters

E. None of the above

8. What is the maximum distance that fiber optic cable can successfully be used.

A. 100 ft.

B. 100 meters

C. 180 ft.

D. 180 meters

E. None of the above

9. Which of the following is a special requirement of fiber optic cable?

A. Devices must be connected to the network cable using T-connectors.

B. Special transceivers must be installed on each end of the cable.

C. Each device must be connected to a port in a hub.

D. Each end of the cable must be terminated with a 50Ω Terminator.

E. Two of the above are true.

F. A FDDI network can be as simple as two network cards and two strands of fiber. Since it is configured in a physical ring, there are no "ends" on which to put transceivers.

10. Which of the following is a special requirement of coaxial cable?

A. Devices must be connected to the network cable using T-connectors.

B. Special transceivers must be installed on each end of the cable.

C. Each device must be connected to a port in a hub.

D. Each end of the cable must be terminated with a 50Ω Terminator.

E. Two of the above are true.

11. Which of the following is a special requirement of twisted pair cable?

A. Devices must be connected to the network cable using T-connectors.

B. Special transceivers must be installed on each end of the cable.

C. Each device must be connected to a port in a hub.

D. Each end of the cable must be terminated with a 50Ω Terminator.

E. Two of the above are true.

12. Network Access . . .

A. Provides a standard by which all devices that wish to communicate on the network must abide.

B. Provides a standard for the encoding method that each packet transmitted on the network must follow.

C. Defines the rights of users on a network.

D. Is only granted if a device agrees to follow established protocols.

E. None of the above.

13. Protocols . . .

    A. Provide a standard by which all devices that wish to communicate on the network must abide.

    B. Define the rights of users on the network.

    C. Establish standards for the transmission of data onto the network that ensure that both the sending and receiving devices are able to communicate.

    D. Are granted only when network access is accepted.

    E. None of the above.

14. Which of the following best describes the bus topology discussed in this chapter?

    A. It is commonly found in coaxial cable-based networks.

    B. Each device is connected to a T-connector and then the T-connector is connected to the cable.

    C. Each end of the cable must be terminated with a 50Ω terminator.

    D. All of the above are true.

    E. None of the above are true.

15. In the event of a cable break, which of the following will **always** result in a total network failure?

    A. Coaxial Cable

    B. Twisted Pair

    C. Fiber Optic

    D. All of the above

    E. None of the above

8

Customer
Satisfaction

Achieving outstanding customer satisfaction is of paramount importance in the business world. Even though the exam only reports this score and it does not determine if you pass or fail the exam, it is extremely important to learn this often-neglected topic. Your professional behavior while working with the customer has the potential of boosting your career immensely. There are many aspects of the art of customer satisfaction, which are discussed in this chapter.

CERTIFICATION OBJECTIVE 8.01

Behaviors to Achieve and Maintain Customer Satisfaction

Achieving and thereafter maintaining customer satisfaction is a complex skill. Once mastered, it can not only help the customer, it can provide you with benefits, too. If you do it correctly, you'll probably notice such career-enhancing events as more frequent pats on the back and phone calls to your boss (and his boss) marveling at what a wonderful technician you are. Customer satisfaction may look effortless to the inexperienced, but in reality, the art of achieving and maintaining a satisfied customer is as challenging as learning any computer technical skills.

Customer satisfaction helps you, it helps the customer, and it helps the business as a whole. Smart business people have always known this—that's why customer satisfaction has always been an important aspect in the service industry. If you look at the companies that have stayed in business the longest, chances are they have stressed the importance of customer satisfaction to their employees. Also, with all the computer jobs being farmed out today, companies are not just interested in computer technicians who will fix their employee's computers, but in the type of computer worker they are. They are looking for a type of worker who is going to make their employees more productive and happy. Computer company owners have spent large amounts of money an amenities to keep their workers happy, such as spacious office buildings, equipment, employee training, and so on. Why would they want to cut corners and send in a bunch of unprofessional computer technicians who would undermine their efforts at employee satisfaction by making the employees frustrated and angry?

What does it take to achieve and maintain customer satisfaction? The first step is to always go the extra mile for the customer. This takes extra time, patience, good listening skills, and the ability to communicate at the user's level of understanding. It also requires the ability to read situations quickly and the ability to anticipate the likely outcome of various ways of doing things. If you use good professional behavior, listen and communicate well, avoid conflict, and fix the customer's PC, you are on your way to achieving customer satisfaction.

One way of framing customer satisfaction is to imagine how the customer perceives you. Think of how when you buy a car you are sent a survey asking you how satisfied you were with the dealership and the car you bought. These surveys usually have a series of questions that ask you to rate the dealerships on a vast array of services performed. What are the issues that determine how you fill out the form? Is it how the salespersons presented themselves? Is it the attention they paid to you? Is it the salesperson's ability to listen to your needs? These are the same elements that make or break an encounter with a customer in any business. Anyone who deals with customer satisfaction in their job should find copies of these kinds of surveys and study them.

Similar surveys may be used when you fix computers. A survey, like the one shown in Figure 8-1, should include: the service performed, timeliness of the service, professionalism of the technician, whether the problem was fixed in one trip, whether the problem recurred, whether the service was done satisfactorily, and if everything else worked correctly after the visit. If your company uses these surveys, make sure to look at them frequently. In this way, you will know exactly where you can improve your customer relation skills.

If a technician fixes a computer, but doesn't have a good grasp of their interpersonal skills, then the technician is not doing their whole job. The technician should always leave the customer's office with the belief that they have treated the customer with dignity, respect, and integrity. Many technicians are not aware of this and they think that if they just fix the

FIGURE 8-1

A Customer Satisfaction
Survey

Customer Satisfaction Survey

Date___/___/___   Time___:___

Reference #_____   Technician's
                                 Name:_____

In order to provide you with the utmost satisfaction with our service,
your response to this questionnaire is greatly appreciated.

Fill in the following:

Did the technician behave   _____
professionally?

Was your service done   _____
promptly?

Was the service done in   _____
one trip?

Is your problem solved?   _____

How satisfied are you with   _____
our service? 1 to 10 scale.

Comments, concerns, questions, ideas:

_____

_____

_____

_____

_____

_____

_____

_____

machines, then the customer is satisfied. This is rarely the case—most users
have no idea of what you are doing and the only way that they can judge
you is by the way you act and the way they are treated. The end result
should be a customer who feels satisfied that you are a professional and
you have done a great job fixing their PC.

Once you achieve the original customer satisfaction, the next step is to maintain it. If you make a customer happy one day, and the next you make them mad, then the end result is that they are mad.

A good start to maintaining a happy customer is good record keeping. Every time you do anything to the user's PC, you should record exactly what you did. This will be helpful for you or whoever else returns to this PC in the future. Keep these lists in a database. Keep track of what you did, and also what the customer has said and how it relates to past and possible future events. A customer absolutely loves it when you go to talk with them and have researched their past repairs and can discuss what has happened before and why it is you are doing what you want to do to the machine.

Good records also are helpful if a repair cannot be completed in one visit, as happens every now and again. For example, the fax software is not working on the user's computer and they need to have a special program shipped in for their particular hardware/software configuration. With your records, you can keep track of who ordered what and when. Let the user know the status either by personally visiting, phoning, or e-mailing them. People don't like to be kept in the dark about things. If you find out that you have received modems to be distributed to a department in a week, let the manager know when you are certain of the date they will receive them.

Many problems require more time to solve. Let the user know what you have done to research them and when you think you will have it fixed. A downed PC can be costly for an organization in terms of money and morale. Every day a PC is out is a day that the user is telling everyone he talks to that his PC is down. This is not good for the reputation of the technicians.

Communicating and Listening

Communicating and listening is of utmost importance in computer repair. It's about knowing when to listen, when to speak, and what to say. But communication is not limited to face-to-face interaction. Communication also includes e-mail, telephone, notes, and having a coworker relay a message. Figure 8-2 shows a typical organization's channels of communication.

FIGURE 8-2   Communication channels in a typical organization

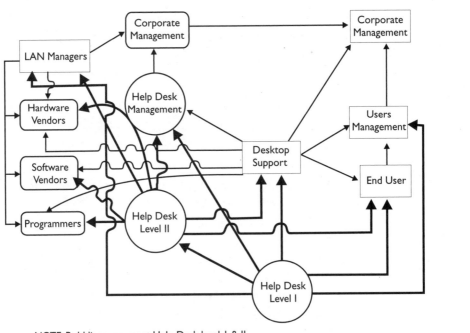

NOTE: Bold lines represent Help Desk level I & II.

When repairing a computer, let the user explain the problem fully before starting to work on it. Many times the exam takes into account exceptions that the technician would run into if they did not listen fully to the customer and ask pertinent questions.

Listening

Let's look at listening first. If nothing else, listening will always bring you more information to think about. It might be right and it might be wrong, but it is always best to listen completely before you do anything. Many technicians jump to the conclusion that they can solve the problem before the user has completely discussed the problem. This is a big mistake and the consequences can be tragic.

Here's an example of a technician coming to a conclusion without fully listening to the customer: A PC is having problems and the technician, without listening to the customer, sees that the network cord is out. Thinking there is a network problem, the technician plugs in the network cord. But what if it was a faulty network card that was causing the problem, and someone had decided to pull it out of the wall so the card would not send out broadcasts flooding the network? If the technician had only waited to listen to the customer tell them that someone working on the hub had disconnected the cord an hour ago, then they would have a different method of troubleshooting. In a similar scenario, if a technician sees that a machine is unplugged and immediately plugs it back in without listening to the user, they might see the machine go up in smoke—which is why the cord was unplugged in the first place.

Communicating

Hand in hand with listening to the customer is how you communicate back to them. Knowing when to ask what is very important. The most obvious—and best—approach to communicating with the customer is first to ask them what problems are occurring. If a solution is not evident, ask them what had changed on the machine preceding the problem. Do not get into the blame game here. Just act matter-of-factly and get the info that you need to solve the problem. Try to get the user into a mode where they remember when and what they were doing when this problem started. Try to get them to duplicate the environment that is causing this problem. Sometimes they can't duplicate the problem at this point and they feel foolish. The problem is simply not recurring at that time. If this is the case and you can't uncover the problem by what they have said and by your own attempts to get the problem to occur, give them your pager number and have them call you if the problem reoccurs. Speaking of pagers, most companies now provide all their techs with pagers. If you don't have one, get one, and give out the number to those who you think will use it responsibly. This gives the customer the safe feeling that if there is an emergency, they have a technician they can get in touch with.

When you are done listening to the user and have asked all of your questions, paraphrase what the user has said and say it back to them. Then ask them if this is what they said. This can be a question, such as "Just to make sure I understand the problem fully, let me say it back to you" then state the problem and ask "Is this what is actually happening?" Users are generally overjoyed that in your large nerdy computer brain you were actually able to process all the information that they inputted and were able to regurgitate it back to them. You are essentially doing two things at once with this technique: The customer is satisfied because they feel you genuinely care about their problem, and you are not on a wild goose chase trying to solve the wrong problem because of miscommunication.

Communicating also involves giving out information about yourself. Always introduce yourself to the users when you meet them. Tell them to ask for you by name if they run into further problems. Find out the user's name and use it when you meet with them. Many names are difficult to pronounce. Keep a list of the phonetic pronunciation of their names along with their record. If you can't pronounce their name, call them on the phone to let them know you are coming out, and write down the pronunciation at this point. One trick for remembering names when you go into their offices is to carry a sheet of paper with the customer's names on it or know where they are written in the office, such as on the door or on their desk. This can be invaluable when you need to call in password problems and what-not. I have found that most people with difficult names respond very well when directly asked, "What is the correct pronunciation of your name?" This removes any guesswork and makes the individual feel like you care about them enough to ask.

One thing that really makes users angry and usually ends up with a call to the help desk or worse, is when a technician does something to a PC and does not leave a note. Many times, users are unaware of hardware upgrades for weeks until they call and find out they had the upgrade done already and the technician did not write a proper note to the user.

Many times, you will be asked as a tech to install hardware or software for an entire floor. Let the users know how long it will take you to do each computer. Ask if anyone's computer should be completed first. Work around the user. Save the busiest people for last. Update the users on how long it will take given the current configurations of that particular department's computer.

When approaching a user's desk, always communicate the basic necessities of fixing their PC. Many a user is not aware that if you are slaving a hard drive, they will have to not only get out of their seat but also clear their desk for you to have room to pop the hood of the computer. Tell them clearly that if they don't mind, you need to sit down in their seat. Have them clear their desk and tell them how long they can expect to have you there. Of course, it is essential that you are polite and not pushy when you tell them this. I've seen too many techs barge into offices and practically push people out of their seat just to get to their machines. Say things like "Take your time, make sure you save all you work." The last thing you want is to ruin your first impression with the user by putting them in such a rush that they don't save the important Word documents they have been working on all day.

Communication does not end at the user's desk. Good communication between technicians is also essential. Many companies use pagers, two-way radios, computers, and cell phones so technicians can get in touch with each other throughout the day to troubleshoot problems. And don't forget to communicate with the other techs when you are all together. Try and eat lunch together, or at least have a time of day when you can all sit down and pick each other's brains about the problems that you are working on. It is truly amazing how much some technicians know about things. Never be afraid to ask simple questions. Chances are that if you are this far in the A+ certification process, you know a lot about computers, but there is always more to learn. If you don't know what you are doing, ask your peers, and if their answer is not satisfactory find the answer from another source.

Technicians should also be able to quickly discern users' technical levels. For this, it helps to know what kind of questions to ask in order to quickly narrow down the problem. And, of course, tact helps too. For example, if a user can't turn the power on, the technician should not assume that the user kicked the plug out of the wall. In this case, instead of asking the user "Is it plugged in?" they should ask such questions as, "When you turn it on, do you hear any beeps?" or "Is there a light on next to the on/off switch?"

Sometimes, technicians have to handle awkward situations. For example, sometimes users will call and try to get things that they should not be getting. They might try to get software and hardware when they haven't received the proper permissions. Other users will try to have someone else's password reset. They will also try to get access on a network that is forbidden for them. This is where your communication skills are essential. You want to find out if these are relevant requests, but you do not want to accuse them of anything or have to call their supervisor to find out if the user has a valid request. Tell the user that it is company policy that so-and-so has to approve all passwords or whatever it is they are trying to get approved. You could try setting up your system so that all users go to a designated person and have them be the only person to call you with requests. Then if a user calls about anything that has been set up in this way, you know instantly that it is an invalid request.

Interpreting Verbal and Nonverbal Cues

Interpreting both verbal and nonverbal cues when dealing with customers is a must. Verbal cues can be obvious or may be very subtle. Nonverbal cues are even subtler. It is paramount to read all of these cues in order to make sure that things run smoothly. By practicing a few techniques, it gets easier to be able to read these cues.

When you first approach a user, listen to their tone of voice. Are they tense, annoyed, mad, rushed, wanting to talk, or just wanting to do their work while you expeditiously repair the machine? You need to read this and act accordingly. If they are annoyed, let them tell you how annoyed they are. Chances are, if they vent all their problems to you about their broken computer, they'll be less likely to tell other people of their frustrations. Even if you don't have a good answer to all their problems, the fact that you are willing to hear them out helps the situation.

Read the mood that they are in. Do they seem like they want to talk about the weather or would they rather just have you fix the problem and be on your merry way? In any corporate climate, moods can vary greatly. Maybe the user just got demoted or yelled at by their boss. Maybe the computer broke just in time to not be able to print the all-important luncheon speech for the foreign dignitary's visit. Read these cues carefully, because they will indeed dictate the approach that you will use in conversing with the customer.

Verbal cues can contain a plethora of information. Listen very closely to what users say. Sometimes they give away information on how they are feeling with the words that they are using. If they're in a bad mood, chances are they're using a lot of negative words.

Nonverbal cues are quite possibly more important than verbal cues. It is said that 80 percent of all communication is done nonverbally. Nonverbal cues can be seen in the face of the user. If the user looks worried when you are moving things around, take note and be careful. The face can tell a lot. There are thousands of moods that people can be in. Learn the facial expression that is associated with each emotion and treat your customer accordingly.

Look for nonverbal cues to help you know how to handle each situation. For example, if you are in a situation where you've been working on a PC for a long time, the user might just want you to leave and fix it the next day. If they are jingling their car keys, putting on their coat, or packing their briefcase, you want to let the user know that the problem is taking longer than originally planned and ask them if they need to be somewhere else. They may want to go to lunch and don't want to leave you in their office. In this situation, tell the user the status of your repair and let them know how long it will take you to complete it. Be willing to work around their schedule.

Always listen to the hints in the user's voice. If they are stressed, it helps to get the user in a trusting, relaxed, and satisfied mood. For example, are they stressed about introducing a new virus into the company's network? In this case, let the user know that you have handled thousands of viruses in your work and it is no big deal. The same goes if they have deleted a crucial document. Evaluate the situation and if you are sure you can fix it, tell the user that everything is all right and calm them down. If they have broken an expensive color laser printer, tell them that you have seen this happen before. It's always a sticky situation—literally—when a user tries to put labels through an ink jet and they clog up the printer. Do not blame them; let them know that this happens all the time. Tell them that the company really ought to put a warning on the printer not to put labels in. Hopefully, you will leave them with a smile on their face when you are done.

If you are calm about a situation, it calms the user. Reassure them. If their problem is hardware-related, let the user know that you have a part that you can swap for them and will be back later in the day to swap it. A calm user is a satisfied user.

And when you're thinking about nonverbal cues, don't forget to notice the cues that you are projecting. Are you calm, confident, and collected or are you tense, anxious, and frustrated? The user will be able to sense the kind of mood you are in by your own nonverbal cues. Make sure that you are projecting the type of cues that you want the user to see. If you look anxious, then the user will start to feel anxious because they think you might not know what you are doing. Users are already worried about their computer and they don't need to get more worried about your skill. Because what you are doing is a mystery to them, they can only see what you are doing by how you act. Even if you are frustrated about something not working, don't show it. Realize that it is part of computer repair. Some things are just going to have to take time and patience. You will find that following network problems can be this way. You are slowly eliminating variables. Many times it takes ten different tests to find them. Just stay calm and realize you can't get everything done in a lightning-fast manner. Confidence breeds success in all fields of work; PC repair is no exception.

exam
ⓦatch

Don't go for the misleading answer, which might solve the problem right away: go for the one that maintains the customer satisfaction requirements.

Responding to the Customer's Technical Level

Responding to the customer's technical level is easy to do, once you get a feel for it. It can save time and help to solve problems. This brings up a very important point. Make sure yourself that you are completely caught up with the latest information on computers. You can do this by reading a few of the hundreds of computer magazines out there. Another way is to simply talk to people about computers.

exam
Watch

Don't assume anything when it comes to a customer's technical level.

Another technique that works well in determining a user's technical ability when you are out in the field is to talk about computers. If the user is talking about a package deal they saw in the paper that threw in two hours of lessons, then you can bet that you are talking to a novice user. On the other hand, if the user is talking about an ad he saw in Computer Shopper for a 32 processor server to host his home Internet site and he is wondering if it will be fast enough, then this user is definitely advanced.

You can always ask the user if they are familiar with a certain program. This can alleviate much wasted time. Remember, it is not only the customer's technical level that is important, but yours also. Figure out creative ways to determine user abilities. Keep a mental record of the abilities of each user. Never put the user in a situation where they have to admit that they are not as smart as they should be. Listen to the language that they use when they are describing things. If they are talking about mapping a drive using an UNC path, for example, chances are they are a smart user. Respect all users regardless of their ability. You will always run into a user who is using a PC for the first time in their lives. Treat them kindly, patiently, and with respect. Try to point them in the right direction, if appropriate.

Most users are casual users. The can get themselves into all sorts of problems. Luckily, the casual and beginning user's problems are the easiest to repair. They get stumped on the same types of problems that you got stuck on eight years ago. Repairing them is second nature to you. One plus common to working with the casual user is that they are easily impressed with your technical ability. Many beginning users, in order to not look stupid, will act like they understand what you are doing when in reality they have no idea. With these users, it is a good idea to glance over at the notes they are taking and determine if they are getting the gist of what you are telling them. If you think that they are not, talk at a level that they will understand and repeat what you say, a few times if it seems necessary. Just don't leave them with the impression that you think they are stupid. Always try to put yourself in the customer's shoes. Think of the first time you ever turned on a PC. Think of how confusing everything was. If somebody started talking about EMS, EMM, or any of these fancy words, you would have been lost and not happy. If, instead, your original trainer made no assumptions about your knowledge of the PC and walked you through the necessary steps, explaining the complex ones as well as the simple ones, you would probably be more satisfied.

All users want to think that they are not as bad at computers as they appear. Sometimes, they give degrading comments about their abilities. When a user is new, they usually struggle to do what they want to do. Take the extra time and give them hints if time permits. Try to explain the big picture to them. Show them how the directories are structured. These short lessons can save you and your company time in the long run. Users are less apt to call the help desk trying to get an explanation over the phone on how to find their lost Word document. These beginning users usually like it when you stop by their desks and watch them do something that appears to be an advanced computer command. When this happens, let them know that they are really getting the hang of things.

On the other end of the spectrum are the advanced users. It is truly a rare pleasure to find a user who has a vast knowledge of computers. When this is the case, talk to the user on their level. Let them explain what has been done to the computer. Listening to the user can be one of the best trouble-shooting techniques. For instance, if they have used Debug, because they read about it somewhere, find out exactly the command that they used when the problem arose. Their help will be key to solving the problem. Even though all of these people may not be total computer wizards, try to let them feel they are. Use comments to show that you realize that they are very good at working with computers.

Never make too many assumptions about the user's knowledge. Some people like to talk a great deal about complex computer topics, when they just maybe have a superficial knowledge of it. While you can get some sort of idea of what they know, don't assume they know everything. If anything, try to assume that they know less than they might know, but don't make it sound like you are talking down to them.

What you say to a customer will stay in their minds for awhile. They will probably think about what you told them when they work. It always astounds me how much users remember of what we say. This is all the more reason not to ever lie to a user or give them a bogus answer.

Being a tech, most people will be in awe of your great computer wisdom. They will take your words as gospel. Please tell them the truth when it comes to computers. Be as knowledgeable as you can about computers and it will be easy to determine the user's abilities with a few questions and observations.

Establishing Personal Rapport with the Customer

Establishing personal rapport with the customer is one of the key elements to maintaining customer satisfaction. Rapport leads to trust, and trust leads to cooperation and a good relationship. Personal rapport includes following up on problems that you judge might end up being a problem again later. It also includes knowing your customers' computer hardware, software, configuration, and history. Finally, it includes knowing your customer on an interpersonal level.

Get to know your users. If you see them in the hall, if appropriate, ask how the last repair you did is working. When you are in their area, stop by their desk and ask them how everything is going if it looks like they are not busy. As is often the case with computers, there will be times when the PC is doing its own thing and there will be dead silence between you and the user. This is the perfect opportunity to get to know them. Look around

FROM THE FIELD

Frank Is His Name and Rapport Is His Game

One day I decided to help our lead tech, Frank, do two computer moves, which incidentally is common for A+ certified techs to do. While I was helping him, I noticed how he developed rapport with clients. Frank has been working in this business for over a decade and everyone he runs into thinks that he is a great tech.

After grabbing a pushcart on which to move the computers, we started to the first location. Frank, of course, made sure he had his tool kit, extra network cords, safety glasses, and so on. We picked up the first computer from a user's desk, at which point Frank called the user that was to receive the computer to let him know we were coming. He also made sure that this was the right PC and that he did, indeed, want it moved right then. On the way over to another building, Frank greeted about 75 percent of the passersby by their first name. They all smiled broadly and greeted him back. One user walked by and Frank asked him how everything was going. The user replied that his printing was still slow. Frank, knowing each person's particular PC (which amounts to thousands of PCs), told the user that the memory module was being ordered. He then said that he had spoken to the person who ordered it, and they had said that it would be in some time next week. As you can see, Frank lived up to many of the principles set forth in this chapter. First, he communicated with a user for whom he had provided a service. He remembered what the user's problem had been. He followed up on the service by asking about the problem and listening to what the user had to say. He had also made sure that the necessary part was ordered, which he communicated to the user (who will likely tell other users about the network printer's memory). He was also confident and positive. The user flashed a big grin and was on his way.

When we showed up at our destination, we knocked on the window and an assistant let us in. Frank made sure that he thanked her. The user was there and we delivered his PC. Frank conversed with this user about non-PC related items. The user then told a joke and Frank laughed out loud, which relaxed the user. We stayed around long enough for the login to the network just to make sure he could grab a DHCP IP address. Frank then talked to three other people in the department and we left. Everybody was happy.

We then went to our next assignment, which was in the middle of a factory. We found the person who wanted a PC moved, but this person was in the middle of something and so gave us directions on how to get to the PC. When we arrived, there was a big argument between two other users about

FROM THE FIELD

whether or not this machine should be moved. Frank quickly determined that he would just move the computer later. It didn't even faze him that delaying the move would mean trekking the cart all the way out here again later to move it. At this point, he didn't just accept that we'd move it later and walk away. Instead, he turned to the angry user, told him a joke, and had him laughing his head off. I'm sure that user will give him a big hello the next time he sees him in the hall. On the way back, Frank suggested we take the long way to say hello to a few more users.

Learn from this tech. People like him so much that he has lifetime job security. He would really have to mess up to get fired, and even then I don't think it would happen. He has learned this through years of knowing what people like and what they don't like. The rapport that he has built in all the years is extraordinary.

—*By Ted Hamilton, MCP, A+ Certified*

their office for interesting conversational items. Talk about the pet they have ten pictures of on the wall. When the customer views you as a person with whom they have a good rapport, they are less likely to withhold important information from you, and they will be more likely to cooperate with you. If you become their friend, then they will be more likely to cooperate with you.

Cooperation is the key to the technician-user relationship. Many times when a PC is messed up, it truly is the user's fault. Never, I repeat, never let them know this. The customer is always right, period. When you have a good rapport with the customer, it is likely that they may actually admit that "somebody" ran FDISK and didn't have the foggiest notion of what they were doing. And being the friendly technician that you are, you buy their story about this "somebody," and gently let them know that this fictitious user should not try to run programs that they are not very familiar with.

The whole goal of rapport is to have the customer happy about their PC experience. This can take the patience of Job with some "problem" users. Many times, you will find a user for whom you have clearly fixed the problem, but they keep asking about other problems and making requests that are not on the work order. You should use discretion. You might share a story that shows you have to tend to many requests. You might "wish" to stay on, but your schedule demands you be on to your next repair. Suggest and encourage them to use the help files or whatever else your company has for learning aid.

Good rapport with customers is the patience to stop when they stop you in the hall, and discuss whatever they want to discuss with you. Many times a user will ask about non-company PC issues. Answer them only if you have the time. If you are busy, politely tell them you are busy and will try and get back with them. Invite them to lunch to discuss the matter if appropriate. Answer their questions to the extent that you can, but make sure that you fully understand the situation that they are facing. Don't have them reload their operating system if, from your judgment, you don't think they are capable of it.

Let users know their PC problems are important. Make them think that your number one goal is to provide the best level of support you possibly can. When you are done fixing a PC, always ask if their problem has been fully resolved and if there are any concerns or other problems that are affecting them. With confidence and a broad smile, wish them a good day/weekend when you leave their office.

Good rapport with the customer can include keeping up with what they talk to you about on a personal basis. If a user talks to you about his car being in the shop, make sure you ask the next time you see him if the car is fixed. Make the whole PC repair as enjoyable as possible. Let users know that you are happy to see them. Even if you do not say this explicitly, make sure that your actions show it. Don't look at problems as a point of frustration. Instead, view them as a learning opportunity. Nothing is more satisfying than learning how to fix a recurring problem on multiple PCs. As part of good rapport, let your fellow techs know what you did to fix the problem so they can fix it quickly if they need to.

Treat every user as if they are a key employee, because they are. Each person contributes to the success of the whole. Showing respect and giving attention to each user builds their morale, which builds company morale. All too often, the low person on the totem pole gets poor service because the techs think that they don't matter as much as others. Treat every person well. You never know when a low-ranking user might get promoted into a key position. Treat all people like they are important in your life. They actually *are* important in your life. If it were not for them, you would not have a job.

Some techs think that the workplace is a good opportunity to meet mates. Go elsewhere for this kind of activity. Many people do not like getting harassed by members of the opposite sex. It can be an embarrassing situation for the user as well as the tech when this type of thing goes on. There are plenty of other places to meet mates. Take the high road and you can't go wrong.

Good rapport with a customer includes listening to their problems and solving the immediate problem and keeping their other annoying problems in the back of your mind. Go back and research the problem on the Internet or TechNet and give the customer a printout of the cause and cure. They will think you are great for this, and if they are ever in a meeting to discuss whether or not they should replace the techs in their company with a competitor, you can guess their answer.

Always think of what you are doing as a service-sector job. Think of all the people who are in the service sector that you have dealt with in your life. Think of the ten worst ones and then the ten best ones. What did the ten worst ones do to turn you off? Never do what they did to you. Now think of what the ten best people did. Concentrate on their behavior and act accordingly. What was it that they did right? How can you integrate this greatness into your own job? Maybe you will be on someone's ten-best list someday. The following checklist might help you make it there:

- ❏ The customer is always right.
- ❏ Treat the customer with respect.
- ❏ Always behave professionally.
- ❏ Always maintain the highest level of integrity.
- ❏ Ask for help if you can't solve a problem.
- ❏ Listen carefully to the customer and ask good questions.

- ❏ Practice good damage control with customers; make sure the customer is not going to complain to everyone about their problems.
- ❏ Ensure that the customers are satisfied when you leave.
- ❏ Always provide superb service, which is above and beyond average service.
- ❏ Don't jump to conclusions and make ungrounded assumptions.
- ❏ Don't be afraid to apologize and own up to your own mistakes.
- ❏ Try not to finger point.
- ❏ Keep accurate logs of repairs on each PC and consult these.
- ❏ Keep users up-to-date on issues that affect them.
- ❏ Do not assume that the customer is comfortable doing things that you might find are easy to do.
- ❏ Try to view things from the standpoint of the user. How would you like to be treated as a user?

Read books on customer relations. Ask other techs when they get a commendation for their work and what it is that they said and did. Also find out what techs did wrong when they get fired or have a customer relations problem so you can learn the pitfalls and avoid them.

Good rapport involves taking the time out to talk to the user about what they want to talk about. Even though you may be done with your repair, provided you are not swamped with work, give the user five minutes of your time and listen to what they have to say. Sometimes listening without even making any recommendations and judgments is what people really like. Think of a relative that you've had, or a friend who will always listen to whatever you say. Even though it may be wrong and the listener might think so, sometime the best listeners don't condemn you and let you find out for yourself that what you are saying is wrong.

Professional Conduct

Professional conduct is essential to understand and achieve in the computer services industry. This encompasses appearance, attitude, time management, integrity, and competence. All too often in this field there are technicians who don't take professionalism seriously. This can make a department, a company, or even collectively the whole industry look bad. Perception is reality to most people and the way that the customer sees you is how they make opinions about you and your department and field.

Appearance

Appearance is very important in the business world. The nature of the work of an A+ Certified Professional will often get you into offices that other people will never be able to get into. How often do people get 20 minutes to talk to the true titans of industry in a relaxed atmosphere? Well, when you are fixing their PCs, often they are there and it is your time to shine. In a situation like this, you are going to want to make sure that your appearance is the best it can be. You should smell nice (avoid strong fragrances) and wear nice clothes that match the dress of the corporation. Work to achieve an overall neat appearance. Think of how embarrassing it would be to watch a fellow employee go into a vice-president's office with their hair looking like a haystack. The higher up the ladder you go, the more important appearance is. These are the people who make corporate decisions about which company to have as their PC technicians. It would be a true shame to ruin your company's image by neglecting your personal appearance.

Attitude

Attitude is important when fixing computers. If you have a good attitude, the user is going to be friendlier and ultimately more satisfied with your work. If you have a lackadaisical attitude about what you are doing, then maybe PC repairs are not for you. Think of your job as fun and be enthusiastic and you will be amazed at how well users treat you.

This brings up the second point on attitude, which is confidence in what you are doing. If you have learned all that you should about computers, then there should be no reason not to be confident. This is not being a braggart or cocky, but having an attitude about yourself that makes users understand that you know what you are doing. This instills a sense of trust in them. It's very important to make the user feel this way about you seeing as you are handling very important data that they might have worked on for years.

Language

Your language is another way people read your attitude. Swearing is unprofessional. We've all seen all too often a frustrated technician swearing at the computer loud enough that the whole department can hear. What this tells people is that the technician has a bad attitude and they assume the technician is incompetent at fixing PCs. Think about it this way: If your physician was swearing and acting frustrated when he was doing a procedure on you, you'd probably be very scared. If you find yourself getting angry on the job and venting, you better ask yourself: Why am I being so negative? The key is to keep your negative emotions contained when you are at the customer's PC. A better place to let out your anger with the machine would be to go back and have a lively discussion with the other techs on what was causing you to be frustrated. PCs inevitably bring you to frustration on occasion. They are not perfect and there will always be problems that make absolutely no sense. Instead of letting the customer know that you have let the machine win, take a breather, do some research, call on your peers, consult TechNet; but don't swear, pout, or do anything that will make the customer think less of the top-notch service that you are capable of providing.

Don't Intrude

Time is a crucial variable that you need to master. Most people are very busy and they get paid by how much work they do. When you are working on their PC, they are usually not productive. It is important to minimize the time spent on each PC. This means that you should be able to anticipate what their problem is before you go over to fix it. In short, do whatever you can to be non-intrusive with the customer's time.

Speaking of non-intrusive, this is very important if you want to be professional. Sometimes work quarters are tight. Do not barge your way into the user's office and cram them in between the chair and desk. If they are on the phone when you go by to help them, either leave or wait far enough away from them so that they don't think that you are eavesdropping on their conversation. If they are in a meeting, do not interrupt them. You can walk by and gesture that you are there and give them enough time to either stop their conversation and welcome you in or schedule another meeting with you.

Patience

Another tricky problem that constantly happens is that the PC technician shows up but the user is not in. It is common for busy professionals to be pulled away or to forget about a service call. Always ask someone in a neighboring office if it is okay to go into the user's office. If you have not worked with the user or if you have any reservations about entering the workspace, then by all means don't go in—try to contact them another way. Make absolutely sure that you know what the problem is and it is the right computer. It's happened before: A tech fixes the wrong computer, only to find out that it was a laptop that the customer had with them that needed to be repaired. In corporations today, there are so many computers and printers around that if there is any slight chance of ambiguity in the user's complaint, do not proceed. Only proceed if the exact repair is obvious.

Integrity

Integrity goes hand-in-hand with professionalism. Integrity means that you are not going to compromise yourself or ask others to in order to achieve something. Never do anything that even appears to be compromising in terms of integrity. Obey all software copyright laws. Never try to break into anything you should not be getting into. If a person tracks the files that you have opened, and you are going into confidential files, you will not have a fun time explaining yourself. If you need a file with which to experiment, open a new one or ask the user what file it is okay to experiment with. Furthermore, make a copy of any file that you are testing, experimenting with, or modifying.

Integrity needs to be a part of software installation. Many organizations get audited for software compliance, and the penalties for unlicensed software are harsh. Get to know all of the rules for the software in your company. Find out what is site-licensed and what is individually licensed. Follow these rules to a "T." Do not install things that are not licensed. Do not bring in shareware for a user knowing that the trial agreement will be violated. Do not bring in bootleg copies of anything. There is now very sophisticated software that can audit each machine and find what does not belong. You will have a tough time explaining this to the user and your boss when these audits unearth something that should not be there in the first place.

This paragraph shouldn't even have to be written for professionals such as yourself. But it does need to be stated. Many times in the PC repair business, with all the expensive hardware around, someone may be tempted to take something home. I've seen thousands of dollars disappear out of rooms by way of hardware components. A trip to a local computer show inevitably unearths a tech who has taken a copy of all Microsoft Word disks that he installed on the computers at work and decided to go sell these at a show. Do not do this! You are a professional and have spent a long time preparing for this great career and it would be horrible to get caught doing something dishonest and have it on your permanent record. If you were hiring techs to handle your hundred-thousand-dollar servers, would you even fathom the idea of hiring a thief? Probably not. Always stay professional —your life will be less stressful and you'll be able to sleep at night. A great philosopher once wrote, "The most comfortable pillow in the world is a clear conscious." Heed these words and stay on the right side of things.

General Professionalism

Much of this chapter has been written about corporate PC repair. Most of the principles apply in other sectors. A person working in a retail setting should treat customers with honesty, integrity, and kindness. A person working in a corporation manufacturing PC equipment should respect their coworkers. They should also respect the way that things are organized and be well aware of company policy.

Business is business, and some things that you would do outside of a company, you would not do inside. Horseplay, pranks, and dirty jokes have no place in most corners of the business world. Stressed executives do not like to see people fooling around. Be aware of the culture in your company and behave accordingly. Some companies are more laid back than others, but be aware of how people act and try to emulate their behavior. Those who don't do this stick out like a sore thumb. These individuals are a definite liability to the corporation. It should go without saying that drugs and alcohol are not part of work life.

In short, professionalism is the image that you want to project. Look in any corporation, and you will soon realize that those who have climbed the ladder of success always act professionally and those who can't get there, don't. It is all in how far up in the business world you want to get. If you are not professional, you may end up in an empty room swapping computer boards all day. On the other hand, act professionally and you may end up being a leader of some sort.

Conflict Avoidance and Resolution

Conflicts can arise in the PC world for a variety of reasons. These are a challenge to your job security in terms of yourself and the rest of the techs. A bad conflict has the potential of harboring bad feelings between the parties for a long period of time. In the extreme, a conflict can get so bad that the users decide to get help elsewhere. Solve all conflicts to the best of your ability, and delegate them if you can't. Do not leave any conflicts unresolved over a long period of time. Also, *avoid* conflicts by not causing a conflict that does not need to happen.

exam
Watch

The customer is always right.

Problem PCs

There will always be a PC that nobody wants to touch. This can be because the software is strange or the hardware has been set up in an unorthodox way. Each person will pass the buck on this machine until it is just put on a back burner and nobody will touch it. Sometimes it may be that the user has such a bad attitude that nobody even wants to come close to him or her. If you have reason to believe that someone other than yourself would be more qualified to work on the machine, approach them. If the tech refuses to work on it, go to a higher authority—ask your boss what should be done. Do what you have to, but just make sure that there is an enforceable resolution. If someone has to get more training to work on this machine, let your boss know and they will usually finance this.

Company Policies

One of the most important things to learn when you are dealing with the computer end user is what your company's policies are regarding various computer-related topics. For example, with a computer, there will always be the employees who would like to play solitaire all day. Well, if the management does not care, fine. But, if the users are installing video games that are messing up the memory on the computers, or if the management does not want their employees playing games all day, then you have a situation where you, as the computer repair person, are going to have to figure out how to resolve the problem while letting management and the employees save face. In this particular situation, it is best to ask management about their policy and not tell them any names. If the company wants to get rid of games, then simply approach the game players and let them know that management has said that no machines are to have games, and you must disable them.

Other conflicts regarding company policy also tend to appear. One user may get one answer from someone while another user gets another answer. Learn company policies. If you work within the framework of what should be done in a circumstance, it gives you a feeling of confidence in what you say to the users. Users are always happy when you have answers ready to their questions on such items as who to call for passwords, hardware, and whatnot. Once you know these policies, you can solve conflict between users who are unsure of policy. In addition, you know how to approach varying situations.

Error Between Keyboard and Chair

One problem that every computer technician will eventually face is the EBKAC error. This is usually very easy to fix, but very difficult to explain. EBKAC is an acronym for Error Between Keyboard and Chair. This usually entails power cords being unplugged, no paper in printer, or power switches being turned off. This is usually quite embarrassing for the user, especially if they are watching the repair. In these situations, in order not to cause animosity, conflict, and other negative emotions, do whatever is in your power to have the user save face. Say something like "I see this type of thing all the time, they should have a light on the printer that says out of paper." Or for the power cord, tell them "The person vacuuming must have dislodged it. I know it is a pain, but if this happens again, could you please look behind the computer and see if the cord has become dislodged?" The user will obviously see what they did wrong and you just want to gracefully leave without making anyone feel stupid.

Know-It-All User

One conflict that will rear its ugly face every now and again is the know-it-all problem user. It seems like they must be technician wannabe's, and they will try and tell you what you, as a technician, are doing wrong and what should be done. Obviously, they don't know all the answers, or they would not have called you in to fix what has been messed up. These people are in need of attention and they must be handled at a very careful level so as not to cause any conflict. Because the customer is always right, never argue with their way of doing things. For example, if they are really convinced that there is not enough RAM and that is why they are getting memory errors in Excel (which you know isn't the case), tell them that you would like to change the memory swap file size. Do not get into the details of how a swap file works. Tweak a couple other things while you are at it. Delete all of the .TMP files. Optimize memory depending on the operating system. Explain to the user that this may indeed fix their problem and you would like them try it out for a few days before resorting to buying RAM. Just make sure that you are not trying to prove a point to the user. Let them understand that this is the departmental policy that software configuration and optimization should be tried before hardware installation.

Angry Users

Another conflict that needs to be resolved is the angry user who is ready to tell the world about his dissatisfaction. These users generally want to talk to the head honchos and anyone else who will listen about their woes. The key to these users is to resolve their anger before it mounts. Get to them quick and resolve the problem promptly and professionally. First of all, listen to their every beef and think of how you will solve their problem. Listen. Show respect for their ideas by giving each one consideration while remaining patient—it can be courageous. Users like this generally are satisfied when you go above and beyond the norm to finally solve their problems. Once they have finally expressed their anger, they generally calm down and are willing to sit down and resolve the problem. Don't point fingers at other people; they may just track down the person you are pointing at and chew them out. The key is controlling the situation. These people do not want excuses, they want resolutions. At this point, do whatever you have to do to please this user. Often, these people end up the most satisfied of all. They remember how they felt before you arrived and how they felt after.

Resolving Your Own Errors

Be willing to apologize for any mistake that you make. Nobody is perfect and we all make mistakes. As a technician you will inevitably mess something up. Make sure that you are willing to do whatever it takes to resolve what you messed up. Approach it professionally and find out what the problem is and fix it promptly. Computers can be surprising. You may fix one problem and cause a problem somewhere else. If the user is knowledgeable enough, explain why it was that you did not realize the side effect that resulted. Don't necessarily volunteer the fact that you messed it up, but if asked, admit that what you did caused the problem elsewhere. Unless grilled for a technical answer, try to keep your explanation understandable to the typical person.

Other Types of Conflict

Another form of conflict is the user who will stop you in the hall with many people around and loudly explain how his PC is messed up after you have left. Even if you know it is not your fault, never embarrass the user. Tell him that you will take a look at it and make sure it works properly. Many users get a kick out of humiliating the technician in front of their peers and the best defense is to act professionally and give an adequate resolution and avoid the situation. Do not let it get to you; some people have insecurities about themselves and they like to project them onto other people.

Many times you will find that you step right in the middle of conflict. One user may want you to do one thing and another will not want you to

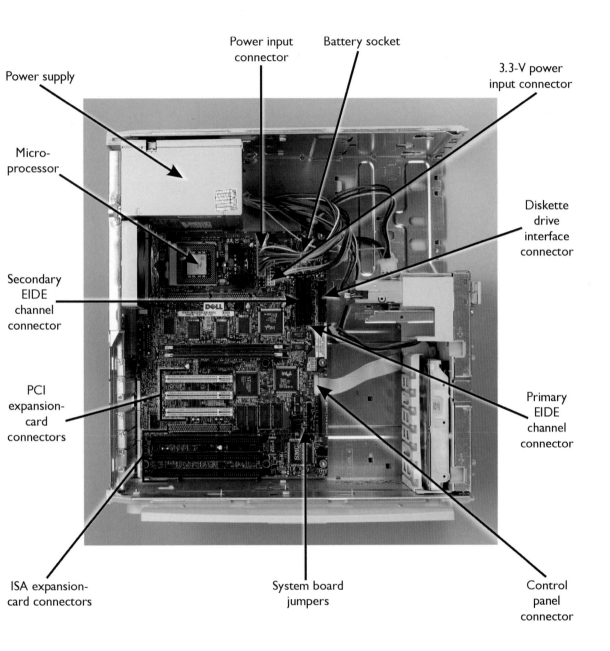

Power input
connector

Battery socket

3.3-V power
input connector

Power supply

Micro-
processor

Diskette
drive
interface
connector

Secondary
EIDE
channel
connector

PCI
expansion-
card
connectors

Primary
EIDE
channel
connector

ISA expansion-
card connectors

System board
jumpers

Control
panel
connector

A typical motherboard and its components (Figure 1-1)

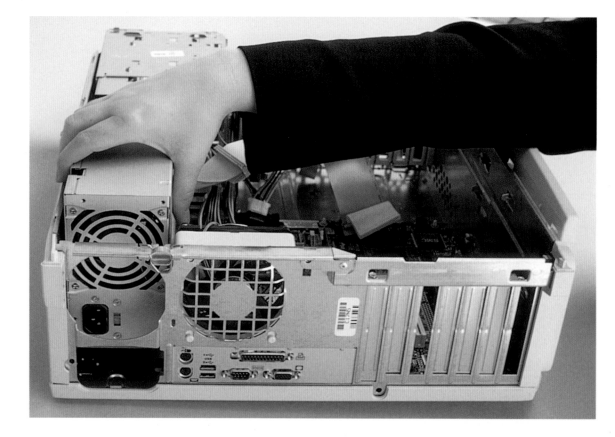

(Figure 1-2) Installing a power supply

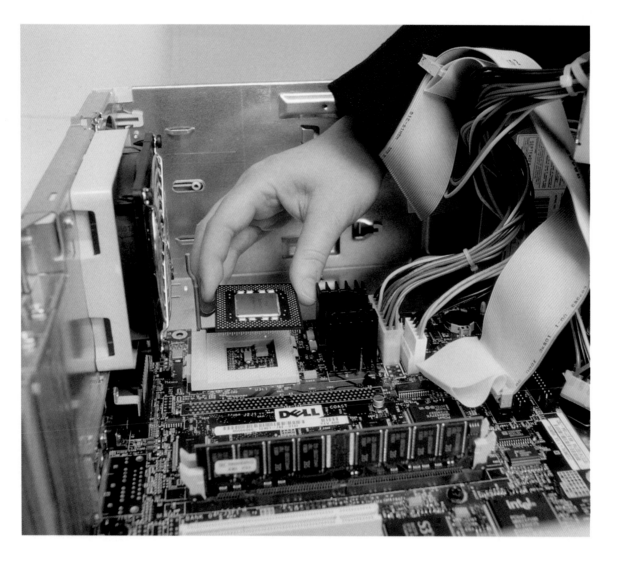

Installing a processor (Figure 1-3)

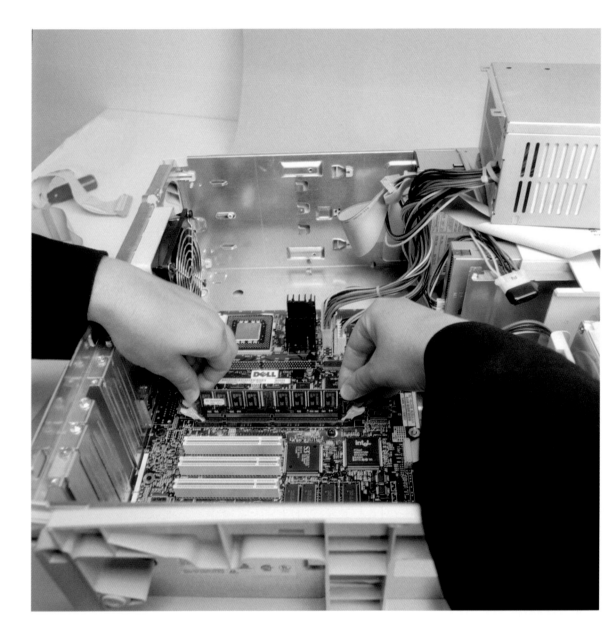

(Figure 1-4) Installing memory

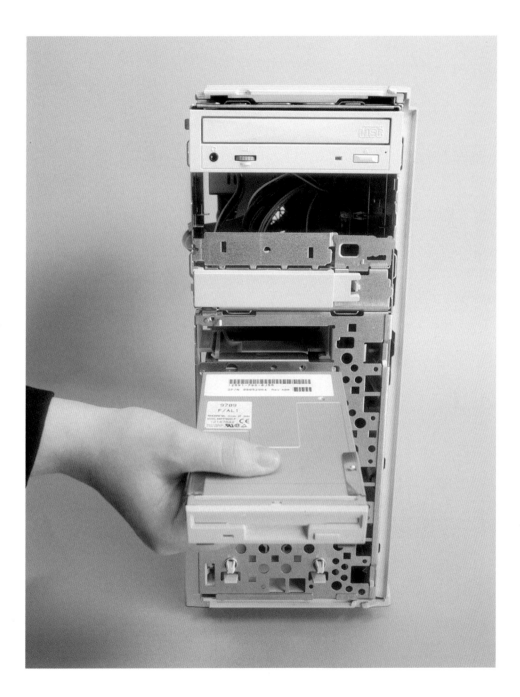

Installing a floppy drive (Figure 1-5)

(Figure 1-6) Installing a CD-ROM drive

Jumpers (Figure 1-7)

Seating an adapter card (Figure 1-8)

(Figure 1-10) Installing a hard drive

Power
input

Centronics
port

A typical printer's system board (Figure 5-1)

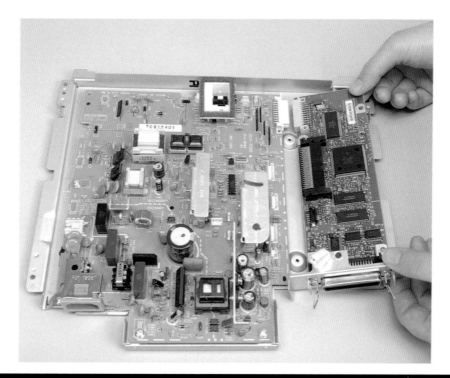

A printer's sub logic board (Figure 5-2)

Printer
motor

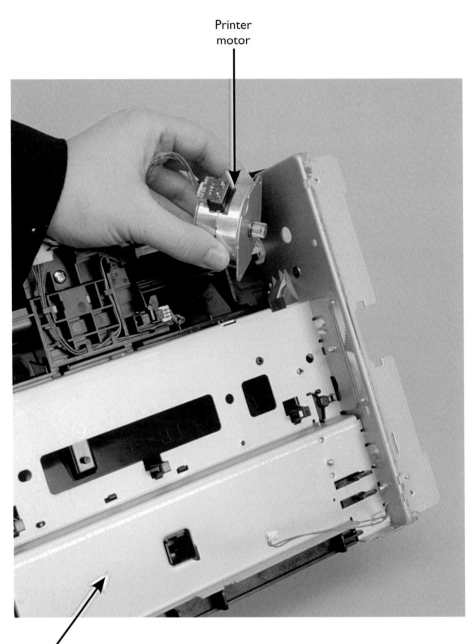

Paper
feed
frame

(Figure 5-3) Typical printer motor

Pickup roller assembly

Delivery assembly

Separation assembly

Printer rollers, front view (Figure 5-4)

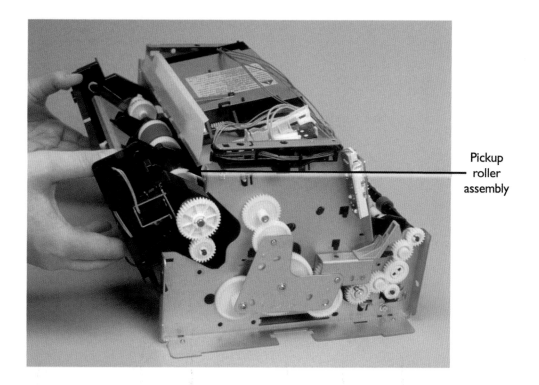

Pickup roller assembly

Printer rollers (assembly), side view (Figure 5-5)

Battery contacts

(Figure 6-1) Installing a portable system battery

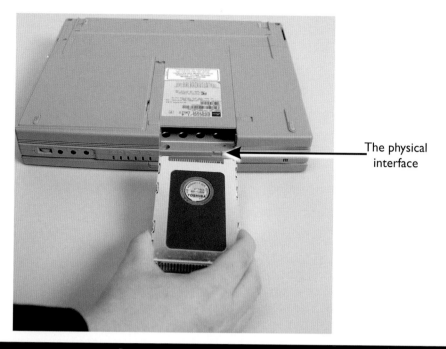

The physical
interface

Removing a hard drive from a portable system (Figure 6-3)

Push tabs   Type II PC Card

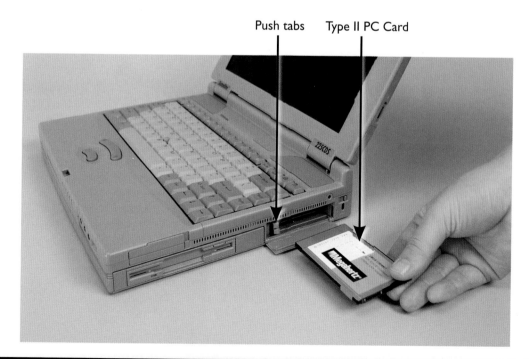

Installing a PC Card in a portable system (Figure 6-4)

Memory
module

Contacts

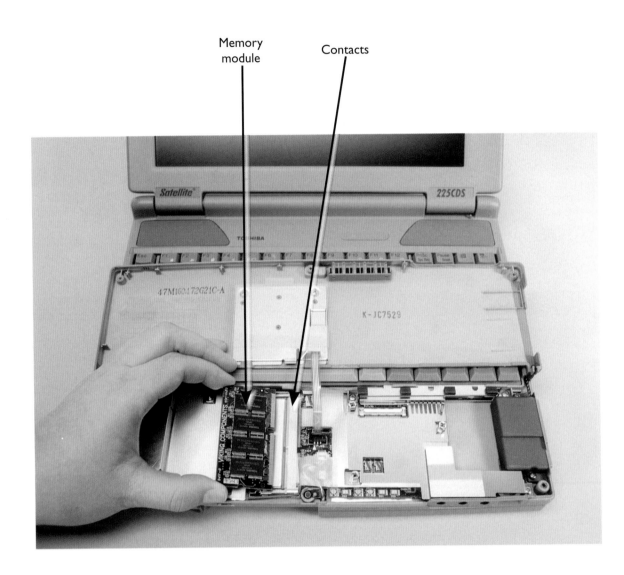

(Figure 6-5) Installing portable computer memory

do that thing. For instance, this may involve moving a computer to a different area. Users may even compete at trying to boss you around by telling you not to listen to what the other person is saying. In this kind of situation, never take a side. Tell them politely that you will wait for them to resolve their argument before you will do anything. If necessary, tell them you will come back at a later time when they finally settle their differences. This type of "not taking sides" is usually a good idea in most arguments when users try to get you in the middle. For example, when they are arguing if SCSI or non-SCSI is better, tell them the merits of both and the drawbacks, but don't side with any of the arguers. This may result in long-held resentment by the person with whom you did not side.

CERTIFICATION SUMMARY

The A+ exam has a pass/fail grading system. Your customer satisfaction questions will not count towards your passing or failing. The score, however, will be reported on the test report. More and more employers are demanding this skill from their technicians. This is a newly added section on the exam and it truly is a call from the employers saying that their technicians are not treating their customers correctly. Take this last lesson as more of a way to act than a way to get high scores on the exam. Just because you pass the exam and do your job thereafter does not guarantee you great promotions in the future. If you truly want to be a superstar in this field, take what has been said in this chapter and use your own knowledge and continue to pursue gaining more knowledge. Put these good techniques to work.

Questions on the exam will be mainly aimed at the following concepts:

- Communicating and listening (face-to-face or over the phone)
- Interpreting verbal and nonverbal cues
- Responding appropriately to the customer's technical ability
- Establishing personal rapport with the customer
- Conflict avoidance and resolution

When you are taking the exam, think of how the question is related to these concepts. Many of the answers will look obvious, but when you think about them, most of the obvious answers will have violated one of these principles. Read each question carefully.

In summary, communicating and listening is crucial if you are going to be able to truly understand what the client's wants, needs, and concerns are. Interpreting verbal and nonverbal cues is second nature for many and can be learned if you try to pay attention to them. Responding to the customer's level of technical skills is essential. It can save you much time and frustration when you can discern advanced users from beginning users. Advanced users can relate to information that, to beginners, seems like a bunch of jargon that is useless to them. Establishing rapport with your customer brings a harmony into the workplace that is desirable for both you and the customer.

Professional conduct will always reward you. Too many techs nowadays do not know how to behave as professionally as they could and end up sticking out like a sore thumb. Learn how to conduct yourself professionally with everyone you interact with and they will view you as a professional. Finally, you have learned about conflict avoidance and resolution. You can save your superiors innumerable headaches if you learn how to resolve conflict without it getting out of hand. Because there are so few techs representing such a large number of users, you are in the trenches for achieving overall satisfaction with the customer. Your superiors can promise whatever service they want to the customer on your behalf. The bottom line is that it is up to you to make the customer happy.

✓ TWO-MINUTE DRILL

- ❑ Customer satisfaction may look effortless to the inexperienced, but in reality, the art of achieving and maintaining a satisfied customer is as challenging as learning any computer technical skills.

- ❑ When you are done listening to the user and have asked all of your questions, paraphrase what the user has said and say it back to them.

❏ One thing that really makes users angry and usually ends up with a call to the help desk or worse, is when a technician does something to a PC and does not leave a note.

❏ Companies are not just interested in computer technicians who will fix their employee's computers, but in technicians who exhibit the highest respect for professionalism.

❏ When you're thinking about nonverbal cues, don't forget to notice the cues that you are projecting.

❏ Communication does not end at the user's desk; good communication between technicians is also essential.

❏ When approaching a user's desk for a repair, make sure they understand what you intend to do and what you expect from them to make the service successful.

❏ It is paramount to read all of a customer's verbal and nonverbal cues in order to make sure that things run smoothly.

❏ Don't assume anything when it comes to a customer's technical level.

❏ Many technicians jump to the conclusion that they can solve the problem before the user has completely discussed the problem. This is a big mistake and the consequences can be tragic.

❏ Nonverbal cues are quite possibly more important than verbal cues.

❏ You will always run into a user who is using a PC for the first time in their lives. Treat them kindly, patiently, and with respect.

❏ Good rapport involves taking the time out to talk to the user about what they want to talk about.

❏ Perception is reality to most people and the way that the customer sees you is how they make opinions about you and your department and field.

❏ When repairing a computer, let the user explain the problem fully before starting to work on it.

❏ Don't go for the misleading answer, which might solve the customer's problem right away; go for the one that maintains the customer satisfaction requirements.

❑   If you have learned all that you should about computers, then there should be no reason not to be confident, which instills a sense of trust in your users.

❑   Integrity means that you are not going to compromise yourself or ask others to in order to achieve something.

❑   The customer is always right!

❑   Solve all conflicts to the best of your ability, and delegate them if you can't.

❑   Avoid taking sides if you get caught in a conflict between two users. Wait for them to settle their differences before you approach the situation again.

SELF TEST

The following Self Test questions will help you measure your understanding of the material presented in this chapter. Read all the choices carefully, as there may be more than one correct answer. Choose all correct answers for each question.

1. The customer states that their problem is with the new monitor they installed and you know it is actually just the setting that needs to be changed. What do you do?

    A. Tell the customer it is just the settings and you'll fix those right away.

    B. Ask them why they think it is the monitor and then explain in technical detail the refresh rates and the drivers that need to be changed.

    C. Tell the user that there are monitor settings that you need to change. Explain to them that it is company policy to try and change the software before changing the hardware. Let them know that if it does not work, you will be more than willing to bring them a new monitor.

    D. Give them a new monitor.

2. You go into an office and see that the user is not in. You are supposed to increase his swap file. What should you do?

    A. Change the swap file size and restart computer.

    B. Close out and save relevant work, change the swap file, and restart the computer.

    C. Ask a neighboring user, if they are not busy, if they know when the user will be back and if they think it would be okay to go in and fix the computer.

    D. Leave a note for the user to page you when they are in so you can fix the PC.

3. A user is starting to ask you to customize their desktop after you fixed their printer. What do you do?

    A. Tell the customer that this was not on their work order and that they should figure it out themselves.

    B. Tell the customer you are busy and you will come back later to help them.

    C. Show the user how to go into the help program and search for Help on how to customize the desktop. Make sure that the user is comfortable in looking through Help and hopefully they will be more self-sufficient.

    D. Go ahead and customize things no matter how long it takes to complete this.

4. You have spent an hour trying to troubleshoot a new optical drive, which is the first one you have ever worked on. Things are not working right and the user is getting impatient. What do you do?

A. Inform the user that you are running into problems that you need to escalate to other techs. Contact your other techs and find out if anyone else has experience with this type of drive. If not, try to get the operating system functional without the drive and tell the user you will call back to arrange a future visit after you have researched the problem. At this point, you would call the company on your time and not theirs.

B. Keep working and tell the user that it should work shortly.

C. Read the 50-page manual on set-up and go though each step once again.

D. Call the company that manufactured the drive and stay on hold until they can help you.

5. The trouble ticket that you have been called on is a monitor that will not work. You enter the office and you notice a monitor that is unplugged. What should you do?

A. Ask the user what is wrong and listen to their long story about the monitor.

B. Plug the monitor back in and try to gracefully not let the user think he is stupid.

C. Ask the user what is wrong with the monitor and ask pertinent questions such as those inquiring about the state of the monitor before it went dead.

D. Tell the user that they should look at this type of thing before they call for service.

6. A user has a mysterious problem in Windows NT that you cannot pinpoint readily. You should:

A. Get the facts and research the problem on your own and go back to fix it when you get a solution.

B. Stay at the user's desk until you get the job done.

C. Cross examine the user and try and find out what they did wrong.

D. Both A and C.

7. You go into an office and the user's name is unpronounceable. What do you do?

A. Don't address them by their name.

B. Try your best to say the name.

C. Hope they introduce themselves.

D. Call them beforehand and let them know you are coming and write their name down phonetically.

8. You need to fix the PC of a Fortune 10 CEO and you were out late the night before. You did not have time in the morning to properly get ready for the day. What do you do?

A. Go to the bathroom to freshen up and comb your hair.

B. Go to the CEO's office anyway and let them accept you for who you are, not how you look.

C. Go home and take a shower.

D. Ask another tech if they would be willing to take this assignment for you.

9. A user is degrading you and saying you are stupid and although the customer is always right, you would like nothing more than to tell the user where they can go. What do you do?

A. Tell the user where they can go! You've earned enough respect on your job and nobody likes this user anyway.

B. Agree with all they say and just keep saying, "You are right."

C. Get another tech on the job; maybe their personalities will interact better.

D. Don't say anything, just get the work done and they will be happy.

10. A user is asking you how he can fix his son's PC at home. The problem sounds pretty complex. What do you do?

A. Stop what you are doing and go the extra mile for his son and write down all the steps needed to fix the PC.

B. Ask the user if they want to discuss it over lunch or during a break, when you don't have other customers to deal with.

C. Tell them that this is non-company business and they should not ask you this again.

D. Quickly tell them all that is needed to be done and hope they get it all.

11. A user is complaining that nothing is on his c:\ drive. Upon further investigation, you realize someone has typed format c: and furthermore you determine that this has occurred at a time when only the user would have been able to do this. What do you do?

A. Reprimand the user and let him know that your investigation has determined that he typed the format command.

B. Mumble something about beginning users and fix the problem.

C. Let the user know that the format command has been run, and even though you don't know who did it, you know that this command should not be run. Let the user know that he should make sure that anyone who is using his computer while he is away should not use this command.

D. Fix the problem and then rename the format command in DOS to a different name.

12. A user says that his Internet connection is not working and asks for your assistance. What do you do?

A. Check out the problem and fix it after they have explained the whole situation.

B. Tell them that they are not allowed to have Internet access and delete the software.

C. Know your software policies and know who is to have what. If he's not allowed Interent access, then delete the software after allowing the user to save his personal files from the software. Notify management if this is company policy.

D. Tell his boss and get him fired because he was not following the rules.

13. A user says that he should be given Microsoft Office Professional on his machine. Furthermore, the user states that his boss thinks he should get the Microsoft Professional installed. What do you do?

A. Because the customer is always right, install the software and assume they are telling the truth about their boss.

B. Immediately call their boss to verify this and then install the software.

C. Know company's policies beforehand. Find out if the user is licensed site-wide or per-individual for this software. If they are not licensed, know the channel to get them licensed and notify the proper people including the user on what is to be done before the install.

D. Because all companies are "site licensed," go ahead and install the software.

14. The user is complaining about a mouse that is shocking him once every half-hour or so. He says that it is an electrical charge. On inspection of the mouse, you see that there is no way in the world that the mouse wire would be shocking him. What do you do?

A. Believe the customer and get him a new mouse. Tell him that if the new one shocks him to call you back.

B. Because this is obviously ESD, make sure that the user is grounded.

C. Perform repeated tests on the mouse to try and replicate the problem.

D. Both A and B.

15. You are fixing a PC and the office workers are having an argument over who messed up the computer. You should:

A. Blame the person that has nonverbal guilt written on their face.

B. Get a hypothesis and then blame the user.

C. Try not to blame anyone and try and ensure that the users are aware of what potentially caused the problem.

D. Side with each user because the customer is always correct.

Part II

DOS/Windows
Examination

9

Function, Structure, Operation, and File Management

This chapter serves to introduce you to some of the inner workings of the PC. It provides an overview of some of the more popular operating systems and contrasts some of their differences. By the time you complete this chapter, you should be familiar with the basic structure and operation of both DOS and Windows.

CERTIFICATION OBJECTIVE 9.01

Functions of DOS, Windows 3.x, and Windows 95

By definition, an operating system (OS) is a set of computer instruction codes, usually *compiled* into executable files, whose purpose is to define input and output devices and connections, and provide instructions for the computer's central processor to operate on to retrieve and display data. The coding is usually broken down into many small, modular component files rather than a few large and complex files.

While there have been several competent, if not commercially successful, operating systems developed for the PC (CP/M, QDOS, NDOS, Dr. DOS, Geoworks, NeXTSTEP, among others), at this time, the PC workstation market belongs primarily to Microsoft, with DOS, Windows, and Windows NT maintaining a healthy market advantage over the various flavors of UNIX and IBM's OS/2. Originally, there were several vendors competing for a share in the "DOS wars," but Microsoft has since dominated the market with its various versions of MS-DOS. MS-DOS reached version 6.22 before being wholly incorporated into Windows 95 as version 7.

DOS is a widely used acronym for Disk Operating System. Microsoft was asked by IBM to develop a disk-based OS for the Personal Computer, which was still in development. Microsoft accepted this challenge and purchased a precursor to DOS from a Seattle company for $50,000. Microsoft modified this OS and created DOS 1.0.

DOS consists of a set of instruction files that include basic commands and drivers to allow a user to load and execute a set of computer instructions, also known as software. These instructions are loaded into the computer through multiple types of hardware devices and storage media.

DOS was created to give PC users easy access to applications and data stored on the PC's storage components. Given the limitations of the then-current hardware, it fulfilled its goal fairly well. It went through several development iterations before reaching a level of adequate device coverage and true stability. Through the use of its internal and external commands placed in scripting or batch files by systems programmers to provide simple task-selection menus, the vagaries of DOS became mostly invisible to the majority of computer users.

At the time DOS was first developed, floppy disks and cassette tapes were the only storage media available for the PC. Hard drives, often known as "Winchesters," taken from the name of one of the first successful manufacturers, were soon to be supported. Modified from their eight-inch version size, used in the large system world, hard drives were changed to fit the smaller PC format.

As DOS has evolved over the years, it has grown to support a multitude of other components, such as sound devices, scanners, CD-ROMs, tape drives, and so forth. It has also been modified to make provisions for networking activity. While most of that function has been off-loaded by the various vendors whose subsistence is drawn from network development, Microsoft has been a networking player since its inception, and the networking capabilities of both Windows and Windows NT are unmatched in their support for most every available networking hardware item.

DOS provides a fairly complete set of utilities and commands to perform most computer operations. However, two of its inherent limitations were that it was text-based, requiring strings of commands to be entered to perform the simplest of tasks, necessitating in-depth knowledge of the command structure and syntax, and that it only allowed a single application to be loaded and executed.

Through research done by the XEROX Corporation's Palo Alto Research Center (PARC) into computer usage, it was demonstrated that through the use of a graphical computer environment, users could achieve a much higher level of production due to the enhanced accessibility of an application's components and features. Developing graphical applications with what was to be known as a "Common User Interface," where the access to compatible features remained consistent across the various applications, provided further enhancement.

This idea was seized on by both Apple Computer with its Macintosh computer, unveiled in the mid-1980s and shipped complete with a graphical OS, and Microsoft, who teamed with IBM to develop their own version of a graphical environment. This co-development became Windows. Version 1.0 of Windows hit the streets in 1985, with a resounding thud. While the Macintosh was delivered from the start with hardware capable of supporting the new graphical environment, Microsoft had the baggage of an already-installed user base of millions of computers already geared to text-based computing. Unlike the Macintosh, whose OS was included and preinstalled since its origin, DOS and Windows are (or were) additional-cost options, licensed separately from the PC on which they resided. These days, most systems vendors preinstall a copy of DOS and/or Windows prior to shipment, and include the cost of the license in their "system package."

Unlike the Mac, with its Motorola 680XX series processors, neither the Intel 8088 microprocessor nor the then-current CGA video standard were capable of better than meager support for high-level graphics. It took the development of the 80286 microprocessor and EGA graphics to get Windows off the ground, and the 80386 and VGA to ensure its success.

Continuous improvements in available system "horsepower" meant that the development of a next-generation OS was needed to take better advantage of the burgeoning hardware and applications that were becoming available for the PC. Microsoft and IBM teamed up together to create a new, more powerful version of DOS and Windows to leverage the new hardware.

DOS was developed as a *16-bit* application, with its internal code segments written to be accessed 16 bits at a time. This fit the 808X processor and memory format. Once Intel moved on to its 80X86 architecture, the processor and system memory were then able to read and write 32 bits of data per clock cycle. The two giants were determined to develop a completely new 32-bit OS that would take full advantage of this feature, and yet would be backward-compatible with all existing DOS and Windows software. This new OS was to become OS/2.

The Microsoft/IBM alliance ended in 1989, when it was decided by both companies in a much-publicized battle to split their development of OS/2. IBM was to keep all rights to existing and future versions of OS/2, and Microsoft got exclusive rights to Windows and further Windows development, soon to be known as Windows NT (New Technology).

The second limitation of DOS, single-task usage, also was hammered down. While a microprocessor could only operate on a single set of instructions (not true now, because Pentium-class processors can now "pipeline" up to 4 concurrent operations) at any given moment, given their speed, task-switching became possible at a rate that produced the effect of multi-tasking. This ability allowed several applications to be loaded into memory concurrently, and a user could then easily switch between them. Windows, OS/2, and the Macintosh, along with some DOS vendors (notably Quarterdeck with its Deskview software) could not only handle the access, but also provided an easy method to exchange data between the concurrently loaded applications. Known as cut and paste, a user could select data, make a copy in memory, and then place the data (usually with its formatting characteristics) into a different application. This made juggling such things as e-mail use, database access, document creation, and event scheduling a snap.

Unlike Windows NT and IBM's OS/2, which are true and complete OSs, Windows (up to Windows 95) is a graphical shell that overlays on DOS, and relies on DOS for its low-level device access. It even requires a separate license from DOS. In order to install Windows (pre-95), a user first had to install a working copy of DOS to the PC. Even though Windows 95 was created to eliminate a requirement for DOS and its reliance on a 16-bit architecture, it still relies on several DOS components, mostly for compatibility reasons. It now also includes the needed DOS components under the same installation and license, and doesn't require a preexisting copy of DOS. The majority of its internal operations are performed 32 bits wide.

CERTIFICATION OBJECTIVE 9.02

Operating System's Files and Structure

Operating systems provide both system access and a set of utilities. The *core* files are also known as the *system* files.

System Files

System files are responsible for all device access and user interface presentation. While they may require the use of additional device drivers for specific hardware items, by themselves they can start up (boot, or IPL) a computer and give a user some access to direct some specific actions.

These core files are listed in the following sections, along with a brief explanation of their function and contents.

DOS

DOS system files include the following:

- AUTOEXEC.BAT
- CONFIG.SYS
- IO.SYS
- MSDOS.SYS
- COMMAND.COM
- HIMEM.SYS
- EMM386.EXE
- ANSI.SYS

AUTOEXEC.BAT is located and automatically executed in the ROOT directory at startup. This file contains commands to modify the PC environment (PATH, COMSPEC, other SET commands), and to execute applications. It can be used to create a menu system, prompt for user input, or *call* other batch files to maintain a modular structure. By default, it carries no attributes, and is NOT required for OS startup.

CONFIG.SYS is located in the ROOT directory and loaded by MSDOS.SYS. This file loads low-level device drivers for specific hardware, and adjusts several system parameters for performance tuning and memory usage. By default, it carries no attributes, and is *not* required for OS startup. Since version 6.*x*, it also may be used in conjunction with an internal menu system to select multiple startup configurations.

IO.SYS is located in the ROOT directory, and defines basic input/output routines for the processor. By default, it carries the hidden, system, and read-only attributes, and *is* required for OS startup.

MSDOS.SYS is located in the ROOT directory, and defines system file locations. By default, it carries the hidden, system, and read-only attributes, and is required for OS startup.

COMMAND.COM is located and automatically executed in the ROOT directory at startup. This file contains the internal command set and error messages. By default, it carries no attributes, and is required for OS startup. It may be executed from a different location and/or renamed if a SHELL command statement is placed in the CONFIG.SYS file pointing to the correct location and name.

e x a m
Ⓦ a t c h

COMMAND.COM displays the DOS prompt.

HIMEM.SYS and EMM386.EXE control memory management and are located in the \DOS directory (\WINDOWS directory in Windows 95). They are not required for system startup (pre-95) and are explained in detail in Chapter 10.

ANSI.SYS is located in the DOS directory and loaded by CONFIG.SYS if required. This file loads an extended character set for use by DOS and DOS applications that includes basic drawing and color capabilities. Normally used for drawing and filling different boxes for menu systems, it is seldom in use today. By default, it carries no attributes, and is not required for OS startup.

Windows 3.x

Windows 3.x system files include the following:

- WIN.INI
- SYSTEM.INI
- USER.EXE
- GDI.EXE
- KRNLXXX.exe (KRNL286.EXE for 80286 processors and KRNL386 for 80386)
- WIN.COM

The WIN.INI file contains configuration information for Windows applications. Errors made in this file seldom have global implications to Window's operation, but can cripple specific applications or features. Printing is also controlled by settings in this file. The WIN.INI file is dynamic, and records the way the user configures how the system looks and behaves. The spacing of the icons, the type of wall paper, screen colors, and other interface features can be customized in the WIN.INI file. This file, as well as the SYSTEM.INI file, are ASCII text files.

The SYSTEM.INI file configures Windows to address specific hardware devices and their associated settings. Errors in this file can and do cause Windows to fail to start, or crash unexpectedly.

The rest of the Windows startup components are explained in detail in the "Components of DOS, Windows 3.x, and Windows 95" section, later in this chapter.

Windows 95

The Windows 95 system files include the following:

- IO.SYS
- MSDOS.SYS
- COMMAND.COM
- WIN.INI

- SYSTEM.INI

- SYSTEM.DAT

- USER.DAT

Because Windows 95 no longer relies on a separate copy of DOS, the fundamentals have changed. While IO.SYS and COMMAND.COM remain for compatibility reasons, MSDOS.SYS no longer contains system code, but allows for special system settings to be user-defined. WIN.INI and SYSTEM.INI are mostly vestigial, allowing for 16-bit (pre-WIN95) applications to still be able to register system variables. The bulk of configuration has now shifted to the SYSTEM.DAT and USER.DAT files. Also, while not listed here, the kernel file, KRNL386.EXE, still teams up with USER.EXE and GDI.EXE to deliver the complete Windows OS.

Components of DOS, Windows 3.*x*, and Windows 95

Because DOS and Windows share a common development heritage and supported hardware, it shouldn't come as a surprise that they share much of the same structure.

DOS installs onto a formatted disk by placing its system files in the root directory. Its external command set and device drivers are then, by default, placed in a directory named DOS just off the root. During installation, an alternate path and name can be chosen, but straying from this default usually leads to trouble.

WIN.COM is a file created by the Setup program when first installing Windows. You won't find a WIN.COM file on any of the distribution media. During installation, Setup takes three files and combines them together to form the WIN.COM file.

When "WIN" is typed on the command line and the ENTER key is pressed, WIN.COM performs three functions. The first function of the WIN.COM is to ascertain what type of processor is in the computer. The file WIN.CNF, also located in the Windows\System subdirectory, performs this function.

The second function that WIN.COM performs is to switch the computer into the appropriate graphics mode by loading a *.LGO file for the logo display. The *.LGO file is selected based on the type of video card Setup determined was in the computer during installation. Setup selects only one graphics mode and adds it to the WIN.COM file. The following files are used by Windows Setup to create WIN.COM. Note that the file used in the creation of WIN.COM is dependent upon the video driver chosen during the setup process. Windows 95 leaves the logo file out of WIN.COM, and moves it to the root directory as LOGO.SYS.

- VGALOGO.LGO for VGA, Super VGA, or 8514/A displays
- EGALOGO.LGO for EGA color displays
- EGAMONO.LGO for EGA monochrome displays
- CGALOGO.LGO for CGA, EGA B&W (64K), and Plasma displays
- HERCLOGO.LGO for Hercules Monochrome Graphics displays

The third function WIN.COM performs is to load the bitmapped graphic advertisement that Windows displays. The file displayed is in a compressed format with a RLE, Run Length Encoded, extension. Setup selects only one of the following available choices and installs it into the WIN.COM file and into the Windows\System subdirectory:

- VGALOGO.RLE for VGA, Super VGA, or 8514/A displays
- EGALOGO.RLE for EGA color displays
- EGAMONO.RLE for EGA monochrome displays
- CGALOGO.RLE for CGA, EGA B&W (64K), and Plasma displays
- HERCLOGO.RLE for Hercules Monochrome Graphics displays

After the three functions of WIN.COM are completed, WIN.COM hands the control of Windows over to either DOSX.EXE (for Standard mode) or WIN386.EXE (for Enhanced mode). Because Windows 95 no longer supports Standard mode, DOSX.EXE has been removed. WIN386.EXE switches the CPU to protected mode, thereby enabling advanced features such as access to all memory in the computer. Windows then loads its kernal, either KRNL286 or KRNL386, and starts a configuration and initialization process. It reads the values stored in the SYSTEM.INI file, and loads the specified device drivers for the display, keyboard and mouse, and other devices. These files include SYSTEM.DRV, KEYBOARD.DRV, MOUSE.DRV, VGA.DRV, MMSOUND.DRV, and COMM.DRV. Basic screen fonts and fonts for DOS applications are loaded next. If VGA mode is selected, the required fonts loaded are VGASYS.FON and VGAOEM.FON for DOS and FONTS.FON, VGAFIX.FON, and OEMFONTS.FON for Windows. The graphics subsystem is then loaded along with the user interface. These files are GDI.EXE and USER.EXE. The display driver, DISPLAY.DRV (used as a label here; the actual driver name will vary) is then loaded. This allows the other drivers to display an error message on screen if they fail to initialize during the next step. Once the DISPLAY.DRV is in control, messages go through Windows. Windows then initializes all drivers and then all fonts.

In the last phase of initialization, Windows 3.x starts a desktop manager, usually Program Manager (PROGMAN.EXE), the default shell that Windows uses unless another desktop manager has been selected in the SYSTEM.INI file. PROGMAN.EXE finishes the Windows initialization by running any startup applications specified in the WIN.INI file, and by starting any applications whose icons are stored in the StartUp Group. The last action PROGMAN.EXE takes is to display its own menus and interfaces for use of the system.

Windows 95 performs much of the same rituals; however, it runs only in *protected mode*, so there is only one kernel, and the WIN.COM file no longer supports switches for *real* or *standard* mode. It still reads the SYSTEM.INI and WIN.INI files, and runs whatever applications are listed in the StartUp folder. The big change, though, is the reliance on the system Registry. Windows 3.x began the move to a Registry-based startup with a REG.DAT file, mostly used to support individual application parameters for Dynamic Data Exchange (DDE). This concept was greatly expanded for Windows NT, and then moved to Windows 95 as well. The Registry is a complex database of settings pertaining to both applications and hardware.

CERTIFICATION OBJECTIVE 9.03

File Allocation Tables, Formatting, and Partitioning

Using the FDISK (for Fixed DISK) utility provided with DOS, a hard drive is prepared for use through the acts of *partitioning* and *formatting*. A partition is created to separate a single physical drive into multiple logical components. Each partition receives a letter, beginning with C:. If a second drive is installed, it is assigned the letter D: automatically. The third becomes E:, and so forth. Additional partitions may be created as desired until the entire drive (or drives) has been allocated. So that the computer knows where to start, one of the partitions (typically C:, but there are sometimes reasons to select a different partition) *must* be set as "active" with FDISK in order to boot from the hard drive.

Various versions of DOS have been stretched to their limit by the ever-expanding capacities of hard drives. In the early days of DOS, circa 1981, a large hard drive was 10 megabytes (MB). Today, drives for home computers are approaching 10 Gigabytes (GB) at about the same cost (~$400). This represents a 10,000 times increase of in storage capacity.

Once partitioned, a drive must be *formatted.* This process divides the drive logically into groups of sectors and tracks. Sector size is usually set at 512 bytes, and physically varies in size depending on whether the sector's track is located in the inner or outer portion of the drive platter. Hard drives consist of a number of platters rotating on a common spindle, with read/write heads mounted on a pivoting assembly that spans all platters concurrently. The sectors are combined logically into groups called *clusters*. When the partition is formatted, an array of addresses that correspond to the physical starting locations of each cluster is created. Known as the File Allocation Table, or FAT, it becomes the pointer for DOS to locate information on the drive.

Due to a limitation in DOS's heritage ("who'da thunk anyone'd need any more?"), the FAT on each hard drive partition can catalog 65,535 (roughly 64K) individual addresses. Depending on the size of the partition, the 64K limit dictates the number of sectors, and therefore the size of each cluster. The cluster is the smallest accessible unit to DOS from the FAT of a hard drive. The smallest cluster used by DOS contains four 512-byte sectors, or 2048 bytes (2KB). Times 65,535, once you reach a partition size of >128MB, cluster size jumps to 4096 (4KB). At >256MB, the jump is to 8KB clusters, at 512MB it goes to 16KB, at 1GB to 32KB, and so forth. Up until recently, DOS wouldn't support a partition greater than 2GB.

These increasing cluster sizes have an inherent drawback, the concept of *slack*. *Slack* is the space left between the end of a file and the end of the cluster in which the file resides. Because the smallest addressable unit is the cluster, once a file is written to a cluster, the cluster is marked as used and can't have anything else written to it until the file in it is erased or overwritten by another copy of the same file. For large files that span several clusters, this is of little consequence. However, say you write a batch file that has 5 lines of code, perhaps 150 bytes in all. When you save the file on a 1GB partition, you've just wasted about 32,000 bytes of space. Multiply this by the literally thousands of small (<2KB) files found on a typical PC, and you can see why it's a good thing large drives have gotten cheap.

When formatting, or afterwards if desired, the partition marked as active must have an operating system installed. In the case of DOS, the *FORMAT C: /S* command formats the C: (boot) drive and puts the DOS system files on the hard drive. At the same time, it puts a pointer in a special location, known as the *boot sector,* which is located in the first cluster on the boot partition. This pointer tells the processor exactly where to find the system files. If for some reason this cluster becomes unusable, the drive can no longer be accessed by DOS. If you choose to add the system files at a later time, the SYS command can be used to reinitialize the boot sector and place the DOS system files in the root directory. Let's try that now, okay? Go to the DOS prompt on your C: drive and type FORMAT C: /S. Just Kidding.

Root Directories, Folders, and Subfolders

Each logical drive contains an initial, or root, directory that is created when it is formatted. Each root directory can hold up to 512 files or other (sub)directories. Also known as folders and subfolders, the files and folders combine into a hierarchical tree known as the directory tree. In DOS, both files and folders are limited to eight characters to the left of a period and three characters to the right, also known as 8 dot 3 naming. The total possible length of a file name, including its *path*, is 128 characters. This is known as the "fully qualified path." In practice, it's best to limit the fully qualified path to less than 60 characters, else some older applications and utilities can display anomalous behavior.

CERTIFICATION OBJECTIVE 9.04

Managing Files and Directories in DOS/Windows

From the DOS command line, there are several commands used to create and manage files and directories. Table 9-1 shows some of the DOS commands. You can get the information listed here at any time by issuing the command with a "/?" extension and pressing the ENTER key. First, in order to change from one drive to another, type in the drive letter to change to, followed by a colon (i.e., to change to drive D, type D: and press the ENTER key).

exam
ⓦatch

Know the command line switches for the XCOPY command very well.

Command Syntax

As you can see from the previous examples, most commands include an array of possible options that are accessed by command line *switches*. These switches are usually preceded by a slash (/), although some use a dash (-). It was the reliance on slash-triggered switches that forced the DOS developers to use the backslash character to distinguish subdirectories. When executing any .BAT, .COM, or .EXE file, the extension may be dropped. Be aware though that there is a hierarchy to execution if multiple commands with the

TABLE 9-1 DOS Command Reference

Command	Command Type	Action Performed	Available Command-Line Switches	Syntax
CD (or CHDIR)	Internal	Displays the name of or changes the current directory	Specifies that you want to change to the parent directory. Type CD drive: to display the current directory in the specified drive. Type CD without parameters to display the current drive and directory.	CHDIR [drive:][path] CHDIR[..] CD [drive:][path] CD[..]
COPY	Internal	Copies one or more files to another location. **Notes:** DOES NOT COPY SUBDIRECTORIES. The switch /Y may be preset using the COPYCMD environment variable. This may be overridden with /-Y on the command line. To append files, specify a single file for destination, but multiple files for source (using wildcards or file1+file2+file3 format). (This is also known as concatenation.)	source Specifies the file or files to be copied. /A Indicates an ASCII text file. /B Indicates a binary file. Destination Specifies the directory and/or filename for the new file(s). /V Verifies that new files are written correctly. /Y Suppresses prompting to confirm you want to overwrite an existing destination file. /-Y Causes prompting to confirm you want to overwrite an existing destination file.	COPY [/A │ /B] source [/A │ /B] [+ source [/A │ /B] [+ ...]] [destination [/A │ /B]] [/V] [/Y │ /-Y] Also; related environment variable, COPYCMD
DIR	Internal	Displays a list of files and subdirectories in a directory. **Notes:** Switches may be preset using the DIRCMD environment variable. You may override preset switches by prefixing any switch with - (hyphen)—for example, /-W.	[drive:][path][filename] Specifies drive, directory, and/or files to list. (Could be enhanced file specification or multiple filespecs.) /P Pauses after each screenful of information. /W Uses wide list format. /A Displays files with specified attributes. *Attributes* D Directories R Read-only files H Hidden files A Files ready for archiving S System files - Prefix meaning not /O List by files in sorted order. *Sortorder* N By name (alphabetic) S By size (smallest first) E By extension (alphabetic) D By date & time (earliest first) G Group directories first - Prefix to reverse order A By Last Access Date (earliest first) /S Displays files in specified directory and all subdirectories.	DIR [drive:][path][filename] [/P] [/W] [/A[[:]attributes]] [/O[[:]sortorder]] [/S] [/B] [/L] [/V] [/4]

TABLE 9-1   DOS Command Reference (continued)

Command	Command Type	Action Performed	Available Command-Line Switches	Syntax
DIR (continued)			/B Uses bare format (no heading information or summary). /L Uses lowercase. /V Verbose mode. /4 Displays year with 4 digits (ignored if /V also given).	
DEL (or ERASE)	Internal	Deletes one or more files.	[drive:][path]filename specifies the file(s) to delete. Specify multiple files by using wildcards. /P Prompts for confirmation before deleting each file.	DEL [drive:][path]filename [/P] ERASE [drive:][path]filename [/P]
MOVE	External	Moves files and renames files and directories.	[drive:][path]filename Specifies the location and name of the file or files you want to move. Destination Specifies the new location of the file. Destination can consist of a drive letter and colon, a directory name, or a combination. If you are moving only one file, you can also include a filename if you want to rename the file when you move it. [drive:][path]dirname1 Specifies the directory you want to rename. dirname2 Specifies the new name of the directory. /Y Suppresses prompting to confirm creation of a directory or overwriting of the destination. /-Y Causes prompting to confirm creation of a directory or overwriting of the destination.	To move one or more files: MOVE [/Y	/-Y] [drive:][path]filename [[,...]] destination To rename a directory: MOVE [/Y	/-Y] [drive:][path]dirname1 dirname2
MD or MKDIR	Internal	Displays the name of or changes the current directory.	None available	MKDIR [drive:]path MD [drive:]path
REN or RENAME	Internal	Renames a file/directory or files/directories.	None available	RENAME [drive:][path][directoryname1	filename1] [directoryname2	filename2] REN [drive:][path][directoryname1	filename1] [directoryname2	filename2]

TABLE 9-1 DOS Command Reference *(continued)*

Command	Command Type	Action Performed	Available Command-Line Switches	Syntax
XCOPY	External	Copies files and directory trees.	Source Specifies the file(s) to copy. Destination Specifies the location and/or name of new files. /A Copies files with the archive attribute set, doesn't change the attribute. /M Copies files with the archive attribute set, turns off the archive attribute. /D:date Copies files changed on or after the specified date. If no date is given, copies only those files whose source time is newer than the destination time. /P Prompts you before creating each destination file. /S Copies directories and subdirectories except empty ones. /E Copies directories and subdirectories, including empty ones. Same as /S /E. May be used to modify /T. /W Prompts you to press a key before copying. /C Continues copying even if errors occur. /I If destination does not exist and copying more than one file, assumes that destination must be a directory. /Q Does not display file names while copying. /F Displays full source and destination file names while copying. /L Displays files that would be copied. /H Copies hidden and system files also. /R Overwrites read-only files. /T Creates directory structure, but does not copy files. Does not include empty directories or subdirectories. /T /E includes empty directories and subdirectories. /U Updates the files that already exist in destination. /K Copies attributes. Normal Xcopy will reset read-only attributes. /Y Overwrites existing files without prompting. /-Y Prompts you before overwriting existing files. /N Copy using the generated short names.	XCOPY *source* [*destination*] [/A | /M] [/D[:*date*]] [/P] [/S [/E] [/W] [/C] [/I] [/Q] [/F] [/L] [/H] [/R] [/T] [/U] [/K] [/N]

same extension are in the same directory (or are executed from a different directory and are in the DOS path). For example, say you issue the NET command from the command line. There may be a NET.COM, NET.BAT, and NET.EXE file all in the path. DOS looks first for .COM files, then .EXE files, then .BAT files. If you ever execute a command and get strange results, be sure and check for the presence of another command with the same name, but a different extension.

Internal Versus External Commands

If you notice, the commands shown in Table 9-1 are listed as either internal or external. Internal commands are present in the COMMAND. COM shell, and can be executed on the command line at any time from any directory location. External commands are those that reside in the DOS directory. External commands must be executed either from there, or from any subdirectory if the DOS directory is included in the DOS path (see PATH Command), or by preceding the command with the fully qualified path to the DOS directory (e.g., C:\DOS\XCOPY).

File Naming Conventions

File management is crucial for the rapid retrieval of information. One method used to organize data is to use logical filenames within the boundaries set by the operating system.

DOS and Windows 3.1 were limited to what is termed an 8.3 (8 "dot" 3) file naming specification. This meant that no filename could exceed eight characters followed by a period and up to three more characters (i.e. FILENAME.EXT). There was also no provision by the operating system for mixed-case names. Everything was in uppercase.

When Windows 95 and Windows NT entered the desktop realm, these limitations were eliminated. Windows 95 and Windows NT provide long filename support on FAT. This essentially links directory entries within the FAT together to create a long filename (up to 250 characters) with mixed case and spaces. Windows NT also provides long filename support with its native file system, NTFS (NT File System).

File Types and Formats

You can save or rename any file to most any combination of eight letters or numbers, a period, and then add a three-letter (or number or combo) extension. DOS only performs an action on certain files based on their three-letter extension. .COM, .EXE, and .BAT files are known as executables. These are the only files that can be executed (or "run") by the computer. These executables can then include additional data or functions by loading additional files. Rather than putting all available functions into a single huge executable file, most developers choose to modularize their applications by creating library files that include additional commands and functions. These additional executable enhancement files are usually referred to as *overlays*. These files usually have a .BIN or .OVL extension. Windows took this one step further and developed *Dynamic Linked Libraries* (.DLL files). These overlays have the additional benefit of being shareable by all of the applications loaded in Windows.

There are additional "conventions" to file naming, but none that must be adhered to at the OS level. Device drivers usually end in .DRV. You can usually count on .TXT and .DOC files to be documents, .HLP to be help files, and so forth.

On the other hand, software applications are usually sticklers at requiring a certain extension to be recognized as a valid file to be opened by the application. Some applications allow the importing of data from several different file types.

Read Only, Hidden, System, and Archive Attributes

Each file accessible to DOS, regardless of media type, has four attributes that may be associated with it. These attributes are READ ONLY, HIDDEN, SYSTEM, and ARCHIVE.

The READ ONLY (RO) attribute prevents a user or application from inadvertently deleting or changing a file. If set, the attribute must be removed before the file can be deleted or overwritten. If the attribute is removed, the file then has READ/WRITE capabilities (RW).

The HIDDEN (H) attribute keeps a file from being displayed when a DIR command is issued. It also prevents the file from being acted upon by standard DOS commands, such as COPY or XCOPY. Some *third-party* applications ignore the HIDDEN attribute, and will operate on the files regardless, but this is rare.

The SYSTEM attribute is usually set by DOS or Windows, and can be modified using ATTRIB or File Manager. SYSTEM files are hidden by the operating system, which helps prevent accidental deletion.

The ARCHIVE attribute is set automatically when a file is created or modified, and is automatically removed by back-up software when the file is backed up.

CERTIFICATION OBJECTIVE 9.05

Viewing and Changing File Attributes

File attributes can be viewed from DOS using either the DIR or ATTRIB command. Windows users can use either File Manager (all versions) or Windows Explorer in Windows 95 to both view and/or modify the attributes of selected files.

Use ATTRIB.EXE

The ATTRIB command displays or changes file attributes, such as the following:

```
ATTRIB [+R | -R] [+A | -A] [+S | -S] [+H | -H]
[[drive:][path]filename] [/S]
```

- ■ +   Sets an attribute.
- ■ -   Clears an attribute.
- ■ R   Read-only file attribute.
- ■ A   Archive file attribute.

- **S**   System file attribute.

- **H**   Hidden file attribute.

- **/S**   Processes files in all directories in the specified path.

Notice this last switch. When using the ATTRIB command on a set of files, using the + will add the attribute to the file, and – will subtract that attribute. For example, the ATTRIB –S <path>\filename will remove the SYSTEM attribute from the file specified, including those set by the operating system. The S switch allows a user to reset the SYSTEM attribute only on those files that were previously set on by the user.

There is a specific hierarchy that must be followed to apply the switches, and this hierarchy varies slightly depending on which version of DOS is in use. For example, if a file is hidden, it must be unhidden before the READ ONLY attribute can be set, but if the file is *already* marked RO, it must be set to RW (using the –R switch) before it can be hidden.

CERTIFICATION OBJECTIVE 9.06

Operating System Navigation

All operating systems provide the user with the ability to manage information. The capabilities vary from one to another, but the goal is a common one. Windows, MacOS, OS/2, and so forth give the user the ability to easily manage their files and programs. Because everything is handled graphically, most functions are present for the user regarding data manipulation, but the features that are present are merely a function of the OS developer's vision of what should be present. In DOS, and other command-line based OSs, ease of use is discarded in favor of power and control. This gap has gradually closed and will continue to do so as the use of the DOS prompt becomes less of a necessity. Keep in mind that a solid grasp of how to accomplish tasks at a DOS prompt will save many hours of frustration when a machine does not boot.

Navigating Through DOS

Earlier in this chapter, Table 9-1 references some of the basic commands used in the DOS environment. Of those commands, the most commonly used commands for navigating the waters of the DOS world are CD (Change Directory) and the DIR (Directory) commands.

The CD command is used in the example shown in Figure 9-1.

The DIR command can be used to search for specific files. This can be accomplished by using the /S (search subdirectories) switch. In most cases, it is best to be in the root, or top, directory of the drive. Figure 9-2 shows an example of this technique.

Navigating Through Windows 3.*x*/Windows 95

Windows pre-95 relies on an application called File Manager to navigate through a user's storage devices. Both local and networked drives can be accessed from this single user interface. File Manager helps to organize files and directories. File management can encompass several tasks, such as formatting floppy disks or creating directories, but the primary task is searching for files and placing them in the appropriate locations. The

FIGURE 9-1

Changing directories in DOS

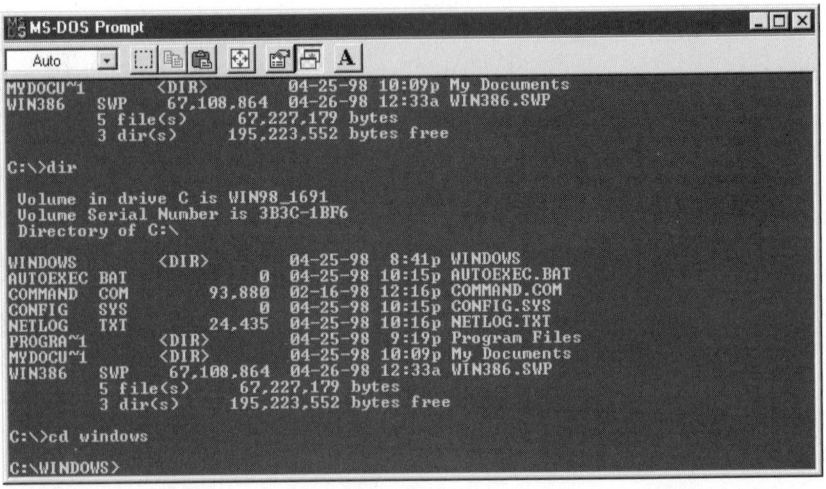

FIGURE 9-2

Using the DIR command to
perform a file search

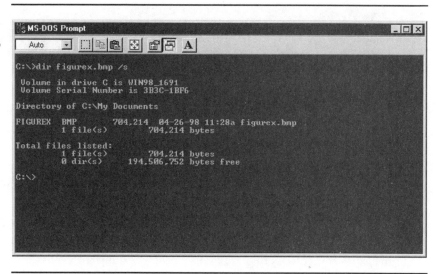

WINFILE.INI is the configuration file that stores the names of the
directories that File Manager displays when starting.

File Manager also dynamically tracks all files on the computer. Messages
are sent by Windows to File Manager of many operations including file
creation and deletion.

File Manager can also be used to start applications. By double-clicking
on any document file, Windows automatically tries to find the application
that works with that document, and then starts that application. File
Manager determines this by the three-character extension of the document
file and then consults with the Windows registration database and the
[EXTENSIONS] section of the WIN.INI. By selecting a document in the
File Manager window and then the File | Run menu option, File Manager
also starts an application. File Manager can also be used to print documents
by selecting them in a File Manager window and then using the File | Print
menu option.

To select a file in File Manager, click on the file's name. To select
multiple files in File Manger, click on one file and then hold down the
SHIFT key when clicking on a second file. File Manager selects the two
specified files and all the files in between them. If the CTRL key is held

FROM THE FIELD

Navigating Through an Operating System Can Be Fun

I always derive pleasure from watching a professional technician navigate through an operating system. I can pick up a few shortcuts while I'm watching. Each operating system has its own structure as well as sharing the structure of other operating systems.

I once watched an administrator fix a system problem through DOS commands. He immediately shelled out of the program manager and started typing very complex commands. After 26 different commands, the network was up and running. Another tech commented that this particular administrator had the ability to think in DOS.

Because much of the work that you will be doing involves navigating through the operating system, you might as well learn as many shortcuts as you can. Your work will not only be quicker, but those who watch you will be impressed. Following is a list of my favorite Windows 95 shortcuts.

—By Ted Hamilton, MCP, A+ Certified

Shortcut	Function	Shortcut	Function
Right click the start button	Launch explorer	CTRL-P	Print
CTRL-ESC	Open the task bar	CTRL-X	Cut
CTRL-TAB	Shuffle Excel windows	CTRL-C	Copy
F5	Update window (good when looking at multiple floppies)	CTRL-V	Paste
CTRL-F	Find	ALT-TAB	Rotate active windows
F1	Help	SHIFT +	Using SHIFT + many shortcuts works in reverse
CTRL-ESC then ALT-M	Minimizes all windows	F10	Activate Menus
ALT-F4	Close the active window (can be used multiple times to close all windows)		

down while selecting files, File Manager allows selection of multiple individual files.

exam
ⓦatch

Windows 95 includes the File Manager utility, but by default loads a newer utility known as the Windows Explorer.

The Windows Explorer is merely a turbo-charged version of File Manager. It provides a more solid integration with the Windows 95 and NT environments than File Manager. Another benefit is the fact that Explorer is highly configurable and extensible by third-party software vendors.

CERTIFICATION OBJECTIVE 9.07

Disk Management

Due to their capacity to store thousands of files coupled with the constant creation and modification of data contained therein, several utilities have been created to help manage hard drive "real estate." Early versions of DOS came with fairly crude utilities, and many companies made a pretty good living by creating better applications to perform disk management functions. Beginning with DOS version 6.0, a disk repair tool (SCANDISK) and a file defragmentation utility (DEFRAG) were included out of the box. Windows brought several new utilities into play. These include file management utilities, such as File Manager and Explorer, graphical versions of SCANDISK and DEFRAG, and also new file-compression utilities to make better use of disk space.

Using Disk Management Utilities

SCANDISK.EXE and DEFRAG.EXE provided with MS-DOS 6.0 and later provide many benefits, as mentioned earlier. Similar functionality is provided with Windows 95's graphical versions of the programs, which are located in the Programs | Accessories | System Tools program folder.

Using SCANDISK.EXE

The Scandisk utility provides the ability to scan and correct some data anomalies on a hard drive before they result in data loss. Typically, it moves the data to a non-damaged portion of the disk whenever possible. Table 9-2 lists the valid command line switches for SCANDISK.EXE.

Using DEFRAG.EXE

The defragmentation utility included with DOS 6.0 and later provides the ability to rearrange the clusters of data on the hard drive in order to achieve greater performance by placing all of the clusters for a given file together in a contiguous fashion. One mistake that is commonly made is that of running DEFRAG to fix errors. It should be noted that DEFRAG does *no* repair and will not make any error disappear.

Typically, the only command line switch that is used is /FULL. This causes a full defragmentation to take place. The command line would appear as shown in Figure 9-3.

TABLE 9-2 Command Line Switches for SCANDISK.EXE	Command Line Switch	Function
	/ALL	Scans all local drives for errors.
	/AUTOFIX	Fixes damage without prompting for user confirmation.
	/CHECKONLY	Checks drive for damage, but does not repair.
	/CUSTOM	Forces SCANDISK to read the SCANDISK.INI file for settings.
	/FRAGMENT	Checks file for fragmentation.
	/MONO	Causes SCANDISK to use a monochrome display.
	/NOSAVE	Used with /AUTOFIX. Deletes lost clusters rather than saving them as a file.
	/NOSUMMARY	Used with /CHECKONLY and /AUTOFIX. Prevents SCANDISK from displaying summary screens.
	/UNDO	Back out of previous repairs.

FIGURE 9-3

Common DEFRAG.EXE
command line syntax

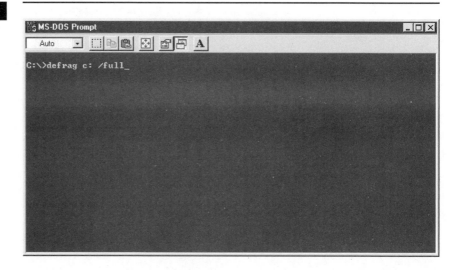

Backing Up

Hard drives are by far the most important part of a computer. That's because they contain the most vital element: your data. As such, it's imperative that the data be kept safe from any failure of the equipment or potential operator error. The best way of doing so is to create a separate copy of the data, also known as a backup. You'd think it would be easy to make copies, because copying files is a feature inherent in DOS, yet this feature has been probably the most problematic of all.

DOS has included backup utilities since version 2.0. Unfortunately, due to the multitude of problems that have arisen, each succeeding version of DOS came with a backup utility that was incompatible with the previous version. This was by far one of the most difficult limitations to overcome. When installing a newer version of DOS, if problems arose with the new install, the new version would be unable to restore the previous version's data, necessitating a reinstallation of the previous DOS version and then often a complete restore. This could take anywhere from hours to days.

Things have gotten better, but not by much. This version incompatibility *still* occurs, even using Windows and/or third-party software. Be aware that no backup can be assumed to be complete and restorable, *unless you actually perform a restore operation and it works correctly.* It's a good idea as part of a prudent disaster-recovery plan to perform occasional full restorations of a backup set to a *different, similarly configured PC* to be sure that what you thought you saved really was saved.

Defragmenting

Another of the problems inherent in the use of the DOS FAT table is file fragmentation. Because DOS writes files to the hard drive by breaking the file into cluster-sized pieces and then storing each piece in the next available cluster, as files are deleted and then rewritten, they can be written in discontiguous clusters scattered all over the disk. To access a file, the heads that actually read the data from the platters must traverse to each cluster in sequence. If the clusters are contiguously stored, the read operation is smooth and fast. However, if the file is fragmented, the heads fly wildly across the platters, picking up each scattered cluster one by one. This can slow down access dramatically.

Recognizing this, developers created utilities that reorganize the files back in a proper, contiguous fashion. They do so by moving several of them to an unused portion of the drive, erasing the previous locations in contiguous clusters, then rewriting the files back in proper sequence. Performed periodically, defragmentation is probably the single best operation a user can perform to maintain a high-performance system. There is both a DOS version and a Windows version of DEFRAG, as well as third-party versions.

SCANDISK

Besides fragmentation, there are a few other things that can go wrong with a hard drive. Actually, there are *two* FATs, identical copies, so that in case one FAT gets messed up, there is a built-in backup. Sometimes, the two get "out of sync," usually when something weird happens. An example might be while saving a file to disk, the power switch is accidentally turned off, or Windows "crashes" while swapping something to disk. Once this happens, the clusters that are marked in disagreement between the two FATs are considered "lost." These lost clusters can be recovered by running the SCANDISK utility.

Also, even though hard drives have become basically bullet-proof, with MTBF (Mean Time Between Failure) readings up in the 100,000 hr + range, occasionally clusters "go bad." These clusters must be detected and "marked" as bad, so that DOS won't try to write data to them. If data exists there already, some of it may be recoverable. SCANDISK notes any bad clusters, attempts to save any data already present, and flags the cluster as unusable. There is both a DOS version and a Windows version of SCANDISK, as well as third-party versions.

Contrasts Between Windows 3.x and Windows 95

Windows versions prior to 95 were all written as 16-bit extensions to DOS. Windows 95 was written as a full 32-bit OS, but still is stuck with some 16-bit calls to some of the PC's subsystems for legacy support, mostly of existing DOS applications. The 32–bit capability virtually doubled throughput to almost all I/O devices and memory, accelerating access to just about everything. Windows 95 also changed virtually everything else, from its networking capabilities to the user interface itself.

e x a m
ⓦ a t c h

Familiarize yourself with the networking capabilities of each of the OSs, as there are invariably questions about this on the exam.

Again for compatibility purposes, Windows 95 retained the WIN.INI and SYSTEM.INI files, but shifted configuration entries to the SYSTEM.DAT and USER.DAT files. The distinction is fairly clear. The SYSTEM.DAT file resides in the WINDOWS directory, and is loaded at startup to provide specific hardware support. It is common to all users of a particular PC. In contrast, the USER.DAT file contains application and environment preferences specific to each user who *logs* on to the PC. These two files in conjunction are known as the Windows *Registry* database. Windows 95 borrows the registry concept from its "big brother," Windows NT. Whereas the SYSTEM.INI and WIN.INI files are ASCII text files that are directly editable, the Registry is a compressed database that requires special tools and skills to manipulate.

Fortunately, for the most part, a user usually doesn't need to mess with the Registry. Its entries are handled automatically by Windows when it comes to hardware, and also by the various applications that are installed. This automaticity is labeled "Plug and Play." If needed, Windows 95 provides a tool, REGEDIT.EXE, to access and edit the registry, but be aware that any changes made are saved immediately. Any changes or deletions must be carefully considered before they are made.

Older versions of Windows used a shell application known as Program Manager to perform its menuing chore. Program Manager organizes applications into groups, with each group displayed in a window that contains a set of application icons. Each group window with individual icons can be viewed, tiled, or cascaded, or the group itself can be minimized to an icon in the Program Manager window. Program Manager stores the information about each group in a .GRP file in the Windows directory.

Major groups (Main, Accessories, StartUp, Games) are formed during installation. The Program Manager File | New menu selection allows creation of new groups. Application installation can also add new groups.

For each of its program icons, Program Manager remembers which *.EXE file should be started when double-clicking on an icon, which directory the *.EXE file resides in, and what title should appear under an icon. The individual groups to be loaded by Program Manager are listed in the PROGMAN.INI file.

Windows 95 now defaults to a "desktop" metaphor, with a hierarchical menu structure accessed from the Start button on the Task bar. All items in the menu and on the desktop are "link" (.LNK) files stored in subdirectories under Windows. If the PC is configured for use by multiple users and set to maintain individual settings for each, then a PROFILES subdirectory is created in the WINDOWS directory and individual user settings (USER.DAT and Program subdirectories that hold .LNK files) are created for each user. These link files contain either Windows-related information about the to-be-launched application if they pertain to a Windows file, or information about "DOS Box" configuration if it is to launch a DOS application. Again, due to their small size (<2KB), link files produce enormous waste of hard drive territory due to slack.

Another change in Windows 95 was to allow file and directory names to have more than the standard 8.3 characters. File names can now be up to 255 characters long, although this also must include the fully qualified path in the count. Also, the ability to use spaces between words is now present. This allows a user to save files with a much more descriptive filename to avoid confusion.

Another big change between Windows 3.x and Windows 95 pertains to the difference in their multitasking capabilities. There are two different types of multitasking, *cooperative* and *preemptive*. Windows 3.x supported 286 and later processors. The 286 had several limitations not present in the 386 and later. The greatest difference is that the 286 supported real and protected modes, but the 386 added virtual x86 mode. This limited the 286 considerably because it could not use virtual memory due to a limitation of the Windows architecture. This was also exacerbated because the 286 only had 24 address lines for memory, which translates to a maximum of 16MB. In contrast, the 386 and later have 32 address lines for memory, which is a maximum of 4GB.

Also, due to the virtual x86 mode not being present, all DOS applications were task switched, meaning that only one could be executing at a time. This was determined by the selected DOS application in the foreground.

On PCs with 386 and later processors, Windows 3.x cooperatively multitasks *all* native Windows applications and preemptively multitasks *all* DOS applications. The older 80286 PCs could load and run only one DOS application at a time.

Cooperative multitasking means that applications must voluntarily relinquish control of the CPU. When an application relinquishes control of the CPU, Windows then decides which application will execute next. The most common way for an application to relinquish control is by asking Windows if any messages are available.

In preemptive multitasking, control is passed from one program to another automatically by the Windows process scheduler. This is accomplished by using specific CPU hardware features of the 386/486/586 processor and the silicon chip timer to tell an application how long the application will be allowed to run. When the preset time expires, the timer interrupts whatever program is running and automatically switches back to the process scheduler. The program is temporarily suspended at this point. Windows is then free to do something else. A very short time later, Windows gives the program another slice of time, then another, and so on. This process of dividing up the time is called *time slicing*. The user perceives all of the running applications to be operating together, when in fact they are actually executing one at a time. Windows uses preemptive multitasking to multitask DOS sessions because DOS programs, unlike Windows programs, were not written to relinquish control of the CPU.

The collection of all the running Windows programs is treated as a single task by the Windows preemptive scheduler. When the collection of Windows programs receives a time slice, the applications multitask cooperatively during that slice of time. This type of "round-robin" scheduling worked pretty well, as long as the running Windows applications were written properly and "behaved well," meaning that they would relinquish control correctly. Errant applications, however, would cause Windows to lock-up, often forcing a reboot.

For this reason, Windows 95 followed Windows NT into the realm of complete preemptive multitasking. The new task-management structure that allows Windows to take control when an application fails to "behave" makes Windows 95 much more stable. Poorly written applications sometimes still misbehave, but now a user can force Windows to take control by pressing the CTRL-ALT-DEL key combination, which brings up the running Task List and allows the user to shut down specific running tasks. Errant applications show up in the Task List with a "(not responding)" entry next to the application's name.

While Windows 3.*x* was fully network-aware, it was geared around a single user. In order to support multiple users on a single PC with independent settings, access to a network server and custom installation procedures were required. Windows 95 allows multiple users to retain their own custom settings on the local PC, much like Windows NT. By default, Windows 95 installs for all users to use the same settings. Accessing the Passwords option in the Control Panel lets an administrator configure the PC for multiple user access.

Windows 95 also added a new feature, System Policies, to allow a network administrator to more easily configure Windows clients on a network. The System Policy editor, POLEDIT.EXE, while not installed with Windows, is located on the Windows 95 CD-ROM. It is used to set common-denominator defaults for all network users, and add certain restrictions on a global basis if deemed necessary.

Virtual File Allocation Table (VFAT)

A new VFAT (VirtualFAT) driver is incorporated in Windows 95, and provides a 32-bit protected-mode code path for manipulating the file system stored on a disk. It is *multithreaded*, providing smoother multitasking performance. The 32-bit file access driver is improved over that provided originally with Windows for Workgroups 3.11 and is compatible with more DOS device drivers and hard drive controllers.

Benefits of the 32-bit file access driver over previous DOS-based driver solutions include:

- Dramatically improved performance and real-mode disk caching
- No conventional memory used (replacement for real-mode SmartDrive)
- Better multitasking when accessing information on disk
- Dynamic cache support

Using DOS and Windows 3.*x*, manipulation of the FAT and writing to or reading from the disk is handled by the Int 21h MS-DOS function and is 16-bit *real-mode* code. Being able to manipulate the disk file system from *protected-mode* removes or reduces the need to transition to real mode in order to write information to the disk through MS-DOS, resulting in a large performance gain while accessing files.

FAT32

FAT32, new to Windows 95 (beginning with the OEM 2 release), provides several enhancements over previous implementations of the FAT file system. While the current FAT supports drives up to 2GB, FAT32 can now address drives up to 2TB (terabytes) in size. FAT32 uses smaller clusters (that is, 4K clusters for drives up to 8GB in size), resulting in 10- to 15-percent more efficient use of disk space relative to large standard FAT (FAT16) drives. FAT32 has the ability to relocate the root directory and use the backup copy of the FAT instead of the default copy. In addition, the boot record on FAT32 drives has been expanded to include a backup of critical data structures. This means that FAT32 drives are less susceptible to a single point of failure than existing FAT16 volumes.

FAT32 was implemented with as little change as possible to Windows 95's existing architecture, internal data structures, Application Programming Interfaces (APIs), and on-disk format. However, in some cases, existing APIs will not work on FAT32 drives. Most programs are unaffected by these changes, and existing tools and drivers should continue to work on FAT32 drives.

All of Microsoft's bundled disk tools (Format, FDISK, Defrag, and MS-DOS-based and Windows-based ScanDisk) have been revised to work with FAT32. In addition, Microsoft is working with leading device driver and disk tool vendors to support them in revising their products to support FAT32.

For most users, FAT32 has a negligible performance impact. Some programs may see a slight performance gain from FAT32. In other programs, particularly those heavily dependent on large sequential read or write operations, FAT32 may result in a modest performance degradation.

CERTIFICATION SUMMARY

There are several available OSs for the Intel-based PC. Of the various choices, the marketplace has been fairly dominated by Microsoft's DOS and Windows in various versions. While complex, this OS combination is now well understood, reasonably stable, and well-documented. Taking the time to learn the various available commands, their syntax, and correct usage can turn an otherwise daunting occupation into an easy and sometimes fun endeavor. By understanding the inner workings of the various components, you, too, can be the expert.

✓ TWO-MINUTE DRILL

❑ At the time DOS was first developed, floppy disks and cassette tapes were the only storage media available for the PC.

❑ DOS commands can be either internal or external. Internal commands are present in the COMMAND.COM shell, and can be executed on the command line at any time from any directory location. External commands are those that reside in the DOS directory.

❑ CP/M, QDOS, NDOS, Dr. DOS, Geoworks, and NEXT, among others, are all examples of competent PC operating systems. However, the PC market belongs primarily to Microsoft, with DOS, Windows, and Windows NT.

❑ DOS was developed as a *16-bit* application, with its internal code segments written to be accessed 16 bits at a time.

❑ Windows (up to Windows 95) is a graphical shell that overlays on DOS, and relies on DOS for its low-level device access.

❑ Because of their small size (<2KB), .LNK files produce enormous waste of hard drive territory due to slack.

❑ System files are responsible for all device access and user interface presentation.

❑ As DOS has evolved over the years, it has grown to support a multitude of components, such as sound devices, scanners, CD-ROMs, tape drives, and so forth.

❑ On the Windows desktop, the spacing of the icons, the type of wall paper, screen colors, and other interface features can be customized in the Windows WIN.INI file.

❑ The bulk of configuration for Windows 95 has shifted to the SYSTEM.DAT and USER.DAT files.

❑ DOS installs onto a formatted disk by placing its system files in the root directory.

❑ By default, the DOS system files AUTOEXEC.BAT, CONFIG.SYS, and ANSI.SYS carry no attributes, and are *not* required for OS startup.

❑ The *.LGO file that WIN.COM selects is based on the type of video card setup determined to be in the computer during installation.

❑ Review Table 9-1 for a DOS command reference.

❑ In Windows 3.*x*, PROGMAN.EXE finishes the Windows initialization by running any startup applications specified in the WIN.INI file, and by starting any applications whose icons are stored in the StartUp Group.

❑ The Windows 95 Registry is a complex database of settings pertaining to both applications and hardware.

❑ DOS is a widely used acronym for Disk Operating System.

❑ Using the FDISK (for Fixed DISK) utility provided with DOS, a hard drive is prepared for use through the acts of partitioning and formatting.

❑ Review Table 9-2 for command line switches for SCANDISK.EXE.

❑ .COM, .EXE, and .BAT files are known as executables.

❑ Cooperative multitasking means that applications must voluntarily relinquish control of the CPU so that other applications may operate.

❑ Hard drives consist of a number of platters rotating on a common spindle, with read/write heads mounted on a pivoting assembly that spans all platters concurrently.

❑ Up until recently, DOS wouldn't support a partition greater than 2GB.

❑ Because the smallest addressable unit is the cluster, once a file is written to a cluster, the cluster is marked as used and can't have anything else written to it until the file in it is erased or overwritten by another copy of the same file.

❑ When formatting, or afterwards if desired, the partition marked as active must have an operating system installed.

❑ In practice, it's best to limit the fully qualified path to less than 60 characters, else some older applications and utilities can display anomalous behavior.

❑ Each file accessible to DOS, regardless of media type, has four attributes that may be associated with it: READ ONLY, HIDDEN, SYSTEM, and ARCHIVE.

❑ The /S switch allows a user to process files in all subdirectories in the specified path.

❑ The best way to keep your data safe from any failure of the equipment or potential operator error is to create a separate copy of the data, also known as a backup.

❑ Performed periodically, defragmentation is probably the single best operation a user can perform to maintain a high-performance system.

❑ Windows Registry entries are handled automatically by Windows when it comes to hardware, and also by the various applications that are installed. This automation is labeled "Plug and Play."

❑ In Windows 95, all items in the menu and on the desktop are "link" (.LNK) files stored in subdirectories under Windows.

❑ Accessing the Passwords option in the Control Panel lets an administrator configure the PC for multiple user access.

SELF TEST

The following Self Test questions will help you measure your understanding of the material presented in this chapter. Read all the choices carefully, as there may be more than one correct answer. Choose all correct answers for each question.

1. In order to install Windows 3.*x* on a PC, the PC must already contain

    A. a CD-ROM drive

    B. a copy of Windows NT

    C. a copy of DOS

    D. Microsoft Schedule +

2. What two files, in conjunction, are known as the Windows Registry database?

    A. USER.DAT and SYSTEM.DAT

    B. SYSTEM.INI and WIN.INI

    C. WIN.INI and USER.DAT

    D. WIN.INI and PROGRAM.INI

3. Which of the following files must be present for a PC to boot from its hard drive?

    A. AUTOEXEC.BAT

    B. IO.SYS

    C. COMMAND.COM

    D. ANSI.SYS

4. Which of the following files *does not need to be* located in the root of the C: drive in order to be processed correctly?

    A. AUTOEXEC.BAT

    B. IO.SYS

    C. COMMAND.COM

    D. CONFIG.SYS

5. From a DOS prompt, you try to execute Windows (pre-95) by typing the WIN command. When doing so, you are greeted by a "Bad command or filename" response. Being the savvy DOS user you are, you issue a DIR win.* /s command from the root of C:, but receive a "0 file(s) found" response. Great. The WIN.COM file is missing. In order to replace it, you must

    A. reinstall Windows

    B. download a new copy from the Internet

    C. copy the file from the installation disks

    D. make a copy of WIN.COM from another PC with Windows installed

6. Time Slicing refers to what process?

    A. The process of the CPU automatically changing its internal clock to accommodate for daylight savings

    B. The process of the CPU dividing up time between applications for preemptive multitasking

    C. The process by which cooperative multitasking operates

    D. The process by which the CPU performs an automatic reboot

7. In order for a hard drive partition to be "bootable," it must be

   A. formatted

   B. configured with an Operating System

   C. set as "Available"

   D. marked as "Active"

8. DOS is a widely-used acronym for

   A. Disk Operating Server

   B. Driver Operating System

   C. Driver Operating Server

   D. Disk Operating System

9. At the time DOS was first developed, what were the only types of storage media available for the PC?

   A. Hard Drives

   B. Floppy Disks

   C. Cassette Tapes

   D. All of the above

10. How many programs could execute at one time with DOS?

    A. One

    B. Two

    C. Three

    D. As many as necessary

11. DOS was developed as a(n) _____-bit application.

    A. 8

    B. 16

    C. 24

    D. 32

12. Which DOS system file contains commands to modify the PC environment and execute applications?

    A. HIMEM.SYS

    B. EMM386.EXE

    C. AUTOEXEC.BAT

    D. MSDOS.SYS

13. Which DOS system file loads low-level device drivers for specific hardware, and adjusts several system parameters for performance tuning and memory usage?

    A. MSDOS.SYS

    B. CONFIG.SYS

    C. IO.SYS

    D. ANSI.SYS

14. USER.EXE is which type of system file?

    A. DOS

    B. Windows 3.*x*

    C. Windows 95

    D. All of the above

15. What is the first function that WIN.COM performs when executed?

    A. It switches the computer into the appropriate graphics mode.

    B. It loads an .LGO file.

    C. It gives control of Windows to either DOSX.EXE or WIN386.EXE.

    D. It determines what type of processor is in the computer.

16. What does the formatting process do to a hard drive?

   A. It separate a single physical drive into multiple logical components.

   B. It increases the capacity of a hard drive.

   C. It divides the drive logically into sectors and tracks.

   D. It creates a complex database of settings pertaining to both applications and hardware.

17. The _____ is the smallest unit accessible to DOS from the FAT of a hard drive.

   A. Cluster

   B. Spindle

   C. Sector

   D. Track

18. _____ is the space left between the end of a file and the end of the cluster in which the file resides.

   A. Scrap

   B. Minibyte

   C. Slack

   D. Drift

19. In DOS, the total possible length of a file name, including its *path*, is:

   A. 32 characters

   B. 64 characters

   C. 128 characters

   D. Limitless

20. The _____ attribute keeps a file from being displayed when a DIR command is issued in DOS.

   A. Read Only

   B. System

   C. Archive

   D. Hidden

10

Memory Management

T

he vagaries of computer memory are often misunderstood. RAM, ROM, PROM, EEPROM, Flash, DIMM, SIMM, DRAM, SRAM, yadda, yadda. Who wouldn't get lost? Take a deep breath, and let's try to unravel the mystery a little.

CERTIFICATION OBJECTIVE 10.01

Types of Memory

While physically, memory is packaged in many sizes and shapes, a PC's central processing unit (CPU) is only able to address two categories of memory. These are labeled *physical memory* and *virtual memory.*

There are several kinds of physical memory. A basic division is between *random access memory* (RAM), which can be both read and written to by the CPU, and programmable read-only memory (PROM a.k.a. ROM). Standard RAM is also known as *volatile* memory, in that it loses its contents when system power is shut down, while ROM is nonvolatile, its contents remaining unchanged even when power is removed. The primary difference between RAM and ROM is that RAM is readable by any application, while ROM is meant for a single instruction set.

RAM is available in several types. The most popular at present are fast-page RAM and EDO RAM (Extended Data Output). Originally, there were only two types, Dynamic and Static. Dynamic RAM (DRAM) had a disadvantage in speed, and it had to be constantly *refreshed* by a clocked supply voltage, or it would lose its contents. Static RAM (SRAM) didn't require the refresh, and was considerably faster (by a factor of five or so), but more than ten times as expensive to make. PC makers chose to stick with DRAM.

exam
Ⓦatch

Physical memory consists of the hardware that handles memory in a PC. This memory is stored in chips that are either ROM—read only memory chips—or RAM—random access memory.

ROM began as a write-once chip. Instruction code was electrically fed to the chip and retained there permanently. In order to update this type of

ROM, the chip must be physically replaced by another chip containing upgraded instruction code. This reduced production costs, but installation costs remained high.

Memory developers quickly realized that upgrades would become a fairly regular occurrence, so they came up with the EPROM chip (erasable programmable read-only memory). The EPROM chip was originally developed to be erased by ultraviolet light, and had a small window on the chip itself. The window was taped over with a small metal-foil cover. Removing the cover and exposing the chip window to ultra-violet would erase it and allow a new instruction set to be loaded. The chips could be changed in this way several times (dozens), but not many (hundreds). Fortunately, ROM is mostly used for specific support of hardware devices, and updates usually are infrequent.

On the heels of the EPROM came the EEPROM (electrically erasable), which could be erased by applying a specific voltage to the chip. These chips still usually required removal and insertion into a PROM "burner" to erase and reprogram. Some inventive hardware manufacturers came up with ways of addressing updates onboard their hardware, but these are the exception.

Besides being difficult to reprogram, ROM was slow in comparison to RAM. While still measured in *nanoseconds* (a millionth of a second), standard RAM access times were under 100 nanoseconds and ROM took 300 or more. A faster version of ROM was finally developed, and labeled *Flash* memory. While still basically developed as ROM, Flash memory could be addressed and loaded *thousands* of times. It also came in sub-100 nanosecond modules. This opened up a method for hardware manufacturers to update their individual system code easily.

Most hardware devices now can be updated by running a program from DOS (or some other Operating System) that can erase and reprogram their device, usually in conjunction with a small ROM chip onboard. In case the upload fails, the ROM chip is there as a backup to continue to seek an operating code set from a specific source in case one is not present in Flash.

Physical memory is usually identified by the actual size, in bytes, of the memory modules, whether they are user-accessible plug-in types or individual chips soldered onto the motherboard or system card. Memory modules remain a moving target in design, as physical dimensions, application, and capacity needs continue to increase.

When the IBM PC first arrived in 1980, memory was quantified in kilobytes (KB) and a standard memory chip had a whopping 4KB. This small memory chip was considered a marvel, compared to memory modules employed by then-existing systems. Still in use at that time were 4KB memory modules powered by vacuum tubes housed in a 6' x 6' x 6' cube that consumed kilowatts (thousands of watts) of electricity.

Today, memory modules come in 2, 4, 8, 16, and 32 *Megabyte (MB)* modules, and consume milliwatts (1000th of a watt) of power, allowing huge quantities of RAM to be contained in portable computers.

Packaging has also come a long way. At its inception, PC memory came in single-chip form. Each chip had 7 or 8 pins on either side of a 1" x ½" rectangular chip, dubbed a DIP (Dual In-Line Package) chip. There was a chip for each connection on the memory bus (a quantity of eight chips) plus an additional parity chip to ensure memory contents remained unaltered.

In the late eighties, RAM manufacturers standardized on the SIMM (Single Inline Memory Module) format, which consisted of placing the 8+1 individual chips onto a small substrate card roughly 4" x 1", which was then mounted in a quick-release connector located on the motherboard. The original 30-pin SIMM format didn't provide sufficient connector density to allow enough for the ever-expanding amount and types of RAM chips, so in 1993, the SIMM chip was lengthened somewhat and the connection contact points more than doubled to 72 pins. 30-pin SIMMs are typically found in 386 and older 486 Intel CPU systems in 1MB and 4MB sizes. Newer 486s and just about all Pentium series systems use 72-pin SIMMs, which have capacities of up to 32MB per SIMM.

exam
ⓦatch

DIP chips are physically soldered to a motherboard. SIMMs are chips that are soldered to a small board that is installed into a slot on the motherboard. Using SIMMs allows the memory to be easily replaced.

Unfortunately, each time the memory module package changed, the motherboard was forced to change as well. This trend of changing format every few years continues today. The newer Pentium II motherboards now use DIMM (Dual Inline Memory Modules) to allow for even greater density and larger capacity in megabytes. The bottom line is: Be careful in the selection of memory upgrade components. The memory module must match the requirements of the motherboard.

Conventional Memory

From its use of *segment/offset* addressing, the architecture of the 808X processor family used in the PC allowed 1MB (1024KB) of address space for system memory. Of this, 640KB was set aside for the applications and the additional 384KB was reserved for hardware to use.

The 640KB of physical memory allocated for the operating system, applications, and data to be loaded in comprises *system memory*. The additional 384KB became *reserved memory*. The 640KB area, while appearing vast at the outset, quickly filled up.

One of the biggest memory consumers was one of the most popular applications at the time: Lotus software's 1-2-3 spreadsheet program. 1-2-3 strained the 640KB system memory limit to the breaking point. Lotus realized they had to find a solution that allowed the processor to address more than 640KB of RAM, in order for 1-2-3 to be able to deal with more complex spreadsheets. Lotus teamed up with Intel, the processor maker, and Microsoft, who developed the operating system, and came up with the Lotus-Intel-Microsoft (LIM) memory specification. The specification renamed system memory to *conventional memory*, and defined additional (above the original 1024KB address limit) areas as *expanded, extended,* and *high* memory. Even though the 808X processor could only address 1024KB, the newer 80X86 series increased from 16-bit to 32-bit memory addressing, and could use up to 16MB (and soon more) RAM for system memory.

Extended/High Memory

Basically, all memory above the 1024KB line is considered *extended memory*. As we shall see, this area can be used in several ways. The basic division, though, is that 808X processors cannot access extended memory at all, but 80X86 processors can. The first 64KB of extended memory was roped off as a control area, and labeled the high-memory area (HMA). This is the area where HIMEM.SYS loads from DOS. As part of the LIM spec, extended memory is addressed through a standard called XMS (eXtended Memory Specification).

By the time DOS 5.0 rolled out, DOS could also load a portion of itself in the HMA. Originally, use of the HMA was reserved for only a single application. Once an application loaded there, it was "done." Microsoft found a way to load HIMEM.SYS, create the HMA, unload itself, and then place up to 64KB of its system code in its place. To enable this feature, you must include the line "DOS=HIGH" in the CONFIG.SYS file along with the "DEVICE=HIMEM.SYS" line.

Enabling XMS required additional work. Two standards for accessing XMS were developed. While Microsoft and Lotus shook hands to develop the LIM specification, they were at odds as to how to best deal with XMS. Microsoft developed the DOS Protected Mode Interface (DPMI) specification, while Lotus embraced a different structure that they inherited from their acquisition of the Phar-Lap company. Lotus's approach was named Virtual Control Program Interface (VCPI), and was totally incompatible with DPMI. This made for a short-term nightmare, as it became impossible to run Lotus 1-2-3, which used VCPI, under Windows 3.1, which used DPMI. Lotus finally conceded, and DPMI effectively has become the standard.

Upper Memory

The HMA is often confused with upper memory. The 384KB of reserved space, which became known as "upper memory" (conventional, below 640KB, being "lower memory"), remained scarcely populated by system boards, and allowed much of it to be used as system memory. In order to take advantage of unused upper memory, memory managers, such as EMM386.EXE, were created. Besides the LIM spec, other vendors, notably Quarterdeck with its QEMM (Quarterdeck Expanded Memory Manager) program, developed ways of digging out every unused portion of the reserved area, and converting it to system memory. On 808X processor machines, any additional space became welcome. The addition of this upper memory to the system memory pool increased the usable system (conventional) memory to as much as 720KB. Of course, this "breathing room" lasted about a week. It was clear that something had to be done to allow 808X processors to remain viable until the newer 80X86 processors could predominate. Enter *expanded* memory.

Virtual Memory and Expanded Memory

The LIM specification took into account the 808X processor's inability to address memory beyond 1024KB through the concept of *virtualizing* RAM. *Virtual memory* is memory that the processor has been "tricked" into using as if it were actual physical memory. The LIM folks created a "frame" of "pages," each page (also known as a window) being 16KB in size, that could be located in free areas of the reserved 384KB hardware address space. Upper memory, remember? The pages could be moved one-at-a-time from the reserved area to either extended memory *or the hard drive.* A small code segment in lower memory looked at every memory address request made by the processor, and adjusted the requested segment/offset value to match a table it created that redefined the asked-for value into a specific page designation. The processor neither knew nor cared about where it got its code from, extended memory or the hard drive. This new type of memory access became the Expanded Memory Specification (EMS).

EMS has a couple of drawbacks when compared to XMS. The paging structure meant that only 64KB could be moved at any one time, and the tabled segment/offset lookups took additional time. What's more, it required that each application be aware that EMS was available to be used. In contrast, XMS was developed for 32-bit processors to access directly, with only a small HMA driver to enable it. Once enabled, the Operating System (OS) could then parse out memory as needed to all running applications.

All of this "mucking around" with the reserved area (a.k.a. upper memory) added to an already existing problem, two devices trying to use the same memory space—a memory conflict.

QUESTIONS AND ANSWERS

When installing new RAM into a 486 PC, the module did not quite fit into the slot. What could be the problem?	Some 486 PCs used 30-pin modules, and newer ones used 72-pin modules. The type of SIMM that was bought for the 486 is the wrong type. The manufacturer should be able to tell you the type of SIMM required for that PC.
When installing a new video adapter card, the PC will no longer boot up into Windows 95. What has occurred?	This is a hard error. The new adapter card has conflicted with an existing card. This is most likely a conflict with the existing video adapter, which may be part of the system board. The video adapter, if a separate card, must be removed from the PC. Or, if a video on the system board, it must be disabled—usually through the system BIOS.

CERTIFICATION OBJECTIVE 10.02

Memory Conflicts and Optimization

Confused yet? It was all supposed to work just right. By loading application and system code "low," and device drivers "high," everything was *supposed* to work perfectly. IBM, with its background in systems hardware, defined specific areas in upper memory to be reserved for specific devices to be accessed by the CPU over the *system bus,* dubbed the *ISA* (Industry Standard Architecture) bus. They just didn't foresee how rapidly newer technologies would add a multitude of new devices installed on the bus that would also need to fit into upper memory.

Network interface cards, graphics boards, SCSI adapters, and the like chomped away at already-overloaded upper memory. Worse yet, because there were no defined standards for these new devices, the default settings chosen often overlapped. Installing a new device without knowing how it and already-existing devices were configured to use a "memory footprint" could result in a *memory conflict.*

Even if you managed to get it to work right, the additional boards ate into those little crannies of memory that were eked out for use by the new memory manager programs. The folks who wrote the memory managers began developing better ways of detecting those areas of upper memory that were free to be used as additional conventional memory.

What Is a Memory Conflict?

Memory conflicts usually show up in one of two ways. If you're lucky, a memory conflict will wait until a specific device driver tries to load, at which time either that device, along with the other conflicting device, ceases to function, or the system will lock up. If you're having a bad day, then you'll install a board that is configured to conflict with something required at startup, such as the display board or hard drive controller, in which case the system will fail to start before the operating system even gets a chance to load. The latter conflicts are usually the easiest to troubleshoot, because they happen immediately upon installation of the offending device, and removal and reconfiguration of it usually meets with success. Conflicts arising from optional devices, such as network cards, can be more difficult to pinpoint.

As long as the boards are populated with switches to make configuration choices, you're home free. Simply by choosing a new switch setting, you can usually resolve conflicts in one or two tries. Newer boards, however, have gotten away from using configuration switches, thanks to the use of EEPROMS or Flash memory, which can be used to store configuration settings. These boards require you to run an installation/configuration program to adjust them, which makes it hard to fix them if you can't start up your computer without it locking up due to a memory or interrupt conflict. Should this occur, if you have another PC available, you can try moving the suspect board to it to see if it will allow the PC to boot, then use the configuration program to change the settings, and move the board back to the original PC. If you don't happen to have an extra PC lying around, then you're stuck with having to remove all the existing cards (remember, it's not going to work without a display adapter) and/or disabling any onboard hardware and then trying again. As long as you can boot the PC and run the configuration program, you can then try a different setting, then replace/re-enable the stuff you removed and try again.

Memory conflicts have been a burr under a PC user's/administrator's saddle for a long time. IBM tried to address them when they developed the *Micro Channel Architecture* (MCA) for their next-generation PCs. When installing a new device, a Produce Definition File (.PDF) would be included by the device manufacturer that instructed the system as to all of the device's available settings. All MCA machines included a setup program that would read the .PDF files of the installed devices and configure them all to defaults that wouldn't overlap—in theory. It *usually* worked. Of course, a user was free to specify their own settings, and the setup program would do its utmost to point out any conflicts that the user might have inadvertently chosen.

Competing vendors created a competing bus standard, Extended Industry Standard Architecture (EISA), which had many of the same configuration features as MCA boards, and included a setup program to configure them.

Recently, a majority of vendors have embraced the Peripheral Component InterConnect (PCI) bus. Many PCs are distributed with a combination of PCI/ISA bus slots so that both the new and older adapter boards can be used. PCI was developed to increase the speed of data transfer between a peripheral and the processor. As newer technologies have increased data transfer speeds, the ISA bus became a bottleneck. This is best represented by the difference between an Ethernet 100BaseT (running at 100 Mbps on the network) PCI network interface card and an Ethernet 100BaseT ISA network interface card. ISA runs at 5 Mbps. PCI runs at 132 Mbps. In the case of an ISA card, a bottleneck exists on the network interface and reduces performance.

PCI supports bus mastering. An intelligent peripheral can take control of (master) the bus in order to accelerate a high-priority task. PCI also allows for concurrency in bus mastering, where the CPU may operate simultaneously with the bus mastering peripherals. This is illustrated by the ability of the CPU to run a mathematical calculation while, at the same time, a network interface card has control of the bus.

Of greatest interest in memory management, PCI supports "Plug and Play"—a specification for automatic configuration of jumper- and switch-free peripherals designed to avoid conflicting settings.

How Do Memory Conflicts Happen?

Besides conflicting hardware, applications themselves can create memory conflicts. The previously listed problems all arise in the reserved area between conflicting hardware. Applications can only reside in system memory. However, occasionally a device will conflict with a portion of upper memory that is being used by a memory manager as system memory. This usually only occurs with peripheral hardware that loads a driver *after* the memory manager loads. Fortunately, memory managers can be forced to *exclude* specific areas to avoid conflicts, and through some careful analysis, a majority of memory conflicts can be resolved.

HIMEM.SYS

The Microsoft driver, HIMEM.SYS, is used to address 80286 and 80386 extended memory, converting it to XMS in accordance with the LIM specification. It also takes the first 64KB of this extended memory area and converts it into the HMA. It is loaded by placing a line—DEVICE= *path*\HIMEM.SYS—in the CONFIG.SYS file. Unless you are using a different memory manager, such as QEMM by Quarterdeck, the HIMEM.SYS file *must* be loaded before EMM386.EXE is loaded so that EMM386 may be used. This also enables an application, or simply the Operating System, to access XMS memory.

Use of Expanded Memory Blocks (Using EMM386.EXE)

EMM386.EXE performs two major functions. It enables and controls EMS, if desired, and enables the use of upper memory as system memory. It is generally conservative in its attempts to locate available upper memory. You can force EMM386 to use specific regions of upper memory by using the *Include* switch on the command line where it is enabled in CONFIG.SYS, and conversely exclude specific regions using the *Exclude* switch.

Employing Utilities

As you can see, trying to resolve memory conflicts can be an incredibly difficult endeavor, because they can come from many sources. Also, "failure-mode analysis" often can't be performed because once the offending device is actually loaded in memory, the system would lock up. Third-party vendors, notably Peter Norton with his Norton Utilities, concentrated on developing a method of checking and reporting on memory allocation usage. Microsoft followed up with its MEM.EXE, MSD.EXE, and MEMMAKER.EXE utilities.

MEM.EXE is a simple command line utility that, using various command switches, can display various reports of memory usage. If you aren't familiar with it, now is a good time to check it out. MEM.EXE is an external command, and should be present in either your DOS directory, or if running Windows 95, in the WINDOWS\COMMAND directory.

```
C:\WINDOWS>mem /?
Displays the amount of used and free memory in your
system.
MEM [/CLASSIFY | /DEBUG | /FREE | /MODULE modulename]
                                              PAGE]

    /CLASSIFY or /C         Classifies programs by memory
                            usage. Lists the size of
                            programs, provides a summary of
                            memory in use, and lists largest
                            memory block available.
    /DEBUG or /D            Displays status of all modules
                            in memory, internal drivers, and
                            other information.
     /FREE or /F            Displays information about the
                            amount of free memory left in
                            both conventional and upper
                            memory.
    /MODULE or /M           Displays a detailed listing of
                            a module's memory use. This
                            option must be followed by the
                            name of a module, optionally
                            separated from /M by a colon.
     /PAGE or /P            Pauses after each screenful of
                            information.
```

From a DOS prompt, executing MEM.EXE yields a brief list of total memory usage.

```
C:\WINDOWS>mem
Memory
Type               Total           Used             Free
---------       --------        --------         --------
Conventional       640K             60K             580K
Upper              155K            155K               0K
Reserved           384K            384K               0K
Extended (XMS)   64,357K             85K          64,272K
---------       --------        --------         --------
Total memory     65,536K            684K          64,852K

Total under 1 MB   795K            214K             580K

Largest executable program size  580K (594,240 bytes)
Largest free upper memory block   0K       (0 bytes)
MS-DOS is resident in the high memory area.
```

Notice the last line, indicating that DOS has been loaded "high" using the DOS=HIGH setting in the CONFIG.SYS file. Otherwise, it shows a breakdown of memory allocation by area and total. Nice to know, but not particularly helpful if you're in trouble.

Using the /C switch gives you quite a bit more to work with.

```
C:\WINDOWS>mem /c
Modules using memory below 1 MB:

    Name          Total        Conventional      Upper
                                                 Memory

    ------     ----------     ------------     -------
    SYSTEM     39,296  (38K)   32,112 (31K)   7,184  (7K)
    HIMEM       1,168   (1K)    1,168  (1K)       0  (0K)
    EMM386      4,320   (4K)    4,320  (4K)       0  (0K)
    DBLBUFF     2,976   (3K)    2,976  (3K)       0  (0K)
    WIN         3,776   (4K)    3,776  (4K)       0  (0K)
    vmm32      10,560  (10K)    8,944  (9K)   1,61   (2K)
    COMMAND     7,504   (7K)    7,504  (7K)       0  (0K)
    DRVSPACE  110,592 (108K)        0  (0K)  110,592(108K)
    OAKCDROM   36,064  (35K)        0  (0K)   36,064 (35K)
    IFSHLP      2,864   (3K)        0  (0K)    2,864  (3K)
Free        594,256 (580K)  594,256 (580K)       0  (0K)
```

```
Memory Summary:

   Type of Memory  Total        Used        Free
   --------------- ------       -----      ----------
   Conventional      655,360     61,104       594,256
   Upper             158,320    158,320             0
   Reserved          393,216    393,216             0
   Extended (XMS) 65,901,968     87,440    65,814,528
   ------------- ----------    ---------   ----------
   Total memory   67,108,864    700,080    66,408,784
   Total under 1 MB  813,680    219,424       594,256
   Largest executable program size   594,240     (580K)
   Largest free upper memory block         0       (0K)
   MS-DOS is resident in the high memory area.
```

Notice that the summary is included as before, but now all loaded applications and drivers are detailed by name and individual memory usage. You can see immediately any changes that have been made from "tweaking" load parameters in AUTOEXEC.BAT or CONFIG.SYS. Changing parameters can add or take away free memory, and using MEM.EXE with the /C switch can help diagnose the results.

Usually, results using the /C switch develop results that cover more than a single screen. Another helpful switch, /P can be used in conjunction with /C (or any others) to "page" the results.

Even more details can be obtained by using the /D switch.

```
Conventional Memory Detail:

   Segment   Total        Name      Type
   -------   -----------  -------   --------
   00000     1,024        (1K)      Interrupt Vector
   00040       256        (0K)      ROM Communication Area
   00050       512        (1K)      DOS Communication Area
   00070     1,424        (1K)      IO System Data
                          CON       System Device Driver
                          AUX       System Device Driver
                          PRN       System Device Driver
                          CLOCK$    System Device Driver
                          A: - H:   System Device Driver
                          COM1      System Device Driver
                          LPT1      System Device Driver
                          LPT2      System Device Driver
                          LPT3      System Device Driver
```

```
                          CONFIG$   System Device Driver
                          COM2      System Device Driver
                          COM3      System Device Driver
                          COM4      System Device Driver
        000C9    04  (7K)  MSDOS     System Data
        0026C 0,528 (30K)  IO        System Data
              1,152  (1K)  XMSXXXX0  Installed
                                      Device=HIMEM
              4,304  (4K)  $MMXXXX0  Installed
                                      Device=EMM386
              2,960  (3K)  DblBuff$  Installed
                                      Device=DBLBUFF
                544  (1K)  Sector buffer
             16,080 (16K)  BUFFERS=30
              2,288  (2K)  LASTDRIVE=Z
              3,072  (3K)  STACKS=9,256
        009E0   80  (0K)  MSDOS     System Program
        009E5   32  (0K)  WIN       Data
        009E7  320  (0K)  WIN       Environment
        009FB 3,424  (3K)  WIN       Program
        00AD1   48  (0K)  vmm32     Data
        00AD4 8,896  (9K)  vmm32     Program
        00D00  336  (0K)  COMMAND   Data
        00D15 5,728  (6K)  COMMAND   Program
        00E7B 1,440  (1K)  COMMAND   Environment
        00ED5  336  (0K)  MEM       Environment
        00EEA 90,464 (88K)  MEM       Program
        02500503,792 (492K) MSDOS     -- Free --
```

Upper Memory Detail:

Segment	Region	Total		Name	Type
0C95C	1	156,656	(153K)	IO	System Data
		110,576	(108K)	DBLSYSH$	Installed Device=DRVSPACE
		36,048	(35K)	MSCD001	Installed Device=OAKCDROM
		2,848	(3K)	IFSHLP	Installed Device=IFSHLP
		1,200	(1K)		Block device tables
		5,616	(5K)		FILES=100
		256	(0K)		FCBS=4
EF9B	1	1,616	(2K)	vmm32	Data

```
Memory Summary:

    Type of Memory    Total       Used          Free
    -----------     ---------   ---------     -----------
    Conventional      655,360      61,104        594,256
    Upper             158,320     158,320              0
    Reserved          393,216     393,216              0
    Extended (XMS) 65,901,968      87,440     65,814,528
    -----------     ----------  -----------   -----------
    Total memory   67,108,864     700,080     66,408,784


    Total under 1 MB  813,680     219,424        594,256

    Memory accessible using Int 15h  0         (0K)
    Largest executable program size  594,240   (580K)
    Largest free upper memory block  0         (0K)
    MS-DOS is resident in the high memory area.

    XMS version  3.00; driver version  3.95
```

This shows not only each loaded application, but each memory segment and its corresponding location for each *piece* of each application.

This tool was a major leap forward for Microsoft to allow a user to visualize changes made in their system. By manually rearranging application and driver loading sequence and related parameters, after much trial and error, you could come up with an optimal configuration that provided the maximum amount of free memory.

Microsoft went one step better when it delivered its MSD.EXE (Microsoft System Diagnostics) program. This little gem roots out almost every conceivable item about your system that you'd ever want to know (and then some!) and displays it in a menu-driven format for you to browse. Conversely, you can run MSD.EXE from the command line, or batch file, and write query results to an output file or printer for a complete analysis using the /P option. An example of the output is included in Appendix G of this book. As you can see, not only is there a full output with statistics equivalent to the MEM.EXE program, but details on the hard drives and their partitioning, and motherboard, video, and networking elements as well. About the only thing missing is the processor speed. Microsoft chose to eliminate MSD.EXE from Windows 95, but in hindsight decided this was a bad idea, and so has posted it as a free download from their Web site.

MemMaker and Other Optimization Utilities

While the MEM.EXE and MSD.EXE programs are excellent tools for memory conflict determination, what was really needed was a tool for problem avoidance. Microsoft delivered this in their MEMMAKER.EXE utility. Running this program automatically determines the best possible configuration and load sequence for a given set of applications and drivers used. Before using MEMMAKER, the PC should be configured for normal operation (i.e. mouse driver, network operation, sound support, and so forth), including any items that are loaded from the AUTOEXEC.BAT and CONFIG.SYS files. MEMMAKER would run through hundreds, sometimes thousands of combinations of command load sequencing and placement, then reboot itself to test its new configuration, and if successful, ask the user to accept its determinations.

MEMMAKER's first version shipped with DOS version 5.0 was not perfected at its release. As often as not, it required multiple runs in order to find a setting that would not hang up the PC when it rebooted. By DOS version 6, MEMMAKER had smoothed out its rough edges and could be counted on to deliver a clean and lean configuration.

Third-party vendors, notably Quarterdeck with its QEMM suite, continued to deliver slightly better, tighter memory configurations, yielding slightly more deliverable RAM. An added benefit to QEMM was its stealth capabilities that were specifically geared to take advantage of the Micro Channel PC's ability to move its board's configurations dynamically, allowing even more available RAM to be recouped.

Windows 95 has now pretty much eliminated the need for memory managers. Previous versions of Windows required that networking elements, often the most memory-hungry components, be loaded in DOS prior to Windows startup. A sometimes annoying feature of Windows was that you couldn't have more memory available for DOS applications run from within Windows than an amount that was slightly less than what you had when you started Windows. Windows 95 now loads virtually everything after it starts, freeing up as much as a full 640KB (or slightly more, if you load DOS high *and* run EMM386.EXE). OS/2 also found a way to deliver as much as 740KB for each DOS session.

System Monitor

Microsoft Windows 95 includes a utility that can be used to monitor the workstation's hardware, applications, and services. Since Windows systems use a significant amount of hard disk space for memory usage in the swap file, monitoring the disk access can be useful in troubleshooting the errors. The System Monitor can be used from a remote computer over a network if the remote registry service has been installed.

When optimizing memory in Windows 95, you should use the System Monitor to see the effect of any changes you have made to the system.

In order to use the System Monitor to track memory, select the Edit menu and choose Add Item. In the Category list window, select the Memory Manager category. Then, in the Item list window, select all the items you wish to monitor.

SMARTDRV

SmartDrive is a system utility that creates a disk cache in extended memory. Caching the disk in extended memory can enhance performance. It is not necessary to start SmartDrive in order to run the system, so if there is any need to reduce the utilities in the AUTOEXEC.BAT, SmartDrive can be remarked out or deleted. The command for this utility is SMARTDRV.EXE.

Although SmartDrive can significantly boost performance in a DOS/Windows 3.1x system, it should not be used in a Windows 95 system. Windows 95 uses an entirely different method of disk caching that makes SMARTDRV unneccessary.

The following is the screen output for the SMARTDRV /? command. It describes the switches that can be used with SMARTDRV.

```
Installs and configures the SMARTDrive disk-caching
utility.

SMARTDRV [/X] [[drive[+|-]]...] [/U] [/C | /R] [/F | /N]
[/L] [/V | /Q | /S]
[InitCacheSize [WinCacheSize]] [/E:ElementSize]
[/B:BufferSize]
```

/X	Disables write-behind caching for all drives.
drive	Sets caching options on specific drive(s). The specified drive(s) will have write-caching disabled unless you add +.
+	Enables write-behind caching for the specified drive.
-	Disables all caching for the specified drive.
/U	Do not load CD-ROM caching module.
/C	Writes all information currently in write-cache to hard disk.
/R	Clears the cache and restarts SMARTDrive.
/F	Writes cached data before command prompt returns (default).
/N	Doesn't write cached data before command prompt returns.
/L	Prevents SMARTDrive from loading itself into upper memory.
/V	Displays SMARTDrive status messages when loading.
/Q	Does not display status information.
/S	Displays additional information about SMARTDrive's status.
InitCacheSize	Specifies XMS memory (KB) for the cache.
WinCacheSize	Specifies XMS memory (KB) for the cache with Windows.
/E:ElementSize	Specifies how many bytes of information to move at one time.
/B:BufferSize	Specifies the size of the read-ahead buffer.

Illegal Operation Occurrences

Every now and then, an error pops up on the screen stating that the program you are running caused an illegal operation and will be shut down. Usually, that error is followed by another stating that there has been a page fault or a general protection fault, and then Windows will crash.

What is an illegal operation? In this case, illegal does not mean against the law, just not allowed by the processor. And illegal operations result from a processor design. The Intel 80x86 (286, 386, 486, Pentium, Pentium Pro,

Pentium II) series of processors are designed to interrupt the execution of a program whenever they detect an abnormal condition. Many times, this abnormal condition is an application trying to access a part of upper memory by mistake. That can be due to a conflicting application or device driver that this application did not expect, using that area of upper memory. Or it can be due to an invalid input from a corrupt file. This type of interrupt is called an exception. If you are familiar with Novell's NetWare server operating system, this error is called an ABEND, which stands for abnormal end—and that pretty much describes what it ends up as.

The operating system normally handles the exception and decides whether to process the exception and return an error, or whether to pass the exception to a handler provided by the application. When the application handles it, you don't see any errors so you never really know when this happens. When the operating system returns an error, the result usually grows to a termination of the application, and many times, of the operating system itself because files are not closed and hardware is not returned to its pre-application state. This, in turn, may lead to lost work and disk errors. Using the DOS CHKDSK command or the SCANDISK command is recommended after an illegal operation to fix the disk errors caused by the files left in an open state. And then, running DEFRAG to defragment the pieces of the files on the hard drive can result in a cleaner FAT table and reduces pesky errors.

Illegal operations can be caused by programs with corrupted files, such as a database program that uses indexes. If you keep getting illegal operations in a database program, find the command that will re-index files or check the database for errors. Bugs in an application can cause illegal operations, too, which can be fixed by applying either operating system or application patches supplied by the manufacturer. And finally, just a glitch in hardware, where a tiny surge in electricity flips a bit (changes it from a "1" to a "0" or vice versa) or two, and the application is doomed. If the glitches occur often and there are all sorts of other error messages, and all other routes (database index, CHKDSK, DEFRAG, applying patches) have been exhausted, this may indicate that RAM or the system board may be going bad. Don't assume hardware first, though—these errors are nearly always caused by an application error.

Conflicts with 16-Bit Applications/Windows 95 Operations

In Windows 3.1, people used to get memory errors all the time. The errors would state that either there was no memory, or that you were running out of system resources. The first error—no memory—referred to a problem with the pagefile, which was created for Virtual Memory.

FROM THE FIELD

Always Check the Swap File Size

Improper swap file size in the real world accounts for a large number of calls to the help desk. Older operating systems, such as Windows 3.1 and Windows for Workgroups, have a horrible problem with memory. The infamous "blue screen of death" was usually attributed to poor memory allocation. Most of the good graphic-intensive programs written for the operating systems would crawl in windows and you would have to run them straight from DOS. Newer operating systems have improved this memory problem, but it still shows up. On Windows NT, if you open too many applications without a large amount of RAM, you still run into out-of-memory problems.

The swap file that is created can sometimes be the cause of the problem instead of just the size of this file. If there is any question about the integrity of the swap file, delete it and reboot to recreate it. A bug in Windows 3.11 caused in some instances a swap file to be put onto a network drive. Imagine this

inefficiency: A 10 Mbps line reading and writing on a distant server. Always make sure that your swap file is within the limits of your hard drive's extra memory or you risk your system sending this file to a network drive.

When you look at a personal computer and wonder what is wrong with it, always look for memory swap file relating to signs of trouble, especially if the system is performing poorly compared to other machines that have equal hardware and are running the same software. Memory can also trigger Dr. Watson errors. Even printing errors are suspect. Most memory problems cause the machine to stop responding. Don't be afraid to increase the swap file; it gives your system more virtual RAM. However, actual RAM may end up to be the ultimate solution in some cases. The larger you make your swap file, the more the hard drive is going to thrash in order to access the memory space.

—By Ted Hamilton, MCP, A+ Certified

In Windows systems, virtual memory is where the operating system allocates more memory than the PC contains, and then pages virtual memory into a file on the hard drive. This means that a PC with 8MB of RAM would look like it had 64MB of RAM if the pagefile was 56MB. The pagefile, also called a swap file, would swap pages of RAM to the 56MB file on the hard drive. It would keep the most recently used memory in RAM, so that the current application would be able to run at optimal speed. The system sounds great, but didn't work all that well, because the pagefile was static in size and had to be configured by the user of the PC who might not know off the top of their head what size that file should be.

In Windows 95, 16-bit Windows (Windows 3.1) applications run in the System VM (Virtual Memory Manager). The VM is the Windows 95 handler of the pagefile. The VM adjusts the pagefile size to an optimal amount automatically. Because of the way Windows 16-bit applications used to work in Windows 3.1, they must run in the same shared memory space with the core components of Windows 95, and shared DLLs. If there is an error that a Windows 16-bit application causes to virtual memory, it is the most likely cause of a system-wide error. (Windows 32-bit applications each run in a separate private address space within the System VM, yet the address space is totally separate from the shared address space where core components and 16-bit applications reside. Therefore, Windows 32-bit applications don't present the problems that Windows 16-bit applications might. MS-DOS-based applications each run in their own VM, completely separate from the System VM.)

To fix these types of errors, the best course of action is to upgrade that 16-bit application with a 32-bit version, if it exists. If that is not possible, then contact the manufacturer and obtain the latest patches and fixes. If there is any question about the way virtual memory is handled, it can be reviewed in the Control Panel System icon under the Performance tab and adjusted in by clicking the Virtual Memory button.

Now remember, the second error that you used to get in Windows 3.1 stated that you were running out of system resources. The only way to get rid of the error was to reboot. System resources degraded over time—some programs would not return all the resources even after they closed, and you simply ran out of them. Often.

Now system resources is rather a cryptic term, because *system resources* refer to small areas of memory called *memory heaps* to be used by the graphics device interface (GDI) and user system components. In Windows 3.1, these heaps were 64KB in size and used 16-bit processing. In Windows 95, the heaps became 32-bit, but the 16-bit heaps didn't go away because of the need for backward-compatibility.

The errors for running out of system resources are rare under Windows 95 because of the 32-bit heaps. But, Windows 16-bit applications using the 16-bit heaps can still cause this error. Especially when that application was one of the programs that behaved badly and wouldn't give back the system resources when it was done with them. The only way to fix system resource errors in the short term is to reboot the PC. The best long-term fix is to contact the manufacturer for a patch or upgrade the application to a 32-bit version.

CERTIFICATION SUMMARY

Memory management is not an easy game to play, nor is resolving memory conflicts and optimization issues. The various flavors of MS-DOS and Windows have each brought with them new concerns with regard to memory management. Hopefully, you leave this chapter with a better understanding of memory placement, how applications and hardware play nicely together, and proper optimization techniques.

✓ TWO-MINUTE DRILL

❑ Standard RAM is also known as *volatile* memory, in that it loses its contents when system power is shut down, while ROM is nonvolatile, its contents remaining unchanged even when power is removed.

❑ You can force EMM386 to use specific regions of upper memory by using the *Include* switch on the command line where it is enabled in CONFIG.SYS, and conversely exclude specific regions using the *Exclude* switch.

❑ ROM began as a write-once chip. Instruction code was electrically fed to the chip and retained there permanently.

❑ The EEPROM (electrically erasable) chip could be erased by applying a specific voltage to the chip.

❑ DIP chips are physically soldered to a motherboard. SIMMs are chips that are soldered to a small board that is installed into a slot on the motherboard. Using SIMMs allows the memory to be easily replaced.

❑ Be careful in the selection of memory upgrade components. The memory module must match the requirements of the motherboard.

❑ The LIM memory specification renamed system memory to *conventional memory*, and defined additional (above the original 1024KB address limit) areas as *expanded, extended,* and *high* memory.

❑ Don't assume hardware first when you receive an illegal operation—these errors are nearly always caused by an application error.

❑ Before using MEMMAKER, a PC should be configured for normal operation (i.e. mouse driver, network operation, sound support, and so forth), including any items that are loaded from the AUTOEXEC.BAT and CONFIG.SYS files.

❑ *Virtual memory* is memory that the processor has been "tricked" into using as if it were actual physical memory.

❑ Under Windows 95, the only way to fix system resource errors in the short term is to reboot the PC. The best long-term fix is to contact the manufacturer for a patch or upgrade the application to a 32-bit version.

❑ MSD.EXE roots out almost every conceivable item about your system that you'd ever want to know (and then some!) and displays it in a menu-driven format for you to browse.

❑ Memory conflicts arising from optional devices, such as network cards, can be difficult to pinpoint.

❑ PCI was developed to increase the speed of data transfer between a peripheral and the processor.

❑ Windows 32-bit applications don't present the problems that Windows 16-bit applications might.

❑ Memory managers can be forced to *exclude* specific areas to avoid conflicts, and through some careful analysis, a majority of memory conflicts can be resolved.

❑ EMM386.EXE performs two major functions. It enables and controls EMS, if desired, and enables the use of upper memory as system memory.

❑ Physical memory consists of the hardware that handles memory in a PC. This memory is stored in chips that are either ROM—read only memory chips—or RAM—random access memory.

❑ MEM.EXE is a simple command line utility that, using various command switches, can display various reports of memory usage

❑ Windows 95 has now pretty much eliminated the need for memory managers.

❑ The Intel 80x86 (286, 386, 486, Pentium, Pentium Pro, Pentium II) series of processors are designed to interrupt the execution of a program whenever they detect an abnormal condition.

SELF TEST

The following Self Test questions will help you measure your understanding of the material presented in this chapter. Read all the choices carefully, as there may be more than one correct answer. Choose all correct answers for each question.

1. What type of memory is RAM?

    A. Upper Memory

    B. High Memory

    C. Virtual Memory

    D. Physical Memory

2. What is the difference between RAM and ROM?

    A. There is no difference.

    B. RAM is readable by any application, ROM is meant for a single instruction set.

    C. ROM is read only by any application, RAM is meant for a single instruction set.

    D. RAM is a single chip, ROM is a long module.

3. Which is more common, SRAM or DRAM, and why?

    A. SRAM, because it is faster and cheaper

    B. DRAM, because it is faster

    C. DRAM, because it is cheaper

    D. SRAM, because it is faster

4. Flash memory is a form of what?

    A. RAM

    B. Upper Memory

    C. Virtual memory

    D. ROM

5. What are the names for random access memory packages?

    A. DIP, SIMM, and DIMM

    B. RAM, DIP, and SIMM

    C. SIMM and DIP

    D. ROM, RAM, and Flash

6. Who created extended memory?

    A. No one—it was always part of a PC

    B. Lotus did—so that their 1-2-3 program would run without running out of memory

    C. Intel did—they design PCs

    D. Lotus, Intel, and Microsoft—because they all wanted the 123 program to work on the processor and the operating system

7. Where is the high memory area?

    A. The first 64KB after the 640KB conventional memory area

    B. The first 64KB of extended memory

    C. The last 64KB of upper memory

    D. The upper memory area

8. What utility can display how memory is allocated?

    A. MEMMAKER

B. CHKDSK

C. MEM

D. DEFRAG

9. Which line should appear first in the CONFIG.SYS?

A. DOS=HIGH

B. DEVICE=EMM386.EXE

C. DOS=UMB

D. DEVICE=HIMEM.SYS

10. How can a System Resources shortage error be resolved?

A. Run SCANDISK

B. DEFRAG the hard drive

C. Reboot the PC

D. Adjust the virtual memory in Control Panel

11

Installation, Configuration, and Upgrading

A ll PCs require that some form of operating system be installed on them. Until mid-1996, the most popular operating system was a combination of DOS and Windows 3.x. Both of these operating systems share many things in common such as requiring that device drivers be installed. Windows 95 introduced Plug and Play, which provided automatic driver installation and resource distribution. In this chapter, we discuss all of these things and a few more as they relate to DOS, Windows 3.x, and Windows 95.

CERTIFICATION OBJECTIVE 11.01

Installing DOS, Windows 3.x, and Windows 95

Installation of operating systems such as DOS, Windows 3.x, and Windows 95 are all fairly simple. There are some steps that are required by each of the installation procedures such as creating a partition, formatting the hard drive, and the usage of a setup utility. These are discussed in the sections that follow.

Partition

In order to install an operating system, the system's disk drives must first be prepared for use. This first step in the preparation for using a new disk drive (or an old drive that you want to erase everything off of for that matter) is to create a partition on the drive. The utility that is used by DOS and Windows systems alike is the FDISK utility shown in Figure 11-1. All that is necessary is that a primary DOS partition is set to actively be created. On a related note, for DOS systems, Windows 3.x, and Windows 95, the maximum size of a partition is 2GB. Windows 95 OSR2 (aka Windows 95 B) is capable of having larger partitions because of its capability to use the FAT32 file system.

Format Drive

Once the partition has been created with FDISK, you must format the drive, or erase all of the information from the partition (see Figure 11-2). In

FIGURE 11-1

The FDISK utility is a DOS-based utility that defines the partition structure of a hard drive

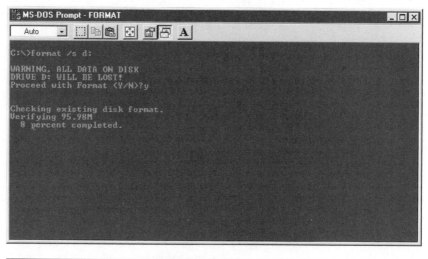

```
MS-DOS Prompt - FDISK

                              FDISK Options

Current fixed disk drive: 1

Choose one of the following:

1. Create DOS partition or Logical DOS Drive
2. Set active partition
3. Delete partition or Logical DOS Drive
4. Display partition information


Enter choice: [1]



Press Esc to exit FDISK
```

FIGURE 11-2

Formatting a drive is a fairly simple process that erases all of the data from a partition

```
MS-DOS Prompt - FORMAT

C:\>format /s d:

WARNING, ALL DATA ON DISK
DRIVE D: WILL BE LOST!
Proceed with Format (Y/N)?y

Checking existing disk format.
Verifying 95.98M
  8 percent completed.
```

addition to erasing all of the information from the partition, formatting can place system files on the partition by issuing the /s switch and check the partition for errors by issuing the /c switch.

If you wish for a drive to be bootable, the drive needs to be formatted with the /s switch. If you do not want to erase all of the data from the drive, the SYS command can also be issued to make the drive bootable.

Setup Utilities

DOS, Windows 3.*x*, and Windows 95 all provide setup utilities that guide you through the installation process. These utilities are all fairly intuitive and don't require a great deal of knowledge. You can expect to be asked for a serial number by the Windows 95 Setup utility, shown in Figure 11-3. In addition, the Windows 95 Setup utility in many cases will ask you to confirm if you have some system devices such as a CD-ROM, Sound Card, or Network Card.

Loading Drivers

Nearly all basic devices require that device drivers be loaded in some shape or form. Most devices, such as Network Interface Cards and sound cards, require that a device driver be loaded.

FIGURE 11-3

The Windows 95 Setup utility provides a graphical user interface that makes the setup process fairly simple

DOS

DOS does not internally provide any support for loading device drivers. You can, however, install device drivers by adding them to CONFIG.SYS or AUTOEXEC.BAT. We cover how to edit CONFIG.SYS and AUTOEXEC.BAT in the later section entitled "Editing AUTOEXEC.BAT and CONFIG.SYS Files." The most common devices that would have been installed in this fashion would be sound cards, mice, and CD-ROM drives.

Windows 3.*x*

In Windows 3.*x*, device drivers are usually installed by a setup program provided by the device manufacturer. Some basic drivers such as mouse and video are built into the Windows 3.*x* setup program.

Windows 95

Windows 95 has the capability and requirement of having a device driver loaded for nearly every device in the system. During the setup process, Windows 95 attempts to automatically detect any devices that exist and then load device drivers for those devices. At the time of installation, Windows 95 should automatically load all device drivers that are necessary for the system to be operational.

CERTIFICATION OBJECTIVE 11.02

Upgrading Operating Systems

The process of upgrading operating systems is a rather simple one in most cases. It is important to remember to always back up all of your data prior to any type of upgrade. No matter how well planned and organized an upgrade is, loss of data is always possible.

Upgrading from DOS to Windows 95

Upgrading from DOS to Windows 95 is a rather simple process. The first, and most obvious, requirement is that you purchase a copy of Windows 95.

On a side note, if you have a system that has DOS installed on it, and is not running Windows 3.x, it might be a good idea to consider upgrading hardware prior to installing Windows 95. In most cases, if Windows 3.x was not installed on the system, it was because of performance issues, in which case Windows 95 will provide worse performance. The published minimum requirements to run Windows 95 are a 386DX-20 with 4MB of memory. Although this machine is capable of running Windows 95, it will be very slow and incapable of running many applications.

Upgrading from Win 3.x to Windows 95

Upgrading from Windows 3.x to Windows 95 is a simple task. Once you have purchased the Windows 95 Upgrade CD, all you need to do is run the setup utility from Windows 3.x's file manager. Windows 95 Upgrade uses the current configuration files for DOS and Windows 3.x to help in the hardware-detection process. In addition, all of your Program Manager groups will be added to the Windows 95 Programs Group under the Start Menu.

Loading Drivers

Once Windows 95 has been installed, nearly all of the necessary device drivers should have been automatically installed for you. If there are any device drivers that you still need to have installed, you can do so by clicking on Add New Hardware. The Add New Hardware Wizard then guides you through the installation process beginning with scanning the system for new devices.

CERTIFICATION OBJECTIVE 11.03

Boot Sequences for DOS, Windows 3.x, and Windows 95

When a PC first starts, it goes through a boot sequence. This boot sequence is the sequence of events that occur during the bootup process. A PC with a standard configuration usually attempts to boot to a floppy drive first. The PC then attempts to boot the first partition on the master hard drive on the primary drive chain.

Windows 3.*x* is not automatically started when the system starts. Many users add a line to the end of the AUTOEXEC.BAT file to start Windows 3.*x* after the AUTOEXEC.BAT has been processed. Windows 95 is automatically started when the system is started.

Booting a System from a Floppy and Hard Drive

In order to boot a system from any type of disk, be it a hard drive or a floppy drive, the partition you wish to boot off of must be set as active (because floppies only have one partition, they are always set as active), and the system files must be copied to the partition. There are two methods of copying the system files to a partition. One of them is the format command with a /s switch (remember, format will delete all of the data currently on the partition). The second method is using the SYS command. SYS simply copies the necessary files to the root directory of the partition. On a related note, DOS, Windows 3.*x*, Windows 95, and Windows 98 require that the system be booted from the first partition of the master drive in the primary drive chain.

Windows 95 Boot Modes

Windows 95 primarily provides three different modes that the system can be started in. The three modes are: Normal Mode, Safe Mode, and DOS Mode.

Normal Mode

Normal Mode is the mode in which Windows 95 is started by default. Normal Mode provides full functionality of the Windows 95 Explorer. Windows 95 loads all of the drivers that are installed on the system.

Safe Mode

Safe Mode is a special diagnostic mode of Windows 95 that starts Windows 95 without any network, CD-ROM, and printer drivers. A standard VGA display and Microsoft mouse drivers are used. This special mode allows you to change an incorrect setting, which will in most cases allow you to return an abnormally functioning system to its correct operation.

DOS Mode

DOS Mode, or DOS Compatibility Mode as it is commonly known, allows execution of some older MS-DOS applications that are not capable of running in Windows 95. These applications are primarily applications that attempt to access hardware that Windows 95 controls directly. Applications that require use of MS-DOS mode are usually blocked from operation within Windows 95. The applications that most commonly require the use of MS-DOS Compatibility Mode include many graphical games.

Multi-Boot Configurations

It is possible to install more than one operating system on a computer. Configuring a system for using more than one operating system is called multi-boot configuration. Configuration of the Boot Options is done by editing the MSDOS.SYS file that is located in the root of the system partition on the master drive on the primary drive chain. This file should be edited following procedures detailed in the Windows 95 Resource Kit.

CERTIFICATION OBJECTIVE 11.04

Windows 95 Plug and Play

Windows 95 Plug and Play automatically configures the resources that Windows 95 Plug and Play-compatible devices use. These resources can include IO Memory Addresses, IRQ Number, and DMA Addresses among other things. Nearly all popular devices that are currently manufactured are Windows 95 Plug and Play-compatible.

Windows 95 Plug and Play automatically configures and tracks resources such as IO Memory Addresses, IRQ Address, and DMA Addresses.

Peripheral Recognition

When Windows 95 is booted for the first time with a particular Windows 95 Plug and Play-compatible device installed, the device is automatically recognized by Windows 95.

Loading Appropriate Drivers

When a new device is first detected, Windows 95 attempts to find a driver from its library of drivers. If Windows 95 finds that the driver is in its library and the driver is already installed on the system, Windows 95 continues as normal. If the driver is in the Windows 95 driver library but has not been installed on the system, Windows 95 prompts you to insert the Windows 95 CD and installs the drivers. If the driver is not in the library, and has not been installed yet, you are prompted for the disks containing the drivers and the operating system installs them from there.

Assigning System Resources

All system resources are assigned to Plug and Play devices automatically using the Plug and Play information that Windows 95 has previously gathered. The new devices are given all of the system resources that they request (so long as they are available) and reports their usage back to Windows 95.

Plug and Play—Working Properly

In proper operation, Windows 95 automatically detects all devices and assigns them the appropriate resources.

Plug and Play—Not Working Properly

In the event that devices are not working correctly, a good troubleshooting method is to delete the device from Device Manager and restart the system. When rebooted, if the device is not redetected and does not work properly, the device is either faulty or Plug and Play is not operating correctly.

CERTIFICATION OBJECTIVE 11.05

Loading/Adding Device Drivers

The process of adding device drivers is a rather simple one. It is important that the procedures outlined in your specific operating system's instructions are followed specifically.

DOS

Any device other than video and the keyboard (and including these in special cases) requires that a device driver be installed in the AUTOEXEC.BAT, CONFIG.SYS, or both. Consult the device's documentation for specific instructions.

Most device driver manufacturers provide an installation program that installs whatever lines need to be added to AUTOEXEC.BAT and CONFIG.SYS automatically. If a device driver does not include such an installation program, the drivers need to be copied onto the hard drive, and then AUTOEXEC.BAT and CONFIG.SYS need to be edited according to the device driver's documentation.

Windows 3.x Procedures

Windows 3.x requires the use of DOS device drivers for some devices such as CD-ROM drives and sound cards. In addition to the use of DOS device drivers, nearly all other major devices require that device drivers be installed. Windows 3.*x* requires device drivers for devices such as video, mice, and many others. Installation of Windows 3.*x* drivers should be done in accordance with the instructions provided by the driver manufacturer.

Windows 95 Procedures

Windows 95 does not rely on DOS device drivers as Windows 3.*x* does but does support them for backward-compatibility. In addition to providing compatibility for DOS device drivers, Windows 95 also provides support for Windows 3.*x* device drivers. If more recent drivers are available, it is highly suggested that you use the Windows 95 driver. To install a device driver in Windows 95, you would simply use the Add New Hardware Wizard shown in Figure 11-4 and follow the directions provided there.

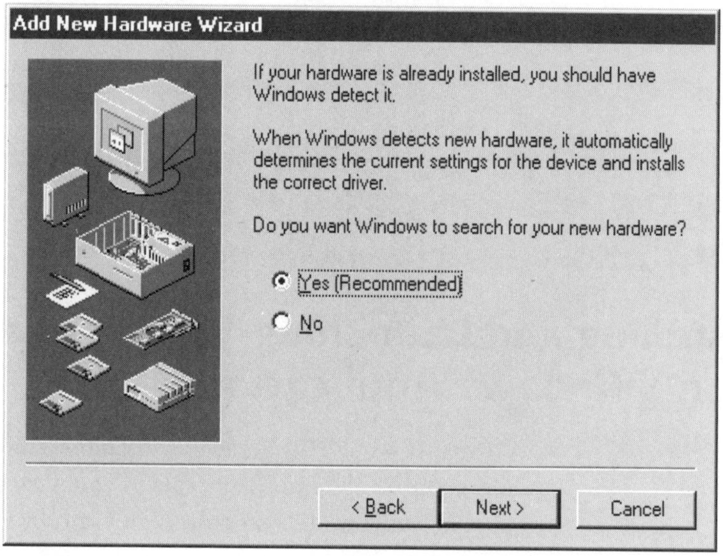

FIGURE 11-4

The Windows 95 Add New Hardware Wizard automatically scans the system for new hardware and installs the appropriate drivers for you

Add New Hardware Wizard

If your hardware is already installed, you should have Windows detect it.

When Windows detects new hardware, it automatically determines the current settings for the device and installs the correct driver.

Do you want Windows to search for your new hardware?

⦿ Yes (Recommended)

○ No

< Back   Next >   Cancel

Changing Options, Configuring, and Using the Windows Printing Subsystem

The Windows printing system is a well-organized system that simplifies the task of printing. DOS-based programs required that the printer be addressed directly by the application. By using the Windows printing subsystem, applications are only required to submit data to be printed to the standardized subsystem. The subsystem then renders the data, and prints it for you.

The Windows Printing Subsystem requires very little configuration. To begin to use the subsystem, a printer must be first installed. To install a printer, double-click on Printers from the Control Panel. Click on Add New Printer and select a driver from the list provided. The Add Printer Wizard shown in Figure 11-5 guides you through the process. In some cases (especially with newer printers), Windows 95 may have auto-detected the printer at system startup and have already installed the drivers for it.

Installing and Launching Windows and Non-Windows Applications

Installation of both Windows and non-Windows applications is extraordinarily simple. In order to complete the installation, all you need to do is follow the instructions provided by the software manufacturer. Windows-based applications should install a shortcut either in Program Manager (in Windows 3.x), or on the desktop or Start menu (in Windows

FIGURE 11-5

The Windows 95 Add
Printer Wizard steps you
through the process of
adding a new printer

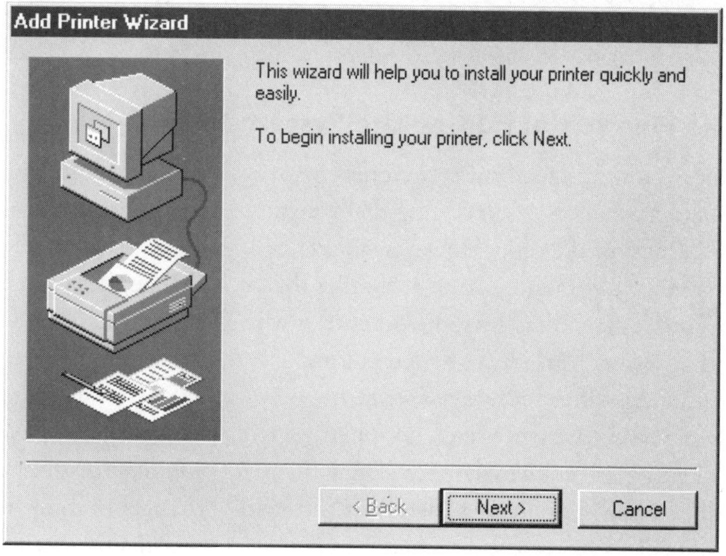

95). If the application is not Windows-based, it can be launched from File
Manager (Windows 3.*x*) or Windows Explorer (Windows 95).

CERTIFICATION OBJECTIVE 11.08

Editing **AUTOEXEC.BAT** and **CONFIG.SYS** Files

AUTOEXEC.BAT and CONFIG.SYS files are two user-editable files.
Any text editor can edit them both. Among other things, CONFIG.SYS
provides the ability to install device drivers. AUTOEXEC.BAT is more
commonly used to invoke device drivers for devices such as the mouse and
the CD-ROM drive. Windows 95 does not require that any settings be
made in either the CONFIG.SYS or AUTOEXEC.BAT file. In fact,
AUTOEXEC.BAT and CONFIG.SYS do not even have to exist for
Windows 95 to function fully.

FROM THE FIELD

The Fine Art of Editing the System Files

Once you understand the system files, you should have no problem editing them, right? Well, most of the time. However, sooner or later you will run into one of these files that was previously edited by some other tech who had his or her own ideas of good editing techniques. Often, the way some techs edit them, you'd have better luck deciphering ancient Egyptian hieroglyphics. These files will probably have many added lines and no comments. I saw one so bad that it took me an hour to even start to understand the logic behind the editing. And, to top it all off, the last editor had only placed one remark in the files, written in all caps: "DO NOT CHANGE ANYTHING." Well, it's common that something will need to be changed in these files as hardware and software are installed, and commenting not to change anything does nothing more than make a workaround next to impossible. Instead of spending the next week on this PC, I looked at the repair log for that computer and found the previous tech who worked on the machine. Luckily, he was still with the company, so I made him edit this file.

When you make a change on a computer, always comment what you do and make your changes understandable to the next person. If you use commands that aren't common, make sure you comment on them and explain them. Back up all previous versions before you change them and remark in the file what you have changed and why. All too often, when things are unclear, a tech will resort to using a skeleton or default version of a system file. This may completely reverse any changes that you have made and any hardware or software changes in these files. You may have to end up reinstalling everything, or stitch together the old file and the new file. Of course there is software that can help you do this, but why spend the time?

One last point to ponder on these files: Make sure that when your system boots, you are not getting errors that are on the screen for the user to see. When your operating system boots up, it usually tells you things like error in config.sys on line 8. Find out why these are happening and fix them. Users don't like to see errors, and furthermore they may be causing other problems. If you know they are not causing problems and are just remnants from an application that was not fully removed, simply REM them out. REMing them out is better, just in case you actually do need them.

—By Ted Hamilton, MCP, A+ Certified

CERTIFICATION SUMMARY

This chapter has offered you a general understanding of installing, configuring, and upgrading the various flavors of Microsoft operating systems and applications. As you have seen throughout this chapter, these processes are relatively simple and straightforward. There are slight differences between performing these functions on DOS, Windows 3.*x*, and Windows 95 systems—with Windows 95 being the most intelligent in this regard—and this chapter has equipped you with the information necessary to be able to perform these functions across the board. Just remember that it's always important to review any specific product's documentation when installing the necessary drivers for it.

✓ TWO-MINUTE DRILL

❑ This first step in the preparation for using a new disk drive (or an old drive that you want to erase everything off of for that matter) is to create a partition on the drive using the FDISK utility.

❑ For DOS systems, Windows 3.*x*, and Windows 95, the maximum size of a partition is 2GB.

❑ If you wish for a drive to be bootable, the drive needs to be formatted with the /s switch. If you do not want to erase all of the data from the drive, the SYS command can also be issued to make the drive bootable.

❑ DOS does not internally provide any support for loading device drivers. You can, however, install device drivers by adding them to CONFIG.SYS or AUTOEXEC.BAT.

❑ If you have a system that has DOS installed on it, and is not running Windows 3.*x*, it might be a good idea to consider upgrading hardware prior to installing Windows 95.

❑ If there are any device drivers that you still need to have installed after you've installed Windows 95, you can do so by clicking on Add New Hardware.

❑ In order to boot a system from any type of disk, be it a hard drive or a floppy drive, the partition you wish to boot off of must be set

❏ as active (because floppies only have one partition, they are always set as active), and the system files must be copied to the partition.

❏ Windows 95 primarily provides three different modes that the system can be started in: Normal Mode, Safe Mode, and DOS Mode.

❏ The Safe mode allows you to change an incorrect setting, which in most cases allows you to return an abnormally functioning system to its correct operation.

❏ DOS Mode, or DOS Compatibility Mode as it is commonly known, allows execution of some older MS-DOS applications that are not capable of running in Windows 95.

❏ Configuring a system for using more than one operating system is called multi-boot configuration.

❏ Windows 95 Plug and Play automatically configures and tracks resources such as IO Memory Addresses, IRQ Address, and DMA Addresses.

❏ In the event that Plug and Play devices are not working correctly, a good troubleshooting method is to delete the device from Device Manager and restart the system.

❏ When adding device drivers, it is important that the procedures outlined in your specific operating system's instructions are followed specifically.

❏ AUTOEXEC.BAT and CONFIG.SYS do not even have to exist for Windows 95 to function fully.

❏ The Windows Printing Subsystem requires very little configuration. To begin to use the subsystem, a printer must be first installed.

❏ Among other things, CONFIG.SYS provides the ability to install device drivers.

❏ AUTOEXEC.BAT is more commonly used to invoke device drivers for devices such as the mouse and the CD-ROM drive.

SELF TEST

The following Self Test questions will help you measure your understanding of the material presented in this chapter. Read all the choices carefully, as there may be more than one correct answer. Choose all correct answers for each question.

1. What is the name of the utility that is used to create partitions on a hard drive?

   A. AUTOEXEC

   B. FORMAT

   C. CONFIG

   D. FDISK

   E. None of the above

2. What utility is used to erase all of the data from a partition on a disk drive?

   A. AUTOEXEC

   B. FORMAT

   C. CONFIG

   D. FDISK

   E. None of the above

3. Which of the following is required to complete the installation of Windows 95?

   A. Valid Serial number

   B. A partition must be created on the hard drive

   C. The partition on the hard drive must be formatted

   D. All of the above

   E. None of the above

4. In order to be able to boot to a floppy disk the floppy disk must . . .

   A. Have a partition created on it with the FDISK utility

   B. Have system files placed on the root directory of the disk

   C. Be set as the active partition

   D. None of the above

   E. All of the above

5. What is the switch that would be used with the FORMAT command to make a disk bootable?

   A. /b

   B. /x

   C. /c

   D. /s

   E. /q

6. What is the utility that would be used to make a disk bootable without erasing all of the data from the disk?

   A. FORMAT

   B. FDISK

   C. SYS

   D. COMMAND

   E. None of the above

7. What is the special diagnostic mode provided by Windows 95?

   A. Safe Mode

   B. DOS Mode

C. Diagnostic Mode

D. Help Mode

E. None of the above

8. Which of the following drivers is **always** loaded by Safe Mode?

A. Network drivers

B. VGA video drivers

C. CD-ROM drivers

D. Sound card drivers

E. All of the above

9. DOS Mode allows . . .

A. Programs that were designed to access hardware directly to be run

B. Most DOS-based programs that will not run in Windows 95 to be run

C. Applications that Windows 95 blocks from operation because of their attempt to access hardware directly to be run

D. All of the above

E. None of the above

10. Windows 95 Plug and Play will automatically detect devices that are installed in the system that are . . .

A. Windows 95 Plug and Play-compatible

B. Listed in the Windows 95 Plug and Play registry

C. Already have device drivers installed for them

D. All of the above

E. None of the above

11. Windows 95 Plug and Play will _____ when it detects a device for the first time that it does not already have installed and is not in the Windows 95 driver library.

A. Automatically download the driver from the internet

B. Prompt the user for the driver from the hardware manufacturer

C. Prompt the user for the Windows 95 CD so the driver can be copied from there

D. All of the above

E. None of the above

12. To install a printer driver in Windows 95, you need to

A. Copy the printer setup program to the Windows\System directory

B. Double-click on Printers from the Control Panel

C. Click on Printers from the Desktop

D. All of the above

E. None of the above

13. To run a DOS-based application from within Windows 95, you would . . .

A. Double-click on the program from File Manager

B. Double-click on the program from Windows Explorer

C. Click on Start and Run, type the applications name, and press ENTER

D. Both A & B are true

E. All of the above are true

14. Both AUTOEXEC.BAT and CONFIG.SYS are . . .

A. User-editable with a text editor

B. Necessary for the operation of both DOS and Windows 95

C. Not able to be edited by the user

D. All of the above

E. None of the above

15. What allows Windows applications to print to a standard interface without worrying about the type of printer that is installed on the workstation?

A. Windows Printing Subsystem

B. DOS Printing Subsystem

C. Windows Printer Driver

D. All of the above

E. None of the above

12

Diagnosing and Troubleshooting

DOS, Windows 3.*x*, and Windows 95 all provide some error messages that can be used to help diagnose common problems, which can be resolved by some common solutions. Whenever you are installing or configuring any type of application, some errors can occur. In this chapter, we discuss some of these common problems and their solutions in addition to some of the tools that can be used to diagnose/fix these problems.

CERTIFICATION OBJECTIVE 12.01

Common Error Codes, Startup Messages, and Icons from the Boot Sequence for DOS, Windows 3.*x*, and Windows 95

All operating systems that have ever been produced have provided some type of error codes to alert the operator to troubles. Unfortunately, many of these error codes are a bit difficult to understand. As we progress into the future, these error codes and startup messages have and will continue to become less incomprehensible. In this section, we discuss some of the common error codes and startup messages, and what they really mean.

DOS

DOS provides three major error messages that are dealt with in this section. These include:

- Incorrect DOS version
- Error in CONFIG.SYS line XX
- Bad or missing COMMAND.COM

Incorrect DOS Version
Whenever a utility is used, it makes some assumptions as to its abilities based on the version of DOS that it is being run on. When the utility first starts, it verifies that it is being run on the version of DOS it was designed

for. If the version of DOS is not the version it was created for, the message "Incorrect DOS version" is displayed.

This problem should be fixed by using applications that were created for the version of DOS that you are using. As a workaround, the SETVER utility can be used to make applications think that they are running on the version of DOS that they want to be running on. To use SETVER, follow the instructions provided when you type "SETVER /?".

Error in CONFIG.SYS Line XX

The message "Error in CONFIG.SYS line XX" (where XX is a number) tells us that there was an error in the CONFIG .SYS file when it was processed. The error can be found by counting the number of lines that are in the CONFIG.SYS file, and finding line number XX. You can then either fix the error by following the instructions that the manufacturer of the driver referenced by that line provides, or by simply deleting the line. The most common cause of this error is a missing file. After determining which driver is creating the error, you should verify that the driver still exists.

Bad or Missing COMMAND.COM

Bad or missing COMMAND.COM most commonly occurs when the COMSPEC parameter is set in CONFIG.SYS, and the COMMAND.COM that COMSPEC references does not exist. This error can also occur when starting Windows 95.

Windows 3.x

Windows 3.x is a bit more advanced than DOS, so there are more advanced error messages that can be displayed from Windows 3.x. Most of the errors in the following list occur after Windows 3.x has begun to load, but the graphical user interface (GUI) is not displayed. The common error messages discussed here are:

- HIMEM.SYS not loaded
- Unable to Initialize Display Adapter

- Swapfile Corrupt
- A device referenced in the WIN.INI could not be found

HIMEM.SYS Not Loaded

Windows 3.*x* requires that the HIMEM.SYS driver be loaded in order to access High Memory. Windows 3.*x* needs to access memory above 640K, and uses the HIMEM.SYS driver to do so. This driver should be the first line in the CONFIG.SYS file. If in Windows you receive the missing HIMEM.SYS error, first verify that the first line of CONFIG.SYS is "DEVICE=C:\WINDOWS\HIMEM.SYS". If the line is in CONFIG.SYS, you should verify that HIMEM.SYS is in the specified location.

Unable to Initialize Display Adapter

Unlike DOS, Windows 3.*x* requires that you identify the video adapter that is installed in your system. If Windows gives you an "Unable to initialize display adapter" error, you should use the Windows setup utility to change the adapter type. If you are unsure of the exact model of adapter you have, VGA should always work, although it does not produce the best results. It is important to note that this error could also be the result of a faulty display adapter, but it is less likely.

Swapfile Corrupt

Windows 3.*x* uses a swapfile in order to create virtual memory. In the event that this file becomes corrupted, Windows operates extremely slowly and gives you the message that the swapfile is corrupt. To remedy this problem, open the Control Panel, and go to 386 Enhanced. Change the swapfile setting to none, save the file, and reboot the machine. After the machine restarts, Windows will be extremely slow. Open the Control Panel again, go to 386 Enhanced, and return the swapfile settings to what they were before.

A Device Referenced in WIN.INI Could Not Be Found

In the event that a device that is referenced from the WIN.INI file cannot be found, you will receive this error. To eliminate this error message, edit the WIN.INI file using any text editor and remove the line that the error is occurring on or place a semicolon in front of the line to comment it out. It is advisable to troubleshoot the problem one step further and determine what is wrong with the device that is not responding.

Windows 95

Windows 95 provides some common error codes that can be used to help troubleshoot a system problem. Many times these error codes are your only suggestion as to the cause of a problem. Knowledge of these common error codes can only speed along the troubleshooting process. The common error messages discussed here are:

- Missing or Corrupt HIMEM.SYS
- No Operating System Found
- Safe Mode
- VFAT Initialization Failure
- Bad or Missing COMMAND.COM

Missing or Corrupt HIMEM.SYS

Like Windows 3.*x*, Windows 95 requires that HIMEM.SYS be loaded for the operating system to function correctly. Windows 3.*x* is dependent on the CONFIG.SYS file correctly loading HIMEM.SYS. Windows 95 automatically loads HIMEM.SYS from the C:\WINDOWS directory prior to processing the CONFIG.SYS file. There are two possible poblems that could cause you to receive the "Missing or Corrupt HIMEM.SYS" error in Windows 95. First, if the file is actually deleted from the C:\WINDOWS directory, and second, if there is a line in CONFIG.SYS referencing another version of HIMEM.SYS. If there is such a line, simply delete it.

No Operating System Found

The message "No Operating System Found" indicates that there is either something wrong with the hard drive of the system or the boot files have been corrupted. Running the Windows 95 setup program should fix any problems related to the boot files being corrupted. If you are unable to write to the hard drive, the problem could be anything from a bad cable to a bad hard drive.

Safe Mode

Any time Windows 95 encounters an error, it automatically starts the system in safe mode. Safe mode is a special diagnostic mode that does not load most of the drivers normally loaded and loads a standard VGA display driver. Safe mode provides a method for you to change system settings in many cases where incorrect settings have rendered the system useless. For example, in the event that an incorrect video driver was installed, safe mode would allow you to correct it, and return the system to its normal functionality.

VFAT Initialization Failure

VFAT initialization failure occurs when the system is unable to initialize the driver that controls the file system on the drive. The first step in attempting to correct this error would be to reboot the system, press F8 when the "Starting Windows 95" message is displayed, and choose "Safe Mode Command Prompt Only" from the list provided. From this command prompt, the SCANDISK utility can be run to attempt to fix physical drive problems. If SCANDISK is unable to fix the error, rerunning Windows 95 setup should correct the problem.

Bad or Missing COMMAND.COM

Windows 95 expects that COMMAND.COM will be installed in the :\WINDOWS\COMMAND directory. In the event that COMMAND.COM is not located in the C:\WINDOWS\COMMAND directory, you should replace it. COMSPEC being set in the CONFIG.SYS file to a directory where COMMAND.COM is not located could cause the problem. In addition, if a manual path statement has been added to the AUTOEXEC.BAT that does not include the C:\WINDOWS\COMMAND directory, this could cause the problem. If none of these possible difficulties exist, rerunning Windows 95 setup should correct the problem.

CERTIFICATION OBJECTIVE 12.02

Correcting a Startup or Boot Problem

There are many startup or boot problems that can occur. The most common and usually easiest solution to these problems is to rerun the setup utility that shipped with your operating system. The setup utility should correct any problems you are having.

CERTIFICATION OBJECTIVE 12.03

Creating an Emergency Boot Disk with Utilities Installed

Windows 95 provides a simple method of creating an emergency boot disk. Follow the procedure outlined in Exercise 12-1.

EXERCISE 12-1

Creating an Emergency Boot Disk

1. Insert a floppy disk into your floppy drive.
2. Click the Start button and choose Settings | Control Panel.
3. Double-click the Add/Remove Programs icon.
4. Select the Startup Disk tab on the far right.
5. Click the Create Disk button.

Figure 12-1 shows the utility that is used to create the Emergency Boot Disk.

Windows 95 can easily
create a startup disk that
can be used to diagnose
and fix problems in the
event of Windows 95 not
working properly

CERTIFICATION OBJECTIVE 12.04

Recognizing Windows-Specific Printing Problems

The Windows printing subsystem simplifies the task of printing a great deal
for both the user and the applications authors. Unfortunately, with the
standardized Windows printing system come some common problems that
could occur. These problems are:

- Print spool is stalled
- Driver is set for bi-directional mode with a uni-directional cable

- Incorrect/incompatible driver for printer
- Printer port not set up correctly in device manager
- Printer is not set to print to correct port

Print Spool Is Stalled

The print spooler can stall itself in order to hopefully prevent the user from losing a print job. In the event that the print spooler does become stalled when it should not be, the problem can be solved by clicking on the File menu from the Printer Properties and selecting Restart Printing.

Driver Is Set for Bi-Directional Printing/User Is Using a Uni-Directional Cable

Some of the newer and more advanced printers have the capability of using a bi-directional mode, meaning that the printer is able to talk back to the computer. This can be extremely useful because it allows the printer to send the user exact error messages that are displayed on the workstation, and helps the spooler to avoid print spooler stalls. In the event that you are unable to communicate with a bi-directional printer, your first step should be to turn off bi-directional printing in the Printer Settings tab. If the printer works after bi-directional support is turned off, you can either leave it that way and be happy, or replace the cable with a bi-directional capable cable. Also note that bi-directional support could be turned off in the systems BIOS (consult the system's manual for details on how to correct this problem).

Incorrect/Incompatible Driver for Printer

It is extraordinarily important to verify that the driver that you are using to print to your printer is the correct version for your printer. The driver should either be specifically manufactured for the printer you are using, or should be listed as a compatible driver by the printer manufacturer. If you need to get a new driver for the printer, either visit the manufacturer's Web site or call their technical support team.

Printer Port Is Not Set Up Correctly in Device Manager (ECP, EPP, Standard)

Windows 95 requires that the port for a printer be installed (installed correctly, to be specific). Windows 95 usually detects and installs ports correctly, but may install a port as Standard when it should be installed as ECP. To correct this problem, use the Add New Hardware Wizard from the Control Panel to add a new port. If after adding the new port you are still having difficulties, you may want to consult your system's documentation to verify that the port is set in the correct mode in the system's BIOS.

Printer Not Set to Print to Correct Port

Having a printer set to the wrong port is undoubtedly one of the most easily solved problems that you can encounter. To change the port that a printer is set to print to, open the properties dialog box of the printer in question, which is shown in Figure 12-2. Next, select the Details tab and change the port setting to the correct one.

CERTIFICATION OBJECTIVE 12.05

Common Problems and Causes

There are some common problems that occur frequently on Windows systems. Whenever one of these problems occurs, it is important to remember that your system may have been rendered in a less-than-optimal state. Even though the system appears to be functioning properly, it may continue to have difficulties. The best solution for most problems is to simply reboot the system.

General Protection Faults

General protection faults (GPFs) occur frequently when an application performs an operation that Windows does not normally permit to happen.

An incorrect port setting can be changed from the Details tab of the Printer Properties dialog box

GPFs can be caused by nearly anything, and can almost be considered a catchall for errors. If an application causes a general protection fault, you should restart the system at your earliest convenience. In many cases, the problem is solved by a simple reboot. In the event that the problem is not solved, you should reinstall the application. If after reinstalling the application the error still continues, it is advisable to contact the program vendor's technical support.

System Lock Up

Applications can easily lock up or hang a system for nearly any reason. In the event that you encounter a lock up, you should simply reboot the system. If lock ups continue, you might want to run SCANDISK and DEFRAG on the system. If after running SCANDISK and DEFRAG, the lock ups still continue, reinstalling the application where they most frequently occur should take care of the problem.

Operating System Will Not Boot

The operating system not booting could be caused by nearly anything, although it is rather rare. Rerunning that operating system's setup program should solve any problems.

Application Will Not Start or Load

In the event that an application does not start, you should first restart the system to attempt to correct the problem. If restarting the system does not solve the problem, reinstalling the application usually does.

Invalid Working Directory

It is not uncommon to have the working directory set incorrectly. If at any time the working directory is wrong, it is possible that a program might not function correctly, or at all. If you are receiving errors about an invalid working directory, you should view the settings of the shortcut and then verify that the working directory exists. If the directory does not exist, modify the setting or create the directory.

Option Will Not Function

It is not unusual for a particular option not to function in the manner that you would expect it to. If this occurs, the best solution is to close all programs and shut down the system. After the system is fully shut down, restart it and see if the option functions properly. If the problem is not solved, the best course of action is to uninstall or reinstall the application.

Cannot Log On to Network

Most times that a system is unable to log on to the network it is caused by external problems such as a broken cable or problem in the wiring closet.

Another common cause is a bad network card. The first course of action that should be taken is to reboot the system. If the problem still continues, removing and reinstalling the network drivers usually takes care of any problems. If the problem is still not solved, it is best to start troubleshooting the network for other difficulties, and determine if the problem is with the particular workstation.

CERTIFICATION OBJECTIVE 12.06

DOS- and Windows-Based Utilities and Commands/Switches

There are many different utilities that are provided with both DOS and Windows 3.*x*/Windows 95 that help in the diagnosing, and in some cases solving, most problems.

DOS

DOS provides some very useful tools that allow us to do anything from gather information about the system to reorganizing the file locations on the hard drive in order to improve performance. The DOS-based tools examined here include:

- MSD.EXE
- SCANDISK.EXE
- DEFRAG.EXE
- MEM.EXE
- EDIT.COM
- FDISK.EXE
- ATTRIB.EXE

MSD.EXE

MSD, Microsoft Diagnostics, is a utility that provides a great deal of information about the system and is demonstrated in Figure 12-3. MSD

FIGURE 12-3

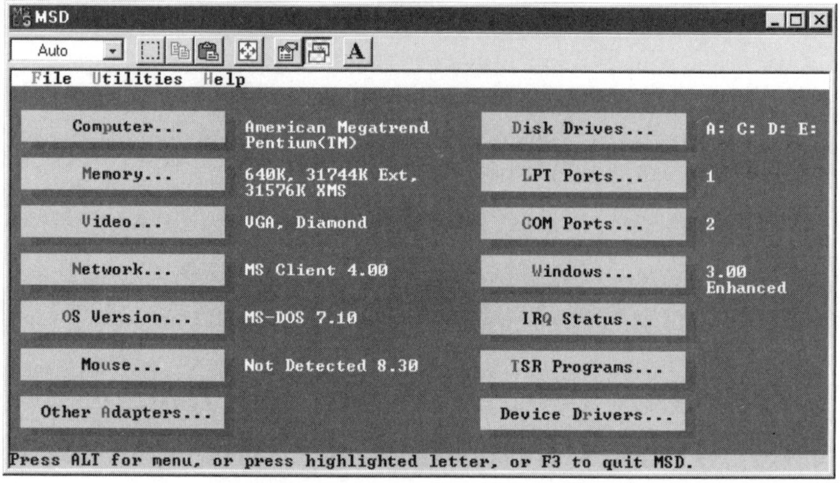

Microsoft Diagnostics
provides a good survey of
the system's features in one
easy-to-read format

is most useful in determining what the system has installed in it, such as
memory and hard drives. This information is available in other forms, but
not all in one group as MSD presents it.

*The Microsoft Diagnostics utility can be used to provide information
about the system. This information can be valuable in determining if a
workstation is capable of being upgraded.*

exam
ⓦatch

SCANDISK.EXE

SCANDISK is a utility that can be used to check disk drives for errors and,
when passed the /f switch, fix them. Many reoccurring problems can be
solved by running the SCANDISK utility.

DEFRAG.EXE

DEFRAG is a utility that can be used to reorganize a hard disk drive.
DEFRAG reorganizes the drive into a fashion that it feels is logical, which
usually results in improved system performance.

MEM.EXE

MEM.EXE provides information about the memory that is installed in
the system, and what it is being used for. Passing the /c switch displays

information on what programs are using the memory, and how much memory they are using. Passing the /f switch provides information about free memory in the system. Many times there is too much information presented on the screen, and you are unable to read it. To alleviate this problem, passing the /p switch pauses after each page of information is displayed. Simply running MEM.EXE, as Figure 12-4 shows, tells how much memory is installed in the system and how much of that is free.

EDIT.COM

EDIT.COM is a simple ASCII text editor. It can be used to modify system files such as AUTOEXEC.BAT and CONFIG.SYS. It is simple to use and provides a basic GUI and mouse support if a mouse driver is loaded.

FDISK.EXE

FDISK.EXE can be used to create and delete partitions on the system's hard disk drives. Be warned that FDISK.EXE makes changes that are permanent and could easily render the system unbootable and make all data on the hard drives inaccessible. Use FDISK with care and ensure that all your data

---

FIGURE 12-4

MEM.EXE can be used to provide information on the memory that is installed in the system and how much of it is available

```
MS-DOS Prompt                                                    _ □ ×
Auto        ▼    □ ▣ ▣ ⊕ ⌗ 🗗 A
C:\>mem

Memory Type         Total       Used        Free
Conventional        640K        52K         589K
Upper               0K          0K          0K
Reserved            384K        384K        0K
Extended (XMS)      31,744K     168K        31,576K

Total memory        32,768K     604K        32,165K

Total under 1 MB    640K        52K         589K

Total Expanded (EMS)                  32M (33,046,528 bytes)
Free Expanded (EMS)                   16M (16,777,216 bytes)

Largest executable program size       588K (602,608 bytes)
Largest free upper memory block       0K      (0 bytes)
MS-DOS is resident in the high memory area.

C:\>
```

is backed up. FDISK, as shown in Figure 12-5, provides an easy-to-use menu-driven interface.

FDISK/MBR can be used to replace the Master Boot Record with a backup copy. This may become necessary if the Master Boot Record becomes infected with a virus. FDISK/MBR is not destructive in any way unless the computer has a third-party boot program installed. These programs are found frequently in older systems with hard drives larger than 540 megabytes installed in them.

ATTRIB.EXE

ATTRIB.EXE is a utility that can be used to change the attributes of a file or group of files. Attributes include Read-Only (r), Archive (a), Hidden (h), and System (s). To turn on attributes, add a plus-sign in front of the letter corresponding to the attribute. To turn off an attribute, add a minus-sign in front of the attribute. To process all of the files in subdirectories, add the /s switch.

FIGURE 12-5

FDISK.EXE can be used to create and delete partitions on a hard disk drive

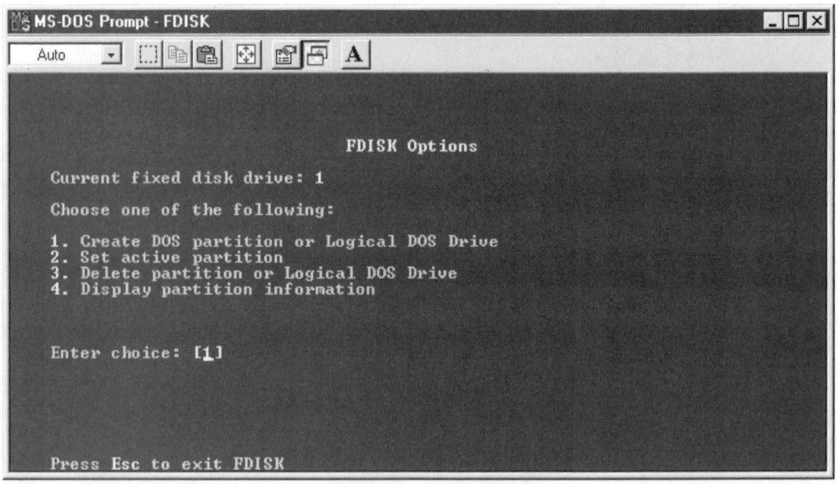

```
MS-DOS Prompt - FDISK                                    _ □ ×

Auto    ▼   □ ⓑⓑ   ⊞   ⓑⓑ   A

                           FDISK Options

        Current fixed disk drive: 1

        Choose one of the following:

        1. Create DOS partition or Logical DOS Drive
        2. Set active partition
        3. Delete partition or Logical DOS Drive
        4. Display partition information


        Enter choice: [1]




        Press Esc to exit FDISK
```

QUESTIONS AND ANSWERS

To make the file . . .	I would use the command . . .
C:\AUTOEXEC.BAT hidden and read-only	attrib c:\autoexec.bat +h +r
C:\AUTOEXEC.BAT unhidden	attrib c:\autoexec.bat –h
C:\AUTOEXEC.BAT system, read-only, not hidden, and archive	attrib c:\autoexec.bat +s +r -h +a
All files in the C:\INFO directory read only	attrib c:\info +r
All files in the C:\INFO directory and all subdirectories	attrib c:\info +r /s

Windows-Based Tools

Windows provides some additional tools and some extensions of the DOS-based tools. The tools discussed here are:

- SCANDISK
- DEFRAG.EXE
- Device Manager
- Conflict Troubleshooter
- SYSEDIT.EXE
- Control Panel
- System General Properties

SCANDISK

Windows SCANDISK, which is shown in Figure 12-6, is nearly exactly the same as the DOS-based SCANDISK. It is capable of detecting and fixing most drive corruption problems that could exist. SCANDISK is capable of fixing errors that it finds without any special parameters, unlike the DOS-based SCANDISK, which requires a /fix switch in order for it to be able to fix problems it finds. SCANDISK operates more efficiently if you close all applications prior to running it.

FIGURE 12-6

SCANDISK can be used to detect and fix most drive corruption problems

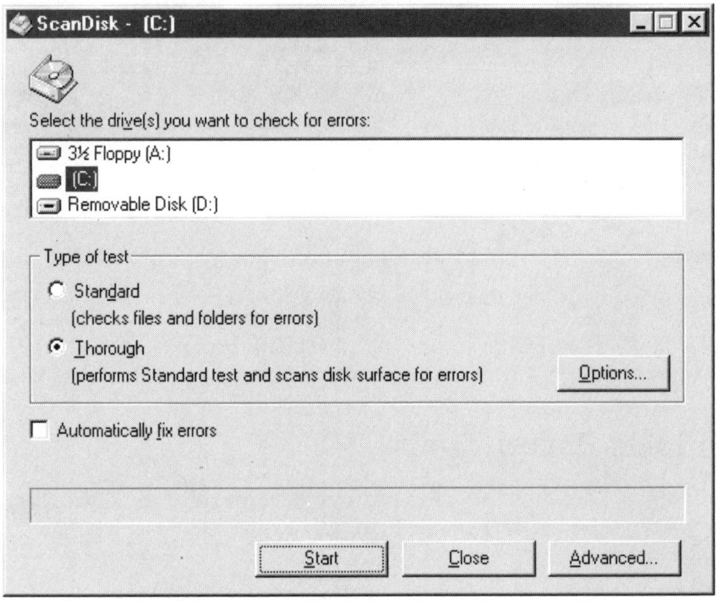

DEFRAG.EXE

Windows DEFRAG is capable of reorganizing the layout of hard disk drives in the same fashion that the DOS-based DEFRAG does. DEFRAG runs more efficiently if all applications are closed prior to running it and after SCANDISK has been run on the drive.

Device Manager

Device Manager is a utility that is provided with Windows 95. Device Manager lists all of the devices that are installed in the system and their properties, as shown in Figure 12-7. Device Manager can be accessed by double-clicking System in the Windows 95 Control Panel and selecting the Device Manager tab.

Conflict Troubleshooter

Conflict Troubleshooter is a utility that is provided with Windows 95 that can be used to help resolve conflicts between two or more devices. Conflict

FIGURE 12-7

Device Manager lists all of the devices that are installed in the system and their properties

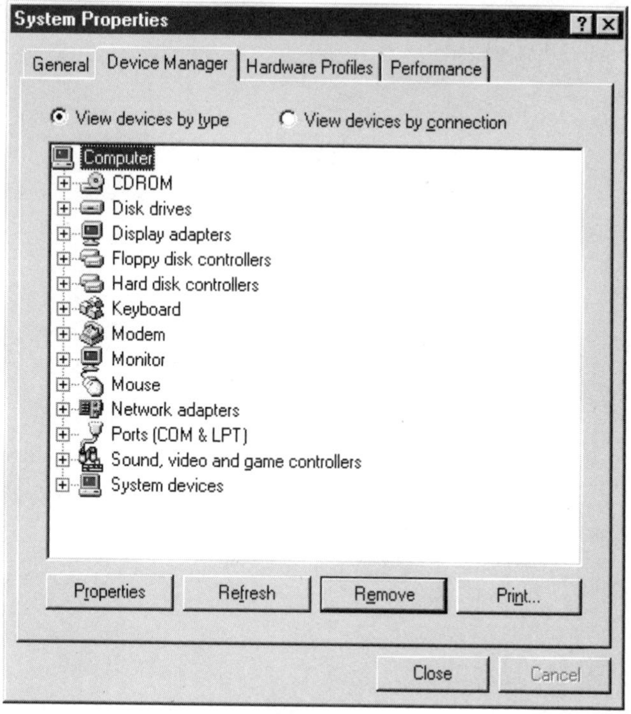

Troubleshooter automatically starts whenever the system starts and detects a conflict.

SYSEDIT.EXE

SYSEDIT.EXE, the System Configuration Editor, is a utility that is provided with both Windows3.*x* and Windows 95. SYSEDIT.EXE, which is shown in Figure 12-8, helps you to easily edit the system configuration files.

The files that SYSEDIT.EXE enables you to edit are:

- MSMAIL.INI
- PROTOCOL.INI
- SYSTEM.INI

FIGURE 12-8

SYSEDIT is a tool that
enables you to edit the
system configuration files
from one easy interface

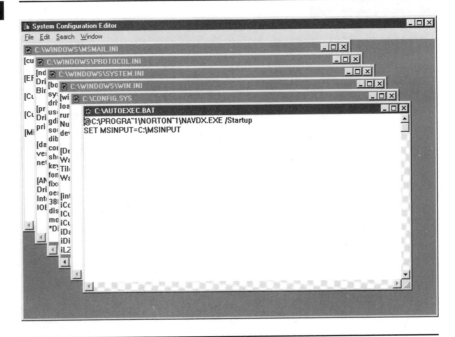

- WIN.INI
- CONFIG.SYS
- AUTOEXEC.BAT

Control Panel

The Control Panel, shown in Figure 12-9, is a utility that can be used to
change the settings of the system. By double-clicking any icon that is listed,
you can change the properties, that are associated with whatever that icon
represents. Note that each system has some core icons such as "Add New
Hardware" and "Add/Remove Programs," but icons that are available vary
according to what is installed on the system.

System General Properties

System General Properties provides information about the computer such
as the version of the operating system, the processor that is installed on the

FIGURE 12-9

The Control Panel provides a method of modifying the configuration of the computer

computer, and the amount of memory that is installed. The System General Properties can be accessed by double-clicking the system icon in the Control Panel.

Registry Editor

The Windows 95 Registry Editor, as shown in Figure 12-10, is the most powerful tool in Windows 95. Be extremely careful when using the Registry Editor. Nearly any setting of the system can be changed within the Registry Editor. You will never be warned if a change you are making could negatively affect the system.

exam
Watch

The Windows 95 Registry Editor can be used to change any of the settings of the system that are stored in the registry. The Registry Editor can cause irreparable harm without any warning.

The Windows 95 Registry Editor is capable of changing nearly any setting on the computer

---

CERTIFICATION OBJECTIVE 12.07

Installing and Configuring DOS Applications, and Potential Problems in Windows 95

Most DOS-based applications can simply be run from within Windows 95 without any difficulties. There are some cases where it is beneficial to make some changes to the configuration of these applications.

Setting Memory

Many DOS programs require that a specific amount of memory be available to the program. Even though there is ample memory available, the programs may attempt to directly access the memory, in which case they can be led to believe there is no memory available. To correct this problem, open the properties for the shortcut to the application that you are dealing with and select the Memory tab, as shown in Figure 12-11. Adjust the memory configuration to the amount the application requires.

Setting Screen Size

Some applications can be difficult to use when they are run in a windowed mode. To change the screen size that an application is run at, select the Screen tab of the Shortcut Properties dialog box, shown in Figure 12-12. From the Screen panel, adjust the initial size to whatever you desire. Remember that a full-screen application can always be forced into windowed mode by pressing ALT-ENTER.

The Memory tab of the Shortcut Properties dialog box can be used to specify how much memory is given to an application

The Screen tab of the Shortcut Properties dialog box can be used to specify the display mode in which an application starts

Determine Whether to Display the Win95 Toolbar

Some applications do not perform well when the Windows 95 Toolbar is displayed. In some cases of applications that were not specifically designed for use with Windows 95, the toolbar may cover vital parts of the application. To prevent the toolbar from displaying, uncheck Display Toolbar from the Screen panel of the Shortcut Properties dialog box.

Enable/Disable Dynamic Memory Allocation

Enabling dynamic memory allocation permits Windows 95 to automatically give an application memory when it needs it and take memory away when the application is not using it. This is good in most cases, but some older applications expect a certain amount of memory to be there, and it may cause problems when it is not. To disable dynamic memory allocation, uncheck Dynamic Memory Allocation from the Screen panel of the Shortcut Properties dialog box.

Illegal Operations Error

Illegal operations, in short, occur when an application attempts to access hardware or memory directly. Windows 95 limits the direct access of any hardware by applications and will repeatedly cause illegal operations in the event that the application attempts this. The best solution to an application that frequently causes illegal operations errors is to force the application to run in MS-DOS mode. Applications can be forced to run in MS-DOS mode by clicking the Advanced button from the Program panel of the Shortcut Properties dialog box, as shown in Figure 12-13. If MS-DOS mode is then checked, the application automatically enters MS-DOS mode (after warning you to save all your work in other applications).

FIGURE 12-13

The Advanced Program Settings dialog box can be used to force an application to run in MS-DOS mode

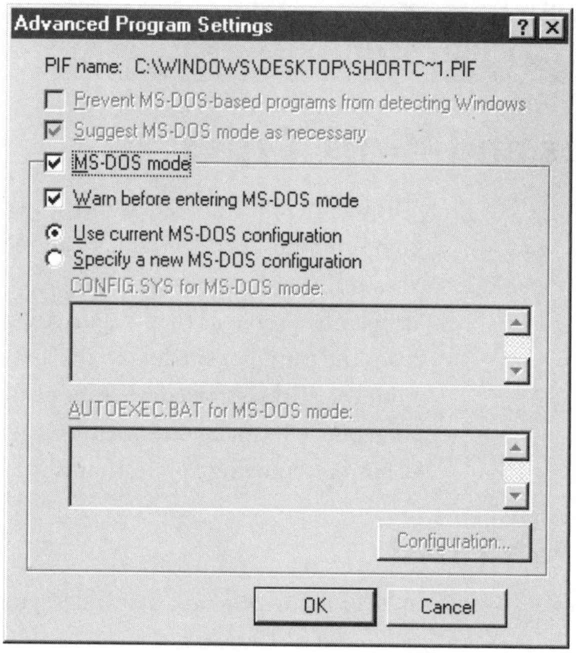

Application May Quit and Windows 95 Stops Functioning

In the event that an application stops functioning, it can frequently hang the entire system and cause the system to appear to be non-functional. Follow the procedures in Exercise 12-2 to remedy this problem.

<table>
<tr><td>EXERCISE 12-2</td></tr>
</table>

Closing a Program That Is Not Responding

1. Press CTRL-ALT-DEL to invoke the Close Program dialog box.

2. Choose the application that is not responding from the list of current applications.

3. Click the End Task button. This returns the system to a functioning state in many cases.

4. If after a few minutes the system does not return to its previous stability, reboot the system. This should return it to normal operation.

CERTIFICATION OBJECTIVE 12.08

Viruses and Virus Types

Viruses are unfortunately something that have become a part of everyday computer life. Any device that can receive data from another device is susceptible to being infected with a computer virus. Viruses are very dangerous problems that plague computing today. They can cause anything from the extreme data loss to the annoying message that pops up every few minutes. Viruses can come from nearly anywhere, but are usually created by someone with malicious intentions. Purchasing and installing a good virus scanning/removing application is the best solution to the virus problem.

What are Viruses?

A virus is any program that is designed with the intention of doing harm to a computer. Viruses can result in anything from damaging your computer's hardware to making a siren blare every day or two. The most common

FROM THE FIELD

The Cost of Viruses to the World

One can only speculate what goes on in the mind of a demented virus creator. Do they think they are being clever? Funny? Brilliant? What? Perhaps in their own little worlds, they are achieving some kind of goal. But in the real world, they are costing the computing society much more than they can comprehend.

Lost corporate time trying to fix these as well as rebuilding that which they destroy is almost incomprehensible. A destructive virus costs companies collectively more than the biggest armed bank heist in history. I wonder if the creators of these know what their creations are costing people, In the near future, the laws should change on these and make them severe felonies.

Money is not the only factor in this damage. Many users out there are not sophisticated enough to be armed with the absolute latest virus checkers, if they are even armed at all. I think of an 80-year-old who is writing his life story and gets zapped by one of these and Bam!, down the drain. Or even for those who are sophisticated enough to have virus checkers, they may not update them regularly.

Viruses are bad news. They can totally destroy your data as well as hardware. Most of you have probably spent tons of time configuring your system and you would hate to have to re-install everything. The moral: Make sure that you and those whose PCs you work on have the latest patches from a reputable virus prevention software company.

—By Ted Hamilton, MCP, A+ Certified

result of viruses is a loss of data of some sort. If your system appears to be operating in a manner that you don't expect it to be, you should scan it for viruses.

Sources

Viruses are in most cases created by persons with the intention of doing harm to other persons' computers. On some occasions, viruses can be created by an unintentional error of a programmer, although this is extremely unlikely.

Spread

Viruses can be spread whenever a computer makes contact with another computer, directly or indirectly. For example, if you download a file from the Internet, the file could be infected with a virus, which could in turn infect your computer. On the contrary, you could infect your computer by opening a file your friend gave you on a floppy disk.

How To Determine Presence

In most cases, the presence of viruses is fairly difficult to detect without a virus detection application. Virus detection applications are available for sale, and are made by many different software companies.

Removal

Most virus detection packages include the ability to remove the virus from the system. By running the virus removal software, most viruses can be removed. In the event that the software is unable to remove the virus, using the FDISK.EXE and FORMAT.COM utilities from a known virus-free boot disk will remove any viruses.

Prevention

Many of the popular virus detection applications also have the capability to scan the system for viruses and detect/clean any that they find. In addition, some of the more progressive software can automatically check each file as it is opened, and scan any files as they are downloaded.

Types of Viruses

There are many different types of viruses that ultimately cause harm to the overall computer, but all exhibit some individual, specific traits. The virus types discussed here are:

- Boot Sector Virus

- FAT Virus
- Memory Virus
- Macro Virus
- CMOS Virus
- Hoax Virus

Boot Sector Virus

A boot sector virus stays resident by infecting the boot sector of the computer. Each time the system is booted, it is re-infected from its own boot sector. Any time a floppy disk is inserted into the drive, the floppy's boot sector is infected. If a machine is booted from or even if an infected floppy disk is left in the floppy drive when the system is rebooted, that computer will then be infected.

FAT Virus

A FAT Virus infects the File Allocation Table of a hard drive. FAT viruses are usually not spread by themselves and are carried along with other viruses. FAT viruses usually cause a loss of files that are on a hard drive, and are usually difficult if not impossible to recover from.

Memory Virus

Memory viruses are viruses that execute and stay resident in memory. Memory viruses usually do not spread themselves, but are carried along with other viruses.

Macro Virus

Macro viruses are viruses that attach themselves to documents in the form of macros. These macros can infect all of the other macros on the system, and all new documents created on the system. Macro viruses most commonly infect Microsoft Word and Microsoft Excel documents, but have the possibility of showing up in any application that includes the ability to create macros.

CMOS Virus

CMOS viruses are viruses that make themselves resident in the CMOS of the computer. These viruses are one of the most difficult to remove. CMOS viruses frequently cause harm to the hardware of the computer.

Hoax Viruses

Hoax viruses are just that, hoaxes. The most common hoax virus began with the title of "Good Times," and has resurfaced under many other names. These virus hoaxes are usually sent as e-mail warnings not to open any e-mails of these titles. In the event that you receive any e-mail similar to this please notify the sender that it is a hoax, and ignore it.

CERTIFICATION SUMMARY

In this chapter, we have examined many of the common errors that you can receive while working on a computer running DOS, Windows 3.*x*, or Windows 95. In addition, we have detailed many of the causes and solutions of these problems and discussed some of the common tools that can be used to repair them.

✓ TWO-MINUTE DRILL

- ❑ The SETVER utility can be used to make applications think that they are running on the version of DOS that they want to be running on.
- ❑ The most common cause of the "Error in CONFIG.SYS line XX" (where XX is a number) error is a missing file.
- ❑ Both Windows 3.*x* and Windows 95 require that the HIMEM.SYS driver be loaded in order to access High Memory.
- ❑ If Windows gives you a "Unable to initialize display adapter" error, you should use the Windows setup utility to change the adapter type.
- ❑ Any time Windows 95 encounters an error, it automatically starts the system in safe mode.

❑ The most common and usually easiest solution to startup or boot problems is to rerun the setup utility that shipped with your operating system.

❑ The message "No Operating System Found" indicates that there is either something wrong with the hard drive of the system or the boot files have been corrupted.

❑ General protection faults (GPFs) can be caused by nearly anything, and can almost be considered a catchall for errors.

❑ The Microsoft Diagnostics utility can be used to provide information about the system. This information can be valuable in determining if a workstation is capable of being upgraded.

❑ DEFRAG is a utility that can be used to reorganize a hard disk drive.

❑ ATTRIB.EXE is a utility that can be used to change the attributes of a file or group of files.

❑ The Windows Device Manager lists all of the devices that are installed in the system and their properties.

❑ Be extremely careful when using the Registry Editor, as nearly any setting of the system can be changed within it and you will never be warned if a change you are making could negatively affect the system.

❑ Enabling dynamic memory allocation permits Windows 95 to automatically give an application memory when it needs it and take memory away when the application is not using it.

❑ Illegal operations, in short, occur when an application attempts to access hardware or memory directly.

❑ The best solution to an application that frequently causes illegal operations errors is to force the application to run in MS-DOS mode.

❑ A virus is any program that is designed with the intention of doing harm to a computer. The best defense against virus infection is to purchase a good virus scanning/removing application.

❑ Memory viruses are viruses that execute and stay resident in memory.

❑ A boot sector virus stays resident by infecting the boot sector of the computer.

❑ FAT viruses are usually not spread by themselves and are carried along with other viruses.

❑ Macro viruses are viruses that attach themselves to documents in the form of macros.

❑ CMOS Viruses are viruses that make themselves resident in the CMOS of the computer and are the most difficult viruses to remove.

❑ The most common hoax virus began with the title of "Good Times," and has resurfaced under many other names.

SELF TEST

The following Self Test questions will help you measure your understanding of the material presented in this chapter. Read all the choices carefully, as there may be more than one correct answer. Choose all correct answers for each question.

1. Which command would you use to change the attributes of all files in the C:\TEMP directory to be read-only and hidden.

   A. ATTRIB C:\TEMP +h

   B. ATTRIB C:\TEMP +h +r

   C. ATTRIB C:\TEMP +h /s

   D. ATTRIB C:\TEMP +h +r /s

   E. None of the above

2. Which DOS-based utility provides information about the computer such as disk drives, memory, and COM ports installed?

   A. SYSEDIT.EXE

   B. Control Panel

   C. MSD.EXE

   D. DEFRAG.EXE

   E. FDISK.EXE

3. Which DOS-based utility can be used to create partitions on a hard disk drive?

   A. SYSEDIT.EXE

   B. Control Panel

   C. MSD.EXE

   D. DEFRAG.EXE

   E. FDISK.EXE

4. Which Windows 95 utility can be used to change the settings of system devices?

   A. SYSEDIT.EXE

   B. Control Panel

   C. MSD.EXE

   D. DEFRAG.EXE

   E. FDISK.EXE

5. Which Windows-based utility can be used to edit many of the system configuration files?

   A. SYSEDIT.EXE

   B. Control Panel

   C. MSD.EXE

   D. DEFRAG.EXE

   E. FDISK.EXE

6. Which utility can be used to reorganize the file locations on a hard drive?

   A. SYSEDIT.EXE

   B. Control Panel

   C. MSD.EXE

   D. DEFRAG.EXE

   E. FDISK.EXE

7. The SETVER utility is used to correct which DOS problem?

A. Incorrect DOS version

B. Bad or Missing COMMAND.COM

C. Error in CONFIG.SYS line XX

D. All of the above

E. None of the above

8. Which type of virus usually is found attached to Microsoft Word and Microsoft Excel documents?

A. Boot Sector virus

B. Memory virus

C. Macro virus

D. FAT virus

E. Hoax virus

9. What type of virus is not actually a virus, and is usually sent in the form of an e-mail warning about a virus?

A. Boot Sector virus

B. Memory virus

C. Macro virus

D. FAT virus

E. Hoax virus

10. What Windows 95-based tool is used to modify the configuration of almost every setting in Windows 95?

A. Control Panel

B. Registry Editor

C. SYSEDIT.EXE

D. Windows SCANDISK

E. Conflict Troubleshooter

11. If an incorrect display adapter is set as the display adapter in DOS, you could _____ in order to fix it.

A. Reinstall the operating system.

B. Use the setup utility to fix the problem.

C. Boot the system in safe mode and then fix the problem.

D. Both A and B are possible solutions.

E. Both A and C are possible solutions.

F. None of the above.

12. If an incorrect display adapter is set as the display adapter in Windows 3.x, you could _____ in order to fix it.

A. Reinstall the operating system.

B. Use the setup utility to fix the problem.

C. Boot the system in safe mode and then fix the problem.

D. Both A and B are possible solutions.

E. Both A and C are possible solutions.

F. None of the above.

13. If an incorrect display adapter is set as the display adapter in Windows 95, you could _____ in order to fix it.

A. Reinstall the operating system.

B. Use the setup utility to fix the problem.

C. Boot the system in safe mode and then fix the problem.

D. Both A and B are possible solutions.

E. Both A and C are possible solutions.

F. None of the above.

14. Which of the following is not true?

A. A printer with a driver set in bi-directional mode must use a bi-directional cable.

B. A printer with a driver not set in bi-directional mode can use a non-bi-directional cable.

C. A printer with a driver not set in bi-directional mode cannot use a non-bi-directional cable.

D. All of the above are true.

E. None of the above are true.

15. Which of the following is true about a "No Operating System Found" error message on a computer running Windows 95?

A. Either the hard drive has a problem or the boot files have been corrupted.

B. The Windows 95 setup program should fix the problem if it is caused by corrupted boot files.

C. If you are unable to write to the hard drive, the problem probably is related to bad hardware.

D. All of the above are true.

E. None of the above are true.

13

Networks

I n this chapter we will discuss networking capabilities such as the sharing of disk drives as well as print and file services. We will talk about accessing the Internet, its basic functions including downloading files, e-mail, and the Web, and what they can do for you.

Networking Capabilities of DOS and Windows

Both DOS and Windows, with the appropriate networking software installed, are capable of sharing files and printers with other persons on the network. Also, with additional software installed, users can access resources available on other computers in places such as the Internet.

Sharing Disk Drives

The sharing of disk drives is the most basic of networking concepts. Sharing disk drives is exactly what it sounds like—sharing disk drives. When drives are shared, other users are given the ability to access the files that you have stored on your drives. Depending on the particular operating system you are using and the permissions you have set on the files, users could read, add, modify, or even delete files.

Sharing Print and File Services

DOS, Windows 3.*x*, and Windows 95 are all capable of sharing files and printers with other users on the network. Each operating system has specific methods of sharing these devices. Refer to the operating system's directions for sharing printers and files.

Installing Software

Each workstation that will be communicating on the network must have software installed on it. This software should include drivers for the NIC, client software that allows the computer to communicate on the network, and software that allows the client software to communicate on the network using the correct protocol.

Network Type and Network Card

DOS, Windows 3.*x*, and Windows 95 are capable of communicating on nearly any type of network, so long as the correct network card and drivers are installed. The installation procedures for the network card and drivers provided by the manufacturer should be followed.

exam
Watch

Whenever installing network drivers, installing network cards, or configuring file and printer sharing, the manufacturer's procedures should be followed.

CERTIFICATION OBJECTIVE 13.02

The Internet and Setting Up a System for Internet Access

In a period of just a few years, the Internet has been transformed from something that only a select few knew about to something only a select few don't know about. The Internet has become something that many people depend on for their day-to-day work. It is important that you have a good working knowledge of the Internet, some of its most basic functions, and how they apply to you. Although the majority of average people do not have Internet access yet, most of those who do have access tend to rely on it.

TCP/IP

TCP/IP, a routable protocol, is very robust and commonly associated with UNIX systems. It has become the standard for the Internet, as well as the networking industry. TCP/IP is actually a suite of protocols with each protocol in the suite having a specific purpose and function. At the time of its origin, TCP/IP was designed to contend with inferior networking conditions. An ability to reroute packets was therefore built in to this

FROM THE FIELD

Web Pages for the Professional Upgrade and Repairperson

Here are some great Web pages that have to do with the A+ certification, hardware repair, and upgrades. Take the time to check them out. There is a huge amount of good information on them.

Where to get a job once you get A+ certified:
http://www.generalcc.com/joblinks/joblinks.htm

First-rate info on the A+ exam:
http://www.comptia.org/atestrept.html

Download an A+ practice test:
http://www.stsware.com/aplus.htm

Download another A+ practice test:
http://www.aplusexam.com/

Online A+ practice exam:
http://www.a1pctraining.com/asample.htm

Register for your A+ exam:
http://www.sylvanprometric.com/

Excellent hardware page:
http://www.sysopt.com/sphelp.html

A must see, with hardware links:
http://www.geocities.com/SiliconValley/Bay/6866/index.html

A good place to find drivers:
http://www.drivershq.com/main.html

Many, many downloads off all types:
http://www.download.com/

—By Ted Hamilton, MCP, A+ Certified

protocol. When setting up a system to access the Internet, your only protocol choice is "TCP/IP". TCP/IP is the only protocol that can be used to access the Internet. Networks running IPX/SPX that do not have TCP/IP installed on each client workstation require an IPX to IP Gateway to convert IPX packets to IP before they can be sent out to the Internet.

Downloading

Downloading is the process of transferring a file or files from one computer to another. In every instance where a file is downloaded, the transfer is initiated at the computer that will be receiving the file(s). Any time you click on a link in a Web browser that transfers a file to your computer, you are downloading that file. By definition, each time you load a Web page, you are truly downloading a file. Each Web page is contained within a file that the Web browser understands how to process. Once the file is being downloaded, the browser begins to process the file, and displays the contents of the file.

E-Mail

E-mail, electronic mail, is quickly becoming one of the most popular communication methods within offices and beyond. The concept of e-mail is that people are able to send electronic messages to you that are stored on a server for you until you read them. In fact, e-mail is very similar in concept to traditional mail (commonly referred to these days as "snail-mail"). In both e-mail and snail-mail messages are sent to you and are stored at a post office until you receive them. The major difference is that e-mail is delivered electronically, which in turn allows message delivery to occur within seconds.

HTML

HTML, Hypertext Markup Language, is the language in which most Web pages are written. HTML is a modular language that is fairly simple to use, and allows for special formatting to be applied to documents without a great deal of work. HTML is what the World Wide Web is based upon. The majority of pages on the World Wide Web are written strictly in HTML.

HTTP

HTTP, Hypertext Transfer Protocol, is the protocol that is most commonly used to transfer information in a Web browser. HTTP was originally used to transfer HTML files to computers, but has been adapted to transfer nearly any type of file. HTTP is the most common transfer protocol on the Internet. HTTP is capable of both downloading and uploading, but is rarely used for uploading.

FTP

FTP, File Transfer Protocol, is used to download files from an FTP server to a client computer. FTP is much older than the HTTP protocol, and was in use prior to the creation of the World Wide Web. FTP is fairly fast and is connection-oriented, meaning that it attempts to verify that files transferred using FTP have not been corrupted during the transfer. FTP is much faster than the HTTP protocol for downloading files.

In addition to downloading files, FTP has the ability to upload files. Uploading is the process of transferring files from one computer to another. Unlike Downloading, uploading is always initiated from the computer that is sending the files.

Domain Names (Web Sites)

Whenever you are visiting a Web page, you can access it by typing in a nice pretty name that can be easily remembered. If you remember back to Computers 101, you were always told that everything with computers involves numbers. How can these sites have nice pretty names if they have to use numbers? These pretty names are called Domain Names. All computers connected to the Internet are required to have an IP address in order to be able to communicate on the Internet. Something called DNS, Domain Name System, is used to resolve these pretty Domain Names into the IP addresses that the computer is able to understand. All of this is done behind your back without any user intervention required. A good example of this can be seen in Figures 13-1 and 13-2, where we display the Syngress Media, Inc. home page using the domain name and by using the IP address that is assigned to it. As you can see, the pages are identical.

ISP

An ISP, Internet Service Provider, is a company that provides access to the Internet. Most ISPs provide dial-up access through modems, but in many cases, they also provide access through higher-speed digital leased lines. In general, any company that provides access to the Internet for customers can be considered an ISP. By saying customers, we are assuming that the people

FIGURE 13-1

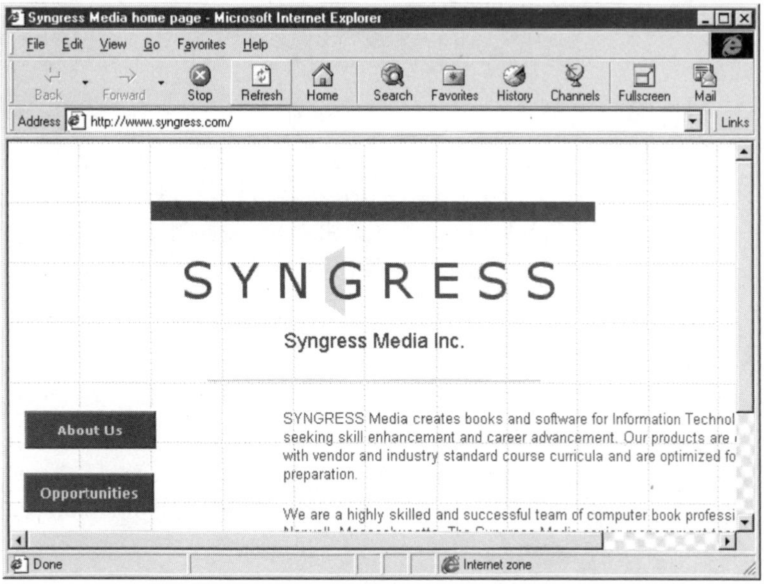

FIGURE 13-1

The Syngress Media, Inc. homepage as displayed using the domain name

FIGURE 13-2

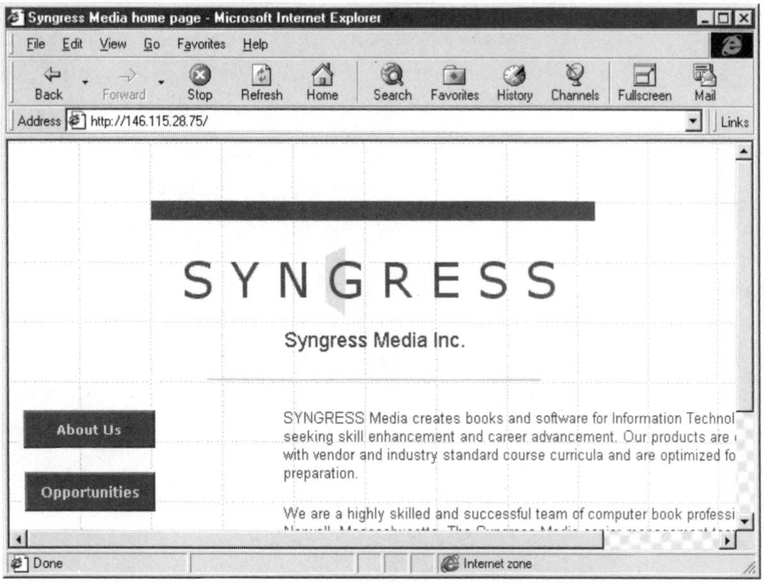

The Syngress Media, Inc. homepage as displayed using the IP address

are paying for the service. A company that gives their employees Internet access through a private bank of modems is usually not considered an ISP.

Dial-Up Access

An ISP usually provides dial-up access to its customers. Dial-up access is defined as access provided to the Internet using a phone line and a modem. More correctly, dial-up access does not have to be a connection to any network, be it the Internet or a corporation's private LAN.

Configuring a Modem

In order for a computer to be able to have dial-up access, a modem must be installed on the system. The modem should be installed according to the modem manufacturer's instructions. After the modem is installed correctly, the dial-up connection must be configured according to the specifications your ISP provides for you.

Configuring Browser

When a browser is first started, there are some basic configuration steps that should be taken. In most cases, you will not be required to perform these configurations, but they will complement the browser and add a great deal of functionality. The settings that should be configured include the default startup Web page, the user's e-mail address, and the user's SMTP server. Figure 13-3 demonstrates some of the common browser settings as they would be entered into Microsoft Internet Explorer 4.0.

E-Mail Set Up

When configuring an e-mail application, you are usually required to provide some information such as e-mail address, user's full name, POP3 server, and SMTP server. If you're confused with these terms, that's fine (and common); the POP3 and SMTP settings should be provided to you by the ISP. Figure 13-4 provides an example of the Properties dialog box used for Microsoft Outlook Express. Figure 13-5 shows the Servers panel of this dialog box.

FIGURE 13-3

FIGURE 13-3

Microsoft Internet Explorer 4.0 provides an easy configuration interface to enter the default startup page

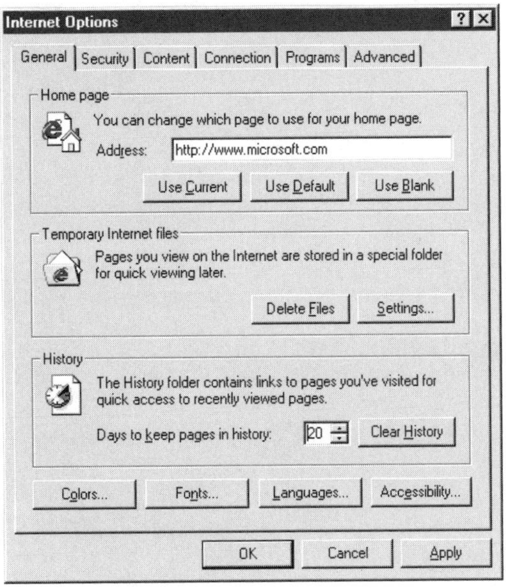

FIGURE 13-4

Microsoft Outlook Express provides a convenient interface to specify the user's full name and e-mail address, in addition to some other optional information

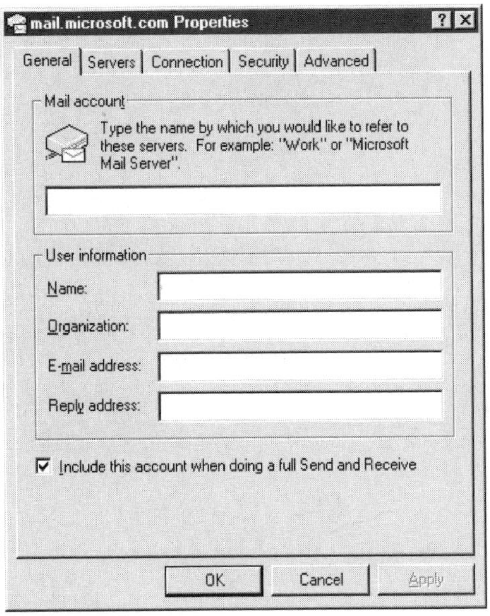

Microsoft Outlook Express
uses a simple interface to
specify the server
information, such as SMTP
and POP3 servers

CERTIFICATION SUMMARY

This chapter outlined some of the networking features that can be
integrated with DOS, Windows 3.*x*, and Windows 95. Some of these
features include anything from sharing files and printers to viewing a Web
page on the World Wide Web.

The Internet provides access to many different types of information.
Some of the information services that the Internet provides access to include
e-mail, the World Wide Web, and FTP.

✓ TWO-MINUTE DRILL

❑ When a Web browser is first started, there are some basic
configuration steps that should be taken, including configuring the
default startup Web page, the user's e-mail address, and the user's
SMTP server.

❑ When drives are shared, other users are given the ability to access the files that you have stored on your drives.

❑ Each workstation that will be communicating on the network must have software installed on it, such as drivers for the NIC, client software that allows the computer to communicate on the network, and software that allows the client software to communicate on the network using the correct protocol.

❑ Whenever installing network drivers, installing network cards, or configuring file and printer sharing, the manufacturer's procedures should be followed.

❑ By definition, each time you load a Web page, you are truly downloading a file.

❑ In addition to downloading files, the File Transfer Protocol (FTP) has the ability to upload files.

❑ When configuring an e-mail application, you are usually required to provide some information such as e-mail address, user's full name, POP3 server, and SMTP server.

❑ Unlike downloading, uploading is always initiated from the computer that is sending the files.

❑ All computers connected to the Internet are required to have an IP address in order to be able to communicate on the Internet.

❑ The Domain Name System is used to resolve Domain Names into the IP addresses that the computer is able to understand.

❑ A company that gives their employees Internet access through a private bank of modems is usually not considered an Internet Service Provider (ISP).

❑ Most ISPs provide dial-up access through modems, but in many cases, they also provide access through higher-speed digital leased lines.

❑ Dial-up access is defined as access provided to the Internet using a phone line and a modem.

SELF TEST

The following Self Test questions will help you measure your understanding of the material presented in this chapter. Read all the choices carefully, as there may be more than one correct answer. Choose all correct answers for each question.

1. What does the acronym HTML stand for?

    A. Hypertext Markup Language

    B. Hypertext Transfer Markup Language

    C. Hybrid Text Markup Language

    D. Hypertext Meta Language

    E. None of the above

2. What does the acronym HTTP stand for?

    A. Hyper Transfer of Text Protocol

    B. Hypo Transfer of Text Protocol

    C. Hypertext Transfer Protocol

    D. Hypertext Transmission Plateau

    E. None of the above

3. What does the acronym FTP stand for?

    A. Folder Transfer Plug

    B. File Transfer Protocol

    C. File Transmission Protocol

    D. File Transfer Plateau

    E. None of the above

4. What does the acronym ISP stand for?

    A. Interim Server Presence

    B. Internet Service Provider

    C. Internet Server Presence

    D. Internetwork Service Presence

    E. None of the above

5. Which of the following are users able to do when disks are shared (depending on configuration)?

    A. Read

    B. Add

    C. Delete

    D. Modify

    E. All of the above

6. Which of the following are usually required when configuring a Web browser?

    A. ISP dial-in number

    B. User e-mail address

    C. Workstation IP address

    D. Web server serial number

    E. None of the above

7. Which of the following are usually required when configuring an e-mail client?

    A. User's e-mail address

    B. SMTP server

    C. User's full name

    D. POP3 server

    E. All of the above

8. Assume computer client A transfers a file to computer server B. The transfer was

initiated by computer A sending the file to computer B. What is this referred to as?

A. Installing

B. Uploading

C. Degrading

D. Downloading

E. None of the above

9. Assume computer server B transfers a file to computer client A. The transfer was initiated by computer A requesting computer B send the file. What is this referred to as?

A. Installing

B. Uploading

C. Degrading

D. Downloading

E. None of the above

10. What protocol can be used for both downloading and uploading?

A. HTML

B. HTTP

C. E-mail

D. FTP

E. None of the above

11. What protocol can be used for downloading files, and is not documented to be capable of uploading?

A. HTML

B. HTTP

C. E-Mail

D. FTP

E. None of the above

12. What type of access does an ISP usually provide?

A. Simple network access

B. Dial-up access

C. Complex network access

D. All of the above

E. None of the above

13. What does the acronym DNS stand for?

A. Direct Name Server

B. Domain Name System

C. Direct Name Service

D. Distributed Name Service

E. None of the above

14. Dial-up access is usually provided using a

_____.

A. Modem

B. Internet

C. Network

D. DNS

E. None of the above

15. Domain Names are resolved to _____ using DNS.

A. Internet names

B. Alternate names

C. Machine addresses

D. MAC addresses

E. None of the above

A

Self Test
Answers

Though the following Self Test questions will help you measure your understanding of the material presented in this chapter. Read all the choices carefully, as there may be more than one correct answer. Choose all correct answers for each question.

Answers to Chapter I Self Test

1. When installing a new power supply, the connectors are attached to the system board by:

   A. Green wires facing each other

   B. Black wires facing away from each other

   C. Green wires facing away from each other

   D. Black wires facing each other

   D. There is no other method. This type of question is important on the A+ exam.

2. When removing an integrated circuit, such as a processor, from the system board you would use a:

   A. Pair of pliers

   B. Pair of tweezers

   C. Chip puller

   D. Your fingers

   C. Never use pliers or tweezers as they can easily crush and integrated circuit. While using your fingers is possible, it is not recommended as you can still damage the pins on the chip itself.

3. When working inside a monitor, you must ensure that you remove your:

   A. Clothing

   B. Jewelry

   C. Electrostatic wrist band

   D. Headphones

   C. Never wear an electrostatic wrist band when working around monitors, as the static electricity buildup could kill you.

4. You have just installed a 16-bit SCSI controller to the computer and are now ready to address your brand new SCSI hard disks. Which of the following address ranges are you permitted to use:

   A. Starting Address: 0; Ending Address: 32

   B. Starting Address: 0; Ending Address: 8

   C. Starting Address: 0; Ending Address: 16

   D. Starting Address: 0; Ending Address: 15

   D. A 16-bit controller allows you to use up to 16 addresses. However, the number 0 counts as one of the numbers, leading to 16 addresses minus 1 address (for the number 0) equals 15 addresses. This was a trick question.

5. A PS/2 mouse uses a

   A. Mini-DIN connector

   B. DB-25 connector

   C. DIN-9 connector

   D. DB-9 connector

   A   A PS/2 mouse uses the new MINI-DIN connector.

6. The work area used by the computer is called:

   A. Central Processing Unit

   B. Cache memory

   C. Memory

   D. BIOS

   C. The central processing unit does the work of directing the computer's components, while the system BIOS stores system settings. While cache memory does provide a work area for frequently accessed instructions, it is a specialized area.

7. When optimizing memory, you want to _____ conventional memory.

   A. Load DOS into

   B. Free up

   C. Remove

   D. Load device drivers into

   B. Optimizing memory entails freeing up conventional memory, not using it.

8. When you transmit a byte of data using several conductors, you are using _____ communications.

   A. Parallel

   B. Byte communications

   C. Network

   D. Serial

   A. Parallel communication uses eight conductors to transmit one bit over each conductor. Eight bits equals a byte.

9. Interference of a signal is called _____.

   A. Noise

   B. Static electricity

   C. ESD

   D. EMI

   D. EMI. Interference of a signal in PCs is always in some form of EMI (and usually, but not always, RFI)

10. Power supplies operate in the _____ range.

    A. ± 5 Vdc and ± 10 Vdc

    B. ± 7 Vdc and ± 10 Vdc

    C. ± 5 Vdc and ± 12 Vdc

    D. ± 4 Vdc and ± 7 Vdc

    C. These are the standard voltages used.

11. A(n) _____ signal is used to indicate that valid data is present when using parallel communications.

    A. Acknowledgment

    B. Data Present

C. Strobe-Asserted

D. Init

C. Acknowledgment is used to indicate that data has been received and Init is used to initialize the parallel device. There is no Data Present signal.

12. Every device that attaches to the computer is connected to the _____.

A. System Board

B. Main Board

C. Motherboard

D. Back Board

A, B, C. These are all terms used to describe the same component.

13. When installing most SIMM memory modules, you place the chip over the slot in a _____ angle.

A. 10 degree

B. 45 degree

C. 90 degree

D. 145 degree

B. This angle is the industry standard.

14. Never use a(n) _____ with a digital monitor.

A. Analog adapter

B. Digital adapter

C. Female D-9 connector

D. EGA monitor

A. Never use an analog adapter with a digital monitor, or vice versa, as you can cause severe damage to the monitor.

15. When you transmit data using asynchronous serial communications, synchronization is performed by:

A. A clock circuit located in both the transmitting and receiving devices

B. Shaking hands

C. A clock circuit located in the transmitting device

D. Using start bits before the data begins and stop bits after the data

A, D. Parallel ports are actually the purest form of asynchronous transmission, using no clock circuits whatsoever, only handshaking of the Data Strobe and Acknowledge lines. It could be argued that RS232 asynch serial ports use timing circuits rather than clock circuits to set the baud rate in both the transmitter and receiver circuits, but that interpretation would make D the only correct answer. Even synchronous serial transmission (rarely used) uses Receiver clock signals only.

16. Tape drives are commonly used to:

A. Store applications

B. Store data

C. Back up the hard drive

D. Play music

C. Application software normally comes on CD-ROM or floppy disk. While data is stored on tape, it is not a good idea because you must read in the data sequentially.

17. Floppy controllers normally use the
    _____ I/O address.

    A. 370 - 37F

    B. 3F0 - 3F7

    C. 2F0 - 2F7

    D. 1F0

    B. This is the address range assigned
    to floppy controllers.

18. When optimizing memory, you include
    the line _____ to load DOS into
    the HMA.

    A. LOAD DOS=UPPER MEMORY

    B. LOAD DOS=1024K

    C. DOS=HIGH

    D. LOAD C:\EMM386.EXE

    C. DOS=HIGH loads DOS into
    upper memory.

19. The _____ signal is used to indicate
    that data has been received.

    A. Acknowledgment

    B. Data Received

    C. Busy

    D. Slct

    A. Busy tells the CPU that it cannot
    receive any more data at this time,
    while Slct is used to select the device.
    There is no Data Received signal.

20. Parallel port LPT1 uses the _____
    I/O address.

    A. 2F0 - 2F7

    B. 378 - 37F

    C. 278 - 27F

    D. 1F0 - 1F8

    B. 378 - 37F is the normal I/O
    address used by LPT1.

21. ESD stands for

    A. Electrostatic Dimming

    B. Electrostatic Discharge

    C. Electrical Sending Device

    D. Electronic Signaling Device

    B. Remember, it is the discharge of
    static electricity.

22. BIOS boot-up settings are stored in the
    _____ Clock/Calendar chip so
    that they may be restored after a computer
    has been turned off.

    A. Complementary Metal-Oxide Service

    B. Computer Module Off Switch

    C. Complementary Metal-Oxide
    Semiconductor

    D. Computer Mode Off Safety

    C. Remember that the CMOS stores
    electronic information, and therefore
    has to *conduct* electrical signals.

23. EGA monitors can display images in
    _____ resolution.

    A. 640 x 350

    B. 720 x 350

    C. 1024 x 800

    D. 600 x 800

    A. The key to this question is *images.*

24. Serial communications use the _____ signal as a reference voltage.

    A. Ground Reference Voltage

    B. Zero

    C. Reference Point

    D. Timer

    A. The other signals do not exist.

25. IRQ 2 is _____.

    A. Keyboard

    B. Mouse

    C. Floppy Controller

    D. Redirected to IRQ 9

    D. It is the only interrupt that is cascaded.

26. When installing two IDE drives on one cable, one is set to be the _____ and one is set to be the _____.

    A. Master, servant

    B. Master, slave

    C. Dominant, submissive

    D. Primary, second best

    B. When you have two IDE hard drives, only one controller can be used.

27. When determining what device drivers and TSRs are in conventional memory, you use the _____ program.

    A. MEMORY.EXE

    B. CONFIG.SYS

    C. MEM.EXE

    D. AUTOEXEC.BAT

    C. MEM.EXE is the MS-DOS program that tells you the memory configuration.

28. You can attach up to _____ EIDE drives to a computer.

    A. 1

    B. 2

    C. 3

    D. 4

    D. IDE drives only allow for two drives.

29. When installing SCSI devices, you must use a _____ on the last drive on the cable and on the adapter.

    A. Resistor

    B. Transmitter

    C. Terminator

    D. End connector

    C. The terminator ensures that the signals that are transmitted on the cable do not stray from the cable.

30. RAM is an acronym for:

    A. Random Access Memory

    B. Random Access Module

    C. Read Access Memory

    D. Read And Memorize

    A. Random Access Memory is the only choice.

31. Parallel port LPT2 uses which IRQ:

    A. IRQ 3

    B. IRQ 5

C. IRQ 7

D. IRQ 12

B. IRQ 3 is used for serial port COM1, IRQ7 for parallel port LPT1, and IRQ 12 is used for the mouse.

32. Your phone uses a(n) _____ connector.

A. RJ-45

B. RJ-11

C. RJ-14

D. DB-9

B. RJ-11 is used to connect telephones. The RJ-11 is used to connect two phone lines, the RJ-45 is normally for networks, and DB-9s are used for video displays and serial ports.

Answers to Chapter 2 Self Test

1. When faced with a laser printer that produces blank pages, the usual suspect is the:

A. Ribbon

B. Paper supply

C. Toner cartridge

D. Tractor feed

C. The key to this question is "laser printer." Ribbons are used with dot matrix printers.

2. Your customer calls you and says, "I can't read my CD." You would:

A. Tell them that the CD is defective and to throw it away.

B. Tell them that the drive needs to be replaced.

C. Go in and check the adapter card.

D. Ask them to try another CD.

D. You cannot automatically assume that the CD is defective or that the drive needs to be replaced. If you automatically go in to check on the various components, you may find that the customer has put the CD in upside down or may not have a CD in the tray.

3. You have reported to a customer site to diagnose a keyboard, and notice that it is dirty. You would first:

A. Replace the keyboard.

B. Change the keyboard port.

C. Clean the keyboard using soap and water.

D. Clean the keyboard using a keyboard cleaning kit.

D. You never replace a component unless you are sure that it is defective. You could clean the keyboard with soap and water, but this is not recommended as tap water contains impurities that may be harmful to the keyboard.

4. At boot time, how many beeps indicate a problem with one of the system components?

A. One

B. Two

C. Three

D. Zero

B. Two beeps usually indicate a problem with one of the system components.

5. Power supply problems are usually indicated by

A. The fan is not working.

B. The computer frequently reboots itself.

C. You get an error code during POST diagnostics.

D. The computer does not boot.

A, B, C, D. All of these are legitimate indications of a power supply problem.

6. When you begin to diagnose a problem, you should first:

A. Isolate the failed component.

B. Gather information.

C. Replace components.

D. Reboot the computer.

B. Without first gathering the information, you will not be able to determine where the problem lies.

7. Once you have determined that a monitor has power and that the brightness/contrast controls are not at fault, the easiest way to determine that the problem isn't with the monitor is to:

A. Check the adapter cable.

B. Replace the monitor with a newer type.

C. Verify the device driver.

D. Replace the monitor with a similar type.

D. The key to this question is "easiest." If you replace the monitor with a newer kind, you have to also replace the adapter card and reinstall the device drivers.

8. Error codes relating to memory problems are in the _____ range.

A. 200 - 299

B. 300 - 399

C. 400 - 499

D. 500 - 599

A. Remember the types of error codes that are generated by the POST diagnostic routine for the exam.

9. You are troubleshooting a modem problem and connect to a remote system. However, you receive garbage characters across the screen that will not stop. This is typically a symptom of:

A. Incorrect stop bit or parity setting

B. Static on the line

C. Modem cable has become loose

D. No power to the modem

A. If it was a phone-line problem, you would get random garbage characters.

10. A printer is beginning to have a problem with page jams. You should check:

A. Paper quality

B. Toner cartridge

C. Adapter card

D. Paper pathway

A, D. The toner cartridge and the adapter card have nothing to do with page faults.

11. You have just installed a floppy drive and turned on the computer. However, the drive light will not go out. You have probably:

A. Put the cable on backwards

B. Forgotten to configure the BIOS settings for the drive

C. Installed a defective drive

D. Incorrectly configured the device drivers

A. Remember that the red stripe must be connected to Pin 1 on both the drive and the adapter.

12. Your customer is complaining that their word processor terminates abnormally when they load a particular document. You probably have to:

A. Replace the hard drive

B. Run a disk-scanning utility

C. Tell them that the file is history

D. Replace the cable

B. The key to this question is "a particular document." In this case, the document probably became corrupted and running a disk-scanning utility may repair the damage.

13. You are diagnosing a laser printer that has excessive page jams. When you attempt to

print several test pages, the paper jams in the same location. This is a symptom of:

A. Poor quality paper

B. A bad toner cartridge

C. Dirt or paper particles impeding the paper from proper movement

D. Static electricity

C. The key to this question is "in the same location."

14. Your customer calls to report that they are unable to perform a tape backup due to an error reported on their only tape cartridge. The mostly likely cause of the problem is:

A. The tape has expired.

B. The tape is not formatted.

C. The drive is about to fail.

D. The cable needs to be replaced.

A. Most backup software puts an internal expiration date to ensure that a tape cartridge is not used beyond a specific time period.

15. You have installed and configured a new SVGA monitor. However, when you boot the computer, you notice that the screen flickers. To resolve this problem, you need to:

A. Replace the monitor.

B. Replace the adapter card.

C. Change the Sync Frequency.

D. Configure the monitor as a VGA.

C. A flickering screen is usually the result of an improperly configured

Sync Frequency. Compare the manufacturer's documentation against the device driver configuration.

16. When walking into the customer's office, you would:

    A. Ask questions.

    B. Remove the case from the computer.

    C. Note the environment for problems.

    D. Put on your wrist strap.

    C. This only takes a moment, and should be done first.

17. Printers that communicate using TCP/IP use _____.

    A. A TCP/IP adapter card

    B. A Jet Direct adapter card

    C. Device drivers

    D. Special cabling

    A, B. A JetDirect card is a NIC and Print Server.

18. You have just installed a new CD-ROM drive, and now the computer does not boot. You would verify:

    A. Address

    B. Cabling

    C. Compact Disk

    D. Application software

    A, B. The compact disk and application software have nothing to do with hardware.

19. One of your customers is attempting to work with several graphic files that have disappeared from the directory in which they were located. You have run the SCANDISK.EXE and MS Defragment programs, and neither reports an error. You also know that the customer attaches to a Novell 3.11 server. You would:

    A. Retrieve the files from the last good backup.

    B. Tell the customer that the files have been deleted.

    C. Ask the system administrator if any network applications have been upgraded.

    D. Replace the hard drive in case other files disappear.

    C. The key to this question is that the customer attaches to a network. A common problem that occurs after a network upgrade is that the drive mappings were not correctly implemented.

20. POST stands for:

    A. Power Off Software Test

    B. Peripheral Operating System Test

    C. Power On Self Test

    D. Peripheral On Self Test

    C. This is the only correct answer.

21. Keyboard errors usually generate a _____ error code.

    A. 1**

    B. 2**

    C. 3**

D. 4**

    C. This is a common question on the exam.

22. While troubleshooting a modem, you make a connection with a remote computer. However, after you have connected, you notice that garbage characters appears at random. This is typically a symptom of:

    A. Incorrect stop bit or parity setting

    B. Static on the phone line

    C. Modem cable on backwards

    D. The remote system software has bugs

    B. The key to this question is "appears at random".

23. A customer calls to complain that their monitor is dead. The first thing you would ask them to try is:

    A. Adjust the brightness/contrast controls.

    B. Power on the monitor.

    C. Check the connection into the monitor.

    D. Nothing. You have to go in and replace it.

    B. The key to this question is "the first thing." Many times the customer will have turned off the monitor and forgotten to turn it back on.

24. Most problems with sound cards stem from:

    A. The card itself

    B. Cabling

    C. DMA channel

    D. IRQ

    C, D. In addition, I/O Addressing is another common problem with sound cards.

25. The method used in troubleshooting that starts with the easiest component and works up to the actual device is called the _____ method.

    A. Top down

    B. Bottom top

    C. Sequential

    D. Bottom up

    D. Bottom up is the only correct answer.

26. You have just replaced a hard drive and restored its contents from tape. However, you are now experiencing printer problems. You check the printer and printer cable without finding any errors. The most likely problem is:

    A. The device driver is corrupted.

    B. The system board is bad.

    C. There is a problem adapter card.

    D. Static electricity.

    A. This question required you to connect the hard drive failure with a printer problem. When a hard drive becomes useless, it has a tendency to take a file or two down with it.

27. You reboot a computer and it gives you a processor error. After opening the case, you press down on the chip and discover that it is loose in its socket. The processor

is said to have suffered from

_____.

A. Old age

B. Chip creep

C. Socket syndrome

D. Post Operational Stress

   B. The rest of the answers are bogus.

28. You are having communication problems between a floppy drive and the computer. You have already checked the address configuration and the cable. The next likely suspect is:

A. Controller card

B. Power connector

C. Floppy drive

D. Device driver

   A. The controller card controls communications between the processor and the floppy drive itself.

29. You have just installed an external modem. However, when you turn it on, none of the lights are active. The most likely suspect is:

A. Corrupted driver

B. Bad RS232-C cable

C. Power connection

D. Address conflict

   C. No lights equals no power.

30. If you are working on a hard drive, you need to ensure that the device driver configuration is correct for _____ types of drives:

A. MTM

B. IDE

C. EIDE

D. SCSI

E. None of the above

   E. Hard drives do not have device drivers. Device drivers are used by the OS for controllers, which act as interfaces to hard drives.

31. Floppy disk media errors can be caused by:

A. Defective disk

B. Adapter cable problems

C. Dirty read/write heads

D. Incompatible floppy drives

   A, C, D. Adapter cable problems have no effect on media errors.

32. A symptom of a dirty mouse is:

A. Little or poor response from mouse

B. No response from mouse

C. Addressing error message

D. POST error message

   A. No response is usually a cable or addressing problem, while POST error messages do not inform you of a dirty mouse.

33. When diagnosing a software error, you would check for:

A. POST error codes

B. Device driver errors

C. Incorrectly addressed adapter

D. Application problems

B, D. The other two are hardware problems.

34. Smudged or poor-quality images from a flat-bed scanner are symptoms of a:

    A. Dirty glass

    B. Application problem

    C. Device driver configuration error

    D. Cable problem

    A. Flat-bed scanners have a glass sheet that the page is put on, and become dirty from fingerprints and dust.

35. The most common problem with the system BIOS is:

    A. Configuration errors

    B. Low CMOS battery

    C. Bad chip

    D. Software errors

    B. The key to this question is "most common."

Answers to Chapter 3 Self Test

1. When working on any monitor, you must first:

    A. Wear gloves

    B. Remove your ESD wrist strap

    C. Wear an ESD wrist strap

    D. Disconnect it from the computer

    B. Remove your wrist strap. *Never* go near a monitor wearing an ESD wrist strap.

2. When disposing of chemical solvents, you can:

    A. Empty them into the sink.

    B. Flush them down a toilet.

    C. Contact the state's environmental regulatory office.

    D. Tightly seal them in a bottle and throw the bottle away.

    C. Contact the state's environmental regulatory office. Chemical solvents are considered hazardous waste and their disposal is regulated by the EPA and your state government.

3. It is a good idea to _____ the inside of a computer whenever you have removed the case.

    A. Dust

    B. Vacuum

    C. Air out

    D. Repair

    B. Vacuum. Dust and dirt, which can carry an electrical charge, tend to collect inside a computer.

4. Catastrophic damage occurs when:

    A. The component is dropped on the floor and rendered inoperable

    B. The component is rendered inoperable due to ESD

    C. The component has ESD damage but continues to function

    D. The component was deluged with water

B. The component is rendered inoperable due to ESD. When the component has ESD damage and continues to function, this is called *degradation.*

5. If you look directly into a CD-ROM's laser while it is on, you risk:

   A. Severe burns

   B. Blindness

   C. Electrocution

   D. Nothing

   B. Blindness. CD-ROM drives employ a low-level laser that does not cause severe burns. Electrocution happens when electricity comes into contact with the body.

6. A brownout is:

   A. A momentary lapse of power

   B. Noise in the line

   C. Total power loss

   D. A fried computer component

   A. A momentary lapse of power. Total power loss is called a blackout.

7. When disposing of a dead battery, you can:

   A. Throw it in the nearest trash can.

   B. Recycle it.

   C. Recharge it.

   D. Reuse it.

   B. Recycle it. Batteries are either recycled or disposed of according to your state's environmental regulatory office.

8. When working around high-voltage equipment, you should never:

   A. Turn the power off

   B. Use both hands on the equipment

   C. Use only one hand on the equipment

   D. Remove your wrist strap

   B. Use both hands on the equipment. By doing so, you make yourself a "live" circuit and risk severe burns and electrocution.

9. When working on a computer, you should:

   A. Follow ESD procedures.

   B. Remove all jewelry.

   C. Turn the computer off.

   D. Remove the power supply.

   A, B, C. Removing the power supply is only necessary when you need to replace it or when it is in the way.

10. A _____ is a special white paper that contains information on possible personal injury.

    A. Materials Supply Data Sheet

    B. Materials Section Display Sheet

    C. Materials Safety Data Sheet

    D. Momentary Surge Dispelling Substance

    C. Materials Safety Data Sheet. The other answers are bogus.

11. You are about to replace the power supply on a customer's computer. Even though the computer has been down for several days, you should still be cautious while

replacing the power supply as you could get a severe electrical shock from:

A. Static electricity.

B. Live current.

C. Nothing. Heat is the true problem.

D. Nothing. The power supply is now safe.

   A. Static electricity. Even after several days, there is still static electricity present in the power supply.

12. To dispose of toner cartridges, you can:

A. Exchange them for new ones.

B. Throw them away.

C. Take them to the landfill.

D. Pour more toner in them.

   A. Toner cartridges are usually accepted by the vendor and a small credit is given for their return.

13. When storing a UPS, you must ensure that:

A. You discharge the UPS

B. You store it in a high-humidity environment

C. You have not discharged the UPS

D. You have put it out of the way

   C. A discharged UPS may loose some of its capacity to hold a charge after a period of time.

14. Prior to performing any preventative maintenance to a computer or its components, you should:

A. Assemble your tools.

B. Remove the cover from the chassis.

C. Review the manufacturer's suggested guidelines.

D. Nothing. Begin the maintenance.

   C. It is important to follow all of the vendor's recommended procedures and to use the cleaning materials that they specify. If you do not, you risk damage to the computer or its components.

15. When discharging a monitor, you wrap a jumper wire around a screwdriver that has a non-conductive shaft. Before you can safely pry the anode lead off of the CRT's glass surface, you must

A. Attach the free end of the jumper wire to the monitor.

B. Attach the free end of the jumper wire to a ground.

C. Attach the free end of the jumper wire to yourself.

D. Nothing. You can proceed with the repair.

   B. Attach the free end of the jumper wire to a ground before prying off the anode lead. If you attach it to the monitor or yourself, you are letting yourself in for a shocking surprise!

16. You need to replace a secondary hard drive in a computer that is still operating from the primary hard drive. You should first:

A. Open the case.

B. Power down the computer.

C. Discharge the hard drive.

D. Remove the power cord.

B. Even if the computer permits you to perform the repair while the power is on, you should not risk burn or shock from the live current flowing inside the computer.

17. When you connect an ESD mat to an electrical ground, you can use:

A. The pin on an electrical outlet

B. The socket on an electrical outlet

C. Another ESD mat

D. Nothing

A. *Never* attach the ESD mat to an electrical socket.

18. To discharge a monitor, you can remove the anode lead from the glass using:

A. Your fingers

B. A gloved hand

C. Screwdriver with a grounded jumper wire

D. Rubber knife

C. Never use your hand, gloved or not, around an anode lead.

19. UPS stands for:

A. Uninterruptible Power Surge

B. Unused Power Supply

C. Uninterruptible Power Supply

D. Unnecessary Power Supply

C. The other answers are all bogus.

20. Never use a(n) _____ when working on high-voltage equipment.

A. ESD mat

B. ESD wrist strap

C. Metal object

D. Table

B. *Never* wear an ESD wrist strap around high-voltage equipment unless you want to be electrocuted.

21. Power supplies tend to generate a lot of _____ from power lost during the power conversion process.

A. Static electricity

B. Current

C. Voltage

D. Heat

D. Heat is also a form of energy.

22. To reduce the potential for static electricity in the room, you can set the humidity level to:

A. Between 10% and 30%

B. Between 30% and 50%

C. Between 50% and 70%

D. Between 70% and 90%

C. Setting the level too low contributes to static electricity, while setting the level too high can cause water condensation on electronic components.

23. Noise present on a power line is caused by _____ .

A. Power surges

B. Brownouts

C. EMI

D. ESD

C. Noise on a power line is caused by Electro-Magnetic Interference.

24. You can use _____ to clean some computer components.

    A. Mild liquid detergents

    B. Isoprophyl alcohol

    C. Pencil eraser

    D. Glass cleaner

    A, B, C, D. All of these items can be used to clean different computer components. However, always consult the manufacturer's documentation to ensure that the component will not be damaged by some materials.

25. When a component has been damaged by ESD, yet still passes the diagnostic software, the device is said to have suffered

    _____.

    A. Degradation.

    B. Catastrophic damage.

    C. ESD damage.

    D. Nothing. The device still functions.

    A. Catastrophic damage is when the device is rendered inoperable. While ESD damage is true, the correct term is *degradation.*

26. To clean the read/write heads of a floppy drive, you would use:

    A. Dust-free cloth

    B. Mild detergent

    C. Special cleaning disk

    D. Rubber blade

    C. This disk comes in a floppy drive cleaning kit and should be used in place of opening the case.

27. To dispose of a functioning monitor, you can:

    A. Donate it to a church or school.

    B. Keep it as a spare.

    C. Throw it away.

    D. See if the vendor will give you credit toward a new one.

    A, B, D. Never throw away a monitor as it may be regulated by your state's environmental regulatory office.

28. _____ labels are used to alert you to possible equipment damage or personal injury.

    A. Caution

    B. Warning

    C. Important

    D. Notice

    B. Caution labels are typically used to inform you of personal injuries but not equipment damage.

29. A _____ is used to reduce noise in power currents and eliminate EMI.

    A. EMI filter

    B. Surge protector

    C. Noise Filter

    D. There is no such thing

    C. EMI filters do not exist, and a surge protector absorbs or blocks excessive power.

30. You are prying the anode lead off of a monitor. As the anode lead becomes detached from the glass, you hear a small "pop." This sound is caused by:

    A. A small electric charge

    B. Rush of air going into the suction cup

    C. The rubber partially melted on the glass

    D. Your imagination

    A. This charge is dispelled into the screwdriver, passed through the jumper wire, and into the ground.

31. ESD is also known as _____ .

    A. Static electricity

    B. Electrostatic Device

    C. Electronic Systems Device

    D. Electronic Safety Device

    A. ESD is electricity that stores up, or remains static, in an object.

32. To prevent possible communications problems with a device's connection, you should:

    A. Periodically replace the device

    B. Periodically clean the contacts

    C. Regularly replace the connectors

    D. There is nothing you can do

    B. Dirty contacts can result in a poor connection and lead to communication problems.

33. "Hidden" ESD refers to:

    A. Dust and dirt particles.

    B. ESD that you cannot feel.

    C. Hidden Electronic Static Data.

    D. Nothing. There is no such thing.

    A, B. The other two are bogus.

34. Common cleaning tools include:

    A. Alcohol

    B. Rubber blade

    C. Screwdriver tip

    D. Dust-free cloths

    A, B, D. Never use a screwdriver tip to clean computer components.

35. A huge increase in power that lasts for a split second is called a _____.

    A. Power surge

    B. Power spike

    C. Noise

    D. Excessive power

    B. While a power surge is an increase in power, it varies in intensity.

Answers to Chapter 4 Self Test

1. RAM stands for:

    A. Random Access Mode

    B. Random Array Memory

    C. Random Access Memory

    D. Random Array Mode

    C. The other answers are all bogus.

2. The 386DX chip could run at speeds of:

A. 16 MHz - 20 MHz

B. 16 MHz - 33 MHz

C. 16 MHz - 133 MHz

D. 20 MHz - 66 MHz

B. The other answers are all bogus.

3. When the computer is rebooted or loses power, the _____ is used to restore those settings.

A. BIOS

B. CMOS

C. Battery

D. OS

B. The CMOS has a battery that can maintain the BIOS settings after the computer has rebooted or lost power.

4. The _____ provides a computer's peripherals with directives that retrieve, display, manipulate, and store information.

A. Memory

B. Adapter

C. Controller

D. Processor

D. Memory does store data but it doesn't provide directives. While the adapter and controller do provide some directives, they do not store information.

5. A _____ is composed of the same track numbers on each disk of the hard drive.

A. Cylinder

B. Sector

C. Track

D. Disk

A. The number of cylinders in a hard drive is also printed on the outside case of the drive itself.

6. The process by which memory chips are constantly updated is called a _____ .

A. Timing

B. Rate

C. Refresh

D. Update

C. This is because the chips are "refreshed" to ensure that signal degradation does not occur.

7. The Pentium, or 586, chip allowed for parallel processing by using a _____.

A. Dual Inter-Dependent Bus Architecture

B. Double Inter-Dependent Bus Architecture

C. Dual Independent Bus Architecture

D. Double Independent Bus Architecture

C. This type of chip is actually composed of two 486 chips inside of one large chip.

8. 3.5" floppy drives come in capacities of:

A. 360KB

B. 720KB

C. 1.44KB

D. 2.77KB

B, C. The 360KB was the capacity of the earliest 5.25" floppy drives. 2.77KB drives do not exist.

9. The _____ is used to receive commands from the processor that are destined for the device attached to the COM port.

   A. Interrupt line

   B. Parity

   C. Serial port

   D. Memory address

   D. The interrupt line is used by the device to get the processor's attention. Parity is an error checking method used by devices.

10. The _____ was built upon ISA architecture, had a 32-bit data bus, and utilized the local bus.

    A. ISA

    B. VL-Bus

    C. EISA

    D. PCI

    B. The VL-Bus was the first bus architecture to take advantage of accessing the local bus.

11. The _____ memory card has memory chips embedded on both sides of the card.

    A. SIMM

    B. ROM

    C. RAM

    D. DIMM

    D. Dual In-Line Memory Module. You can remember this from the "D" for "double."

12. _____ is a form of error checking where the sum of 1s is added up.

A. CRC

B. Parity

C. Even

D. Odd

   B. CRC is a different form of error checking, while even and odd are types of parity.

13. If you want the computer to request a password before completing the boot sequence, you would enable the _____ password.

    A. DOS

    B. Windows

    C. BIOS

    D. CMOS

    D. DOS and Windows are loaded after the boot sequence.

14. The difference between the 486 SX and 486 DX processors was that the _____ was disabled on the _____ CPU.

    A. Cache Memory, 486DX

    B. Math Co-Processor, 486DX

    C. Cache Memory, 486SX

    D. Math Co-Processor, 486SX

    D. The 486SX processor was released prior to the 486DX and was less expensive.

15. Dynamic Random Access Memory chips used _____ to store small electrical charges.

    A. Transistors

B. Capacitors

C. Cells

D. Electricity

> **B.** This allows for DRAM chips to store more data in the same amount of space.

16. A computer stores information in the form of 1s and 0s, called _____ .

A. Electrical charges

B. Binary

C. Switches

D. Capacitors

> **B.** Binary is the language that your computer understands.

17. When modifying the CMOS settings on a computer that has more than one hard drive, which controller is used to control the hard drive?

A. Master

B. Second

C. Primary

D. Slave

> **A.** The other hard drives are the *slaves.*

18. What is used by a device to get the processor's attention?

A. Memory address

B. Dynamic Memory Access channel

C. Interrupt line

D. Nothing

> **C.** The memory address is where the device expects to receive requests, and a DMA channel is used to bypass the processor.

19. Which type of RAM does not need a constant refresh rate?

A. DRAM

B. EDO RAM

C. WRAM

D. SRAM

> **D.** Remember the "S" for *static.*

20. The problem with using parity as an error-checking mechanism is that:

A. It does not work.

B. If only 1 bit is changed, the data will be accepted.

C. If only 2 bits are changed, the data will be accepted.

D. There is no problem with using parity.

> **C.** Remember that an even number of bits that are switched will pass the data. However, if an odd number of bits are changed the bad data is caught.

21. To calculate the size of a hard drive, you would use which of the following formulas?

A. cylinders * sectors * tracks * heads * 0.5

B. cylinders * sectors * heads * 0.5

C. cylinders * tracks * heads * 0.5

D. sectors * tracks * heads * 0.5

B. Even though the size of the hard drive is actually calculated when entering CMOS settings, the A+ exam has been known to have a question on it at times.

22. SIMMs come in what pin sizes?

    A. 16-pin

    B. 30-pin

    C. 64-pin

    D. 72-pin

    B, D. When dealing with computers and their components, it's easy to forget that there are numbers other than multiples of 8.

23. The Pentium II chip runs in speeds ranging between _____

    A. 33 - 66

    B. 66 - 133

    C. 133 - 166

    D. 233 - 266

    D. Remember the speeds of each processor for the exam.

24. The 8088 chip used a _____-bit data bus.

    A. 8

    B. 16

    C. 20

    D. 24

    A. The 8088 chip the first processor in use.

25. External devices attach to the motherboard through the:

    A. Cable

    B. Adapter

    C. Communications port

    D. Connector

    C. The key to this question was the *external* devices.

26. What type of memory is used to store frequently accessed instructions and data?

    A. Cache

    B. Extended

    C. RAM

    D. ROM

    A. Remember that the information is stored separately from regular RAM so that it is more easily accessed.

27. Which bus uses a special bridging circuit and special configuration software to allow it to be processor independent?

    A. ISA

    B. EISA

    C. VL-BUS

    D. PCI

    D. Until this bus architecture was developed, the bus was processor dependent.

28. Which bus architecture used a 16-bit data bus and was the first to provide an industry standard?

    A. ISA

    B. EISA

    C. VL-Bus

D. PCI

A. Remember that ISA stands for Industry Standard Architecture.

29. Which bus architecture was originally developed for small, handheld computers?

A. EISA

B. MCA

C. PCI

D. PCMCIA

D. This long acronym is also known as the PC Card.

30. The _____ tells the computer where to locate the files and settings, as well as the search order, that it needs to boot.

A. Boot sequence

B. Power On Self Test

C. CMOS

D. BIOS

A. The entire boot process falls under this category.

31. EISA is an acronym for:

A. Extended Independent System Architecture

B. Extended Industry Standard Architecture

C. Enhanced Independent System Architecture

D. Enhanced Industry Standard Architecture

B. This is an extended, or upgraded, version of ISA.

32. The VL-Bus is more commonly used for:

A. Hard drive components

B. Video components

C. Floppy drive components

D. Audio components

B. Remember that the "V" stands for Video.

33. What types of communication ports are available on the motherboard?

A. Serial

B. Dual

C. Parallel

D. Single

A, C. There is no such thing as a Single or Dual communications port on the motherboard.

34. What is used to connect the processor to the motherboard?

A. Processor socket

B. Processor connector

C. Cable

D. Processor port

A. The other answers are bogus.

35. Which processor was the first to have the SX and DX designations?

A. 80286

B. 80386

C. 80486

D. Pentium

B. Also known as the 386SX or 386DX. This was the first time that Intel did not license its technology to its competitors, which led to the extra designation.

Answers to Chapter 5 Self Test

1. Which is the correct sequence for the EP printing process?

   A. Charging, Cleaning, Writing, Transferring, Fusing, Developing

   B. Cleaning, Charging, Writing, Developing, Fusing, Transferring

   C. Cleaning, Charging, Writing, Developing, Transferring, Fusing

   D. Charging, Cleaning, Writing, Developing, Transferring, Fusing

   C. This is the only correct sequence in the EP printing process.

2. Toner cartridges should be _____ when they run out.

   A. Refilled with the correct toner

   B. Replaced with a new toner cartridge

   C. Replaced with an ink cartridge

   D. Serviced

   B. For quality image output, the toner cartridge should be replaced.

3. What is the maximum recommended cable length for a parallel cable?

   A. 5 feet

   B. 10 feet

   C. 20 feet

   D. 50 feet

   B. Anything longer than 10 feet runs the risk of signal degradation due to attenuation and crosstalk.

4. Which component transfers the toner from the electrostatic drum to the paper?

   A. Fuser

   B. Transfer corona

   C. Transfer assembly

   D. Primary corona

   B. The transfer corona provides the strong positive charge necessary to pull the toner away from the photo-sensitive drum to the paper.

5. Which type(s) of printers can be used to print multi-part forms?

   A. Dot matrix printers

   B. Daisy wheel printers

   C. Laser printers

   D. Bubble jet printers

   A, B. Dot matrix and daisy wheel printers are impact type printers, capable of printing multi-part forms.

6. Which of the following are possible interfaces for printers?

   A. Parallel

   B. IDE

   C. Serial

   D. Network

   E. Game port

A, C, D. Currently the most standard printer interfaces are parallel, serial, and network.

7. The most likely cause for random specs of ink on a laser printed page is:

    A. Improper voltage on corona wire

    B. Parallel cable too long

    C. Photosensitive drum dirty

    D. Improper paper type

    C. If you are getting specs on the page, the photosensitive drum is not properly being cleaned in the cleaning step of the EP process.

8. Which type of printer is most similar to a typewriter?

    A. Page printer

    B. Typeset printer

    C. Laser printer

    D. Daisy wheel printer

    D. Daisy wheel printers have a wheel with raised letters and symbols on it, much like a typewriter.

9. In the charging step of the EP process, the voltage can reach to as high as:

    A. 120 volts

    B. 1200 volts

    C. 5000 volts

    D. 50,000 volts

    C. Charging involves applying a high-voltage negative charge to the photosensitive drum.

10. The most likely cause for a white line across the page while printing with a dot matrix printer is:

    A. Pin not firing

    B. Clogged nozzle

    C. Print head misalignment

    D. Ink ribbon needs replacement

    A. A pin not firing would cause a white line in the same position on each printed line.

11. In order to permanently bond a laser's toner particles to paper, a _____ process must take place.

    A. Chemical

    B. Magnetic

    C. Charging

    D. Fusing

    D. Fusing is the last step in the EP process.

12. _____ is the dot matrix mode by which characters are stored in ROM.

    A. ROM addressable

    B. Memory mapping

    C. Font addressable

    D. Font matrix

    C. The printer receives the instruction to print a character in font addressable mode and looks up the pin sequence to print that character in its ROM table.

13. Concerning the EP printing process, the primary corona wire has a _____ charge, the transfer corona has a _____ charge, and toner naturally has a _____ charge.

    A. negative, positive, positive
    B. positive, negative, negative
    C. negative, positive, negative
    D. positive, positive, negative

    C. The primary corona has a highly negative charge. The transfer has a highly positive charge to attract the toner to the page. Toner by nature is negatively charged.

14. What does "PDL" stand for?

    A. Printer-Defined Language
    B. Page Description Language
    C. Paper Driver Latch
    D. Printer Device Logic

    B. The other answers are all bogus.

15. The print head on a dot matrix printer is a series of pins each controlled by a:

    A. Capacitive coil
    B. Resistive coil
    C. Solenoid
    D. Spring coil

    B, C. A solenoid and resistive coil are the same thing. They control pin motion on a dot matrix printer.

Answers to Chapter 6 Self Test

1. Of the different battery types currently available, which provides the most power with the lease amount of weight?

    A. Nickel Cadmium
    B. Lithium Ion
    C. Nickel Metal Hydride
    D. Lead Acid

    B. Lithium Ion batteries provide more power per pound than any of the other portable computer battery types. Lead Acid batteries are usually found under the hood of your car.

2. After using her laptop for only a short time, Mary recharged the battery in her computer. She is complaining now that her battery only holds a charge for a short time. You know Mary's computer uses a NiCad battery. What could be the problem?

    A. Mary's computer is not configured properly for that type of battery.
    B. Mary's computer is using a high color display that uses a great deal of power.
    C. Mary's battery is suffering from "memory effect" and will need to be replaced.
    D. Mary's battery needs to be fully discharged before it will fully recharge again.

C. By not fully discharging her battery before it was recharged, Mary's battery is now suffering from the "memory effect" and will not ever fully charge again. Even fully discharging the battery will not erase this effect.

3. The AC adapter on a portable computer changes one type of power to another. What types?

   A. 110v AC to 220v AC

   B. 220v AC to 110v AC

   C. 110v AC or 220v AC to DC

   D. 12v DC to 110v AC

   C. The AC adapter transforms either 110v AC or 220v AC to usable DC for both charging the battery and powering the computer.

4. Portable computers now use which type of display technology?

   A. Liquid Crystal

   B. Light Emitting Diode

   C. Cathode Ray Tube

   D. 8514/A

   A. Today's portable computers use Liquid Crystal Displays (LCDs). Just about the only place you will see a CRT display in a portable is in a museum.

5. Which type of display uses a transistor at each pixel?

   A. Cathode Ray Tube

   B. 8514/A

   C. Light Emitting Diode

   D. Active Matrix

   D. Active matrix, or Thin Film Transistor (TFT), displays have a transistor at each pixel location.

6. Joe is complaining that when he moves his mouse quickly, his cursor disappears. What can you do to help him out?

   A. Change his display mode from Passive to Active.

   B. Set the mouse trails option to On.

   C. Adjust the contrast of the display.

   D. Tell him not to move the mouse as quickly.

   B. The mouse trails option exists just for this purpose. Mouse trails makes the cursor appear much more easily.

7. A docking station can provide which of the following?

   A. PCI slots

   B. ISA slots

   C. Enhanced sound capabilities

   D. All of the above

   D. Docking station can give a portable all of the same capabilities as a desktop computer, including expansion slots and full-size drive bays.

8. Docking stations use what type of connector?

   A. Centronix

   B. DB-50

C. DIN

D. Proprietary

D. Docking stations use proprietary connectors. You must use a docking station designed for the portable you are using.

9. Patty wants to upgrade the hard drive in her portable computer. You have many new hard drives for other portable computers in your office. What should you do to upgrade her system?

A. Use one of the hard drives that you already have.

B. Compare the old hard drive with a new one. If they look the same, it should work.

C. Buy a hard drive made for her particular computer.

D. Suggest that Mary get a new portable computer. You cannot upgrade a hard drive in a portable.

C. You should only use hard drives specifically designed for your particular computer. Manufacturers use different physical interfaces and footprints. An improper match may damage the drive, or worse, damage the motherboard.

10. PC Cards were originally intended for what technology?

A. Hard drives.

B. Hard drive adapters

C. Memory

D. Network adapters

C. The original specification from PCMCIA is intended for memory technologies.

11. Type III PC Cards are intended for what type of peripherals?

A. Modems

B. LAN cards

C. Rotating mass storage

D. Memory

C. Type III Cards are 10.5mm thick and are intended to be used for rotating mass storage devices, like hard drives.

12. This BIOS level software detects insertion or removal of PC Cards.

A. Card Services

B. Socket Services

C. Windows 95

D. DOS

B. Socket Services is charged with detecting the insertion and removal of PC Cards.

13. This software manages the allocation of system resources once a PC Card has been inserted.

A. Card Services

B. Socket Services

C. Windows 95

D. DOS

A. Card Services manages the allocation of resources once the Socket Services detects a PC Card has been inserted or removed.

14. Uses for PC Cards today include:

A. Hard drives

B. Network cards

C. Memory cards

D. Global Positioning System cards

E. All of the above

E. PC Cards are used many areas, including all of the above.

15. What types of pointing devices are found in portable computers today?

A. Trackballs

B. Touch pads

C. Pointing stick

D. All of the above

D. All of the above types of pointing devices can be found in portable computers today.

16. This type of pointing device has the most moving parts.

A. Trackballs

B. Touch pads

C. Pointing stick

D. Mouse

A. Track balls use many moving parts and as a result, require the most maintenance.

Answers to Chapter 7 Self Test

1. What does the acronym NIC stand for?

A. Network Interface Card

B. Network Interference Carrier

C. Network Interface Carrier

D. Network Interference Card

E. None of the above

A. Network Interface Cards, NICs, are the devices that, when installed in a PC, connect the PC to the network cable.

2. What does the acronym CSMA/CD stand for?

A. Carrier Sense Multiple Address/Carrier Detection

B. Carrier Sense Multiple Access/Carrier Detection

C. Collision Sense Multiple Access/Carrier Detection

D. Carrier Sense Multiple Access/Collision Detection

E. None of the above

D. Carrier Sense Multiple Access/Collision Detection, CSMA/CD, detects if any other devices have transmitted onto the network at the same time. If it detects that another device has transmitted data onto the network, the device then waits an unspecified random amount of time and retransmits its data.

3. What does the acronym TCP/IP stand for?

    A. Timely Cautious Protocol/Internet Protocol

    B. Transmission Control Protocol/Internet Protocol

    C. Totally Controlling Packets/Internet Protocol

    D. Time Controlled Packets/Internet Protocol

    E. None of the above

    B. TCP/IP, Transmission Control/Internet Protocol, is the most common protocol used today. TCP/IP is the protocol that the Internet is built upon.

4. The basic networking concepts introduced in this chapter include all of the following except:

    A. Cabling

    B. Network Interface Cards

    C. Network Access

    D. Network Repairs

    E. Protocols

    D. The basic networking concepts introduced here include cabling, network interface cards, network access, and protocols. A firm grasp of these concepts will help improve your networking skills.

5. A common cable type used for networks is:

    A. Twisted Pair

    B. Fiber Optic

    C. Coaxial

D. All of the above

E. None of the above

    D. The three types of cabling introduced are twisted pair, coaxial, and fiber optic.

6. What is the maximum distance that coaxial cable can successfully be used?

    A. 100 ft.

    B. 100 meters

    C. 180 ft.

    D. 180 meters

    E. None of the above

    D. Coaxial cable is capable of successfully transmitting at lengths up to 180 meters.

7. What is the maximum distance that twisted pair cable can be successfully be used?

    A. 100 ft.

    B. 100 meters

    C. 180 ft.

    D. 180 meters

    E. None of the above

    B. Twisted pair cable is capable of successfully transmitting at lengths of up to 100 meters.

8. What is the maximum distance that fiber optic cable can successfully be used.

    A. 100 ft.

    B. 100 meters

    C. 180 ft.

    D. 180 meters

    E. None of the above

E. Fiber optic cable theoretically has no limit to its maximum transmission distance. Using fiber optic cable for extremely long spans could, however, be cost-prohibitive.

9. Which of the following is a special requirement of fiber optic cable?

A. Devices must be connected to the network cable using T-connectors.

B. Special transceivers must be installed on each end of the cable.

C. Each device must be connected to a port in a hub.

D. Each end of the cable must be terminated with a 50Ω Terminator.

E. Two of the above are true.

F. A FDDI network can be as simple as two network cards and two strands of fiber. Since it is configured in a physical ring, there are no "ends" on which to put transceivers.

B. Fiber optic cable requires that a fiber optic transceiver be installed at each end of the cable.

10. Which of the following is a special requirement of coaxial cable?

A. Devices must be connected to the network cable using T-connectors.

B. Special transceivers must be installed on each end of the cable.

C. Each device must be connected to a port in a hub.

D. Each end of the cable must be terminated with a 50Ω Terminator.

E. Two of the above are true.

E. Coaxial cable requires that each device must be connected to the network using T-connectors. In addition, each end of the cable must be terminated with a 50Ω Terminator.

11. Which of the following is a special requirement of twisted pair cable?

A. Devices must be connected to the network cable using T-connectors.

B. Special transceivers must be installed on each end of the cable.

C. Each device must be connected to a port in a hub.

D. Each end of the cable must be terminated with a 50Ω Terminator.

E. Two of the above are true.

C. Twisted pair cable requires that each device on the network be connected to a port in a hub.

12. Network Access . . .

A. Provides a standard by which all devices that wish to communicate on the network must abide.

B. Provides a standard for the encoding method that each packet transmitted on the network must follow.

C. Defines the rights of users on a network.

D. Is only granted if a device agrees to follow established protocols.

E. None of the above.

A. Network access provides a standard by which all devices that wish to communicate on the network must abide.

13. Protocols . . .

    A. Provide a standard by which all devices that wish to communicate on the network must abide.

    B. Define the rights of users on the network.

    C. Establish standards for the transmission of data onto the network that ensure that both the sending and receiving devices are able to communicate.

    D. Are granted only when network access is accepted.

    E. None of the above.

    C. Protocols establish standards for the transmission of data onto the network. Both the sending and receiving device must be capable of communicating using the same protocols.

14. Which of the following best describes the bus topology discussed in this chapter?

    A. It is commonly found in coaxial cable-based networks.

    B. Each device is connected to a T-connector and then the T-connector is connected to the cable.

    C. Each end of the cable must be terminated with a 50Ω terminator.

    D. All of the above are true.

    E. None of the above are true.

D. In a bus topology, each device must be connected to a T-connector. Each T-connector is connected to the next with a coaxial cable. After all of the devices are connected, the ends of the cable must then be terminated with a 50Ω terminator.

15. In the event of a cable break, which of the following will **always** result in a total network failure?

    A. Coaxial Cable

    B. Twisted Pair

    C. Fiber Optic

    D. All of the above

    E. None of the above

    A. In the event of a cable break, the entire network is **always** rendered useless when coaxial cable is used. Twisted pair usually results in one device being rendered useless, while fiber optic (in its standard configuration) would not have any major effects.

Answers to Chapter 8 Self Test

1. The customer states that their problem is with the new monitor they installed and you know it is actually just the setting that needs to be changed. What do you do?

    A. Tell the customer it is just the settings and you'll fix those right away.

B. Ask them why they think it is the monitor and then explain in technical detail the refresh rates and the drivers that need to be changed.

C. Tell the user that there are monitor settings that you need to change. Explain to them that it is company policy to try and change the software before changing the hardware. Let them know that if it does not work, you will be more than willing to bring them a new monitor.

D. Give them a new monitor.

C. Even though the customer is always right, it may be necessary to figure out a way to deal with the situation without trying to show them that you are right. In this case, you are just following corporate hardware repair guidelines.

2. You go into an office and see that the user is not in. You are supposed to increase his swap file. What should you do?

A. Change the swap file size and restart computer.

B. Close out and save relevant work, change the swap file, and restart the computer.

C. Ask a neighboring user, if they are not busy, if they know when the user will be back and if they think it would be okay to go in and fix the computer.

D. Leave a note for the user to page you when they are in so you can fix the PC.

D. The user may have a laptop computer with him that needs the adjustment. You would not know this by doing A, B, or C.

3. A user is starting to ask you to customize their desktop after you fixed their printer. What do you do?

A. Tell the customer that this was not on their work order and that they should figure it out themselves.

B. Tell the customer you are busy and you will come back later to help them.

C. Show the user how to go into the help program and search for Help on how to customize the desktop. Make sure that the user is comfortable in looking through Help and hopefully they will be more self-sufficient.

D. Go ahead and customize things no matter how long it takes to complete this.

C. Show the user in a polite way how to change these, because they may want to change them in future and you do not want to be called on these annoyance calls.

4. You have spent an hour trying to troubleshoot a new optical drive, which is the first one you have ever worked on. Things are not working right and the user is getting impatient. What do you do?

A. Inform the user that you are running into problems that you need to escalate to other techs. Contact your other techs and find out if anyone else has experience with this type of drive. If not, try to get the operating system functional without the drive and tell the user you will call back to arrange a future visit after you have researched the problem. At this point, you would call the company on your time and not theirs.

B. Keep working and tell the user that it should work shortly.

C. Read the 50-page manual on set-up and go though each step once again.

D. Call the company that manufactured the drive and stay on hold until they can help you.

A. Do whatever you can to not waste the customer's time.

5. The trouble ticket that you have been called on is a monitor that will not work. You enter the office and you notice a monitor that is unplugged. What should you do?

A. Ask the user what is wrong and listen to their long story about the monitor.

B. Plug the monitor back in and try to gracefully not let the user think he is stupid.

C. Ask the user what is wrong with the monitor and ask pertinent questions such as those inquiring about the state of the monitor before it went dead.

D. Tell the user that they should look at this type of thing before they call for service.

C. By asking questions, you might find that this monitor was actually popping and smoking and that is why it was unplugged. Keep it unplugged until it can be repaired or replaced.

6. A user has a mysterious problem in Windows NT that you cannot pinpoint readily. You should:

A. Get the facts and research the problem on your own and go back to fix it when you get a solution.

B. Stay at the user's desk until you get the job done.

C. Cross examine the user and try and find out what they did wrong.

D. Both A and C.

A. The customer's time is valuable.

7. You go into an office and the user's name is unpronounceable. What do you do?

A. Don't address them by their name.

B. Try your best to say the name.

C. Hope they introduce themselves.

D. Call them beforehand and let them know you are coming and write their name down phonetically.

D. People get offended when their names are mispronounced.

8. You need to fix the PC of a Fortune 10 CEO and you were out late the night before. You did not have time in the morning to properly get ready for the day. What do you do?

A. Go to the bathroom to freshen up and comb your hair.

B. Go to the CEO's office anyway and let them accept you for who you are, not how you look.

C. Go home and take a shower.

D. Ask another tech if they would be willing to take this assignment for you.

D. Professionalism means always looking your best and having the courage to ask for help when it is needed.

9. A user is degrading you and saying you are stupid and although the customer is always right, you would like nothing more than to tell the user where they can go. What do you do?

A. Tell the user where they can go! You've earned enough respect on your job and nobody likes this user anyway.

B. Agree with all they say and just keep saying, "You are right."

C. Get another tech on the job; maybe their personalities will interact better.

D. Don't say anything, just get the work done and they will be happy.

C. Many techs thrive on difficult personalities. The other choices are clearly wrong.

10. A user is asking you how he can fix his son's PC at home. The problem sounds pretty complex. What do you do?

A. Stop what you are doing and go the extra mile for his son and write down all the steps needed to fix the PC.

B. Ask the user if they want to discuss it over lunch or during a break, when you don't have other customers to deal with.

C. Tell them that this is non-company business and they should not ask you this again.

D. Quickly tell them all that is needed to be done and hope they get it all.

D. As part of integrity, you should not spend company time on your customer's personal problems. Helping him out is going the extra mile. It is not necessary, but they really appreciate you going out of the way.

11. A user is complaining that nothing is on his c:\ drive. Upon further investigation, you realize someone has typed format c: and furthermore you identify that this has occurred at the time that only the user would have been able to do this. What do you do?

A. Reprimand the user and let him know that your investigation has determined that he typed the format command.

B. Mumble something about beginning users and fix the problem.

C. Let the user know that the format command has been run, and even though you don't know who did it, you know that this command should not be run. Let the user know that he should make sure that anyone who is using his computer while he is away should not use this command.

D. Fix the problem then rename the format command in DOS to a different name.

C. Do not blame, humiliate, or otherwise act unprofessionally before the user. Most of the time, it is not important to know who caused the problem, but what is important is not to let it happen again, which choice C accomplishes.

12. A user says that his Internet connection is not working and asks for your assistance. What do you do?

A. Check out the problem and fix it after they have explained the whole situation.

B. Tell them that they are not allowed to have Internet access and delete the software.

C. Know your company's software policies and know who is to have what. If he is not allowed Interent access, then delete the software after allowing the user to save his personal files from the software. Notify management if this is company policy.

D. Tell his boss and get him fired because he was not following the rules.

C. Know your company's policies. Also, make sure before you delete to spare any data that should not be deleted.

13. A user says that he should be given Microsoft Office Professional on his machine. Furthermore, the user states that

his boss thinks he should get the Microsoft Professional installed. What do you do?

A. Because the customer is always right, install the software and assume they are telling the truth about their boss.

B. Immediately call their boss to verify this and then install the software.

C. Know company's policies beforehand. Find out if the user is licensed site-wide or per-individual for this software. If they are not licensed, know the channel to get them licensed and notify the proper people including the user on what is to be done before the install.

D. Because all companies are "site licensed," go ahead and install the software.

C. Know the company's policies and do not embarrass the user.

14. The user is complaining about a mouse that is shocking him once every half-hour or so. He says that it is an electrical charge. On inspection of the mouse, you see that there is no way in the world that the mouse wire would be shocking him. What do you do?

A. Believe the customer and get him a new mouse. Tell him that if the new one shocks him to call you back.

B. Because this is obviously ESD, make sure that the user is grounded.

C. Perform repeated tests on the mouse to try and replicate the problem.

D. Both A and B.

D. First of all, the customer is always right. Secondly, by knowing it was a mouse problem before approaching the user, you should have brought a new mouse with you. By giving him the new mouse, you are not saying that the user is wrong and because swapping a mouse is so easy, it is a small price to pay to keep up the user's perception of himself.

15. You are fixing a PC and the office workers are having an argument over who messed up the computer. You should:

   A. Blame the person that has nonverbal guilt written on their face.

   B. Get a hypothesis and then blame the user.

   C. Try not to blame anyone and try and ensure that the users are aware of what potentially caused the problem.

   D. Side with each user because the customer is always correct.

      C. You should try to avoid potentially conflict-inducing situations. Also, you should not place blame or prejudgments on anybody.

Answers to Chapter 9 Self Test

1. In order to install Windows 3.*x* on a PC, the PC must already contain:

   A. A CD-ROM drive

   B. A copy of Windows NT

   C. A copy of DOS

   D. Microsoft Schedule +

      C. DOS must be already loaded for Windows 3.*x* to be installed.

2. What two files, in conjunction, are known as the Windows Registry database?

   A. USER.DAT and SYSTEM.DAT

   B. SYSTEM.INI and WIN.INI

   C. WIN.INI and USER.DAT

   D. WIN.INI and PROGRAM.INI

      A. The Registry is a compressed database that requires special tools and skills to manipulate

3. Which of the following files must be present for a PC to boot from its hard drive:

   A. AUTOEXEC.BAT

   B. IO.SYS

   C. COMMAND.COM

   D. ANSI.SYS

      B, C. ANSI.SYS and AUTOEXEC.BAT are optional.

4. Which of the following files *does not need to be* located in the root of the C: drive in order to be processed correctly?

   A. AUTOEXEC.BAT

   B. IO.SYS

   C. COMMAND.COM

   D. CONFIG.SYS

      C. COMMAND.COM may be located anywhere on the drive and referenced by a SHELL statement in the CONFIG.SYS file.

5. From a DOS prompt, you try to execute Windows (pre-95) by typing the WIN command. When doing so, you are greeted by a "Bad command or filename" response. Being the savvy DOS user you are, you issue a DIR win.* /s command from the root of C:, but receive a "0 file(s) found" response. Great. The WIN.COM file is missing. In order to replace it, you must:

A. Reinstall Windows

B. Download a new copy from the Internet

C. Copy the file from the installation disks

D. Make a copy of WIN.COM from another PC with Windows installed

A or D. You won't find the file on the install disks. A copy of WIN.COM may be used from a different PC. The worst thing that will happen is that the startup screen might be distorted if it was made for a different screen resolution. Of course, you can always reinstall Windows. If you're really ambitious, you can also perform a concatenation copy of the three WIN.COM internal components and make your own.

6. Time Slicing refers to what process?

A. The process of the CPU automatically changing its internal clock to accommodate for daylight savings

B. The process of the CPU dividing up time between applications for preemptive multitasking

C. The process by which cooperative multitasking operates

D. The process by which the CPU performs an automatic reboot

B. The other answers are all bogus.

7. In order for a hard drive partition to be "bootable," it must be

A. Formatted

B. Configured with an Operating System

C. Set as "Available"

D. Marked as "Active"

A, B, D. There is no way to set a hard drive as Available.

8. DOS is a widely-used acronym for:

A. Disk Operating Server

B. Driver Operating System

C. Driver Operating Server

D. Disk Operating System

D. The other answers are all bogus.

9. At the time DOS was first developed, what were the only types of storage media available for the PC?

A. Hard Drives

B. Floppy Disks

C. Cassette Tapes

D. All of the above

B, C. Hard drives, also known as "Winchesters," came shortly thereafter.

10. How many programs could execute at one time with DOS?

A. One

B. Two

C. Three

D. As many as necessary

> **A.** This, along with its being entirely text-based, was one of DOS's limitations.

11. DOS was developed as a _____-bit application.

A. 8

B. 16

C. 24

D. 32

> **B.** It wasn't until Intel moved on to its 80x86 architecture that the processor and system memory were able to read and write 32 bits of data per clock cycle.

12. Which DOS system file contains commands to modify the PC environment and execute applications?

A. HIMEM.SYS

B. EMM386.EXE

C. AUTOEXEC.BAT

D. MSDOS.SYS

> **C.** In addition, note that AUTOEXEC.BAT isn't required for system startup.

13. Which DOS system file loads low-level device drivers for specific hardware, and adjusts several system parameters for performance tuning and memory usage?

A. MSDOS.SYS

B. CONFIG.SYS

C. IO.SYS

D. ANSI.SYS

> **B.** CONFIG.SYS is loaded by MSDOS.SYS, and is not required for OS startup.

14. USER.EXE is which type of system file?

A. DOS

B. Windows 3.*x*

C. Windows 95

D. All of the above

> **B, C.** USER.EXE, along with GDI.EXE, is responsible for graphical interface for the Windows OS.

15. What is the first function that WIN.COM performs when executed?

A. It switches the computer into the appropriate graphics mode.

B. It loads an .LGO file.

C. It gives control of Windows to either DOSX.EXE or WIN386.EXE.

D. It determines what type of processor is in the computer.

> **D.** After the processor type is ascertained, WIN.COM switches the computer to the appropriate graphics mode, and then gives control of Windows to DOSX.EXE (for Standard mode) or WIN386.EXE (for Enhanced mode).

16. What does the formatting process do to a hard drive?

    A. It separate a single physical drive into multiple logical components.

    B. It increases the capacity of a hard drive.

    C. It divides the drive logically into sectors and tracks.

    D. It creates a complex database of settings pertaining to both applications and hardware.

    C. A drive must be partitioned before it is formatted. Partitioning separates the drive into multiple logical components.

17. The _____ is the smallest accessible unit to DOS from the FAT of a hard drive.

    A. Cluster

    B. Spindle

    C. Sector

    D. Track

    A. Sectors are combined logically into groups, which are called clusters.

18. _____ is the space left between the end of a file and the end of the cluster in which the file resides.

    A. Scrap

    B. Minibyte

    C. Slack

    D. Drift

    C. The other answers are all bogus.

19. In DOS, the total possible length of a file name, including its *path*, is:

    A. 32 characters

    B. 64 characters

    C. 128 characters

    D. Limitless

    C. A file name that utilizes all 128 characters is known as a fully qualified path.

20. The _____ attribute keeps a file from being displayed when a DIR command is issued in DOS.

    A. Read Only

    B. System

    C. Archive

    D. Hidden

    B, D. The other attributes perform different functions.

Answers to Chapter 10 Self Test

1. What type of memory is RAM?

    A. Upper Memory

    B. High Memory

    C. Virtual Memory

    D. Physical Memory

    D. RAM is a form of physical memory. It is a hardware component of the PC.

2. What is the difference between RAM and ROM?

    A. There is no difference.

B. RAM is readable by any application, ROM is meant for a single instruction set.

C. ROM is read only by any application, RAM is meant for a single instruction set.

D. RAM is a single chip, ROM is a long module.

   B. RAM is randomly accessible by any application. ROM is meant for a single instruction set.

3. Which is more common, SRAM or DRAM, and why?

A. SRAM because it is faster and cheaper

B. DRAM because it is faster

C. DRAM because it is cheaper

D. SRAM because it is faster

   C. DRAM is more common than SRAM because it is cheaper to produce, even though it is slower.

4. Flash memory is a form of what?

A. RAM

B. Upper Memory

C. Virtual memory

D. ROM

   D. Flash memory is a form of ROM that allows the instruction set to be loaded from a diskette, created to no longer force the PC to be physically opened each time that ROM needed to be upgraded.

5. What are the names for random access memory packages?

A. DIP, SIMM, and DIMM

B. RAM, DIP, and SIMM

C. SIMM and DIP

D. ROM, RAM, and Flash

   A. The packages for RAM are the DIP (dual inline package) chip, SIMM (single inline memory module), and DIMM (dual inline memory module).

6. Who created extended memory?

A. No one—it was always part of a PC.

B. Lotus did—so that their 1-2-3 program would run without running out of memory

C. Intel did—they design PCs

D. Lotus, Intel, and Microsoft—because they all wanted the 1-2-3 program to work on the processor and the operating system.

   D. Extended memory came out of the LIM specification—designed by Lotus, Intel, and Microsoft.

7. Where is the high memory area?

A. The first 64KB after the 640KB conventional memory area

B. The first 64KB of extended memory

C. The last 64KB of upper memory

D. The upper memory area

B. 640KB is conventional, 384KB is upper, everything after that is extended. The first 64KB of extended is called high memory.

8. What utility can display how memory is allocated?

   A. MEMMAKER
   B. CHKDSK
   C. MEM
   D. DEFRAG

   C. MEM, along with various switches, can display how memory is allocated.

9. Which line should appear first in the CONFIG.SYS?

   A. DOS=HIGH
   B. DEVICE=EMM386.EXE
   C. DOS=UMB
   D. DEVICE=HIMEM.SYS

   D. Loading HIMEM.SYS first allows the other commands listed here to work correctly.

10. How can a System Resources shortage error be resolved?

    A. Run SCANDISK
    B. DEFRAG the hard drive
    C. Reboot the PC
    D. Adjust the virtual memory in Control Panel

    C. The only way to refresh system resources is to reboot the PC.

Answers to Chapter 11 Self Test

1. What is the name of the utility that is used to create partitions on a hard drive?

   A. AUTOEXEC
   B. FORMAT
   C. CONFIG
   D. FDISK
   E. None of the above

   D. FDISK is used to create partitions on a hard disk drive. In addition to partition creation, FDISK can also be used for deletion.

2. What utility is used to erase all of the data from a partition on a disk drive?

   A. AUTOEXEC
   B. FORMAT
   C. CONFIG
   D. FDISK
   E. None of the above

   B. FORMAT is used to erase all of the information from the partition. In addition to erasing all of the information from the partition, formatting can place system files on the partition by issuing the /s switch and check the partition for errors by issuing the /c switch.

3. Which of the following is required to complete the installation of Windows 95?

A. Valid Serial number

B. A partition must be created on the hard drive

C. The partition on the hard drive must be formatted.

D. All of the above

E. None of the above

> **D.** In order to install Windows 95 a partition must be created on the hard drive and be formatted. A valid serial number will be required by the setup utility.

4. In order to be able to boot to a floppy disk the floppy disk must

A. have a partition created on it with the FDISK utility

B. have system files placed on the root directory of the disk

C. be set as the active partition

D. None of the above

E. All of the above.

> **B.** The only requirement for a floppy disk to be bootable is that the system files be placed in the root directory of the disk. FDISK does not support floppy disks because they are only capable of having one partition.

5. What is the switch that would be used with the FORMAT command to make a disk bootable?

A. /b

B. /x

C. /c

D. /s

E. /q

> **D.** The FORMAT utility with the /s switch will erase all of the data from a disk and copy the system files to the disk.

6. What is the utility that would be used to make a disk bootable without erasing all of the data from the disk?

A. FORMAT

B. FDISK

C. SYS

D. COMMAND

E. None of the above

> **C.** The SYS utility is used to copy the system files to a disk and make the disk bootable without erasing all of the data from the disk drive.

7. What is the special diagnostic mode provided by Windows 95?

A. Safe Mode

B. DOS Mode

C. Diagnostic Mode

D. Help Mode

E. None of the above

> **A.** Safe Mode is a special diagnostic mode of Windows 95 that allows you to change an incorrect setting, which in most cases allows you to return an

abnormally functioning system to its correct operation.

8. Which of the following drivers is **always** loaded by Safe Mode?

   A. Network drivers

   B. VGA video drivers

   C. CD-ROM drivers

   D. Sound card drivers

   E. All of the above

   B. Safe mode is a special diagnostic mode of Windows 95 that starts Windows 95 without any Network, CD-ROM, and printer drivers. A standard VGA display and Microsoft mouse drivers are used. This special mode allows you to change an incorrect setting, which will in most cases allow you to return an abnormally functioning system to its correct operation.

9. DOS Mode allows

   A. Programs that were designed to access hardware directly to be run

   B. Most DOS-based programs that will not run in Windows 95 to be run

   C. Applications that Windows 95 blocks from operation because of their attempt to access hardware directly to be run

   D. All of the above

   E. None of the above

   D. DOS Mode, or DOS Compatibility Mode as it is commonly known, allows some older MS-DOS applications to run that are not capable of running in

Windows 95. These applications are primarily applications that attempt to access hardware that Windows 95 controls directly. Applications that require use of MS-DOS mode are usually blocked from operation within Windows 95. The applications that most commonly require the use of MS-DOS compatibility mode include many graphical games.

10. Windows 95 Plug and Play will automatically detect devices that are installed in the system that are

    A. Windows 95 Plug and Play-compatible

    B. listed in the Windows 95 Plug and Play registry

    C. already have device drivers installed for them

    D. All of the above

    E. None of the above

    A. After a device has been added for the first time, it is automatically detected if the device is Windows 95 Plug and Play-compatible.

11. Windows 95 Plug and Play will _____ when it detects a device for the first time that it does not already have installed and is not in the Windows 95 driver library.

    A. Automatically download the driver from the internet

    B. Prompt the user for the driver from the hardware manufacturer

C. Prompt the user for the Windows 95 CD so the driver can be copied from there

D. All of the above

E. None of the above

B. Whenever Windows 95 detects a new device for which it does not already have the driver installed that is not in the Windows 95 driver library, the user is prompted for the driver.

12. To install a printer driver in Windows 95, you need to

A. Copy the printer setup program to the Windows\System directory

B. Double-click Printers from the Control Panel

C. Click Add New Printer from the Desktop

D. All of the above

E. None of the above

B. To install a printer, double-click Printers from the Control Panel. Click Add New Printer and select a driver from the list provided. In some cases (especially with newer printers) Windows 95 may have auto-detected the printer at system startup and have already installed the drivers for it.

13. To run a DOS-based application from within Windows 95, you would

A. Double-click the program from file manager

B. Double-click the program from windows explorer

C. Click Start and Run, type the applications name, and press ENTER

D. Both A and B are true

E. All of the above are true

D. A DOS-based application can be run by double-clicking the program from file manager or by double-clicking the program from Windows Explorer.

14. Both AUTOEXEC.BAT and CONFIG.SYS are

A. User-editable with a text editor

B. Necessary for the operation of both DOS and Windows 95

C. Not able to be edited by the user

D. All of the above

E. None of the above

A. AUTOEXEC.BAT and CONFIG.SYS files are two easily user-editable files. Any text editor can edit them both. CONFIG.SYS provides the ability to install device drivers among other things. AUTOEXEC.BAT is more commonly used to invoke device drivers for devices such as the mouse and the CD-ROM drive. Windows 95 does not require that any settings be made in either the CONFIG.SYS or AUTOEXEC.BAT file. In fact, AUTOEXEC.BAT and CONFIG.SYS do not even have to exist for Windows 95 to function fully.

15. What allows Windows applications to print to a standard interface without worrying about the type of printer that is installed on the workstation.

   A. Windows Printing Subsystem

   B. DOS Printing Subsystem

   C. Windows Printer Driver

   D. All of the above

   E. None of the above

   A. By using the Windows printing subsystem, applications are only required to submit data to be printed to the standardized subsystem. The subsystem then renders the data, and prints it for you.

Answers to Chapter 12 Self Test

1. Which command would you use to change the attributes of all files in the C:\TEMP directory to be read-only and hidden.

   A. ATTRIB C:\TEMP +h

   B. ATTRIB C:\TEMP +h +r

   C. ATTRIB C:\TEMP +h /s

   D. ATTRIB C:\TEMP +h +r /s

   E. None of the above

   B. The command "ATTRIB C:\TEMP +h +r" changes the attributes of all files in the C:\TEMP directory to read-only and hidden. Although option D is tempting, it also sets the attributes of any files in subdirectories to read-only and hidden, which was not the question.

2. Which DOS-based utility provides information about the computer such as disk drives, memory, and COM ports installed?

   A. SYSEDIT.EXE

   B. Control Panel

   C. MSD.EXE

   D. DEFRAG.EXE

   E. FDISK.EXE

   C. MSD, Microsoft Diagnostics, is a utility that provides a great deal of information about the system. MSD is most useful in determining what the system has installed in it, such as memory and hard drives.

3. Which DOS-based utility can be used to create partitions on a hard disk drive?

   A. SYSEDIT.EXE

   B. Control Panel

   C. MSD.EXE

   D. DEFRAG.EXE

   E. FDISK.EXE

   E. FDISK.EXE can be used to create and delete partitions on the system's hard disk drives.

4. Which Windows 95 utility can be used to change the settings of system devices?

A. SYSEDIT.EXE

B. Control Panel

C. MSD.EXE

D. DEFRAG.EXE

E. FDISK.EXE

B. The Control Panel is a utility that can be used to change the settings of the system. By double-clicking on any icon that is listed in the Control Panel, you can change the properties that are associated with whatever that icon represents.

5. Which Windows-based utility can be used to edit many of the system configuration files?

A. SYSEDIT.EXE

B. Control Panel

C. MSD.EXE

D. DEFRAG.EXE

E. FDISK.EXE

A. SYSEDIT.EXE, System Configuration Editor, is a utility that is provided with both Windows 3.*x* and Windows 95 that helps you to easily edit the system configuration files.

6. Which utility can be used to reorganize the file locations on a hard drive?

A. SYSEDIT.EXE

B. Control Panel

C. MSD.EXE

D. DEFRAG.EXE

E. FDISK.EXE

D. DEFRAG is a utility that is used to reorganize a hard disk drive. DEFRAG reorganizes the drive in a fashion that it feels is logical, which usually results in improved system performance.

7. The SETVER utility is used to correct which DOS problem?

A. Incorrect DOS version

B. Bad or Missing COMMAND.COM

C. Error in CONFIG.SYS line XX

D. All of the above

E. None of the above

A. The SETVER utility is used to make applications think that they are running on the version of DOS that they want to be running on.

8. Which type of virus usually is found attached to Microsoft Word and Microsoft Excel documents?

A. Boot Sector virus

B. Memory virus

C. Macro virus

D. FAT virus

E. Hoax virus

C. Macro viruses are viruses that attach themselves to documents in the form of macros. These macros can infect all of the other macros on the system, and all new documents created on the system. Macro viruses most commonly infect Microsoft Word and Microsoft Excel documents, but have the possibility of showing up in any application that includes the ability to create macros.

9. What type of virus is not actually a virus, and is usually sent in the form of an e-mail warning about a virus?

A. Boot Sector virus

B. Memory virus

C. Macro virus

D. FAT virus

E. Hoax virus

E. Hoax viruses are just that, hoaxes. The most common hoax virus began with the title of "Good Times," and has resurfaced under many other names. These virus hoaxes are usually sent as e-mail warnings not to open any e-mails of these titles. In the event that you receive any e-mail similar to this, please notify the sender that it is a hoax, and ignore it.

10. What Windows 95-based tool is used to modify the configuration of almost every setting in Windows 95?

A. Control Panel

B. Registry Editor

C. SYSEDIT.EXE

D. Windows SCANDISK

E. Conflict Troubleshooter

B. The Windows 95 Registry Editor is used to change nearly any setting in Windows 95. It is undoubtedly the most powerful configuration tool in Windows 95.

11. If an incorrect display adapter is set as the display adapter in DOS, you could _____ in order to fix it.

A. Reinstall the operating system.

B. Use the setup utility to fix the problem.

C. Boot the system in safe mode and then fix the problem.

D. Both A and B are possible solutions.

E. Both A and C are possible solutions.

F. None of the above.

F. DOS does not require that the display adapter be configured for the system.

12. If an incorrect display adapter is set as the display adapter in Windows 3.x, you could _____ in order to fix it.

A. Reinstall the operating system.

B. Use the setup utility to fix the problem.

C. Boot the system in safe mode and then fix the problem.

D. Both A and B are possible solutions.

E. Both A and C are possible solutions.

F. None of the above.

D. Windows 3.x, when configured for an incorrect display adapter, can be fixed by either running the setup utility or reinstalling the operating system.

13. If an incorrect display adapter is set as the display adapter in Windows 95, you could _____ in order to fix it.

    A. Reinstall the operating system.

    B. Use the setup utility to fix the problem.

    C. Boot the system in safe mode and then fix the problem.

    D. Both A and B are possible solutions.

    E. Both A and C are possible solutions.

    F. None of the above.

    D. Windows 95, when configured for an incorrect display adapter, can be fixed by either booting the system in safe mode or reinstalling the operating system.

14. Which of the following is not true?

    A. A printer with a driver set in bi-directional mode must use a bi-directional cable.

    B. A printer with a driver not set in bi-directional mode can use a non-bi-directional cable.

    C. A printer with a driver not set in bi-directional mode cannot use a non-bi-directional cable.

    D. All of the above are true.

    E. None of the above are true.

    C. A printer with a driver set in bi-directional mode must use a bi-directional cable. However, a printer with the driver not set in bi-directional mode can use either a bi-directional or non-bi-directional cable.

15. Which of the following is true about a "No Operating System Found" error message on a computer running Windows 95?

    A. Either the hard drive has a problem or the boot files have been corrupted.

    B. The Windows 95 setup program should fix the problem if it is caused by corrupted boot files.

    C. If you are unable to write to the hard drive, the problem probably is related to bad hardware.

    D. All of the above are true.

    E. None of the above are true.

    D. The message "No Operating System Found" indicates that there is either something wrong with the hard drive of the system or the boot files have been corrupted. Running the Windows 95 setup program should fix any problems related with the boot files being corrupted. If you are unable to write to the hard drive, the problem could be anything from a bad cable to a bad hard drive.

Answers to Chapter 13 Self Test

1. What does the acronym HTML stand for?

    A. Hypertext Markup Language

    B. Hypertext Transfer Markup Language

    C. Hybrid Text Markup Language

    D. Hypertext Meta Language

E. None of the above

A. Hypertext Markup Language (HTML) is the language in which most Web pages are written.

2. What does the acronym HTTP stand for?

A. Hyper Transfer of Text Protocol

B. Hypo Transfer of Text Protocol

C. Hypertext Transfer Protocol

D. Hypertext Transmission Plateau

E. None of the above

C. HTTP, Hypertext Transfer Protocol, is the protocol that is most commonly used to transfer information in a web browser. HTTP was originally used to transfer HTML files to computers, but has been adapted to transfer nearly any type of file.

3. What does the acronym FTP stand for?

A. Folder Transfer Plug

B. File Transfer Protocol

C. File Transmission Protocol

D. File Transfer Plateau

E. None of the above

B. FTP, File Transfer Protocol, is used to download files from an FTP server to a client computer. FTP is much older than the HTTP protocol, and was in use prior to the creation of the World Wide Web.

4. What does the acronym ISP stand for?

A. Interim Server Presence

B. Internet Service Provider

C. Internet Server Presence

D. Internetwork Service Presence

E. None of the above

B. An ISP, Internet Service Provider, is a company that provides access to the Internet. Most ISPs provide dial-up access through modems, but in many cases, they also provide access through higher-speed digital leased lines.

5. Which of the following are users able to do when disks are shared (depending on configuration)?

A. Read

B. Add

C. Delete

D. Modify

E. All of the above

E. When sharing files, depending on your particular configuration, users can Read, Add, Delete, and Modify files.

6. Which of the following are usually required when configuring a Web browser?

A. ISP dial-in number

B. User e-mail address

C. Workstation IP address

D. Web server serial number

E. None of the above

B. Configuration of a Web browser usually requires the user's e-mail address, SMTP server, and default startup page.

7. Which of the following are usually required when configuring an e-mail client?

   A. User's e-mail address

   B. SMTP server

   C. User's full name

   D. POP3 server

   E. All of the above

   E. When configuring an e-mail application, you are usually required to provide some information such as e-mail address, user's full name, POP3 server, and SMTP server.

8. Assume computer client A transfers a file to computer server B. The transfer was initiated by computer A sending the file to computer B. What is this referred to as?

   A. Installing

   B. Uploading

   C. Degrading

   D. Downloading

   E. None of the above

   B. Uploading is the process of transferring a file from a client to a server. The client always initiates the upload.

9. Assume computer server B transfers a file to computer client A. The transfer was initiated by computer A requesting computer B send the file. What is this referred to as?

A. Installing

B. Uploading

C. Degrading

D. Downloading

E. None of the above

D. Downloading is the process of transferring a file from a server to a client after the client requests that the file be transferred.

10. What protocol can be used for both downloading and uploading?

    A. HTML

    B. HTTP

    C. E-mail

    D. FTP

    E. None of the above

    B, D. HTTP and FTP can be used to both upload and download files.

11. What protocol can be used for downloading files, and is not documented to be capable of uploading?

    A. HTML

    B. HTTP

    C. E-mail

    D. FTP

    E. None of the above

    E. HTML is not a protocol but a language for creating Web pages. HTTP and FTP are both protocols that are capable of both downloads and uploads. E-mail is also not a protocol.

12. What type of access does an ISP usually provide?

    A. Simple network access

    B. Dial-up access

    C. Complex network access

    D. All of the above

    E. None of the above

    B. ISPs usually provide dial-up access as their primary service. Some ISP's also may provide high-speed digital access among other services.

13. What does the acronym DNS stand for?

    A. Direct Name Server

    B. Domain Name System

    C. Direct Name Service

    D. Distributed Name Service

    E. None of the above

    B. Called DNS, Domain Name System is used to resolve Domain Names into the IP addresses that the computer is able to understand.

14. Dial-up access is usually provided using a _____.

    A. Modem

    B. Internet

    C. Network

    D. DNS

    E. None of the above

    A. Dial-up access is defined as access provided to the Internet using a phone line and a modem. More correctly, dial-up access does not have to be a connection to any network, be it the Internet or a corporation's private LAN.

15. Domain Names are resolved to _____ using DNS.

    A. Internet names

    B. Alternate names

    C. Machine addresses

    D. MAC addresses

    E. None of the above

    E. Domain Names are resolved to IP Addresses using DNS. All computers connected to the Internet are required to have an IP address in order to be able to communicate on the Internet. DNS is used to resolve Domain Names into the IP addresses that the computer is able to understand.

B

About the CD

CD-ROM Instructions

This CD-ROM contains a full web site accessible to you via your web browser. Browse to or double-click **Click Here.htm** at the root of the CD-ROM and you will find instructions for navigating the web site and for installing the various software components.

Electronic Book

An electronic version of the entire book in HTML format.

Interactive Self-Study Module

An electronic self-study test bank is linked to the electronic book to help you instantly review key exam topics that may still be unclear. This module contains over 500 review questions, the same questions that appear at the end of each chapter. If you answer a multiple choice question correctly by clicking on the right answer, you will automatically link to the next question. If you answer incorrectly, you will be linked to the appropriate section in the electronic book for further study.

Installing Sample Exams

Included on the CD-ROM are sample exams from some of the leading practice test vendors. Launch the web site by double-clicking on the **Click Here.htm** file in the root of the CD-ROM. This will launch your default browser and bring up the web's home page. From the Home Page, click on the "Sample Exams" button. You will be instructed that some of the exams can be launched directly from the web page by Internet Explorer by clicking on the hyperlinks and choosing the "open the file" option when prompted. Others exams will require additional installation steps. Carefully read the instructions for each exam.

If you have problems installing from Internet Explorer, or you are using another browser such as Navigator, you should install directly from

Windows Explorer by opening the Demo Exams folder on the CD-ROM and following the installation instructions below:

1. The Self-Test Software A+ Exam cannot be installed from your web browser. In Windows Explorer, double-click on the following file: Demo Exams\STS APlus exam\APlus.exe

2. To install MindWorks PRELIM from Windows Explorer, double-click on the file: Demo Exams\Prelim\Setup.exe. Once it is installed, run "MWTest " via the "Start Programs" taskbar on your desktop. When prompted, enter a Username and Password of your choice. Select the A+ Demo and enter key code **MK13893527** in the appropriate field. Click on Validate to start the demo exam.

3. To install the MaxIT A+ Certification Exam Testing Demo from Windows Explorer, double-click on the file: Demo Exams\MaxIT APlus Cert Demo\install.exe and then launch the exam by double-clicking on Demo Exams\MaxIT APlus Cert Demo\N_test.dtz. You must enter your first and last name, but you can ignore the "Department" and "Identification Number" fields.

4. To install IBID A+ Certification from Windows Explorer, double-click on the file: Demo Exams\IBID\ClickMe.htm.

5. To install Dali Design PREP! for A+ from Windows Explorer, double-click on the following file: Demo Exams\Prep!for A Plus \preplus.exe.

Once they are installed, you should run the programs via the "Start Programs" taskbar on your desktop.

C

About the Web Site

Access Global Knowledge Network

As you know by now, Global Knowledge Network is the largest independent IT training company in the world. Just by purchasing this book, you have also secured a free subscription to the Access Global web site and its many resources. You can find it at:

http://access.globalknowledge.com

You can log in directly at the Access Global site. You will be e-mailed a new, secure password immediately upon registering.

What You'll Find There. . .

You will find a lot of information at the Global Knowledge site, most of which can be broken down into three categories:

Skills Gap Analysis

Global Knowledge offers several ways for you to analyze your networking skills and discover where they may be lacking. Using Global Knowledge Network's trademarked Competence Key Tool, you can do a skills gap analysis and get recommendations for where you may need to do some more studying (sorry, it just may not end with this book!).

Networking

You'll also gain valuable access to another asset: people. At the Access Global site, you'll find threaded discussions as well as live discussions.

Product Offerings

Of course, Global Knowledge also offers its products here—and you may find some valuable items for purchase: CBTs, books, courses. Browse freely and see if there's something that could help you.

D

DOS Command Reference

ATTRIB

The DOS ATTRIB command can be used to set the attributes on a file. Attributes are properties of a file, such as its ability to be written to. The attributes that can be set are:

- **Read-only**   When the file can only be read. The read-only attribute can be used to keep important files from being written to.
- **Archive**   Used to mark the archive status of files. In most cases, backup utilities skip files that do not have the archive attribute.
- **System**   Used to mark files that are vital to the system. In most cases, the operating system does not allow files that have the system attribute to be deleted.
- **Hidden**   Used to mark files that are to be hidden. Files are not visible in standard directory listings. (They can, however, be seen easily using the dir/a command.)

Each attribute can be turned on by placing a + in front of the attribute. In turn, they can be turned off by placing a – in front of the attribute.

Switches

The only switch that the attribute command accepts is /s. The /s switch applies the attributes to the selected directory, and all subdirectories. ATTRIB without any switches is applied only to the particular file / directory. ATTRIB without any attributes specified displays the attributes of the selected file / directory.

Usage

The syntax of the ATTRIB command is as follows:

```
Attrib <attributes> <filename and/or path> [/s]
```

CHKDSK

CHKDSK is used to check the integrity of the file system. CHKDSK can, if told to do so, fix most of the problems that it encounters.

Switches

- **/f** Tells CHKDSK that it is permitted to fix the errors that it encounters
- **/v** Displays the full path of each file as it checks them

Usage

```
Chkdsk <disk and/or path and/or filename> [/f][/v]
```

DELTREE

The DELTREE command is used to delete a tree of files. In other words, DELTREE deletes a directory and all of the directories below it. DELTREE is an extremely powerful tool that can be extremely useful, but in turn can cause a great deal of trouble. DELTREE is capable of deleting files with the Hidden, System, and Read-only attributes without any additional steps.

Switches

The only switch that DELTREE accepts is /y. DELTREE /y is used to delete trees of files without any confirmation. The files are simply deleted. Be warned that this command deletes *everything* below the directory you specify without asking you otherwise.

Usage

```
Deltree [/y] <directory(s) or filename(s)>
```

DISKCOPY

DISKCOPY copies the contents of one disk onto another. The contents are copied exactly, including any system files. A boot disk can be copied using DISKCOPY and results in another working boot disk.

Switches

- **/1**   Used to specify that only the first disk should be copied (older switch rarely used).

- **/m**   Used to specify that the source disk should only be copied to memory. This switch copies as much of the source disk into memory as possible, and then requests that the target disk be put into the drive. The information that was copied into memory is then copied onto the target, and the process is repeated until the entire disk is copied. (This is the default for DOS 6.*x* and earlier.)

- **/v**   Used to specify that the copy should be verified after completion.

Usage

```
Diskcopy <source drive> <destination drive>
```

EDIT

EDIT is a text editor with color pull-down menus and support for the mouse. EDIT can be used to modify text files. EDIT's most common use is to modify system files such as the AUTOEXEC.BAT and the CONFIG.SYS, but it can be used for anything that requires a text editor.

Switches

- **/b**   Forces EDIT to be started in a monochrome mode rather than the standard color VGA mode.

- **/h** Forces EDIT to be run displaying on the maximum number of lines that your computer can use. In most cases, more of a text file is displayed on the screen at one time making modifications a bit easier.

- **/r** Forces EDIT to load the file in read-only mode, no matter what the file attributes are.

Usage

```
edit [/b][/h][/r] <file name>
```

FDISK

The FDISK command can be used to create and delete partitions on the system's hard drives. Be warned that FDISK.EXE makes changes that are permanent and could easily render the system unbootable and make all data on the hard drives inaccessible. Use FDISK with care and ensure that all your data is backed up.

Switches

- **/status** Displays information about the current configuration of the drives in the computer. No changes can be made, this is merely for informational purposes.

- **/mbr** Replaces the master boot record with a backup copy. This is sometimes useful for removing viruses that have become resident in the boot record of a computer.

Usage

```
Fdisk [/status][/mbr]
```

FORMAT

FORMAT is used to erase all of the data from a partition of a drive. FORMAT is destructive and *will* erase all of the data on the partition it is used on.

Switches

- **/v** Followed by a colon and some text, this switch specifies the volume label that the disk will be given after the format.

- **/q** Forces a quick format. The files are not erased from the partition; the file allocation table is deleted with a new blank one put in its place. This does *not* remove viruses from infected floppy disks.

- **/f** Followed by a colon, this switch specifies the size of floppy disk to format. Possible sizes are: 160, 180, 320, 360, 720, 1.2, 1.44, 2.88, assuming your hardware supports them.

- **/b** Allocates space on the disk for system files to be put into, but does not put them there.

- **/s** Allocates space on the disk for system files and puts them there.

- **/c** Checks all of the clusters on the drive that are marked as bad to verify that they are not recoverable.

Usage

```
Format <drive letter> [/V:label][/q][/f:size][/b][/s][/c]
```

LABEL

LABEL changes the disk label of the specified drive. LABEL is not used very frequently, but is useful to be familiar with. LABEL is invoked by typing:

```
Label <drive letter>
```

MEM

The MEM command displays information on the programs that are currently in memory and how much memory they are using. In addition MEM tells how much memory the system has installed in it, and how much of that is available.

Switches

- **/c** Displays the amount of memory that is in use by each program
- **/d** Displays the amount of each segment of memory that is used by each program
- **/f** Displays information on the amount of memory that is free
- **/p** Pauses after each full screen of text is displayed

Usage

```
Mem [/c][/d][/f][/p]
```

MORE

MORE displays the contents of a file one page at a time. MORE is very helpful in reading long text files and program documentation. MORE is invoked by typing **more** and the file name you wish to read.

MOVE

MOVE is a command that moves all of the files and/or directories from one location to another.

Switches

- ■ **/y**   Used to force all files to be moved without prompting for confirmation. Be warned that this could be dangerous.
- ■ **/-y**   Used to force move to prompt you for each file.

Usage

```
Move [/y] <source file or directory> <destination file or
directory>
```

SUBST

The SUBST command is a command that can be used to substitute a drive letter for another drive letter or a path on a disk. SUBST cannot be used on network drives.

Switches

- ■ **/d**   Deletes the substituted drive

Usage

```
Subst <new drive letter> <source drive and path> [/d]
```

SYS

The SYS command copies the system files to a disk and make the disk bootable. This is accomplished by typing **sys** and the drive letter to which you wish to have the files copied. Obviously, there must be enough free space on the drive for the system files to be copied.

XCOPY

XCOPY copies all of the files from one location to another location. XCOPY is extremely sophisticated and is capable of much more than a standard copy of files.

Switches

- **/a**   Copies all files with the archive attribute set, and does not modify the archive attribute.

- **/m**   Copies all files with the archive attribute set, and turns off the archive attribute.

- **/d**   Followed by a colon and a date, this switch copies all files modified after the specified date.

- **/p**   Prompts the user prior to creation of each destination file.

- **/s**   Copies specified directories, subdirectories, and files except empty subdirectories.

- **/e**   Copies specified directories, subdirectories, and files including empty subdirectories.

- **/c**   Keeps copying if errors are encountered.

- **/q**   Does not display file names while copying.

- **/f**   Displays full source and destination paths and file names while copying.

- **/h**   Copies hidden and system files also.

- **/r**   Overwrites read-only files.

- **/t**   Copies directory structure but does not copy files. Does not copy empty subdirectories.

- ■ **/t /e**   Copies directory structure but does not copy files. Copies empty subdirectories.

- ■ **/u**   Updates files that already exist in destination.

- ■ **/k**   Copies attributes.

- ■ **/y**   Overwrites existing files without prompting the user for input.

- ■ **/-y**   Prompts user prior to overwriting existing files.

Usage

```
Xcopy <source> <destination>
[/a][/m][/d][/p][/s][/e][/c][/q][/f][/h][/r][/t][/u][/k]
[/y][/-y]
```

E

Network Troubleshooting Guide

N etworks are a great tool for us. Unfortunately, they can become an enormous hassle when they don't work as you would expect them to. In the event that your network is not operating as you suspect it should be, there are some steps you can take to help troubleshoot the problem. Because TCP/IP networks are most common, we focus on them.

Reboot

Before starting to troubleshoot the problem, reboot the machine to verify that there is an existing problem that reoccurs, not something that is user induced.

Neighborhood Watch

The first step in troubleshooting a possible network connection problem is to see what nearby users are doing. Are they able to access information or is it isolated to one machine? If all of the machines are having trouble, the problem is likely a network outage (this outage could be caused by one computer, though).

Ping Test

A ping test can be used to verify connectivity. Pinging can be accomplished by typing the command **ping** *<destination address>*. There are seven destination addresses you should try. These are:

1. **The IP Address of the machine on which you are working** This verifies that the machine is able to communicate on the network in the most basic way.

2. **The IP Address of the machine's gateway** This tests communication between the machine and the outside world. If you are unable to ping the gateway, either the machine has a local problem or the entire local network is down. Because you should have already verified that other

users are able to connect, the problem is likely to be with this specific machine.

3. **The IP Address of a remote host that you should be able to get to**
This verifies that you are able to communicate with a host while knowing its IP address. (A host I like to use is one of the Internic Web servers at 198.41.0.5.) If your connection to the Internet is behind a firewall, the results of this test could be misleading. Contact your Network Administrator if you think this is a problem you may be having.

4. **The IP Address of the machine's name server** By pinging the name server, you are verifying that the domain name service server is up and you are able to communicate with it.

5. **The name of a remote host that you should be able to connect to**
This verifies that you are able to communicate with hosts on outside networks as you would normally expect. (A host I like to use is www.internic.net.)

6. **A computer located on the same physical network segment** This verifies that your problem is with all computers, and not just ones outside your local area.

7. **A computer located on another subnet** If you are unsure of what to use for this test, contact your Network Administrator.

Trace the Route

You can use the tracert command to trace where your problem is occurring. If the ping test is successful for 3 or 5, you can skip this step. Type the command **tracert** www.internic.net. Tracert should tell you where your network trouble is occurring. You should then contact the proper authority to report the outage.

Test the Connection on the Wall (Method 1 *Cheaper)

In many cases, this can be accomplished with a handy dandy 30-foot cable. Simply disconnect your machine from its regular network connection, plug it into a longer network cable, and run that cable to the nearest connection. Repeat the ping tests. If the connection now works, plug the longer network cable into the connection in the wall the machine was originally plugged into. If the machine successfully completes a ping test, trash the old cable and replace it with a new one (of an appropriate length, of course).

Test the Connection on the Wall (Method 2 *Easier)

Disconnect the cable from the machine and plug it into a laptop computer. If the ping test is successful, the problem is with the machine. If the ping test is unsuccessful, replace the cable with a new one and test it again. If the ping test is still unsuccessful, the problem is in the wall and you need to contact the proper authorities; otherwise, the cable was bad.

Workstation Configuration

Verify that the IP Address, Subnet Mask, Gateway Address, and DNS Server address are configured correctly. Verify that the correct Network Interface Card drivers are installed. (I usually take this a step further and simply delete the drivers for the NIC and re-install it. I then reenter the information to verify that it is correct.)

Bad Ethernet Card?

If all else fails, check the Ethernet card in the workstation. A quick way to test that is to replace it with another and see if the problem reoccurs.

F

Networking Language

his appendix presents you with some of the common networking terminology. While most of these terms also appear in this book's Glossary, some of them do not because of the cryptic nature of the term. You should be at least familiar with all of these terms.

Topologies

Topology is defined as the physical layout of computers, cables, and other components on a network. Any network design encountered will be a variation on or combination of the three basic networking topologies:

- Bus
- Ring
- Star

Bus

A bus topology is when all of the devices that are connected to the network are connected to a central line or bus. In most instances of cable breaks, the entire network becomes inoperable.

Ring

A ring topology is when all of the devices are connected to a virtual (and usually physical) ring. Devices are not allowed to communicate on the network until a token has been passed around the ring to it. Only the device with the token is allowed to transmit. In most instances of cable breaks, the entire network becomes inoperable.

Star

A star topology is when all of the devices are connected to a central device that allows them to communicate with each other. In most instances of cable breaks, only the machine(s) directly attached to the broken network cable is affected.

Cabling and Physical Connectors

In order to create a network, you must physically connect the devices that will be on the network. This is accomplished using cables. There are many different types of cables, each having its own advantages and disadvantages.

10BaseT

10BaseT cable is also referred to as Twisted Pair or Unshielded Twisted Pair (UTP). 10BaseT is the most commonly used type of network cable. 10BaseT is capable of transmitting a maximum of 10 megabits/second at a maximum distance of 100 meters. Networks utilizing 10BaseT can be wired with either Category 3 or Category 5 cabling. 10BaseT is wired in a star topology.

100BaseT

100BaseT cabling has all of the characteristics of 10BaseT except that it is capable of transmitting at a maximum speed of 100 megabits/second and can only be wired with Category 5 cabling.

10Base2

10Base2 cable is also referred to as BNC Coax or Thinwire Coax. 10Base2 is capable of transmitting a maximum of 10 megabits/second at a maximum distance of 180 meters. Networks utilizing 10Base2 are wired in a bus topology.

10Base5

10Base5 cable is also referred to as AUI or Thickwire. 10Base5 is capable of transmitting a maximum of 10 megabits/second at a maximum distance of 500 meters. Networks utilizing 10Base5 are wired in a bus topology.

Category 3 (aka Cat 3)

Category 3 cable is the cable that is most commonly used to wire phones. It can be used for 10BaseT networks. It is, however, recommended that all new wiring be done utilizing Category 5.

Category 5 (aka Cat 5)

Category 5 cable can be used for both 10BaseT and 100BaseT networks. Category 5 is the preferred cable for new network installations.

T-Adapter

Each device in a 10Base2 network must be connected to a T-Adapter, which in turn is connected to the network cable.

Terminator

Each end of the network cable in a 10Base2 network must be connected to a 50 Ω terminator.

Connectivity Devices

Network connectivity devices have a wide range of uses, from keeping your network's configuration in a physically organized fashion to improving the overall performance of the network.

Hub

A hub is a networking device that takes input from each of its ports and re-transmits it out all of the other ports on the hub. A hub is the device that is used in a network of star topology to connect each of the devices on the network.

Repeater

A repeater is a device that allows network cabling to exceed its maximum distances. A repeater simply accepts communication from one side and re-transmits it out the other.

Router

A router is a device that connects two separate networks. The router intercepts traffic and determines if it is destined for the network on the other side of the router. If the traffic is destined for the other side of the router, it is allowed to cross.

Switch

A switch is a device that can be used in place of a hub. A switch allows devices on the network to communicate with each other without transmitting the data over the entire network. A switch determines what devices are on each port, and only send packets that are destined to one of those devices or are broadcasts to those ports.

G

MSD.EXE
Output

A s you saw in Chapter 10, memory conflicts are difficult to diagnose because they can come from many different sources, and are therefore difficult to troubleshoot. One of the most dynamic tools for checking and reporting on memory allocation usage is Microsoft's own MSD.EXE, which is available as a free download at their Web site. This tool provides a full output of every conceivable detail about your system. A sample output follows.

```
Microsoft Diagnostics version 2.13    4/21/98   11:49am   Page  1


===================================================================

--------------------- Summary Information ---------------------

              Computer: Award/Award, Pentium(TM)
                Memory: 640K, 64512K Ext, 64272K XMS
                 Video: VGA, Unknown
               Network: Windows 95 Client
            OS Version: MS-DOS 7.10
                 Mouse: Not Detected 8.30
         Other Adapters: Game Adapter
           Disk Drives: A: B: C: D: E: F: G: H:
             LPT Ports: 1
             COM Ports: 3
   Windows Information: 4.10, Enhanced

------------------------- Computer -------------------------

         Computer Name: Award
      BIOS Manufacturer: Award
          BIOS Version: Award Modular BIOS v4.50PG
         BIOS Category: IBM PC/AT
         BIOS ID Bytes: FC 01 00
             BIOS Date: 03/14/96
             Processor: Pentium(TM)
       Math Coprocessor: Internal
              Keyboard: Enhanced
              Bus Type: ISA/AT/Classic Bus
        DMA Controller: Yes
          Cascaded IRQ2: Yes
     BIOS Data Segment: None
```

Microsoft Diagnostics version 2.13   4/21/98   11:49am   Page 2

===

------------------------- Memory -------------------------
Legend: Available " " RAM "##" ROM "RR" Possibly Available ".."
   EMS Page Frame "PP" Used UMBs "UU" Free UMBs "FF"
 1024K FC00 RRRRRRRRRRRRRRRR FFFF Conventional Memory
       F800 RRRRRRRRRRRRRRRR FBFF   Total: 640K
       F400 RRRRRRRRRRRRRRRR F7FF   Available: 580K
  960K F000 RRRRRRRRRRRRRRRR F3FF   594240
                                                        bytes

       EC00 UUUUUUUUUUUUUUUU EFFF
       E800 UUUUUUUUUUUUUUUU EBFF Extended Memory
       E400 UUUUUUUUUUUUUUUU E7FF   Total: 64512K
  896K E000 UUUUUUUUUUUUUUUU E3FF
       DC00 UUUUUUUUUUUUUUUU DFFF MS-DOS Upper Memory Blocks
       D800 UUUUUUUUUUUUUUUU DBFF   Total UMBs: 154K
       D400 UUUUUUUUUUUUUUUU D7FF   Total Free UMBs: 0K
  832K D000 UUUUUUUUUUUUUUUU D3FF   Largest Free Block: 0K
       CC00 UUUUUUUUUUUUUUUU CFFF
       C800 .....UUUUUUUUUUU CBFF XMS Information
       C400 RRRRRRRRRRRRRRRR C7FF   XMS Version: 3.00
  768K C000 RRRRRRRRRRRRRRRR C3FF   Driver Version: 3.5f
       BC00 .... BFFF   A20 Address Line: Enabled
       B800 .... BBFF   High Memory Area: In use
       B400 .... B7FF   Available: 64272K
  704K B000 .... B3FF Largest Free Block: 2048K
       AC00 .... AFFF   Available SXMS: 64272K
       A800 .... ABFF   Largest Free SXMS: 2048K
       A400 .... A7FF
  640K A000 .... A3FF DPMI Information
                                          DPMI Detected: Yes
                                               Version: 0.90

------------------------- Video -------------------------

       Video Adapter Type: VGA
              Manufacturer: Unknown
                     Model:

```
                    Display Type: VGA Color
                      Video Mode: 3
                Number of Columns: 80
                   Number of Rows: 50
             Video BIOS Version: S3 86C325 Video BIOS. Version 1.00-10
                 Video BIOS Date: 08/02/96
         VESA Support Installed: Yes
                   VESA Version: 1.02
                  VESA OEM Name: S3 Incorporated. 86C325
              Secondary Adapter: None


   Microsoft Diagnostics version 2.13    4/21/98   11:49am    Page   3


   ====================================================================

   -------------------------- Network --------------------------

                     Network Running: Yes
                        Network Name: Windows 95 Client
         MS-DOS Network Functions: Supported
                     Computer Name: DA_MACHINE
                   NetBIOS Present: Yes
             NetBIOS INT 5C Address: 0AEE:000F
                       Network Root: C:\WINDOWS
                          User Name: DUDE
              Workgroup: DUDES
    Server Connection: Established
                     Mailslot Support: Yes
                          API Support: Yes
   NetBIOS Card Information:
                   Net01 ID: 0207011BB875
                   Active Sessions for Net01


   -------------------------- OS Version --------------------------

                   Operating System: MS-DOS 7.10
                   Internal Revision: 00
                   OEM Serial Number: FFH
                   User Serial Number: 000000H
                   OEM Version String: Windows 98 [Version
                                                   4.10.1650]
```

```
                     DOS Located in: HMA
                        Boot Drive: C:
                Path to Program: F:\LIBRARY\TEMP\MSD.EXE


                         Environment Strings
----------------------------------------------------------------
PROMPT=$p$g
winbootdir=C:\WINDOWS
COMSPEC=C:\WINDOWS\COMMAND.COM
SOUND=f:\HARDWARE\CREATI~1
MIDI=SYNTH:1 MAP:E MODE:0
TEMP=G:\temp
TMP=g:\temp
PATH=C:\WINDOWS;C:\WINDOWS\COMMAND;..;F:\DOSUTILS;O:\OFFICE\OFFICE;
windir=C:\WINDOWS
BLASTER=A220 I10 D1 H6 P330 T6
CMDLINE=msd /P test2.txt



Microsoft Diagnostics version 2.13    4/21/98   11:49am   Page  4


================================================================


-------------------------- Mouse ----------------------------


                Mouse Hardware: Not Detected
           Driver Manufacturer: Microsoft
               DOS Driver Type: Serial Mouse
              Driver File Type: .SYS File
            DOS Driver Version: 8.30
                     Mouse IRQ: 4
                Mouse COM Port: COM1:
        Mouse COM Port Address: 03F8H
       Number of Mouse Buttons: 2
         Horizontal Sensitivity: 50
          Mouse to Cursor Ratio: 1 : 1
           Vertical Sensitivity: 50
          Mouse to Cursor Ratio: 1 : 1
                Threshold Speed: 0
                Mouse Language: English
```

```
----------------------- Other Adapters ------------------------

                 Game Adapter: Detected
             Joystick A - X: 103
                         Y: 29
                   Button 1: On
                   Button 2: On
             Joystick B - X: 0
                         Y: 141
                   Button 1: On
                   Button 2: On



  Microsoft Diagnostics version 2.13    4/21/98   11:49am   Page  5

========================================================================

----------------------- Disk Drives ------------------------
Drive  Type                                 Free Space  Total Size
-----  ----------------------------------   ----------  ----------
  A:   Floppy Drive, 3.5" 1.44M
          80 Cylinders, 2 Heads
          512 Bytes/Sector, 18 Sectors/Track
  B:   Floppy Drive, 5.25" 1.2M
          80 Cylinders, 2 Heads
          512 Bytes/Sector, 15 Sectors/Track
  C:   Fixed Disk, CMOS Type 46                76M         401M
          102 Cylinders, 128 Heads
          512 Bytes/Sector, 63 Sectors/Track
       CMOS Fixed Disk Parameters
          622 Cylinders, 128 Heads
          63 Sectors/Track
  D:   Fixed Disk, CMOS Type 46               121M         507M
          258 Cylinders, 64 Heads
          512 Bytes/Sector, 63 Sectors/Track
       CMOS Fixed Disk Parameters
          516 Cylinders, 64 Heads
          63 Sectors/Track
  E:   Fixed Disk, CMOS Type 46                68M         495M
          126 Cylinders, 128 Heads
          512 Bytes/Sector, 63 Sectors/Track
       CMOS Fixed Disk Parameters
          516 Cylinders, 64 Heads
          63 Sectors/Track
```

```
F:   Fixed Disk, CMOS Type 46                          26M        495M
       126 Cylinders, 128 Heads
       512 Bytes/Sector, 63 Sectors/Track
     CMOS Fixed Disk Parameters
       516 Cylinders, 64 Heads
       63 Sectors/Track
G:   Fixed Disk, CMOS Type 46                         354M        507M
       129 Cylinders, 128 Heads
       512 Bytes/Sector, 63 Sectors/Track
     CMOS Fixed Disk Parameters
       516 Cylinders, 64 Heads
       63 Sectors/Track
H:   Fixed Disk, CMOS Type 46                          25M        505M
       257 Cylinders, 64 Heads
       512 Bytes/Sector, 63 Sectors/Track
     CMOS Fixed Disk Parameters
       516 Cylinders, 64 Heads
       63 Sectors/Track
I:   CD-ROM Drive
J:   DriveSpace Drive                                  71M        563M
       Actual Free Space                               0K
       CVF Filename Is H:\DRVSPACE.001
K:   CD-ROM Drive
L:   CD-ROM Drive
M:   CD-ROM Drive
O:   DriveSpace Drive                                  63M        529M
```

Microsoft Diagnostics version 2.13   4/21/98   11:49am   Page   6
===
```
         Actual Free Space                             0K
         CVF Filename Is E:\DRVSPACE.001    U:   DriveSpace Drive
53M     132M            Actual Free Space                        0K
         CVF Filename Is E:\DRVSPACE.002
     SHARE Installed
     MSCDEX Version 2.95 Installed
     LASTDRIVE=Z:
```

------------------------- LPT Ports -------------------------

Port	Port Address	On Line	Paper Out	I/O Error	Time Out	Busy	ACK
LPT1:	0378H	Yes	No	No	No	No	No
LPT2:	-	-	-	-	-	-	-
LPT3:	-	-	-	-	-	-	-

```
-------------------- COM Ports ---------------------

                       COM1:      COM2:      COM3:     COM4:
                       -----      -----      -----     -----
Port Address           03F8H      02F8H      02E8H      N/A
Baud Rate              1200       2400       2400
Parity                 None       None       None
Data Bits              7          8          8
Stop Bits              1          1          1
Carrier Detect (CD)    No         No         No
Ring Indicator (RI)    No         No         No
Data Set Ready (DSR)   No         Yes        Yes
Clear To Send (CTS)    No         Yes        Yes
UART Chip Used         8250       8250       16550AF

---------------- Windows Information -------------------

             Windows version: 4.10
                Windows mode: Enhanced
           Windows Directory: C:\WINDOWS
            System Directory: C:\WINDOWS\SYSTEM
           Virtual Machine ID: 2
       Display driver version: 0.00
          Display resolution: 1024 x 768
              Bits per pixel: 24
        Number of bit planes: 1

Filename                      Size         Date       Time
--------------------    ---------------   --------    -----
DVA.386                          5195      7/13/96     0:00
BI-DI.386                       26670      6/14/96     4:20
MSMOUSE.VXD                     15809     12/03/97     8:52
VWAVSYN.386                    249144      3/14/97     4:01


Microsoft Diagnostics version 2.13    4/21/98   11:49am
                                                   Page 7


============================================================
```

```
--------------------- IRQ Status ---------------------

IRQ   Address   Description      Detected        Handled By
---   -------   --------------   -------------   ----------
 0    0AE3:0000  Timer Click      Yes                   (
 1    0920:0028  Keyboard         Yes          Default Handlers
 2    F000:EF6F  Second 8259A     Yes                 BIOS
 3    F000:EF6F  COM2: COM4:      COM2:               BIOS
 4    F000:EF6F  COM1: COM3:      COM1: COM3: Not DeteBIOS
 5    F000:EF6F  LPT2:            No                  BIOS
 6    0920:009A  Floppy Disk      Yes          Default Handlers
 7    0070:0465  LPT1:            Yes              System Area
 8    0920:0035  Real-Time Clock  Yes          Default Handlers
 9    F000:ECF3  Redirected IRQ2  Yes                 BIOS
10    F000:EF6F  (Reserved)                           BIOS
11    F000:EF6F  (Reserved)                           BIOS
12    F000:EF6F  (Reserved)                           BIOS
13    F000:F0FC  Math Coprocessor Yes                 BIOS
14    0920:00FA  Fixed Disk       Yes          Default Handlers
15    0920:0112  (Reserved)                    Default Handlers


Microsoft Diagnostics version 2.13    4/21/98    11:49am
Page  8


=============================================================

--------------------- TSR Programs ---------------------
Program Name      Address   Size   Command Line Parameters
---------------   -------   ------  -----------------------
 System Data       026C     30512
  HIMEM            026E      1152   XMSXXXX0
  EMM386           02B7      4304   $MMXXXX0
  DBLBUFF          03C5      2960   DblBuff$
  ùË.VSRQP         047F       544   Block Device
  BUFFERS          04A2     16080
Directories        0890      2288
Default Handlers   0920      3072
System Code        09E0        64
```

```
COMMAND.COM        09E5        16
=C:\WIND           09E7       304
WIN                09FB      3408
(                  0AD1        32
(                  0AD4      8880
???                0D00       320    /P test2.txt
COMMAND.COM        0D15      5712    /P test2.txt
???                0E7B      1424    /P test2.txt
MSD.EXE            0ED5       336    /P test2.txt
MSD.EXE            0EEB    335024    /P test2.txt
MSD.EXE            60B7      8192    /P test2.txt
Free Memory        62B8    250976
Excluded UMB Area  9FFF    169408
System Data        C95C    156640
  DRVSPACE         C95E    110576    DBLSYSH$
  OAKCDROM         E45E     36048    MSCD001
  IFSHLP           ED2C      2848    IFS$HLP$
    t.< r$w        EDDF      1200    Block Device
  File Handles     EE2B      5616
  FCBS             EF8B       256
(                  EF9B      1600
```

```
Microsoft Diagnostics version 2.13   4/21/98  11:49am
                                                Page 9
```

```
============================================================

------------------ Device Drivers --------------------

Device        Filename  Units    Header      Attributes
-----------   --------  -----   --------    ----------------
NUL                             00C9:0048   1.............1..
IFS$HLP$      IFSHLP            ED2C:0000   11.1............
MSCD001       OAKCDROM          E45E:0000   11..1...........
DBLSYSH$      DRVSPACE          C95E:0000   1...............
DblBuff$      DBLBUFF           03C5:0000   11..1....1......
$MMXXXX0      EMM386            02B7:0000   11..............
XMSXXXX0      HIMEM             026E:0000   1.1.............
Block Device  DBLSPACE    18    021E:0000   .11.1....1....1.
CON                             0070:0016   1.........1..11
AUX                             0070:0028   1...............
PRN                             0070:003A   1.1.....11......
```

```
CLOCK$                          0070:004C  1...........1...
Block Device              8     0070:005E  ....1...11....1.
COM1                            0070:006A  1...............
LPT1                            0070:007C  1.1.....11......
LPT2                            0070:008E  1.1.....11......
LPT3                            0070:00A0  1.1.....11......
CONFIG$                         0070:012D  11..............
COM2                            0070:00B8  1...............
COM3                            0070:00CA  1...............
COM4                            0070:00DC  1...............
&MMXXXX0                        0ADE:0000  11..............
mscd$$$$                        0AE6:0000  11..1...........
```

_____
_____
_____
_____
_____

Glossary

Access Methods   Also known as *network access*, these are the methods by which a device communicates on a network. Network access provides a standard that all devices that wish to communicate on a network must abide by in order to eliminate communication conflicts.

Active Matrix Display   Active matrix displays are based on Thin Film Transistor technology. Instead of having two rows of transistors, active matrix displays have a transistor at every pixel, which enables much quicker display changes than passive matrix displays and produces display quality comparable to a CRT.

ANSI.SYS   ANSI.SYS is a DOS system file that is loaded by CONFIG.SYS if required. This file loads an extended character set for use by DOS and DOS applications that includes basic drawing and color capabilities. Normally used for drawing and filling different boxes for menu systems, it is seldom in use today. By default, it carries no attributes, and is not required for OS startup.

ARCHIVE Attribute   The ARCHIVE attribute is set automatically when a file is created or modified, and is automatically removed by back-up software when the file is backed up.

ATTRIB.EXE   ATTRIB.EXE is a utility that can be used to change the attributes of a file or group of files.

AUTOEXEC.BAT   A user-editable system file, AUTOEXEC.BAT contains commands to modify the PC environment (PATH, COMSPEC, other SET commands), and to execute applications. It can be used to create a menu system, prompt for user input, or *call* other batch files to maintain a modular structure. By default, it carries no attributes, and is not required for OS startup.

Basic Input Output System   See BIOS.

Bi-Directional Print Mode Most common in some of the newer and more advanced printers, bi-directional print mode means that the printer is able to talk back to the computer, enabling, for example, the printer to send the user exact error messages that are displayed on the workstation. It also helps the spooler to avoid print spooler stalls.

BIOS Most commonly known as BIOS, Basic Input Output System is a standard set of instructions or programs that handle boot operations. When an application needs to perform an I/O operation on a computer, the operating system makes the request to the system BIOS, which in turn translates the request into the appropriate instruction set used by the hardware device.

Brownout Momentary lapses in power supply. Brownouts can cause problems with computer components that are not designed to withstand these events.

Bus A bus is the actual pathway used to transmit electronic signals from one computer device to another.

Bus Topology In a local area network, a bus topology has each device on the network connected to a central cable, or bus. Most common with coaxial cabling.

Cache Memory Cache memory is used to store frequently used instructions and data so that they can be accessed quickly by the computer.

Carrier Sense Multiple Access/Collision Detection See CSMA/CD.

Central Processing Unit See CPU.

Chip Creep A phenomenon whereby a computer chip becomes loose within its socket.

Cleaning Blade   This rubber blade inside a laser printer extends the length of the photosensitive drum. It removes excess toner after the print process has completed and deposits it into a reservoir for re-use.

CMOS   The Complementary Metal-Oxide Semiconductor (or CMOS) is an integrated circuit composed of a metal oxide that is located directly on the system board. The CMOS, which is similar to RAM in that data can be written to the chip, enables a computer to store essential operating parameters after the computer has been turned off, enabling a faster system boot.

Coaxial Cable   A high-bandwidth network cable that consists of a central wire surrounded by a screen of fine wires.

COMMAND.COM   COMMAND.COM is a DOS system file that is automatically executed in the ROOT directory at startup. This file contains the internal command set and error messages. By default, it carries no attributes, but is required for OS startup.

Complementary Metal-Oxide Semiconductor   See CMOS.

CONFIG.SYS   A user-editable system file that provides the ability to install device drivers. Windows 95 does not require any specific settings to be made in CONFIG.SYS.

Cooperative Multitasking   There are two different types of multitasking: cooperative and preemptive. Cooperative multitasking means that applications must voluntarily relinquish control of the CPU. When an application relinquishes control of the CPU, Windows then decides which application will execute next. The most common way for an application to relinquish control is by asking Windows if any messages are available.

CPU   The CPU (Central Processing Unit) is the operations center of a computer. Its job is to provide the devices attached to the computer with directives that retrieve, display, manipulate, and store information.

CSMA/CD   Most commonly found on Ethernet networks, carrier sense multiple access/collision detection (CSMA/CD) is a network communication protocol and operates in much the same way as humans communicate. With CSMA/CD, a device transmits data onto the network. The device then detects if any other devices have transmitted onto the network at the same time. If it detects that another device has transmitted data onto the network at the same time, the device then waits an unspecified random amount of time and retransmits its data.

Defragmentation   A process that reorganizes fragmented files back in a proper, contiguous fashion. This is done by moving several of them to an unused portion of the drive, erasing the previous locations in contiguous clusters, then rewriting the files back in proper sequence. Performed periodically, defragmentation is probably the single best operation a user can perform to maintain a high-performance system.

Device Driver   Device drivers are programs that translate necessary information between the operating system and the specific peripheral device for which they are configured, such as a printer.

Dial-Up Access   Dial-up access is defined as access provided to the Internet, a LAN, or even another computer by using a phone line and a modem. Dial-up access does not have to be a connection to any network.

Dial-Up Networking   Refers to the type of network in which a modem is used to connect two or more workstations.

DIMM   A Dual In-line Memory Module (DIMM) is very similar to a SIMM; it's a small plug-in circuit board that contains the memory chips that you need to add certain increments of RAM to your computer. Because the memory chips run along both sides of the chip, DIMM chips can hold twice as much memory as SIMM chips.

DIP Switch   Dual In-line Package (DIP) switches are very tiny boxes with switches embedded in them. Each switch sets a value of 0 or 1, depending on how they are set. These switches are used to provide user-accessible configuration settings for computers and peripheral devices.

Direct Memory Access   See DMA.

Dirty Current   Noise present on a power line is referred to as dirty current. This noise is caused by *electro-magnetic interference (EMI)* and can stray, or leak, from the current into nearby components. When EMI leaks from power current, it is called a magnetic field and can easily damage computer components.

DMA   Direct memory access (DMA) is a facility by which a peripheral can communicate directly with RAM, without intervention by the CPU.

DNS   Domain Name System (DNS) is the Internet-based system that resolves symbolic names to IP addresses (which are a series of numbers) that the computer is able to understand.

Docking Station   Docking stations allow users to add "desktop-like" capabilities, such as a mouse, monitor, or keyboard, to their portable computer by plugging these components into a docking station and connecting their portable only to the docking station, rather than to each individual component.

Domain Name System   See DNS.

DOS Mode   DOS Mode, or DOS Compatibility Mode as it is commonly known, allows execution of some older MS-DOS applications that are not capable of running in Windows 95. Applications that require use of MS-DOS mode are usually blocked from operation within Windows 95. DOS itself stands for Disk Operating System.

Download   Downloading refers to the process of transferring a file or files from one computer to another. Unlike uploading, the transfer is always initiated by the computer that will be receiving the file(s).

Downtime   Downtime is the time wasted as a result of a malfunctioning computer or network.

DRAM   Dynamic Random Access Memory (DRAM) chips abandoned the idea of using the unwieldy transistors and switches in favor of using the smaller capacitors that could represent 0s and 1s as an electronic charge. This resulted in the ability to store more information on a single chip, but also meant that the chip needed a constant refresh and hence more power.

Dual In-line Memory Module   See DIMM.

Dual In-line Package Switch   See DIP Switch.

Dynamic RAM   See DRAM.

EBKAC Error   A common error that most technicians face, the EBKAC error stands for Error Between Keyboard and Chair. As that implies, EBKAC errors are not technical errors, but rather errors on the part of the end user. Common EBKAC errors include power cords being unplugged, no paper in printer, and power switches being turned off.

ECP   ECP (Extended Capability Port) is a parallel printer interface designed to speed up data transfer rates by bypassing the processor and writing the data directly to memory.

EDO RAM   Extended Data Output RAM (EDO RAM) is a type of DRAM chip designed for processor access speeds of approximately 10 to 15 percent above fast-page mode memory.

EISA   Extended Industry Standard Architecture (EISA) is an industry standard bus architecture that allows for peripherals to utilize the 32-bit data bus that is available with 386 and 486 processors.

Electrophotographic Printing Process   See EP Process.

EMM386.EXE   EMM386.EXE is a DOS system file that, along with HIMEM.SYS, controls memory management. It is not required for system startup in pre-Windows 95 machines. Basically, this is an expanded memory emulator that performs two major functions: It enables and controls EMS, if desired, and enables the use of upper memory as system memory.

EMS   Meaning Expanded Memory Specification, EMS is an expanded memory standard that allows programs that recognize it to work with more than 640K of RAM.

Enhanced Parallel Port   See EPP.

EP Process   The EP (Electrophotographic Printing) process is the six-step process that a laser printer goes through to put an image on a page. The process follows these six steps: Cleaning, Charging, Writing, Developing, Transferring, and Fusing.

EPP   EPP (Enhanced Parallel Port) is an expansion bus that offers an extended control code set. With EPP mode, data travels both from the computer to the printer and vice versa.

Error Between Keyboard and Chair   See EBKAC Error.

Exit Roller   One of four different types of rollers found in printers, exit rollers aid in the transfer and control of the paper as it leaves the printer. Depending on the printer type, they direct the paper to a tray where it can be collated, sorted, or even stapled.

Expanded Memory Specification   See EMS.

Extended Capability Port   See ECP.

Extended Data Output RAM   See EDO RAM.

Extended Industry Standard Architecture   See EISA.

eXtended Memory Specification   See XMS.

FDISK   A DOS-based utility program used to partition a hard disk in preparation for installing an operating system.

Feed Roller   One of four different types of rollers found in printers. Also known as paper pickup roller, the feed roller, when activated, rotates against the top page in the paper tray and rolls it into the printer. The feed roller works together with a special rubber pad to prevent more than one sheet from being fed into the printer at a time.

Fiber Optic Cable   Extremely high-speed network cable that consists of glass fibers that carry light signals instead of electrical signals. Fiber optic cable is best used for transmission over long distances, and is much less susceptible to environmental difficulties, such as radiation.

File Transfer Protocol   See FTP.

Flash Memory   A faster version of ROM that, while still basically developed as ROM, can be addressed and loaded *thousands* of times.

Fragmentation   Because DOS writes files to the hard disk by breaking the file into cluster-sized pieces and then storing each piece in the next available cluster, as files are deleted and then rewritten, they can be written in noncontiguous clusters scattered all over the disk. This is known as file fragmentation.

FTP   Much older than the HTTP protocol, the File Transfer Protocol (FTP) is the protocol used to download files from an FTP server to a client computer. FTP is much faster than HTTP.

Fully Qualified Path   A fully qualified path is the entire path of a file, starting from the root of the file system, to the file being referenced.

Fusing Rollers   One of four different types of rollers found in laser printers, fusing rollers comprise the final stage of the Electrophotographic Printing (EP) process, bonding the toner particles to the page to prevent smearing. The roller on the toner side of the page has a non-stick surface that is heated to a high temperature to permanently bond the toner to the paper.

Ghosted Image   "Ghosting" is what occurs when a portion of an image previously printed to a page is printed again, only not as dark. One cause of this is if the erasure lamp of the laser printer sometimes fails to operate correctly, not completely erasing the previous image from the EP drum. Another cause of ghosting may be a malfunction in the cleaning blade such that it doesn't adequately scrape away the residual toner.

Handshaking   The process by which two connecting modems agree on the method of communication to be used.

HIDDEN Attribute   The Hidden attribute keeps a file from being displayed when a DIR command is issued.

HIMEM.SYS   HIMEM.SYS is a DOS system file that, along with EMM386.EXE, controls memory management. It is not required for system startup in pre-Windows 95 machines.

Hot Dock   Hot docking is the ability of a system to accept new accessories while it is plugged in.

HTML   Derived from the Standard General Markup Language (SGML), the Hypertext Markup Language (HTML) is the markup language that dictates the layout and design of a Web page.

HTTP   Hypertext Transfer Protocol (HTTP) is the TCP/IP-based protocol that is most commonly used for client/server communications on the World Wide Web.

Hub   Hubs are common connection points for devices in a network. Hubs contain multiple ports and are commonly used to connect segments of a LAN.

Hypertext Markup Language   See HTML.

Hypertext Transfer Protocol   See HTTP.

Impact Printer   Impact printers, like the name suggests, require the impact with an ink ribbon to print characters and images. An example of an impact printer is a daisy wheel.

Industry Standard Architecture   See ISA.

Input Device   Input devices take data from a user, such as the click of a mouse or the typing on a keyboard, and convert that data into electrical signals used by your computer. Several devices that provide input are: keyboards, mice, trackballs, pointing devices, digitized tablets, and touch screens.

Internet Service Provider   See ISP.

Internetwork Packet Exchange/Sequenced Packet Exchange
See IPX/SPX.

Interrupt Request Line   See IRQ.

IO.SYS   IO.SYS is a DOS system file that defines basic input/output routines for the processor. By default, it carries the hidden, system, and read-only attributes, and *is* required for OS startup.

IPX/SPX   Internetwork Packet Exchange/Sequenced Packet Exchange (IPX/SPX) is a very fast and highly established network protocol most commonly used with Novell NetWare.

IRQ   Interrupt Request (IRQ) lines are the physical lines over which system components such as modems or printers communicate directly with the CPU when the device is ready to send or receive data.

ISA   Industry Standard Architecture (ISA) is an industry standard bus architecture that allows for peripherals to utilize the 16-bit data bus that is available with 286 and 386 processors.

ISP   An Internet Service Provider (ISP), as its name suggests, is a company that provides users with access to the Internet, usually for a fee. On the other hand, a company that gives their employees Internet access through a private bank of modems is usually not considered an ISP.

Jumper   Jumpers, like DIP switches, are used to accomplish configuration manually. Jumpers are actually made of two separate components: a row of metal pins on the hardware itself and a small plastic cap that has a metal insert inside of it. The two parts together form a circuit that sets the configuration. This form of configuration device is only used to set one value for a feature at a time, as opposed to DIP switches, which can handle multiple configurations.

LAN   A local area network (LAN) is created whenever two or more computers in a limited geographic area (within about a two-mile radius) are linked by high-performance cables so that users can exchange information, share peripheral devices, or access a common server.

Local Area Network   See LAN.

Material Safety Data Sheets   See MSDS.

MEM.EXE   MEM.EXE is a simple command line utility that, using various command switches, can display various reports of memory usage.

MEMMAKER.EXE   A Microsoft utility that automatically determines the best possible configuration and load sequence for a given set of applications and drivers used. Before using MEMMAKER, the PC should be configured for normal operation (i.e., mouse driver, network operation, sound support, and so forth), including any items that are loaded from the AUTOEXEC.BAT and CONFIG.SYS files.

Memory Address   The memory address is used to receive commands from the processor that are destined for any device attached to a computer. Each device must have a unique memory address in order for it to function.

Memory Bank   A memory bank is the actual slot that memory goes into.

Memory Effect   When a Nickel Cadmium, or NiCad, battery is recharged before it is fully discharged, the battery loses the ability to fully recharge again, which is known as the memory effect.

MSD.EXE   MSD, Microsoft Diagnostics, is a DOS-based utility that provides a great deal of information about the system. It is most useful in determining what the system has installed in it, such as memory and hard drives.

MSDOS.SYS   MSDOS.SYS is a DOS system file that defines system file locations. By default, it carries the hidden, system, and read-only attributes, and is required for OS startup.

MSDS   Material Safety Data Sheets (MSDS) are white pages that contain information on any substance that is deemed hazardous, most notably cleaning solvents. The purpose of MSDS is to inform employees about the dangers inherent in hazardous materials and the proper use of these items to prevent potential injuries from occurring.

Multi-Boot Configuration   A system that has been configured to use more than one operating system.

Multimeter   A multimeter is a device that measures current, resistance, or voltage, used to determine whether certain computer components are functioning correctly based on these electrical measurements.

NetBEUI   The NetBIOS Extended User Interface (NetBEUI) is an extremely fast network transport protocol that is most commonly found on smaller networks.

NetBIOS Extended User Interface   See NetBEUI.

Network Interface Card   See NIC.

Network Topology   The arrangement of cable links in a local area network. There are three principal network topologies: bus, ring, and star.

NIC   A network interface card (NIC) is used to connect a PC to a network cable.

Noise Filter   UPS's contain a special filter, called a *noise filter*, that reduces the amount of noise present in electrical current and eliminates magnetic fields caused by noise, thus providing some protection to the components that utilize the current or are nearby.

Non-Impact Printer   Non-impact printers do not use an ink ribbon, and therefore do not require direct contact with the paper for printing. An example of a non-impact printer is a laser printer.

Normal Mode   Normal Mode is the mode in which Windows 95 is started by default, which provides full functionality of the Windows 95 Explorer.

Null Modem Cable   A null modem cable is a special cable that has the send and receive lines reversed on the connector. It enables you to connect two computers directly, without using a modem.

Operating System   See OS.

Operator Error   Operator error occurs when the customer inadvertently makes a configuration change.

OS   By definition, an Operating System (OS) is a set of computer instruction codes, usually *compiled* into executable files, whose purpose is to define input and output devices and connections, and provide instructions for the computer's central processor to operate on to retrieve and display data.

Output Device   Output devices take electronic signals *from* a computer and convert them into a format that the user can use. Examples of output devices include monitors and printers.

Overlays   Rather than put all available functions into a single huge executable file, most developers choose to modularize their applications by creating library files that include additional commands and functions. These additional executable enhancement files are usually referred to as overlays.

Page Description Language   See PDL.

Parallel Port   One of two types of communication ports found on a motherboard (the other is the serial port), the parallel port is used to connect a peripheral device (most commonly a printer for this type of port) to the computer. A parallel port allows transmission of data over eight conductors at one time. The processor socket is the actual socket used to attach the processor to the motherboard.

Parallel Processing   The Intel 586 (Pentium) chip combines two 486DX chips into one, called the *Dual Independent Bus Architecture*. This allows each processor inside the chip to execute instructions simultaneously and independently from each other, which is called parallel processing.

Parity   Parity is an error-checking mechanism that enables the device to recognize single-bit errors.

Partition   A section of the storage area on a computer's hard disk. A hard disk must be partitioned before an operating system can be installed.

Passive Matrix Display   Most common on portable systems, the passive matrix display is made from a grid of horizontal and vertical wires.

At the end of each wire is a transistor. In order to light a pixel at (X, Y), a signal is sent to the X and Y transistors. In turn, these transistors then send voltage down the wire, which turns on the LCD at the intersection of the two wires.

PC Card   The PC Card (Personal Computer Memory Card International Association, or PCMCIA) bus was first created to expand the memory capabilities in small, hand-held computers. It is a type of bus used mostly with laptop computers that provides a convenient way to interchange PCMCIA-compatible devices. The card itself is only slightly larger than a credit card.

PCI   The Peripheral Component Interconnect (PCI) was designed in response to the Pentium class processor's utilization of a 64-bit bus. PCI buses are designed to be processor-independent.

PCMCIA   See PC Card.

PDL   Laser printers use a Page Description Language (PDL) to send and receive print job instructions one page at a time, rather than one dot at a time, as with other types of printers.

Peripheral Component Interconnect   See PCI.

Personal Computer Memory Card International Association
See PC Card.

Photosensitive Drum   This light-sensitive drum is the core of the electrophotographic process inside the laser printer. This drum is affected by the cleaning, charging, writing, and transferring processes in the six-step laser printing process.

Plug and Play   Introduced with Microsoft Windows 95, Plug and Play offers automatic driver installation as soon as hardware or software is "plugged in," or installed.

Pointing Stick   One of the three most common types of pointing devices found on portable systems, the pointing stick is a small pencil-eraser-size piece of rubber in the center of the keyboard. The on-screen pointer is controlled by simply pushing the pointing stick in the desired direction.

Point-to-Point Protocol   See PPP.

POLEDIT.EXE   The Windows 95 System Policy feature, POLEDIT.EXE, is used to set common-denominator defaults for all network users, and add certain restrictions on a global basis if deemed necessary.

POP   Post Office Protocol (POP) is a system by which an Internet server lets you receive e-mail and download it from the server to your own machine.

POST   As its name suggests, a Power On Self Test (POST) is self test performed by the computer that occurs during boot time. It is used to diagnose system-related problems.

Post Office Protocol   See POP.

Power On Self Test   See POST.

Power Spike   When there is a power spike, there is a sudden, huge increase in power that lasts for a split second. Power spikes can literally burn out computer components.

PPP   The Point-to-Point protocol (PPP) is a serial communications protocol used to connect two computers over a phone line via a modem. SLIP is the alternate protocol that is acceptable to most browsers, though it's not as common as PPP.

Preemptive Multitasking   There are two different types of multitasking: cooperative and preemptive. Preemptive multitasking means that control is passed from one program to another automatically by the Windows process scheduler.

Primary Corona Wire   This highly negatively charged wire inside a laser printer is responsible for electrically erasing the photosensitive drum, preparing it to be written with a new image in the writing stage of the laser print process.

Processor Socket   The processor socket is the actual socket used to attach the processor to the motherboard.

Protocol   A set of communication standards between two computers on a network. Common protocols include TCP/IP, NetBEUI, and IPX/SPX.

READ ONLY Attribute   The READ ONLY attribute prevents a user or application from inadvertently deleting or changing a file.

Refresh   Refresh refers to the automatic process of constantly updating memory chips to ensure that their signals are correct. The refresh rate is the frequency by which chips are refreshed, usually about every 60 to 70 thousandths of a second.

Registration Roller   One of four different types of rollers found in laser printers, the registration roller synchronizes the paper movement with the writing process inside the EP cartridge. Registration rollers do not advance the paper until the EP cartridge is ready to process the next line of the image.

Ring Topology   In a local area network, a ring topology has each device arranged around a closed-loop cable. This is most commonly used with fiber optic cabling.

Rollers   Rollers are located inside a printer to aid in the movement of paper through the printer. There are four main types of rollers: feed, registration, fuser, and exit.

Safe Mode   Safe Mode is a special diagnostic mode of Windows 95 that starts the operating system without any network, CD-ROM, and printer drivers. This special mode allows you to change an incorrect setting, which will in most cases allow you to return an abnormally functioning system to its correct operation.

Serial Port   One of two types of communication ports found on a motherboard (the other is the parallel port), the serial port connects to a serial line that leads to a computer peripheral—the type used most commonly with modems and mice. The serial port transmits data sequentially, bit by bit over a single conductor.

SIMD   Single Instruction Multiple Data (SIMD) works by allowing a single instruction to operate on multiple pieces of data when an application is performing a repetitive loop.

SIMM   A Single In-line Memory Module (SIMM) is a small plug-in circuit board that contains the memory chips that you need to add certain increments of RAM to your computer. The chips are positioned along one side of the board.

Simple Mail Transfer Protocol   See SMTP.

Single In-line Memory Module   See SIMM.

Single Instruction Multiple Data   See SIMD.

Slack   Slack is the space left between the end of a file and the end of the cluster in which the file resides.

SLIP   The Serial Line Interface Protocol, SLIP is a protocol used to manage telecommunications between a client and a server over a phone line. PPP is the alternate protocol that is acceptable to most browsers, and is in fact the most common.

SMTP   Simple Mail Transfer Protocol (SMTP) is the underlying protocol for Internet-based e-mail.

Socket Services   Socket Services is a layer of BIOS-level software that isolates PC Card software from the computer hardware and detects the insertion or removal of PC Cards.

Solenoid   The solenoid is a resistive coil found in dot matrix and daisy wheel printers. When the solenoid is energized, the pin is forced away from the printhead and impacts the printer ribbon and ultimately the paper, thus impressing the image on the page.

SRAM   Unlike DRAM, Static RAM (SRAM) retains its value as long as power is supplied. It is not constantly refreshed. However, SRAM does require a periodic update and tends to use excessive amounts of power when it does so.

Star Topology   In a local area network, a star topology has each device on the network connected to a central processor, usually a hub. This is most commonly used with twisted pair cabling.

Static RAM   See SRAM.

Stylus   Shaped like a pen, a stylus is used to select menu options and the like on a monitor screen or to draw line art on a graphics tablet.

Sync Frequency   Monitors use a *sync frequency* to control the refresh rate, which is the rate at which the display device is repainted. If this setting is incorrect, you get symptoms such as: a "dead" monitor, lines running through the display, a flickering screen, and a reduced or enlarged image.

SYSTEM Attribute   The SYSTEM attribute is usually set by DOS or Windows, and cannot be modified using standard DOS or Windows commands, including the ATTRIB command or File Manager.

SYSTEM.INI   SYSTEM.INI is a Windows system file that configures Windows to address specific hardware devices and their associated settings. Errors in this file can and do cause Windows to fail to start, or crash unexpectedly.

TCP/IP   The most common protocol in use today, Transmission Control Protocol/Internet Protocol (TCP/IP) is the protocol upon which the Internet was built. It refers to the communication standards for data transmission over the Internet.

Time Slicing   The process of the CPU dividing up time between applications for preemptive multitasking is called time slicing.

Token Passing   Token passing is a network communication protocol by which a token is passed from device to device around a virtual (and frequently physical) ring on a network. Whenever a device receives the token, it is then allowed to transmit onto the network.

Toner   Toner is comprised of finely divided particles of plastic resin and organic compounds bonded to iron particles. It is naturally negatively charged, which aids in attracting it to the written areas of the photosensitive drum during the transfer step of the laser printing process.

Touch Pad   A touch pad is a stationary pointing device commonly used on laptop computers in replace of a mouse or trackball. They are pads that have either thin wires running through them, or specialized surfaces that can sense the pressure of your finger on them. You slide your finger across the touchpad to control the pointer or cursor on the screen.

Trackball   Most commonly, trackballs are used in older portable computers to replace a mouse. Trackballs are built the same way as an opto-mechanical mouse, except upside-down with the ball on top.

Transfer Corona   This roller inside a laser printer contains a positively charged wire designed to pull the toner off of the photosensitive drum and place it on the page.

Transistor   A transistor is the most fundamental component of electronic circuits. A CPU chip, for example, contains thousands to millions of transistors, which are used to process information in the form of electronic signals. The more transistors a CPU has, the faster it can process data.

Transmission Control Protocol/Internet Protocol   See TCP/IP.

Twisted Pair   By far the most common type of network cable, twisted pair consists of two insulated wires wrapped around each other to help avoid interference from other wires.

Uninterruptible Power Supply   See UPS.

Upload   Uploading is the process of transferring files from one computer to another. Unlike downloading, uploading is always initiated from the computer that is sending the files.

UPS The uninterruptible power supply (UPS) is a device that was designed to protect your computer and its components from possible injury from the problems that are inherent with today's existing power supply structure.

VESA Local Bus See VL-Bus.

Virtual Memory Virtual memory is memory that the processor borrows from the hard drive as if it were actual physical RAM.

Virus Any program that is written with the intent of doing harm to a computer. Viruses have the ability to replicate themselves by attaching themselves to programs or documents. They range in activity from extreme data loss to an annoying message that pops up every few minutes.

VL-Bus Originally created to address performance issues, the VESA Local Bus (VL-Bus) was meant to enable earlier bus designs to handle a maximum clock speed equivalent to that of processors.

WAN A wide area network (WAN) is created whenever two or more computers are linked by long-distance communication lines that traverse distances greater than those supported by LANs (or, greater than about two miles).

Wide Area Network See WAN.

WIN.INI WIN.INI is a dynamic Windows system file that contains configuration information for Windows applications. Errors made in this file seldom have global implications to Window's operation, but can cripple specific applications or features. Printing is also controlled by settings in this file.

Windows Accelerator Card RAM See WRAM.

WINFILE.INI   In pre-Windows 95 systems, this is the configuration file that stores the names of the directories that File Manager displays when starting.

WRAM   The Windows Accelerator Card was introduced into the market out of a need to assist some environments with running Microsoft Windows. WRAM utilizes memory that resides on the card itself to perform the Windows-specific functions, and therefore speeds up the OS.

XMS   Meaning eXtended Memory Specification, XMS is a set of standards that allows applications to access extended memory.

Zoomed Video   See ZV.

ZV   Zoomed Video (ZV) is a direct data connection between a PC Card and host system that allows a PC Card to write video data directly to the video controller.

INDEX

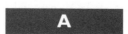

E

S

U

Custom Corporate Network Training

Train on Cutting Edge Technology   We can bring the best in skill-based training to your facility to create a real-world hands-on training experience. Global Knowledge Network has invested millions of dollars in network hardware and software to train our students on the same equipment they will work with on the job. Our relationships with vendors allow us to incorporate the latest equipment and platforms into your on-site labs.

Maximize Your Training Budget   Global Knowledge Network provides experienced instructors, comprehensive course materials, and all the networking equipment needed to deliver high quality training. You provide the students; we provide the knowledge.

Avoid Travel Expenses   On-site courses allow you to schedule technical training at your convenience, saving time, expense, and the opportunity cost of travel away from the workplace.

Discuss Confidential Topics   Private on-site training permits the open discussion of sensitive issues such as security, access, and network design. We can work with your existing network's proprietary files while demonstrating the latest technologies.

Customize Course Content   Global Knowledge Network can tailor your courses to include the technologies and the topics which have the greatest impact on your business. We can complement your internal training efforts or provide a total solution to your training needs.

Corporate Pass   The Corporate Pass Discount Program rewards our best network training customers with preferred pricing on public courses, discounts on multimedia training packages, and an array of career planning services.

Global Knowledge Network Training Lifecycle: Supporting the Dynamic and Specialized Training Requirements of Information Technology Professionals

- Define Profile
- Assess Skills
- Design Training
- Deliver Training
- Test Knowledge
- Update Profile
- Use New Skills

College Credit Recommendation Program   The American Council on Education's CREDIT program recommends 53 Global Knowledge Network courses for college credit. Now our network training can help you earn your college degree while you learn the technical skills needed for your job. When you attend an ACE-certified Global Knowledge Network course and pass the associated exam, you earn college credit recommendations for that course. Global Knowledge Network can establish a transcript record for you with ACE which you can use to gain credit at a college or as a written record of your professional training that you can attach to your resume.

Registration Information

COURSE FEE: The fee covers course tuition, refreshments, and all course materials. Any parking expenses that may be incurred are not included. Payment or government training form must be received six business days prior to the course date. We will also accept Visa/MasterCard and American Express. For non-U.S. credit card users, charges will be in U.S. funds and will be converted by your credit card company. Checks drawn on Canadian banks in Canadian funds are acceptable.

COURSE SCHEDULE: Registration is at 8:00 a.m. on the first day. The program begins at 8:30 a.m. and concludes at 4:30 p.m. each day.

CANCELLATION POLICY: Cancellation and full refund will be allowed if written cancellation is received in our office at least six business days prior to the course start date. Registrants who do not attend the course or do not cancel more than six business days in advance are responsible for the full registration fee; you may transfer to a later date provided the course fee has been paid in full. Substitutions may be made at any time. If Global Knowledge Network must cancel a course for any reason, liability is limited to the registration fee only.

GLOBAL KNOWLEDGE NETWORK: Global Knowledge Network programs are developed and presented by industry professionals with "real-world" experience. Designed to help professionals meet today's interconnectivity and interoperability challenges, most of our programs feature hands-on labs that incorporate state-of-the-art communication components and equipment.

ON-SITE TEAM TRAINING: Bring Global Knowledge Network's powerful training programs to your company. At Global Knowledge Network, we will custom design courses to meet your specific network requirements. Call (919)-461-8686 for more information.

YOUR GUARANTEE: Global Knowledge Network believes its courses offer the best possible training in this field. If during the first day you are not satisfied and wish to withdraw from the course, simply notify the instructor, return all course materials and receive a 100% refund.

In the US:

CALL: 1 888 762 4442

FAX: 1 919 469 7070

VISIT OUR WEBSITE:

www.globalknowledge.com

MAIL CHECK AND THIS FORM TO:

Global Knowledge Network

Suite 200

114 Edinburgh South

P.O. Box 1187

Cary, NC 27512

In Canada:

CALL: 1 800 465 2226

FAX: 1 613 567 3899

VISIT OUR WEBSITE:

www.globalknowledge.com.ca

MAIL CHECK AND THIS FORM TO:

Global Knowledge Network

Suite 1601

393 University Ave.

Toronto, ON M5G 1E6

REGISTRATION INFORMATION:

Course title _____

Course location _____ Course date _____

Name/title _____ Company _____

Name/title _____ Company _____

Name/title _____ Company _____

Address _____ Telephone _____ Fax _____

City _____ State/Province _____ Zip/Postal Code _____

Credit card _____ Card # _____ Expiration date _____

Signature _____